"Of particular value in Angelica Löwe's book a
of my father's work. She helps us feel our wa
Erich Neumann's inner world. Of all the interpr
presented in this volume are the most profound.
for her work."

Professor Micha Neumann, Psychoanalyst, Tel Aviv

"Löwe's psychological and historical insights are remarkable. I learned a great
deal about Jung and Neumann—and Palestine—from what she has researched.
It made me rethink many things. I found her compassion as valuable as her
scholarship. And the contemporary resonances shone through."

Andrew Samuels, Jungian analyst, Professor emeritus,
University of Essex

"Erich Neumann described his world as 'sitting between all faculties' and
therefore was able to reflect more deeply on it than the majority of his generation. Angelica Löwe brings this to light in her great book. Her expertise is
stupendous, and her style elegant. Löwe's book portrays Neumann and Julie
Neumann as well as their practice in Israel. Two people with stunted German
roots who reinvent themselves in C.G. Jung's footsteps: Neumann as one of the
most prominent Jungians and the couple as part of intellectual production communities between Tel Aviv and Ticino, where the famous Eranos Circle met.
Angelica Löwe's book is insightful and deserves wide attention."

Hildegard Keller, author and director, Zurich

"Nowadays, when a new book is published, one rarely gets the impression that
it closes a gap … yet this is exactly what Angelica Löwe's work does beyond
any shade of doubt."

Roman Lesmeister, Jungian analyst, Hamburg

"Erich Neumann's book *The Great Mother* enjoyed cult status in the '70s.
The connections to C.G. Jung and the Eranos Circle were well known. But
the author's personality disappeared behind the Great Mother. Angelica Löwe
has saved the Berlin-born German-Jewish intellectual from oblivion. She masterfully portrays his career and his work against the background of dramatic
times. The result is a brilliant biographical study."

Daniel Krochmalnik, Professor of Jewish Religion and Philosophy,
University of Potsdam

"Reading the life history of Erich Neumann and tracing the development of his
theory in parallel to historical events, one can feel and understand his unique
contribution to the world of analytical psychology and to Jung's thoughts in
particular, his deep understanding of the feminine and morality, and finally
the development of consciousness through life. Angelica Löwe's wonderful
account of Neumann's relationship with Jung, his Jewish destiny, the search
for his Jewish-Israeli identity and the development of his theory presents
Neumann as the man and genius that he was."

Avi Bauman, Jungian analyst, Jerusalem

"An excellent biography!"

Paul Mendes-Flohr, Professor emeritus,
University of Chicago, Divinity School

"One can only hope that Löwe's book will stimulate further research and editions and that it will also help to strengthen the methodological and historical self-reflection of psychoanalysis. Its questions, those of a 'grammar of the depths,' also touch on the concerns of philosophy."

Harald Seubert, Professor of Theology,
Basel School of Divinity, Gießen School of Divinity

"Angelica Löwe masterfully strings the scattered pearls of Neumann's life and thought on a well organised biographical chain. Between 1925 and 1956, Neumann lived in Berlin, Erlangen, Heidelberg, Zurich, Tel Aviv, Jerusalem and Ascona. During this period, he developed an important variant of depth psychology, mainly by shedding unprecedented light on the feminine in his famous *The Great Mother*. Löwe paints an impressively coherent and detailed picture of Neumann's intellectual struggle for Jewish identity—beginning with his partly unpublished early work and correspondence, and ending with insightful interpretations of his classical works."

Manfred Oeming, Professor of Old Testament Theology,
University of Heidelberg

"Erich Neumann is the subject of this excellent biography by Angelica Löwe. In Löwe's biography, the full extent of Neumann's life and work is explored. Recommended to all interested in Jung, Neumann, Analytical Psychology and the history of psychoanalytical thinking."

Erel Shalit, editor of *Erich Neumann's Jacob and Esau:
The Collective Symbolism of the Brother Motif* (2016)

"The author's outstanding style makes the book a pleasure to read."

Information Philosophie, 2015,
No. 2/2015 (Philosophical Quarterly)

Life and Work of Erich Neumann

Life and Work of Erich Neumann: On the Side of the Inner Voice is the first book to discuss Erich Neumann's life, work and relationship with C.G. Jung. Neumann (1905–1960) is considered Jung's most important student, and in this deeply personal and unique volume, Angelica Löwe casts Neumann's comprehensive work in a completely new light.

Based on conversations with Neumann's children, Rali Loewenthal-Neumann and Professor Micha Neumann, Löwe explores Neumann's childhood and adolescent years in Part I, including how he met his wife and muse Julie Blumenfeld. In Part II the book traces their life and work in Tel Aviv, where they moved in the early 1930s amid growing anti-Jewish tensions in Hitler's Germany. Finally, in Part III, Löwe analyses Neumann's most famous works.

This is the first book-length discussion of the existential questions motivating Neumann's work, as well as the socio-historical circumstances pertaining to the problem of Jewish identity formation against rising anti-Semitism in the early 20th century. It will be essential reading for Jungian analysts and analytical psychologists in practice and in training, as well as for scholars of Jungian and post-Jungian studies and Jewish studies.

Angelica Löwe, MA, is a Jungian analyst in private practice in Vienna. She is a member of the C.G. Jung Institute in Munich, Germany, and other memberships include the DGAP and IAAP. She has published widely on various topics and serves as chief editor of *Analytische Psychologie.*

Life and Work of Erich Neumann

On the Side of the Inner Voice

Angelica Löwe

Translated by Mark Kyburz
Foreword by Micha Neumann

 Routledge
Taylor & Francis Group

LONDON AND NEW YORK

Published in English 2020
by Routledge
2 Park Square, Milton Park, Abingdon, Oxon OX14 4RN

and by Routledge
52 Vanderbilt Avenue, New York, NY 10017

Routledge is an imprint of the Taylor & Francis Group, an informa business

First published in German
Angelica Löwe, "Auf Seiten der inneren Stimme …". Erich Neumann -
Leben und Werk © 2017 Karl Alber Verlag part of Verlag Herder GmbH,
Freiburg im Breisgau.

British Library Cataloguing-in-Publication Data
A catalogue record for this book is available from the British Library

Library of Congress Cataloging-in-Publication Data
Names: Löwe, Angelica, author.
Title: Life and work of Erich Neumann: on the side of the inner voice
/ authored by Angelica Löwe; translated by Mark Kyburz; foreword by
Micha Neumann.
Other titles: "Auf Seiten der inneren Stimme..." English
Description: Abingdon, Oxon; New York, NY: Routledge, 2020. |
Includes bibliographical references and index.
Identifiers: LCCN 2020003491 (print) | LCCN 2020003492 (ebook) |
ISBN 9780815382355 (hardback) | ISBN 9780815382379 (paperback) |
ISBN 9781351208710 (ebook)
Subjects: LCSH: Neumann, Erich. | Psychologists–Germany–Biography. |
Psychology–History.
Classification: LCC BF109.N48 L64913 2020 (print) | LCC BF109.N48
(ebook) | DDC 150.19/5092 [B]–dc23
LC record available at https://lccn.loc.gov/2020003491
LC ebook record available at https://lccn.loc.gov/2020003492

ISBN: 978-0-8153-8235-5 (hbk)
ISBN: 978-0-8153-8237-9 (pbk)
ISBN: 978-1-351-20871-0 (ebk)

Typeset in Times
by Deanta Global Publishing Services, Chennai, India

Contents

Figures

Foreword

Angelica Löwe has undertaken the difficult task of writing the first-ever book-length account of the work and life of Erich Neumann. This volume is now before us, thanks to Ms Löwe's courage, spirited inquiry, patience and attention to detail. She has gathered an unprecedented wealth of information about Neumann, through which she brings to life his personality and his hitherto unexplored and hence unknown life. This book also provides the interested reader with access to Neumann's work, which includes many of his unpublished writings about Judaism. After more than 50 years, which have passed since Neumann's premature death in 1960, we now finally have a work before us that offers so many insights of which I, as his son, was unaware.

My father was a very busy man. He was always at his desk, writing, and could not be disturbed. When he was not writing, he looked after his many patients. The breaks from work that he granted himself, and during which he found time to talk to me, were few and far between. The exception was Sabbath, when he enjoyed playing with me and told me stories, in particular from the Bible. He would sometimes paint beautiful colour pictures to accompany those stories.

In the battle for my father's attention, I had numerous rivals, including some of great importance—first and foremost my mother, Julie Neumann, of course. My sister and I knew that our father's relationship with our mother took priority. Others rivals included C.G. Jung and Olga Fröbe-Kapteyn, with whom my father corresponded for many years, and then of course his favourite places: Moscia on Lago Maggiore, where the Eranos conferences were held every year; and Sils Maria in the Upper Engadin, where my mother and he went to recuperate. Last but not least, there were his other children: his books.

My father was not at all like my friends' fathers. I felt and knew that he loved me and that I mattered a lot to him. Yet from an early age I also realised that his life was determined by great and important tasks. Because I understood this, I never reproached him. Often, I identified with him and imagined that, at some stage, I might also matter to so many people.

Of particular value in Angelica Löwe's book are her excellent interpretations of my father's work. She helps us feel our way into and thus to experience Erich Neumann's inner world. The language and structure of her book provide subtle access to his complex and at times difficult ideas. Of all the interpretations that I have read, those presented in this volume are the most profound. I am most grateful to Ms Löwe for her work. This is a very well-written, highly absorbing and beautiful book. It makes exciting and gratifying reading. Not once did I feel like putting it down.

For me, as Erich Neumann's son, this book is therefore of particular importance. It gives me great pleasure to wish that *Life and Work of Erich Neumann* will attract the large and interested readership it fully deserves.

Micha Neumann, Tel Aviv, 2015

Preface to the 2014 German edition

Erich Neumann is widely considered C.G. Jung's most important student. His extensive work, translated into many languages, is still read today. Of particular importance are *The Origins and History of Consciousness*, *Depth Psychology and a New Ethic*, *The Great Mother* and *Amor and Psyche*. And yet the fact that Neumann's life, his relationship with C.G. Jung or the evolution of his work have received precious little attention (or indeed none) is striking as much as it is baffling. Thus, we have engaged with an important body of work, not only for the Jungian world, without the slightest knowledge of its creator. This has suggested that this lack of knowledge was a blind spot, reflective of historical obliviousness and symptomatic of failing to recall the exodus of the Jewish intellect brought about by National Socialism.

In essence, the development of this book is closely linked to the activities of the working group for "Analytical Psychology and History."[1] One of the group's main concerns is to remember the Jewish colleagues who were persecuted by the Nazi regime.[2] A conference held in Vienna in 2005, entitled "100 Years of Erich Neumann, 130 Years of C.G. Jung," provided further impetus for pursuing the project of a book about Neumann's life and work. The children of Erich and Julie Neumann—Micha Neumann and Rali Loewenthal-Neumann (who both reside in Israel)—were invited to the conference to deliver lectures, which provided an initial opportunity for discussion. Further interviews and research took place at a later stage in Israel, Moscia near Ascona, the site of the Eranos conferences, and London, where I met Julie Neumann's youngest (and now deceased) sister.

This project began with an admission: I realised that not only I knew almost nothing about Neumann's Jewish background, but that very little was known about his life in either Germany or Israel. The outcome of my research is a book whose main sources are my conversations with those people who knew Neumann, as well as his unpublished letters and manuscripts; it is an attempt to paint a lively picture of the life and work of a man who was characterised by his strong desire for independence, by his immense creativity and by tremendous intuition. He was a scholar and writer whose work, in his own assessment, "sits between all faculties." Neumann himself did not see his cultural, philosophical and critical writings in the context of the emergence of psychoanalytic theory, but as contributions to "cultural therapy" or metapsychology. They were the work of "a proud Jew," as Gershom Scholem described Neumann in his obituary.

To return to the strange misalignment between the active reception of Neumann's work and a lack of biographical knowledge:[3] Neumann and C.G. Jung engaged in an intense and at times even dramatic correspondence. These letters, whose publication in 2015 will mark one of the most important events in the history of analytical psychology, bears witness to a complex intellectual dialogue, an essential part of which concerns the examination of Jewish identity.[4] For this reason, Erich Neumann's life can only be adequately retraced if it is understood as a historical-critical examination of Jewish life and of the political situation prevailing in Germany before and after the Nazi's rise to power in 1933. This perspective also means taking into account the history of German Zionism, which exercised a lasting influence on Neumann. The present examination of Neumann's biography places personal statements and aspects of his work in the context of the massive rupture caused by a series of political catastrophes. No such inquiry can be guided by the idea of a "German-Jewish conversation," which, as Gershom Scholem observed, takes place "in an empty fictitious space."[5] It attempts, instead, to reveal the fault lines of a dialogue that is in many respects inadequate, and even severed. Thus, this biographical account of Neumann's life and work also contributes to the historiography of psychoanalysis.

I have divided this book into three parts:

Part I traces the origins of Erich and Julie Neumann. It considers the historical and socio-political conditions of Jewish life in Germany, in particular in Berlin during the first quarter of the 20th century. It reviews the key intellectual currents that shaped Neumann's thinking, first and foremost Martin Buber's "Jewish Renaissance" and Kurt Blumenfeld's concept of post-assimilation (Chapter 1). Chapter 2 discusses Julie Blumenfeld's family background and social engagement at the beginning of her career as an analyst. Chapter 3 illumines Neumann's early writings, including his doctoral dissertation, his (unpublished) studies on Franz Kafka and excerpts from his (also unpublished) novel *Der Anfang* (The Beginning). On the one hand, it is important to delineate the lines running between Neumann's early and later work, and on the other to convey a palpable sense of the young Neumann's intellectual independence, which later led him to develop the concept of "mystical anthropology." My main purpose throughout is to trace the emergence of Neumann's key concepts from his early, unpublished works to his later writings. Those early works were, as becomes evident, a "quarry" for the later ones.

Part II explores the correspondence between Erich Neumann and C.G. Jung, in order to bring into view Neumann's chief concern: his struggle for Jewish identity. We will, however, be able to assess the definitive scope of the Jung–Neumann correspondence only after the publication of Neumann's complete letters. Chapters 4, 6 and 7 explore Neumann's intellectual debate with Jung. These chapters consider Jung's examination of Judaism, his statements in various publications, which are nothing other than anti-Semitic, and also his theorising of the unconscious and its effect on the young Jewish intellectual, who had decided to place Jungian theory over others. Jung's theory of the Jewish unconscious is particularly significant in this respect. Chapter 6 involves a brief excursion into the history of ideas. It provides a brief overview of Martin Buber's *Reden an das Judentum* (On Judaism), which concerns emigration to Palestine, in comparison with Jung's deliberations on the relationship between the collective unconscious and the "soil." Chapter 8, which considers Neumann's life in Tel Aviv, draws on manuscripts gratefully provided by Rali Loewenthal-Neumann and Dvora Kutzinski, and on Neumann's unpublished letters to Olga Fröbe-Kapteyn, the founder of the Eranos conferences. Chapter 9, which conjures up the spirit and flair of the annual Eranos conferences on Lake Maggiore in southern Switzerland, is also based on a close reading of Neumann's unpublished letters to Olga Fröbe-Kapteyn, the "Magna Mater" of Eranos. Neumann was one of the most important speakers at the gathering, from 1948 until his untimely death in 1960.

Part III discusses Neumann's key works in the context of his long unpublished manuscripts on the *Psychologie des jüdischen Menschen* (Psychology of the Jewish Person), which he began writing in the 1930s. Published in 2019 as *The Roots of Jewish Consciousness*, only this early work enables one to open up the impressive and highly significant world of thought that would emerge in Neumann's later work. Here, in these early manuscripts, Neumann devotes himself to the fundamental philosophical question of how consciousness forms time and space. The crucial concept of time in Jewish thought is *messianism*, from which Neumann developed his concept of *actualised messianism* (Chapter 10).

Neumann places the theme of space within the highly charged, dichotomous debate over "land, home, earth, soil," which Martin Buber and C.G. Jung both addressed from their different ideological perspectives (Chapter 6). Here, Neumann develops, not least as part of his critique of Jewish theology, which he believes fails to respect the feminine, and influenced by Rilke's *Duino Elegies*, a line of thought that addresses *the transparency of the earthly* (Chapter 11). The chapter on his *Depth Psychology and a New Ethics* examines Neumann's "new ethic" in terms of its Nietzschean influence and places this work in the context of *Jewish Nietzscheanism* (Chapter 12). Chapter 12 discusses a vision that Neumann wrote to Jung about in one of his letters. Its interpretation is based on the philosophy and basic ideas of the French philosopher Emmanuel Lévinas (Chapter 13). The last two chapters are dedicated to the "heroic path" of the modern human being. This theme assumes many mythological guises, in which Neumann found the development of human consciousness (i.e. ego complex) delineated in metaphorical terms. Characteristic of Neumann's work in this respect is his distinction between the development of male and female consciousness. Thus, Chapter 14, in discussing the central theses of his *Origins and History of Consciousness*, focuses on Neumann's critique of the Freudian concept of the Oedipus complex. The final chapter, an account of Apuleius's tale of *Amor and Psyche*, traces woman's "heroic path."

This book also presents various ancillary materials, including chronological tables and documents about Erich and Julie Neumann. Also included is the commemorative speech given by the author on the occasion of the unveiling of a memorial plaque for the Neumanns in May 2007 in Berlin Wilmersdorf.

Vienna, January 2014

Notes

1 The working group has existed since 2015. Its current members include Michael Lindner (Berlin), Angelica Löwe (Vienna), Elke Metzner and Martin Schimkus (both Nuremberg).
2 Thus, in 2007, following Regine Lockot's project "Freud in Berlin," a commemorative plaque for Erich and Julie Neumann was mounted and unveiled in Berlin. This was followed by plaques honouring Ernst Bernhard and Gerhard Adler, who had also been raised or spent their lives in Berlin. A plaque for Sabina Spielrein had already been unveiled in March 2007.
3 No complete critical edition of his work exists to date.
4 The letters will be published as *Analytical Psychology in Exile: The Correspondence of C.G. Jung and Erich Neumann*. Edited by Martin Liebscher. Translated by Heather McCartney (Princeton, NJ: Princeton University Press, 2015); the German edition will also be published next year.
5 Gershom Scholem, "Wider den Mythos vom deutsch-jüdischen Gespräch," *Bulletin des Leo Baeck Instituts* 27 (1964), p. 278f.; from a letter written by Scholem dated 18 December 1962.

Preface to the English edition

Shortly after the publication of the first (German) edition of this book in the autumn of 2014, Neumann's reception in English-speaking countries entered a new phase. The decisive factor in the subsequent increase in interest was the publication of the English edition of Neumann's correspondence with C.G. Jung in the spring of 2015.[1] The occasion was duly celebrated at an international conference held in April 2015 at Shefayim Kibbutz Hotel near Tel Aviv.[2] Representative of the renewed interest in Erich Neumann's work are the comprehensive conference proceedings published by Erel Shalit and Murray Stein in the autumn of 2016.[3] The Jung–Neumann correspondence was published in German in 2016.[4]

Neumann's unpublished works have also begun attracting wider interest: They include *Jacob and Esau*, edited by Erel Shalit and indispensable to understanding Neumann's later works.[5] Professor Micha Neumann, Neumann's son, has published a very personal and highly important account of the correspondence between Neumann and Jung.[6] Another important unpublished work by Neumann from the 1930s was published in 2019: his two manuscripts on the psychology of the Jewish person.[7]

It is thus fair to speak of a Neumann revival in analytical psychology. It gives me much pleasure to meet the ongoing interest in Neumann's life and work with the second (German) edition of this volume. It serves as the basis for the English translation, which contains several corrections to the first edition and an extended version of the final chapter. I am delighted that Micha Neumann has contributed a foreword to this edition.

Vienna, July 2019

Notes

1 Martin Liebscher (ed.), Analytical Psychology in Exile: The Correspondence of C.G. Jung and Erich Neumann, translated by Heather McCartney (Princeton, NJ: Princeton University Press, 2015). The German edition, published by Patmos, also appeared in 2015.
2 See The Jung-Neumann Letters, An International Conference in Celebration of a Creative Relationship, April 24–26, 2015, Israel.

3 Erel Shalit and Murray Stein (eds.), *Turbulent Times, Creative Minds: Erich Neumann and C.G. Jung in Relationship (1933–1960)* (Asheville, NC: Chiron, 2016).
4 Martin Liebscher (ed.), *C.G. Jung und Erich Neumann: Die Briefe 1933–1959. Analytische Psychologie im Exil* (Ostfildern: Patmos, 2015).
5 Erich Neumann, *Jacob and Esau: On the Collective Symbolism of the Brother Motif.* Edited by Erel Shalit, translated by Mark Kyburz (Asheville, NC: Chiron, 2016).
6 Micha Neumann, *The Relationship between C.G. Jung and Erich Neumann based on their Correspondence* (Asheville, NC: Chiron, 2016).
7 Erich Neumann, *The Roots of Jewish Consciousness*, 2 vols., edited by Ann Conrad Lammers; translated by Mark Kyburz and Ann Conrad Lammers (London and New York: Routledge, 2019).

Acknowledgments

I am indebted first and foremost to the children of Erich and Julie Neumann—Rali Loewenthal-Neumann and Professor Micha Neumann—who offered me such generous insight into the lives of their parents during several long conversations. In addition, Rali Loewenthal-Neumann entrusted me with a large number of unpublished manuscripts and photographs, which form the basis of many essential aspects of this book.

Many thanks are due to my friends and colleagues, who have been such good discussion partners. I am most grateful to my colleague Michael Lindner for his valuable advice and for his careful editing of parts of the German manuscript. Elke Metzner's encouragement and initiative gave me the opportunity to present some of my thoughts about Erich Neumann to an interested audience in the Jungian community. Daniel Krochmalnik, professor at the School of Jewish Theology at Potsdam University, gave me valuable hints and has been an important and stimulating discussion partner for many years. My thanks also go to Professor Lutz Müller, who provided me with a digitised version of Neumann's unpublished letters and unpublished manuscripts on the depth psychology of the Jewish person, which did not exist in printed form at the time. I am also grateful to Giovanni Sorge and Herbert Springer for their advice. I am also most grateful to my translator Mark Kyburz, whose musical ear and circumspect handling of language, as well as his ability to reproduce complex thoughts with stylistic elegance—not least his patience—formed the basis of an extraordinarily good and friendly cooperation.

I owe particular thanks to the DGAP (The German Association of Analytical Psychology) for bearing the publishing costs of the German edition. My gratitude also extends to the various places that inspired me while I was writing this book: I have fond memories of a Buddhist monastery in the Palani Hills in Tamil Nadu, India, and of a small farmhouse belonging to the Köster family in Szalafö in eastern Hungary.

Finally, I extend my deepest thanks to my husband, Roland Hegnauer: Without his patience and generosity it would not have been possible to have this book translated into English.

Credit Lines

Published with permission from the Neumann Estate.

Amor and Psyche: The Psychic Development of the Feminine: A Commentary on the Tale of Apulelus, Erich Neumann, Routledge and Paul Kegan, 1971, used with permission from Princeton University Press, Copyright Clearance Center.

Analytical Psychology in Exile: The Correspondence of C. G. Jung and Erich Neumann, C. G. Jung, Martin Liebscher, and Erich Neumann, 2015, used with permission from Princeton University Press, Copyright Clearance Center.

The Roots of Jewish Consciousness, Volume One: Revelation and Apocalypse and The Roots of Jewish Consciousness, Volume Two: Hasidism, by Erich Neumann, edited by Ann Conrad Lammers, Routledge, 2019, used with permission.

Abbreviations

AP	Erich Neumann, *Amor and Psyche: The Psychic Development of the Feminine, A Commentary on the Tale by Apuleius*, Bollingen Series LIV (New York: Princeton University Press, 1956); orig. published as *Apuleius: Amor und Psyche, mit einem Kommentar von Erich Neumann: Ein Beitrag zur seelischen Entwicklung des Weiblichen* (Zurich: Rascher Verlag, 1952).
CW	*The Collected Works of C.G. Jung.* Edited by Gerhard Adler, Michael Fordham, Herbert Read and William McGuire. 20 vols. Translated by R.F.C. Hull, Bollingen Series XX (New York and Princeton, NJ, and London: Princeton University Press, and Routledge and Kegan Paul, 1951–1979).
DA	Erich Neumann, *Der Anfang* (The Beginning), an unpublished novel.
DPNE	Erich Neumann, *Depth Psychology and a New Ethic* (published in German in 1949; the English edition first appeared in 1969).
DS	Erich Neumann's doctoral dissertation: *Johann Arnold Kanne. Ein vergessener Romantiker. Ein Beitrag zur Geschichte der mystischen Sprachphilosophie* (Berlin: Reuther and Reichard, 1927).
FF	Erich Neumann, *The Fear of the Feminine and Other Essays on Feminine Psychology*, ed. William McGuire, Bollingen Series LXI/4 (Princeton, NJ: Princeton University Press, 1994).
FFI	Erich Neumann, "Freud and the Father Image," *Creative Man: Five Essays*, trans. Eugene Rolfe, Bollingen Series LXI:2 (Princeton, NJ: Princeton University Press, 1979).
GM	Erich Neumann, *Die Grosse Mutter: Der Archetyp des grossen Weiblichen* (Zurich: Rhein Verlag, 1956); translated into English by Ralph Manheim as *The Great Mother: An Analysis*

	of the Archetype (London: Routledge and Kegan Paul, 1955).
KC	Erich Neumann, "Kafka Commentary," unpublished manuscript, completed in 1933.
KUE	Erich Neumann, *Krise und Erneuerung* (Crisis and Renewal) (Zurich: Rhein Verlag, 1961); reprinted in vol. 5 of Neumann's Eranos Vorträge (Rütte: Johanna Norländer Verlag, 2009), pp. 96–187. Not translated into English.
JE	Erich Neumann, "Jakob und Esau" (unpublished typescript, 1934); English translation: *Jacob and Esau: On the Collective Symbolism of the Brother Motif.* Edited by Erel Shalit. Translated by Mark Kyburz (Asheville, NC: Chiron, 2015).
JNC	*Analytical Psychology in Exile: The Correspondence of C. G. Jung and Erich Neumann.* Edited by Martin Liebscher. Translated by Heather McCartney (Princeton, NJ: Princeton University Press, 2015).
Major Trends	Gershom Scholem, *Major Trends in Jewish Mysticism* (New York: Schocken Books, 1995; first published in English in 1941; German ed. 1957).
MEA	Erich Neumann, "Die Bedeutung des Erdarchetyps für die Neuzeit," in *Mensch und Erde I*, Eranos Yearbook 1953 (Zurich: Rhein Verlag, 1954); translated into English as "The Meaning of the Earth Archetype for Modern Times," trans. Eugene Rolfe and Michael Cullingworth, *Harvest: International Journal for Jungian Studies* 27 (1980) and vol. 29 (1982); cited here from *The Fear of the Feminine and Other Essays on Feminine Psychology*, ed. William McGuire, Bollingen Series LXI/4 (Princeton, NJ: Princeton University Press, 1994), pp. 165–226.
MDR	C.G. Jung, *Memories, Dreams, Reflections.* Recorded and edited by Aniela Jaffé. Translated by Richard and Clara Winston (London: Collins, and Routledge and Kegan Paul, 1963).
MM	Erich Neumann, "Der mystische Mensch," *Der Mensch* (2), Eranos Yearbook 1948 (Zurich: Rhein-Verlag), pp. 317–374; reprinted in *Kulturentwicklung und Religion*, Eranos Vorträge, vol. 1, ed. Regula Bühlmann (Rütte: Johanna Nordländer Verlag, 2007), pp. 100–140. English translation as "Mystical Man," published in *The Mystic Vision*, ed. Joseph Campbell (Princeton, NJ: Princeton University Press, 1968), pp. 375–415.
MMF	Erich Neumann, "Zu Mozart's Zauberflöte" (1950); English translation as "On Mozart's Magic Flute," by Esther Doughty, *Quadrant* 11, no. 2 (1978), pp. 5–32; cited here from the revised

	translation by Boris Matthew in Erich Neumann, *The Fear of the Feminine and Other Essays on Feminine Psychology*, ed. William McGuire, Bollingen Series LXI/4 (Princeton, NJ: Princeton University Press, 1994), pp. 119–164.
NOF	Erich Neumann's letters to Olga Fröbe-Kapteyn (unpublished).
OHC	Erich Neumann, *The Origins and History of Consciousness* (German ed. 1949; English ed. 1954).
Psych & Rel	C.G. Jung, *Psychology and Religion* (1938) (CW 11,1).
Roots I, II	Erich Neumann, *The Roots of Jewish Consciousness.* 2 vols. Edited by Ann C. Lammers. Translated by Mark Kyburz and Ann Conrad Lammers (London: Routledge, 2019).
UD	Erich Neumann, unpublished diary (undated, probably written between 1926 and 1927).
Z	Friedrich Nietzsche, *Thus Spoke Zarathustra*. Translated by R. J. Hollingdale (London: Penguin, 1961/2003).

Part I

Germany

"I am a Jew and hold Prussian citizenship"

The cultural and political reorientation of a generation

"I was born on 23 January 1905 in Berlin-Charlottenburg, as the son of the merchant Eduard Neumann and his wife Selma née Brodnitz. I am a Jew and hold Prussian citizenship." These are the first two sentences of the curriculum vitae that Erich Neumann, aged 22 at the time, appended to his doctoral dissertation on its submission in 1927.

Couched in dry factuality, Neumann's self-description encapsulates a cosmos of backgrounds, allusions and reflections that, upon closer scrutiny, reveal the coordinates of the complex and difficult Jewish–German relations of an age, in which the German Empire, once founded in splendour and glory, had brought about its own demise through rushing blindly into a disastrous war. The young republic, which struggled to establish democratic structures in the aftermath of humiliating defeat, and engulfed in a profound economic crisis, came to a brutal end with the rise of National Socialism.

"I am a Jew and hold Prussian citizenship": The fact that Erich Neumann refers to himself first as a Jew and only then as a Prussian citizen is remarkable. This suggests that he rejected not only the complete integration of Jewish citizens into German life, which was widely called for by public opinion at the time, but also the greatest possible alignment with German thought and culture, aspired to by many Jewish citizens in the early 20th century. Leading figures of the Jewish community made countless attempts to bring together Judaism and *Deutschtum* ("Germanness"), as it was then called, so that their relationship could become a formula for future life in Germany. These endeavours ranged from demanding total assimilation, inner and outer, to the resigned observation that, in spite of all efforts, however painstaking, such rapprochement would ultimately prove impossible.

A veritable deluge of autobiographical writings by German Jews revealed just how far this dualism had not only become the pervasive theme of life at the time, but beyond that also prompted the search for synthesis. The wide array of perspectives and the heightening of this inner conflict suggest that, historically, this amounted to a very complex problem of personal and cultural identity.[1]

The grammatical structure of Neumann's terse assertion, "I am Jewish and have Prussian citizenship," indicates how he viewed this wide-reaching problem:

He favoured his Jewishness. "I am Jewish" reflects a need to reassure himself of his identity, whereas the second clause, "and have Prussian citizenship," almost comes as an afterthought. It articulates the young Neumann's perceived entitlement to dispose of his citizenship as he saw fit while distancing himself from it at the same time. This brief statement resonates with the inner struggle that preoccupied a considerable number of Jews in their search for synthesis during the German Empire and the Weimar Republic. There are, as we will see, good enough reasons to doubt whether such a synthesis could exist for Neumann.

Being born as a Jew in 1905 in Berlin-Charlottenburg corresponded to the following historical panorama: Berlin had been the capital of the German Empire since 1871, the very year in which German Jews were ensured equality before the law. The Jews, now freed from the previous legal strictures, began moving increasingly into the cities. In 1871, 36,326 Jews lived in Berlin and its suburbs; by 1910, their number had soared to 142,289; purely numerically, though also in religious, intellectual, economic and cultural terms, Berlin eventually became the centre of Jewish life in Germany.[2] More than 30 per cent of all German Jews lived in Berlin.[3] One quarter of the Jews living in Berlin were of foreign origin and lacked German citizenship. The so-called "Eastern Jews" (*Ostjuden*) came largely from Poland, Russia and Galicia, but also from other parts of the Habsburg monarchy. Many belonged to an Eastern Jewish proletariat of workers and small traders in Berlin. In the same period, however, an ever greater number of Jewish students, writers and artists from Eastern Europe and Vienna also began flocking to the imperial capital, which soon became the intellectual centre of European Jews. Hebrew and Yiddish books were published in large numbers in Berlin. The economic, cultural and religious differences between the Jews living in Berlin were enormous—only the anti-Semites regarded all Jews as a single entity.[4]

Charlottenburg was a preferred residential area among Jews in early 20th century Berlin. While in the 19th century, the northern part of *Berlin Mitte*, the city's central district, still constituted the Jewish centre of Berlin,[5] large-scale Jewish migration to the western districts, in particular Charlottenburg and Tiergarten, and later also Schöneberg and Wilmersdorf,[6] soon resulted from the increasing social advancement of Jews in the German Empire. Within these bourgeois districts, Jewish residential areas such as the Hansaviertel and the area around Bayerischer Platz soon emerged. Large synagogues were built in these western districts. The latest addition to this growing number was located at Wilmersdorfer Prinzregentenstrasse and had a capacity of 2,000 seats. The newly arriving Eastern European Jews often settled in the so-called Scheunenviertel, an impoverished area to the west of Alexanderplatz. Petty-bourgeois Eastern Jews preferred Prenzlauer Berg, while upper-class Jews lived in the Grunewald district.[7]

Erich Neumann's life began at 30 Joachimsthaler Strasse in Berlin-Charlottenburg, as the third child of assimilated Jews. His older siblings were named Lotte and Franz. Lotte was born on 1 August 1897, Franz on 3 March 1899.

Figure 1.1 Two-year-old Erich (centre) with his siblings Lotte and Franz

The Neumanns were well-to-do: Erich's father, Eduard Neumann, who was born on 29 March 1866 in Schlochau, the former province of Posen-West Prussia, was a grain merchant; his mother, Selma Neumann, born on 21 May 1872 in Posen (province of Posen), ran the Neumann household. The family belonged to the German middle class. The Neumanns could refer to themselves as citizens in two senses of the word: as members of the German Empire, and as part of a specific social class, the bourgeoisie.[8] For the vast majority of 19th-century Jews, becoming part of bourgeois society was an important, if not *the* most important goal: Integrating into and adapting to middle-class customs and traditions, and achieving distinction within that class, were considered the measure of social success or failure. Indeed, for the Jews, becoming bourgeois involved complete adaptation to middle-class styles and morals. Paradigmatic of this near-total assimilation—even if they seem grotesquely exaggerated today—are the words of the young Walther Rathenau: He demanded that the Jews did everything in their power to educate themselves and to work their way up from "the sultry ghetto into the clear air of the German forests and mountains."[9]

Most early 20th-century German Jews were highly acculturated. Consequently, a sense of upward mobility, paired with a craving for education, opportunities for self-representation and social recognition were regarded as the essential forces driving the intellectual and moral climate in the Neumann household. The sparse facts about Erich Neumann's childhood indicate that his family was in many respects a typical example of a widespread tendency. In the majority of Jewish families—in parallel to wide-reaching social secularisation—a drastic erosion of family-based religious and ritual traditions occurred in early 20th century Germany. Non-observance of the Sabbath became increasingly common: Shops closing on the Sabbath or on public holidays became a rare event, and public holidays also lost their previous significance and appeal. Like Christians, who attended church only to celebrate the highest feasts, there was now talk of "Three-Day Jews,"[10] those who came to the synagogue only on Rosh Hashanah (the two-day celebration of the New Year) and on Yom Kippur (Reconciliation Day).

Other widespread tendencies towards dissolution included many members leaving the Jewish community to convert to the Christian faith. Some practised such a Judeo-Christian symbiosis by observing Jewish holidays while celebrating Christmas and Easter. Others adapted even more strongly to their non-Jewish environment by marrying non-Jewish partners and founding mixed families.

Until the onset of modernity, Jewish culture had been widely identified with the Jewish religion. Its loss of importance is reflected in the situation of the Jewish communities, which were on the verge of collapse: Of the approximately 900 communities in Prussia in 1925, only 63 had a rabbi, 285 a teacher, and only half had a synagogue or a cemetery.[11] In his study "Zur Sozialpsychologie der Juden in Deutschland 1900–1930" (On the Social Psychology of Jews in Germany 1900–1930),[12] Gershom Scholem distinguished three different layers of assimilation among German Jews:

1. "Totally Germanised" Jews, who considered themselves Germans and, as Scholem wrote, "did not need to participate in the Jewish heritage nor felt any obligations towards it." Or, as he further observed, "of course, the Jewish element also played an unconscious role in this group and, perhaps because it was consciously suppressed, an even greater one."[13]
2. The class of rich Jews, "who largely exhibited the features of the nouveaux riches": Characteristic of this group was the desire to be on good terms with non-Jewish high society, as well as with the non-Jewish intelligentsia and cultural elite. Aside from a few exceptions, this layer became completely assimilated and was also open to baptism as a possible means of integration.[14] Its members raised their children as staunch patriots.
3. The largest group was the liberal Jewish middle class (to which the Neumanns belonged). The "substance of Judaism" had largely been lost, though without being completely abandoned. As Scholem remarked, certain Jewish rituals were practised in this group, including

> the observance of the high holidays, of Friday and Passover evenings, of women attending the synagogue on festive days to commemorate their deceased parents and children. The *Bar Mitzvah* celebration at the age of 14 was also maintained by the majority of this group. Religious education to the end of the 14th year, as prescribed by state law, was seldom.[15]

Scholem asserted that all three layers—although to different extents—were characterised by an "often secretive, manifest contradiction in terms, between an ideology that proclaimed assimilation, or which claimed its existence, and everyday behaviour, in particular in important life situations and in psychological reality."[16]

According to his children (Rali and Micha), Neumann's relationship with his parents was neither particularly close nor particularly cordial. Of all his family members, he was most fond of his sister Lotte. The atmosphere in the Neumann household seems to have been prosaic and sober, offering scant opportunities to talk about one's inner life.[17]

Neumann's (as yet) unpublished studies of Kafka's stories and novels contain a number of passages that reveal the young Erich's stance towards the world and life. The following passage is from his interpretation of Kafka's *Das Urteil* (The Judgment), in which an elderly father sentences his son Georg to death:

Figure 1.2 Twelve-year-old Erich (seated) with his brother Franz and their parents

> Georg's historical situation means that he lacks a sense of solidarity or ancestral lineage, which would establish ties with his forefathers and identity. But his mother has also died and with her any reassurance that he might have gained through faith, other people and the earth. The world in which Georg finds himself is already fatally narrow and endangered.[18]

Education and social advancement rather than tradition: Quite possibly, this equation applied to the Neumann household. The cultivated conditions at home offered Erich and his siblings a place where—sheltered from the outside world—they could develop their talents and embark on their academic careers. Lotte and Franz studied medicine and became doctors, while Erich first turned to the humanities before also pursuing medical studies.

Education was of paramount importance in middle-class Jewish homes. Jewish parents like Neumann's were determined to provide not only their sons but also their daughters an academic education. This was yet another sign of how strongly they identified with the social class to which they proudly belonged—the educated middle class—and which promised further opportunities for advancement. The better education of Jewish boys compared to their German peers could be observed over several generations.[19]

Erich attended the Mommsen Gymnasium (a liberal arts grammar school) on Wormserstrasse in Charlottenburg. German was his favourite subject. He also loved the Latin and Greek classics, including Virgil and Cicero. Even years later,

Figure 1.3 Eduard Neumann, Erich's father

Figure 1.4 Neumann's mother Selma Neumann (second from left) with her five sisters (from left) Regina, Clara, Hedwig, Marie and Käthe

he could still quote Homer by heart. His school-leaving certificate states that he was "going on to study German." Neumann's artistic inclinations became apparent at an early age and manifested themselves first and foremost in a series of literary experiments. From this vantage point—and seen in terms of his family background and talents—young Erich could have looked forward to a brilliant academic career under different, more favourable historical circumstances. Yet during his time at grammar school, the painfully dissonant sounds of collective sabre-rattling and euphoric warmongering blended with the harmonious sounds of humanistic ideals intent on nurturing individual development. The situation for German Jews became more and more critical, not least since their civic rights, previously guaranteed by the Empire, now came under ever greater pressure from the massive resurgence of anti-Semitism.

Circumstances compelled the generation of German Jews born around 1900 to painfully struggle for its own identity: amid the contradictory tensions created by their parents' assimilatory efforts on the one hand, and by the rapid succession of historical upheavals on the other, which seriously called into question the possibilities for integration. The most seismic event in this regard was unquestionably World War I and the post-war aftermath.[20] The year 1916 in particular became a year of unprecedented crisis for Germany's Jewish population.

In August 1914, many Jews still believed that the old "Jewish question" would soon be overcome once and for all. When war erupted, and after the declaration of a "truce," amid an "atmosphere of national solidarity," the Jews could now consider themselves an integral part of the German nation.[21] Enthusiastic expressions of loyalty and nationalistic commitment rang out in Jewish public life. Without exception, Jewish associations called upon their members to join the war effort. In the face of impending danger, and fuelled by staunch patriotism, the Jews were prepared to sacrifice everything. Widespread Jewish participation in the war coincided with a noticeable waning of anti-Semitic tendencies.

And yet, the frontline experience, which was meant to strengthen Jewish integration into German public life, precipitated radical disillusionment. When the anticipated crushing victory failed to materialise, the previous anti-Semitism once again reared its ugly head. The Jews were accused wholesale for the military setbacks and the hardship suffered back home; they were denounced as pacifists, slackers or profiteers.[22]

Under the influence of anti-Semitic associations, which began polemicising sharply against the alleged Jewish "shirkers," the Prussian Minister of War ordered a statistical survey on the Jewish contribution to the war effort. Conducted in 1916, this government measure suggested that the allegations of the Jew haters were considered justified until proven otherwise. The state's breach of loyalty towards the Jews was compounded by the fact that the findings were never published.[23] While the Jews obviously perceived the survey as anti-Semitic, Jewish organisations felt compelled to play down the crisis; they reassured the German public of their members' unconditional loyalty to the Empire. However, this diplomatic gesture could not conceal the far-reaching disappointment at the lost illusion of eventually "merging" into—and flourishing amid—Germanness.[24] The younger generation of Jews was profoundly unsettled by the self-evident contradiction between its legal predicament, its political and social equality, post-war impoverishment and mass unemployment on the one hand, and the resurgence of anti-Semitism on the other.[25] While their parents tended to trivialise matters, and maintained their faith in the future, intellectually minded young Jews in particular responded both more sceptically and more hesitantly to the change in public mood. More often than not, they flatly rejected their parents' life and adaptation strategies.

Even if Erich took good advantage of the education that his gymnasium offered its students, above all the opportunity to learn foreign languages, he dismissed school as a place of learning. With no teachers to revere, he often missed classes, earning himself poor marks for diligence and application. He preferred to meet his friends, including his classmate Carl Frankenstein, at a Jewish debating society, which he joined already at the age of 16. The group debated current political affairs and philosophy, forged its own worldview, which gravitated around Jewish identity, and took private lessons in modern Hebrew.

Neumann also undertook various poetic experiments, in which he explored the contours of a potential future Jewish identity. One of his expressionist-visionary poems, many of which he wrote while at grammar school, reflect his feelings about the fate of the Jewish people:

Figure 1.5 Erich as a grammar school student

Is God, sunken for a thousand years, emerging?
Are stone tombstones now bursting asunder?
Is God's new fate quivering from sunken vaults, overshadowing time?
You people, overwhelmed with millennia of God's steely wrath.
Almost crushed under the weight of the vanished deity
Transformed, gratingly, from divine kings, Saul, David, Solomon
Overflamed by the glow of Yahweh's fire
A faintly glimmering flock, sunken in the sludge and ash of the past.

Yet soaring high, in despair, ablaze in Elias's glowing wagon
Once every millennium.
To burn the fall of the people into God.

Is the earthly chasm opening once again?
To recall its people
In a sea of fire and lightning
New Sinai,

Eternal Annunciation Rebirth?
Look up
The earth is faltering
And one writes with flashes of lightning
The signs of his covenant in heaven.[26]

Since the typical Jewish home offered almost no visible traces of what might have been considered an expression of a remembered Jewish identity,[27] the young Jewish generation set out in search of a new definition of Judaism. What meaning could Judaism have for them? If religion was merely a fragile basis for highly secularised German Jews, and thus no longer the place "on which identity could be founded," what could replace it?

Erich Neumann's choice of university subjects suggests where he hoped he might find answers to these pressing questions. After graduating from grammar school in 1923, he enrolled at the University of Erlangen, where he read philosophy, psychology, education, the history of literature and art, and Semitic studies. His humanistic orientation seems to have further deepened the basic questions he had been asking himself already at school. His friend Gerhard Adler, who later also became a well known Jungian analyst, and with whom Neumann maintained a lifelong friendship, recalls how intensely the young Erich took part in fundamental debates:

> Even then, as a student and young man, his creative personality was clearly and impressively evident. We belonged to a circle of friends deeply interested in and committed to engaging with the problems of the post-war period—problems for which Germany provided a focal point at the time: philosophy, psychology, poetry and art, and not least the Jewish question. How many nights did we spend locked in intense, never-ending conversations about the questions of life! In search of answers, he [Neumann] contributed his views, his passionate nature, his original and creative answers.[28]

An entry in a private diary that Neumann kept during his student years illumines his relationship with Adler and also contains the following self-assessment:[29]

> In response to some remark I made yesterday, Gerhard [Adler] said: This is what you have over me, your unconditional self-confidence. I am always embarrassed when I am told that. Because I do not like people finding me quite so "arrogant." In fact, it is not arrogance at all. For my self-confidence, which I have without a doubt, is identical with my inferiority, even if it involves no "inferiority feeling." I am most certainly self-critical. I know my negative points, but keep turning them into what drives me, not what troubles me. When I think about what I want and should achieve, I am quite sceptical. Saying that, I know that I will always have a central connection, even if no one else sees it. Still, I believe I possess something indestructible.

(UD)

Another entry reveals Neumann's passion for debating life and its questions with his friends:

> Harmlessness, enjoyment, bodily activity, pleasure: Everything is possible, even naivete and childishness, though hardly Siegfried's ignorance. ... In the end, I do not believe in God, but am sure of him. The absurdity of the world, and its unimaginability, which is nevertheless related to something, forces itself upon me, just as it remains within us. This, in my eyes, is the devastating aspect of Christianity. In the unspeakable godlessness of the world, they [Christians] crucify a prophet and worship him as God, merely to create something like themselves, a human being. The Jews are not so naive. We felt God once, and once one has experienced that connection there is nothing else to be content with. Hence all the scepticism. Nothing will be able to destroy the Jews, for they will always search for the One. This "urge" is stronger than any other. There is no God, at least not for the time being. That is precisely why this urge is so strong ... The metaphysical meaning of the moment, that is the problem, the flash that strikes the centre. No effect on time. Direct contact. If it exists. This exists among people, so why not otherwise?
>
> (UD)

Attending discussion groups and self-organised lectures was the order of the day among grammar school and university students in the Weimar Republic. For this generation, the developmental stage during which "self-experimental life"[30] normally begins was overshadowed by massive social and political problems, amid which any personal circumstances receded into the background or were symptomatic of social upheaval. The discussion groups mainly involved young middle-class people.[31] It was precisely the fact that they came from assimilated families, who were familiar with the varieties of and variations on cultural and political assimilation, and who grew up in an atmosphere of material security, that heightened the conflict between demarcation and reorientation for young Jewish intellectuals like Erich Neumann. The difficult early years of the Weimar Republic provided the backdrop against which the generation around 1900 began forging new plans. The cultural upheaval when the Empire collapsed—which coincided with the end of World War I—was felt to be a revolutionary turning point, one that wrenched the young generation[32] from its dreams and challenged it to develop a new life plan.

What began as a genuine generational conflict now turned into a revolt of Jewish sons intent on leapfrogging the legacy of their assimilated fathers. In their quest for elements that might be shaped into a "symbolic identity,"[33] these young men explored the customs and traditions of earlier generations that had since fallen into oblivion. Against this venerable backdrop, their fathers appeared at best as pale shadows.[34] Thus, a large number of youth groups had emerged by the turn of the century. This phenomenon has commonly been referred to as the "youth movement."[35] When anti-Semitism forced its way, disastrously, into the youth associations, the Jews founded their own groups. In the 1920s, about one third of German Jews belonged to a Jewish youth organisation.[36]

Even if Neumann did not (as far as we know) belong to an organised group, he grew up in the spirit of this youth culture. Strikingly, Jewish youth culture at the time shared a considerable number of aims and positions across otherwise strong political divides. They all attached great importance to the search for Jewish identity. What preoccupied their members, whose number was not particularly large, was the central question of Jewish existence in a secularised society. How could a modern form of Judaism be created? What might be its contents? From these questions ensued a search for Jewish authenticity and originality, for spiritual reorientation.[37] So-called "isms" (e.g. rationalism, liberalism and materialism) were rejected as hostile to life and as fragmenting. Stale bourgeois existence was subjected to fierce criticism, which erupted in stinging remarks about the hectic pace of urban life and its decadence, widespread mechanisation, and parental and educational impositions, for instance, those of institutions like schools, which were felt to deform rather than build character. The generation of 1900 envisaged a new society. This, they believed, would replace the perpetual and ultimately futile struggle of interests, and the materialistic orientation of life, with a community based on idealistic values.

The search for Jewish identity idealised rural life. Nature became the guiding concept of this neo-romantic movement. Unmistakable in this regard are the manifold associations with the contemporaneous life reform movement, with Nietzsche's philosophy of life and cultural criticism, which indirectly revived Rousseau's adoration of nature, and with art nouveau.[38] Key philosophical terms at the time included wholeness and originality, which were said to exist in Eastern European Judaism, in particular among the Hasidim, whose mystical depth exerted a profound fascination on the young generation of Jews. In addition to Theodor Herzl's *Altneuland* (The Old New Land) and Martin Buber's *Die Erzählungen der Chassidim* (Tales of the Hasidim), the reading list for aspiring young Jewish intellectuals included Hermann Hesse's novel *Demian*, Stefan George's poems or Oswald Spengler's *Untergang des Abendlandes* (The Decline of the West), a monumental study in cultural pessimism. Together, these writings formed the seedbed for the young generation's search for authenticity. Martin Buber dubbed this quest the "Jewish Renaissance" as early as 1900.[39]

The forces driving the "Jewish Renaissance" included many figures, Zionists and non-Zionists, dedicated to modernising and reformulating Jewish tradition and culture. First and foremost among them were Martin Buber, Franz Rosenzweig and their students, who gathered at the *Freies Jüdisches Lehrhaus* (Liberal Jewish Teaching Centre) in Frankfurt during the 1920s.

Many figures who later made a name for themselves under completely different circumstances were fascinated by the project of a Jewish Renaissance and actively participated in this movement during their school or student days.[40] One pivotal influence was what Gershom Scholem later described as "tendencies that promoted the rediscovery by the Jews of their own selves and their history." These, he remarked, would enable "spiritual, cultural, and, above all, social rebirth."[41] Nevertheless, realising the potential slumbering in Judaism only seemed possible if, as Scholem asserted, "the Jew would encounter himself, his people, and his roots."[42]

A passage in Neumann's diary reflects his views on these ideas:

> Again and again I am surprised by my dislike of the purely scientific ... my urge towards what I would almost call religious efficacy. Not that I wish to preach or anything of the sort. Yet I feel God in everything ... This is now an evil phrase, but I do not know how to express it any better ... Here, too, lies a source of my awareness of the selectness of the Jews. I feel it in my essence that my ancestors have had an intimate relationship with God for thousands of years. All Jews must have that, for we are those upon whom he relies. If, however, this chain runs through all generations and families, then each one of us must also conquer direct intimacy ... Thus we must forever replenish the stock, which we pass on.
>
> (UD)

In his programmatic *On the Jewish Renaissance* (1903), Buber advances his ideas of ancestral lineage, though particularly his concept of the people. His views are reminiscent of Johann Gottfried Herder's national concept of individuality:

> We live in a time that seems to introduce an epoch of cultural seeds. We see national groups gathering around new flags ... Not ... the territorial expansion of nations now strives to live out its full potential, but their individual nuances. The souls of the peoples are contemplating themselves. One wants to make the unconscious development of the national psyche conscious: one wants to condense the specific characteristics of a blood tribe and to exploit these creatively; one wants to make the national instincts more productive by proclaiming their kind. Goethe's dream of a world literature assumes new shapes: only when each people speaks from its essence does it increase the common treasure.[43]

Buber's call to renew the *Volkseele* (the people's soul)—a term that is perhaps difficult to understand today—reflected the spirit of the *fin de siècle*, for which the beginning of the new century represented the awakening of modernity, whose many facets sparkled in manifold and highly contradictory ways. Buber's *Tales of the Hasidim* (first published in German in 1906) attracted widespread acclaim and formed the basis of a renewed interest in Judaism among many assimilated Jews in Germany. One of the reasons for the successful reception of these stories was the growing popularisation of myths and mysticism. The poet Stefan George and his circle drew on Germanic myths and Eastern spiritual ideas as sources for modern literary creativity. The publisher Eugen Diederichs published classical mystical texts in modern translations. In the same year (1906) that saw the publication of Buber's *Rabbi Nachman*, and Gustav Landauer published the first modern translation of the German mystic Meister Eckhart.[44]

In turning to Hasidism, Buber not only followed the contemporaneous awakening of mystical traditions, but also resisted the "science of Judaism." Shaped by 19th-century positivism, this endeavour had sought to present Judaism as a "pure," rational religion devoid of mysticism and superstition. Buber linked Jewish mysticism to the German mystic tradition of Jakob Böhme, thus enabling emancipated Jews to discover their tradition, whose depth and significance had previously remained elusive.[45] A considerable number of Jews—influenced by Buber's tales—returned either to Jewish religion or became Zionists. Buber's mystical reorientation provided an alternative to the German-bourgeois educational ideal, hitherto steeped in the Enlightenment and deeply internalised in the Jewish world.

Thus, Buber significantly influenced the emerging debate on religious tradition. Nevertheless, it was impossible to simply restore Jewish traditions or to reverse the fundamental socio-economic and intellectual changes experienced by previous generations.[46] The process initiated under the slogans "renewal of Judaism" and "revivification of the heart"[47] made it possible, although eclectically, to discard seemingly useless mythisations, and to foreground others, in what constituted a process of creative reappropriation. By returning to traditional sources, Martin Buber, Oskar Goldberg and Erich Unger[48]—the latter two deserve mention for their strong influence on Neumann—reinvigorated messianic historical thinking. This nurtured the hope of awakening individual creative forces and the capacity for social renewal. As he wrote in his diary, Neumann considered messianic thinking to be crucial:

> I have done some more philosophical work, and am once again scared by my *daimonion*. What had occurred to me intuitively a year or more previously, without me noticing, now suddenly became clear. My entire work forms a coherent inner unity. Even the wrong thing, in fact this of all things, clearly points in one and the same direction. All of sudden there transpired "The Philosophy of Messianism," for which everything else had merely been preliminary work.
>
> (UD)

Gershom Scholem, who engaged in a lifelong intellectual debate with Buber, recalled the latter's influence in his memoirs:

> There can be no doubt that Martin Buber was the most influential proponent of a radical new beginning among German-speaking Zionists. In his *Reden über das Judentum* [Addresses on Judaism] he took Achad Ha'amism[49] in a new, distinctly religious-romantic direction, thus confronting a "religion" that had grown formally rigid with a "religiosity" that would be creative and truly central. Buber later abandoned this antithesis, which was quite popular

in Germany at that time, and struck out in other directions … He found a fair number of disciples who were prepared to adopt his catchword about "*Urjudentum*," a primal Judaism that was to be revived from rigidified rabbinism. A number of publications in this vein, particularly the collection *Vom Judentum* [On Judaism], which was inspired by Buber and issued by Kurt Wolff in 1913, aroused violent controversies.[50]

Buber delivered his *Reden über das Judentum* at "Bar Kochba," the Prague Jewish student association, between 1909 and 1913, leaving in particular the young Zionists in attendance deeply impressed. The religious-romantic colouring of these addresses, in which Buber presented a new form of Jewish self-reflection as a return to origins and ancestry, along with his affirmation of the peculiar destiny of the Jewish people, as it emerges from its history, ushered in a veritable Buber cult. Under his influence, Jewish themes became questions about individual life and conscience. In 1913, in the wake of Buber's *Reden*, Zionist students in Prague published an anthology in which the established Jewish bourgeois lifestyle was vehemently rejected; its philistine, mendacious character was denounced, while its vibrant yet meaningless activity was deplored.[51] Hans Kohn articulated this sentiment in his preface to the collection:

> We see the Jewish people, barely a people any more, a torn, lost flock, anxious and cowardly, inactive and dull, devoted to everyday life, in awe solely of its conditions, perceiving its weakness as normal. Nowhere exists a great emotion capable of tearing asunder the web of circumstance, nor of confronting it with a new realm, from which sprouted a spirit and an idea that formed all matter; nowhere is there a great will that bears testimony to a creative act.

Kohn's pathos echoes Fichte's *Reden an die deutsche Nation* (Addresses to the German Nation) and is unmistakably that of the youth movement.[52] Kurt Blumenfeld, the intellectual pioneer of the German Zionist movement, adopted the same tone. He accused western Judaism of being "rootless" and of possessing a "hermaphroditic soul." He was also contemptuous of the "comfort" in which the Jews lived. Zionism, along with its resolutely political thrust, could also be seen as a cultural revolution brought about by the rise of anti-Semitism.[53] One of its main concerns was to redefine Jewish identity. Its respective lines of argumentation attempted to deal with the anti-Jewish stereotypes to the point of a painfully exaggerated self-criticism. These stereotypes had changed decisively in the first two decades of the 20th century. Jews now represented the anti-thesis to the prevailing neo-romantic ideal of the time: They were largely urbanised, not bound to a native soil, homeless and lacked living popular traditions. Judaism, once attacked for its "superstition," was now criticised for being a rational religion. Thus, for instance, the "restless age" and the "restless Jew" merged into the signature of an ominous epoch. The fact that German Jews were highly urbanised suggested that anti-Semitic slogans might have some truth. The bourgeois Jews in the large cities had become the "distorted image of modernity," in particular for neo-conservative ideologists. This distorted image perturbed those whose own image was distorted.

This stereotype is evident, for instance, in one of the most widely read anti-Semitic books at the time: Julius Langbehn's *Rembrandt als Erzieher* (1890), which juxtaposes pre-modern and modern Jews:

> Rembrandt's Jews were real Jews who wanted to be nothing other than Jews. Moreover, they had character. The Jews of today embody exactly the opposite: They want to be Germans, English, French, etc. and have thus become characterless.[54]

To free themselves from their role as outsiders, and to shield themselves against the anti-Semitic projection of being "modern, decomposing and soulless," German Jews needed to immunise themselves against the majority verdict. These strategies involved taking up traditional strands capable of discontinuing the past and of disrupting German-Jewish culture from within. The search for such a new identity was labelled "post-assimilatory," a term coined by Kurt Blumenfeld. It epitomised the struggle to restore personal dignity, inner truth and freedom all at once. Thus, initiatives for achieving post-assimilation were welcome. They included purging one's own character, turning towards one's origins by reinvigorating one's traditions, the concept of nature and the humanistic ideal of education. The zenith, however, was performing the "Zionist act" par excellence: emigration to Palestine.

The fact that Neumann joined the *Berliner Zionistische Vereinigung* (Zionist Union of Berlin), at the suggestion of his friend Erwin Loewenson, may be said to have outwardly manifested a clear political stance. This much is evident from the official confirmation, dated 2 March 1924, of Neumann joining the *Vereinigung*. His corresponding diary entry reads: "I am conscious of the fact that my whole life is harnessed into the great task, and that everything individual only becomes meaningful in relation to this goal" (UD).

Neumann was mostly likely strongly influenced by Zionist ideals during his student days, not least owing to his friendship with Erwin Loewenson. Seventeen years his senior, Loewenson worked for several literary magazines and was a founding member of the *Neuer Club*. He is considered one of the pioneers of early literary expressionism and served as secretary of the German-Palestine Relief Organisation. He was actively involved in the Zionist Association as a journalist and events organiser. The philosophical foundation underpinning Neumann's early notion of Jewish identity sprang from the vibrant culture of discussion among and the publications of "Goldberg's crowd," as Walter Benjamin once called this group somewhat disparagingly.[55] Loewenson, a classmate of Goldberg's and Erich Unger's,[56] was consistently present and active in these circles, which had emerged from a literary-philosophical association of lower secondary students at Friedrich Gymnasium in Berlin Lichterfelde. It was the philosophical ideas of these two "guiding intellectual forces" that Loewenson passed on to the young

Neumann. Loewenson can be regarded as Neumann's early intellectual role model, from which—as his diary reveals—he struggled to distance himself, since amicable "devotion" became entangled with Zionist commitment, which required the individual to step back behind the collective "cause":[57]

> And Erwin? On the one hand I am absolutely his student. I would be unthinkable without him; yet time and again, without any vanity whatsoever, I believe a difference exists somewhere, also philosophically. However, I consciously apply myself to support him. I do not seek to gain any independence from him, since this is not my cause, nor indeed barely our cause, but the *cause*. And it would be to its detriment.
>
> (UD; original emphasis)

It is not unlikely that Loewenson introduced Neumann to Hannah Arendt, with whom he had had a brief liaison.[58] Arendt had relocated from Marburg to Heidelberg in 1926 to pursue doctoral work with Karl Jaspers. Her acquaintances in Heidelberg included Hans Jonas, Benno von Wiese, Friedrich Gundolf, Kurt Blumenfeld and Erich Neumann.[59] Loewenson also seemed to have been a role model in private matters. Here, however, Neumann draws the sharpest line, or indeed even expresses a sense of superiority over his much older friend. In his diary, he tells Julie:

> We thrive on closeness, on living the moment to the full, which is infinitely rich and independent. That's the private part. Erwin is rather opposed to such a thing and probably calls it individualism, yet that is mistaken. … I often feel superior to him. Especially when he talks about women.
>
> (UD)

His relationship with Loewenson also required Neumann to position himself vis-à-vis his commitment to the "cause." The following entry in his diary reveals how he set himself apart from Zionist heroism, though without abandoning the role model as which the Zionists saw themselves:

> I find it very strange that the Jews have no heroes in the same sense as the other peoples. (In the Bible this is another matter.) I do not think this can be explained by inferiority etc. Strangely, they have almost never resisted pogroms, etc. Here exists a centredness on God, which strongly points towards fatalism (or is it guilt or perhaps even a weariness of life?) Here lies a danger! Zionism should not "just" become heroic! Everyone must feel this responsibility in their blood, and must live as if the Jews could die without them—but I do not believe this is true. The Jews are not dying. We don't know their sources. If, however, the split-off, reformed Western Jews could become people like us! The Jews do not die that easily.
>
> (UD)

Figure 1.6 Erich and Hannah Arendt wearing fancy dress

Neumann's entry into the Zionist Union had a polarising effect on his family, and perhaps even caused irreconcilable differences—as it would have done in many other Jewish homes at the time. These divisions reflected the tensions created by the conflicting ideological concepts typifying the confrontation with the political situation in the Weimar Republic. Gershom Scholem, a Zionist, who had also been raised in an assimilated, liberal household like Neumann, later recalled:

> If I may say so, based on my own experience, and that of the friends of my youth, these contradictions lay between the conscious general assertions staunchly defended in domestic debates and the unacknowledged, largely also expressly denied emotional attitudes.[60]

The Zionists fiercely contested, indeed even refuted, the notion of assimilation and the attitudes associated with it. They had challenged its originally positive meaning from the outset. In the course of the Zionist clashes with their adversaries, the term "assimilation" became increasingly synonymous with Jewish self-denial, as well as with a blindness to the hostilities facing the Jews amid intensifying anti-Semitism. Standing up for Zionism meant committing oneself to a position that was not only under fierce attack from many sides but also rejected by the majority of German Jews.

The political attitudes held by German Jews in the early 20th century were as follows: About 60 per cent—including Neumann's parents—were liberals. Emancipated and saturated, they were anti-Marxist, yet tolerant, willing to enter coalitions and voted DDP (German Democratic Party).[61] Their official lobby was the "Centralverein deutscher Staatsbürger jüdischen Glaubens" (Central Association of German Citizens of the Jewish Faith),[62] whose main task was combatting anti-Semitism. Ideologically, liberal Jews aspired to symbiosis, that is, a humanitarian "German-Jewish worldview." They understood the association between Germans and Jews primarily in terms of the explicit appreciation and defence of the bourgeois, enlightened cultural tradition. And yet, they strongly objected to a "Jewish-national solution to the Jewish question" along Zionist lines.[63]

The other two groups were law-abiding Jews and Zionists. Both expressed far more serious reservations about German society than the liberal majority.[64] The German Zionist Association, which had been under the stewardship of Kurt Blumenfeld since 1924, was relatively small. In 1930, it had approximately 20,000 members, that is, roughly 3.5 per cent of German Jews.[65] Nevertheless, the Zionist theses were unmistakably sharp-edged.[66] They called upon Jews to finally become "conscious Jews" again and to overcome their attachment to German culture. Rather than assimilation, the Zionists propagated the "conscious Jewification" of the Jews.[67] German Zionism saw its task chiefly as raising awareness, so as to ensure a "return to Judaism before returning to Jewish land," as Herzl's striking formulation had put it.[68]

In spite of their radical aversion, from German culture towards their own traditions, the Zionist influence on the debate over the position of Jews within German culture should not be underestimated, least of all since many of their followers were intellectuals. The Zionist press found an interested readership far beyond its subscribers.[69] On balance, public discussion within German Judaism was determined by the ideological debate between the two most prominent factions: the C.V. ("Central-Verein") and the ZVfD ("Zionistische Vereinigung," the Zionist Association").[70]

Thus, the decision to become a Zionist—as Erich Neumann did—had serious consequences for one's political stance and at the same time for one's position within the Jewish discursive community. The consequences were serious, among others, since this decision was associated with the intention to emigrate and to begin a new life under wholly uncertain circumstances.

Notes

1 The title of Jakob Wassermann's autobiographical account (1921)—*Mein Weg als Deutscher und Jude* (My Path as a German and as a Jew)—bears witness to this conflict.

2 See the anthology *Juden in Berlin 1671–1945: Ein Lesebuch* (Berlin: Nicolaische Buchhandlung, 1988), p. 127.

3 After Berlin, Frankfurt and Wroclaw had the largest Jewish populations; see Jost Hermand, "Am Endpunkt der Emanzipation: Juden in der Kultur der Weimarer Republik," in his *Judentum und deutsche Kultur: Beispiele einer schmerzhaften Symbiose* (Cologne, Weimar, Vienna: Böhlau, 1996), p. 143.

4 See *Juden in Berlin.*

5 The "Stiftung Neue Synagoge Berlin – Centrum Judaicum" at Oranienburgerstrasse still bears witness to this today.

6 These were middle-class Jews, whose average income was twice or even three times higher than that of their fellow Jewish citizens. The number of self-employed Jews amounted to 46 per cent in 1933, while it was only 16 per cent among non-Jews. Most German Jews were active in commercial or academic professions. The proportion of doctors and lawyers was astonishingly high, as was the number of Jews in cultural life. It was highest among editors and lawyers (5 per cent). Four per cent of male students were of Jewish descent, 7 per cent of female students; see Hermand, "Am Endpunkt der Emanzipation," p. 143.

7 Ibid., p. 180.

8 Shulamit Volkov, "Die Verbürgerlichung der Juden in Deutschland als Paradigma," in his *Antisemitismus als kultureller Code* (Munich: Beck'sche Reihe, 1990), p. 111.

9 Walther Rathenau, "Höre Israel!" *Die Zukunft* (1897); see Harry Graf Kessler, *Walther Rathenau: Sein Leben und sein Werk* (Frankfurt am Main: Fischer, 1988; first published 1928), p. 41.

10 Trude Maurer, "Die Juden in der Weimarer Republik," in Dirk Blasius and Dan Diner (eds.), *Zerbrochene Geschichte: Leben und Selbstverständnis der Juden in Deutschland* (Frankfurt am Main: Fischer, 1991), p. 115.

11 Moshe Zimmermann, *Die Deutschen Juden 1914–1945* (Munich: De Gruyter, 1997), p. 37.

12 Gershom Scholem, "Zur Sozialpsychologie der Juden in Deutschland, 1900–1930," *Judaica 4* (Frankfurt am Main, 1984).

13 Ibid., pp. 235–236.

14 Ibid., p. 236ff.

15 Ibid., p. 238f.

16 Ibid., p. 240.

17 Rali Loewenthal-Neumann and Prof. Micha Neumann, personal communication.

18 *Das Urteil*, unpublished manuscript by Erich Neumann dating from the early 1930s, p. 17.

19 The gap became plainly obvious in the early 20th century. In Prussia, the number of Jewish children educated beyond primary school was eight times higher than among non-Jewish children. In Berlin, one quarter of gymnasium (i.e. grammar school) students were Jewish, although Germany's Jewish population amounted to slightly less than 1 per cent. At that time, the proportion of Jewish residents in Berlin was 4.26 per cent; see Shulamit Volkov, "Jüdische Assimilation und Eigenart in Deutschland," in his *Jüdisches Leben und Antisemitismus in Deutschland im 19. und 20. Jahrhundert* (Munich: C.H. Beck, 1990), p. 142.

20 In his preface to his *The Spirit of Utopia* (first published in German as *Geist der Utopie* in 1918; Stanford: Stanford University Press, 2000), Ernst Bloch commented on the war as follows: "There has never been a more dismal military objective than Imperial Germany's: a suffocating coercion imposed by mediocrities and tolerated by mediocrities; a triumph of stupidity, guarded by the gendarme, acclaimed by the intellectuals who did not have enough brains to provide slogans" (p. 1).

21 Volkov, "Die Juden in Deutschland 1780–1918," *Enzyklopädie deutscher Geschichte*, 2nd rev. ed., ed. Lothar Gall (Munich: De Gruyter, 2000), p. 67.

22 Ibid., p. 68.
23 Arno Herzig, *Jüdische Geschichte in Deutschland: Von den Anfängen bis zur Gegenwart*, 2nd ed. (Munich: C.H. Beck, 2002), p. 211. According to Jewish statistics, 12,000 Jewish soldiers died in World War I, a percentage of 12.5 compared to the general percentage of 13.4. About 100,000 Jews, including 19,835 from Greater Berlin, fought for Germany during World War I.
24 Georg Hermann, a well-known Jewish writer, observed that while his German identity had declined as a result of the war, his Jewish identity had increased; see Moshe Zimmermann, *Die Deutschen Juden 1914–1945* (Munich: De Gruyter, 1997), p. 5.
25 See Detlev J. K. Peukert, *Die Weimarer Republik: Krisenjahre der Klassischen Moderne* (Frankfurt am Main: Suhrkamp, 1987).
26 From a collection of unpublished poems by Erich Neumann, age 19 at the time.
27 Two memoirs are worth noting in this respect: Gershom Scholem, *From Berlin to Jerusalem* (Philadelphia: Paul Dry Books, 2012; orig. *Von Berlin nach Jerusalem*, 1997) and Richard Lichtheim, *Rückkehr: Lebenserinnerungen aus der Frühzeit des deutschen Zionismus* (Stuttgart: DVA, 1970).
28 H. Dieckmann, C.A. Meier and H.J. Wilke (eds.), *Kreativität des Unbewussten. Zum 75. Geburtstag von Erich Neumann (1905–1960)* (Basel: Karger, 1980), p. 10.
29 Written in epistolary form, Neumann dedicated his diary (undated, handwritten, ca. 40 pages) to Julie Blumenfeld, his future wife. It probably dates from 1926 to 1927; cited hereafter as UD.
30 Karl Mannheim, *Das Problem der Generationen in Wissenssoziologie*. Edited by K.H. Wolff (Berlin: Luchterhand, 1964), pp. 509–565.
31 As Gershom Scholem reports in his memoirs, "Jung Juda" (Young Judea) was a Zionist youth movement that consisted largely of pupils from West Berlin secondary schools and students; it met in a café at Tiergarten railway station; see *From Berlin to Jerusalem*, pp. 43–44.
32 A glance at the blossoming youth cult around 1900—commonly referred to as the "youth movement"—reveals that young people were discovering and asserting their independence on an unprecedented scale. In the first three decades of the 20th century, "youth" became a suggestive concept of society, whose charisma conjured up a wide range of emotions, as well as a wealth of associations with alternative life forms. What was negotiated here far transcended an adolescence in crisis. The phenomenon is widely known as the "incarnation of vitalism," in which not only young people were involved; rather, adults also made youth their business. In addition to socialist designs on history and nationalist prophecies, a third message can be heard: salvation by youth. A previously neglected "natural law," represented by adolescence, now became recognised. Youth became a myth, one that sought the profound revaluation of (above all bourgeois) values. Concepts and ways of life beyond modern industrial society were considered, discussed and experimented with. The resulting concepts manifested the quest for a "different" life, moreover a "different" society. The movement drew its impetus from the revolt of middle-class sons and daughters; see Thomas Koebner, Rolf-Peter Janz and Frank Trommler (eds.), *Mit uns zieht die neue Zeit: Der Mythos Jugend* (Frankfurt am Main: Suhrkamp, 1985).
33 In this regard, Herbert J. Gans speaks of "symbolic ethnicity." He also coined the term "symbolic identity," and in this context speaks of "subjective ethnic identity." An identity thus created differs fundamentally from an unquestionable rootedness in tradition; see Elisabeth Beck-Gernsheim, *Juden, Deutsche und andere Erinnerungslandschaften* (Frankfurt am Main: Suhrkamp, 1999), p. 246.
34 Gert Mattenklott, "Nicht durch Kampfesmacht und nicht durch Körperkraft: Alternativen jüdischer Jugendbewegung in Deutschland vom Anfang bis 1933," in Koebner et al. (eds.), *Mit uns zieht die neue Zeit*, p. 346.
35 Ibid.

36 Michael Brenner, *The Renaissance of Jewish Culture in Weimar Germany* (New Haven and London: Yale University Press, 1996), p. 47

37 A deeper, dissimilatory development, quasi-contrapuntal to assimilation, pervaded the Jewish population, as it were underground, and encouraged Jews to reconsider their self-image. Since the mid-1890s, signs of a new, wide-reaching preoccupation with Judaism became evident among German Jews. Numerous associations dedicated to promoting reflection on the roots of Jewish culture, without having to renounce one's German "heritage," were founded. Orthodox and liberal communities both participated in disseminating knowledge about religious, literary, historical and political topics; see Volkov, "Die Erfindung einer Tradition: Zur Entstehung des modernen Judentums in Deutschland," in his *Das jüdische Projekt der Moderne* (Munich: Beck'sche, 2001), pp. 118–137.

38 Hans Mommsen, "Generationskonflikt und Jugendrevolte in der Weimarer Republik," in Koebner et al. (eds.), *Mit uns zieht die neue Zeit*, pp. 50–67.

39 Martin Buber, "Jüdische Renaissance," first published in *Ost-West*, later reprinted in *Die jüdische Bewegung: Gesammelte Aufsätze und Ansprachen (1900–1914)* (Berlin: Jüdischer Verlag, 1920), pp. 7–16.

40 Jörg Hackeschmidt, *Von Kurt Blumenfeld zu Norbert Elias: Die Erfindung einer jüdischen Nation* (Hamburg: Europäische Verlagsanstalt, 1997), p. 9.

41 Scholem, *From Berlin to Jerusalem*, p. 54.

42 Ibid.

43 Martin Buber, *Die jüdische Bewegung. Gesammelte Aufsätze und Ansprachen* (1900–1914) (Berlin: Jüdischer Verlag, 1920), p. 7f.—Trans.

44 Brenner, *The Renaissance of Jewish Culture in Weimar Germany*, p. 29.

45 As George L. Mosse has remarked: "All of a sudden, the young Georg Lukacs discovered his possibly Hasidic ancestry. Under the same influence, Walther Rathenau briefly became an avid student of Hebrew"; see Mosse, *Jüdische Intellektuelle in Deutschland: Zwischen Religion und Nationalismus* (Frankfurt am Main: Campus Verlag, 1992), p. 65.

46 Eric Hobsbawm has described the formation of tradition as follows: "the peculiarity of 'invented' traditions is that the continuity with it is largely factitious. In short, they are responses to novel situations which take the form of reference to old situations, or which establish their own past by quasi obligatory repetition"; see Eric Hobsbawm and Terence Ranger, *The Invention of Tradition* (Cambridge: Cambridge University Press, 1984), p. 2.

47 Scholem, *From Berlin to Jerusalem*, p. 54.

48 See Manfred Voigts, *Oskar Goldberg: Der mythische Experimentalwissenschaftler. Ein verdrängtes Kapitel jüdischer Geschichte* (Berlin: Agora-Verlag, 1992); see also Henning Ritter, "Von Berlin-Lichterfelde nach New York," *Frankfurter Allgemeine Zeitung* (28 November 2007), p. N 3; *Lexikon deutsch-jüdischer Autoren*, vol. 9 (Munich: Saur, 2001), pp. 67–71.

49 The most important spokesman of a cultural, ostensibly non-political Zionism was the essayist Ascher Ginsberg, who became famous under the pseudonym Achad Ha'am. Some of his essays were available in German at the time.

50 Scholem, *From Berlin to Jerusalem*, p. 55.

51 Bar Kochba, Verein jüdischer Hochschüler (ed.), *Vom Judentum: Ein Sammelbuch* (Leipzig: Kurt Wolff Verlag, 1913).

52 This reproduces Fichte's pathos of Germany's struggle for survival against the French.

53 Kurt Blumenfeld speaks of a "cultural conflict" in this respect.

54 Julius Langbehn, *Rembrandt als Erzieher* (Weimar: Duncker, 1928).

55 Henning Ritter, "Von Berlin-Lichterfelde nach New York," *Frankfurter Allgemeine Zeitung* (28 November 2007), p. N 3.

56 Ibid.
57 Hans Tramer, "Berliner Frühexpressionisten: Leben und Schaffen von Erwin Loewenson," *Bulletin des Leo Baeck Instituts*, 6 (1963), pp. 245–254; Christoph Grubitz, "Erwin Loewenson (Golo Gangi)," in Andreas Kilcher (ed.), *Metzler-Lexikon der deutsch-jüdischen Literaturgeschichte: Jüdische Autorinnen und Autoren deutscher Sprache von der Aufklärung bis zur Gegenwart* (Stuttgart: Metzler, 2000), pp. 396–398.
58 Elisabeth Young-Brühl, *Hannah Arendt: Leben, Werk und Zeit* (Frankfurt am Main: Fischer, 2004).
59 Wolfgang Heuer, Bernd Heiter and Stefanie Rosenmüller (eds.), *Arendt Handbuch: Leben-Werk-Wirkung* (Stuttgart: Metzler, 2011).
60 Gershom Scholem, "Zur Sozialpsychologie der Juden in Deutschlang 1900–1930," p. 240.
61 Ideologically closest to the C.V. was the "Reichsbund jüdischer Frontsoldaten." Founded in 1918, its goal was to stave off anti-Semitism. It was the second largest Jewish organisation after the C.V. Its patriotism was surpassed by the "Verband nationaldeutscher Juden" (Association of National German Jews), which supported the right-wing DVP, later even the anti-Semitic DNVP, in order to convince the political right of the patriotic and anti-Marxist stance of German Jews. "The German vanguard, the Fellowship of German Jews," a youth club led by Hans-Joachim Schoeps, represented the most extreme position. Its slogan was: "Bereit für Deutschland" (Prepared for Germany). These groups adhered deeply to German bourgeois culture; see Hermand, "Am Endpunkt der Emanzipation," p. 144.
62 Alarmed by the election campaign of the anti-Semitic parties in 1893, in which they won 263,000 votes and 16 seats in the Reichstag, the C.V. was founded in 1893 as a liberal Jewish lobby. From its humble beginnings, the C.V. grew into the largest Jewish organisation in Germany. In 1918, it had over 38,000 individual and over a hundred corporate members, thus representing probably half of all German Jews; see Raymond Wolff, "Zwischen formaler Gleichberechtigung, Zionismus und Antisemitismus," in *Juden in Berlin*, p. 129.
63 Hermand, "Am Endpunkt der Emanzipation," p. 144.
64 In 1920, Orthodox Jews joined ranks in the "Bund gesetzestreuer jüdischer Gemeinden" (Union of Law-abiding Jewish Communities). They did not, however, play a decisive role in the subsequent cultural debates.
65 Hermand, "Am Endpunkt der Emanzipation," p. 147.
66 In contrast to the C.V., which vehemently affirmed its members' *Deutschtum* (Germanness), the idea of Jewish nationalism and Jewish self-emancipation, which had first appeared in Russia, now emerged. Its most prominent advocate was the journalist Theodor Herzl (1860–1904). Born in Budapest, Herzl published the Zionist pamphlet *Der Judenstaat* (The Jews' State) in 1896, in which he called for the founding of a Jewish state. Following the first Zionist Congress, held in Basel in 1887, the "Zionistische Vereinigung für Deutschland" (Zionist Association for Germany) was founded by various German delegates. "Jung Israel" (Young Israel) was founded in Berlin in 1892. From it arose the "Berliner zionistische Vereinigung" (Berlin Zionist Association), which was supplemented by Zionist student associations. Although its Zionist membership steadily increased, it could not rival the C.V. The Zionists declared the assimilation project a failure and demanded a Jewish home in Palestine. Not all German Zionists, on the other hand, represented a strict Jewish nationalism, but pleaded instead for extensive acculturation in Germany.
67 Hermand, "Am Endpunkt der Emanzipation," p. 146.
68 Ibid.

69 The most important Zionist publications, which were famous for their outstanding journalism, were *Ost und West*, an illustrated monthly for modern Judaism (1901–1923), and Buber's *Der Jude* (1916–1924).

70 The cosmopolitans, left-wing liberals, leftists and Marxists also deserve mention. The followers of the C.V. considered themselves close to the cosmopolitans, who had a considerable number of members for a short period of time. As one of their most prominent representatives, the writer Lion Feuchtwanger, declared: In a world in which there would be no more "borders," the Jews would play a decisive role on account of their "cosmopolitanism," that is "their non-rootedness in the soil," in particular in the field of culture.

Chapter 2

"Our paths will cross again!"
Erich Neumann and Julie Blumenfeld

Erich Neumann met Julie Blumenfeld, his future wife, as a 15-year-old grammar school student in Berlin. Also aged 15 at the time, Julie had joined "Blau-Weiss," a Zionist Youth Alliance, much to the displeasure of her parents, affluent, assimilated Jews. They allowed Julie to belong to Blau-Weiss, the *Bund für jüdisches Jugendwandern in Deutschland* (German Association of Jewish Youth Hiking Groups) if she agreed to cultivate her elegance and femininity instead of turning into a "child of nature."[1] This "cultivation programme" also included dance lessons.

Erich, too, was supposed to learn to dance.[2] The dance school was located at Pariserstrasse 4 in Berlin-Wilmersdorf, not far from his home. The Blumenfelds had lived on Kronprinzenufer 30 before relocating to an apartment one floor above the dance school. Julius Blumenfeld, Julie's father, had begun looking for an apartment where his family could play music without disturbing the neighbours. After an extensive search, he eventually found suitable accommodation (in 1918) at Pariserstrasse 4 in Berlin-Charlottenburg. Located on the ground floor was a private school for Jewish and Christian children, founded in 1918 by Anne Peletson, a Jewess who had converted to the Protestant faith (she was later murdered at Theresienstadt concentration camp).

The Blumenfelds moved onto the third floor, immediately above the dance school. Julie's father Julius (born on 21 June 1863 in Hamburg) came from a large Orthodox family. He had five sisters. His mother died in childbirth, and his father soon remarried. The second marriage produced two more sons. One of the family's hallmarks was its musical talent: Three of Julius's sisters became piano teachers, while two of his half-brothers also worked as musicians (one of them later became a celebrated violinist in America). Julius, who was also very musical, took up a commercial profession and began earning a living as a carpet trader.

In 1893, he married Ida Silbermann (born on 14 June 1869 in Berlin). Her parents had immigrated from Upper Silesia to Berlin and were well off: Ida's father was the director of a private bank. She had four sisters and a brother, who lived as an architect in Frankfurt an der Oder. When Julius married Ida, he entered the Reform Synagogue, since Ida's father was a member of the Reform community.

The couple had five children: Martin, Lotte and Paul were followed by Julie, who was born on 28 April 1905. Ruth, Julie's youngest sister, was born in 1909.

The apartment on Pariserstrasse was spacious: It had seven rooms; the two main rooms had large windows, and together with the dining room and the salon, where the piano stood, they lent the Blumenfeld's home a representative air. Julie's mother looked after the children. She was an excellent cook and sewed clothing for her sons and daughters. The family had several maids, who performed the numerous household chores for many years. It seems that Ida Blumenfeld managed to appease her husband's frequently effervescent temper, so that relations in the Blumenfeld household were largely harmonious. Julius Blumenfeld loved to travel a lot, including America, where three of his sisters and his two half-brothers lived.

The Blumenfelds were open-minded in religious matters. They attended the synagogue only on high holidays. Occasionally, though irregularly, they celebrated Sabbath and also Christmas. Julius justified these festivities as a concession to the maids. A small Christmas tree was bought for their room.

The family's musical talents were also evident in this generation: Lotte, Julie's eldest sister, became a pianist and piano teacher; her brother Paul a cellist. Her father, who had not learned to play an instrument in his youth, had a fine ear. If anyone played a wrong note, his voice would boom from the next room: "Wrong!" Ruth, Julie's youngest sister, was also an enthusiastic pianist. Ida's mother, who lived with her daughter's family during the final years of her life, often played pieces composed for four hands with one of her grandchildren.

Figure 2.1 The Blumenfelds, 1911: Julius Blumenfeld (front left), Ruth on her grandmother's lap, mother Ida with Julie, between the two women Paul, at the back Lotte and Martin between two relatives

Julie's musical talent could not match that of her siblings (like her, they did not enjoy school either). A highly formative influence during her teenage years, and indeed for her entire life, occurred when a friend persuaded Julie to join Blau-Weiss, a Jewish hiking association affiliated with a Zionist youth organisation. She was 13 years old at the time.[3] Blau-Weiss was not a "debating society," but an "activity club," as its founder Felix Rosenblüth once said.[4] It offered Jewish teenagers the opportunity to play games and attend events in keeping with the principles of the "Wandervogel" (Wayfaring Association), which focused on developing its young members' ideological outlook along national Jewish lines. The community spirit and the many outdoor experiences were greeted with storms of enthusiasm, making membership highly popular among 10- to 15-year-olds. However, most important to the association's founders—beyond any social romanticism—was a return to Judaism and the establishment of a collective, forward-looking Jewish identity.[5]

The Blumenfelds, like other liberal Jewish families, were not very pleased about Julie's decision to join a Zionist organisation. Even less so since she also persuaded her youngest sister Ruth to become a member of Blau-Weiss. Julie, a fervent activist, at least managed to have Hanukkah celebrated at home instead of Christmas. Hanukkah celebrations at Blau-Weiss meetings were part of the association's identity-forming educational work: Jewish youth groups celebrated Hanukkah by performing heroic scenes from Jewish tradition—among others, Moses's Exodus from Israel or the Bar Kochba uprising—as well as musical comedies; campfires were also hugely popular.[6]

Figure 2.2 The Blumenfelds, 1919: (front) Ruth, between their parents; (back, from left) Martin, Lotte, Julie and Paul

The fact that Julie, whose mind was brimming with Zionist ideas and who derived precious little pleasure from the temptations of bourgeois life, eventually attended the dance school one floor down from her home was the result of her parent's pressure. The Blumenfelds feared losing their daughter to a youth movement whose attraction was mistrusted by both liberal and orthodox Judaism.

Ruth, Julie's youngest sister, later recounted the following anecdote about Erich and Julie: "After one lesson, young Erich offered to take Julie home. She replied that wouldn't be necessary, since she lived upstairs. Erich made a disappointed face, but before long he was frequently and happily scaling the three flights up to the Blumenfeld's apartment."[7] Their acquaintance lasted six months. Julie ended it since she felt that Erich was far more mature than her, even if they were the same age. On 28 April 1921, Julie's 16th birthday, Erich gave her a book by Martin Buber with the dedication: "Our paths will cross!"[8] He later noted in his diary:

> Believe me, my "precociousness" comes more from deep down than from anything wide-ranging … I was too proud, that is, perhaps hurt too soon when I realised that I was not a woman's equal.

(UD)

Meeting and leaving Erich marked the beginning of Julie's professional orientation. Unlike him, whose later intellectual career was foreshadowed in his early writing activities, Julie's talents lay elsewhere. Her main interest, which probably grew from joining Blau-Weiss at such a young age, was to help others. She was keenly interested in children's social work and social care. There was, however, one obstacle: Julie had left Hohenzollern Lyceum at the end of Year 1. From October 1921 to Easter 1922, she worked as a volunteer in a refugee home for Eastern Jewish children.

A brief digression on Eastern Judaism is warranted here, since it influenced Julie and Erich's generation in various ways. Moreover, it is only against the historical background of the early 20th century that we can better appreciate what committing oneself to helping Eastern Jewish children meant in post-war Germany.

After World War I, Germany faced a tremendous influx of Jewish refugees from those regions that warfare had separated from the country's main territory. Other groups flocking to Germany included pogrom survivors and refugees from areas now under Ukrainian and Soviet control. According to estimates of the Jewish Welfare Office, approximately 100,000 Jews had escaped to Germany between 1914 and 1921. About 20,000 Eastern Jews now lived in Berlin. In the major cities, they accounted for roughly one quarter of the Jewish population, almost twice as much compared to the pre-war period.[9] The "Eastern Jew" soon became a political issue, above all in anti-Semitic election campaigns. The image of the Eastern Jews—even among acculturated Western German Jews—was largely stereotypical: They were viewed as the opposite of the assimilated Jew; they were said to be lazy and contaminated and were branded the carriers of infectious diseases, criminals, Asians and revolutionaries. In the eyes of assimilated Jews, the Eastern Jews kept alive a negative image of Jews and stood for everything that they rejected. The Eastern Jews therefore aroused highly mixed feelings among Western German Jews, who were overly concerned about preserving their status:

> With regard to status, the Eastern Jews were regarded as the greatest source of embarrassment, causing the better situated, better acculturated and better assimilated Jews sleepless nights. Shame and embarrassment were this generation's most important emotional extremes. One felt ashamed if one forgot or ignored the strict rules of the game of civilisation even for one moment. The inappropriate behaviour of others caused embarrassment. Given the strict behavioural rules that German Jews imposed upon themselves, shame was a persistent feeling. Their particular sense of solidarity was the source of constant embarrassment.[10]

The image of the Eastern Jews polarised the German-Jewish population. While assimilated Jews fretted over their status, Zionists and Orthodox Jews explicitly welcomed the Jews from Eastern Europe, whose arrival they believed would enrich their own Judaism.[11] Some Jews even felt compelled to finally renounce their Jewish ancestry, while others only now began to recognise the extent of their confrontation with their Jewishness:

> In view of the influx of Eastern Jews ... new definitions of their existence as Jews had to be searched for. They were about to transcend the limits of their own smug, solid bourgeois German identity.[12]

The "Eastern Jewish question" became one of the most fiercely debated issues and soon heightened the generational conflict in assimilated Jewish families. While the older generation was most intent on preserving its prestige, education and property, which had been attained with great difficulty over recent decades, the younger generation adopted a relatively relaxed attitude towards social advancement, if not even rejecting outright the necessity of "getting on" in life. At the same time, young Jews were more open to "recognising and acknowledging themselves in strangers and outsiders."[13] Thus, for instance, the philosopher Franz Rosenzweig wrote to his parents as early as 1916:

> There is no more unreasonable writing about Eastern Jews than about Western Jews ... there is no Eastern Jewish question, but only one Jewish question—and even that does not properly exist ... By the way, just consider the fact that none of the German fear of the Eastern Jews is aimed at Eastern Jews as such, but rather at them as future Western Jews (that is, people like yourselves).[14]

The Eastern Jewish question provided a considerable, yet well established Jewish minority, in particular the Zionists, an opportunity to examine their own Jewish identity. Heterogeneity and pluralism could now increasingly be viewed as positive values, in whose context the limitations of assimilation became apparent. Self-respect was barely possible without feeling solidarity with the dispossessed.

One practical form of solidarity, among many others, was doing social work with Eastern Jewish refugees. The premises at Auguststrasse 14–17 served as the headquarters of the *Ostjudenfürsorge* (Eastern Jewish Welfare Organisation), not only in Berlin but also for the whole of Germany.[15] To stem the onrush of needy and harried new arrivals at Auguststrasse, many able and willing hands from various professions were needed in addition to the extensive administrative apparatus. In 1920, the "Ahawah" children's home was built at Auguststrasse 14. Under its director Beate Berger, this facility soon became a model organisation. The Ahawah attended to the many refugee orphans and half-orphans arriving in Berlin in the post-war period.[16] The vast majority of volunteers were young people from the "Volksheim" (People's Home), from Zionist student circles and from the ranks of workers and refugees.[17] Julie Blumenfeld was one of the many auxiliaries eager to express her solidarity through steadfast idealism and commitment:

> For many of these people, some of whom worked all day without pay, others for low wages, working at Auguststrasse marked a vital career decision. From these volunteers grew a new generation of Jewish social workers in Germany. Working with refugees provided many leading Jewish social workers with excellent basic training.[18]

Julie's work at Ahawah[19] gradually crystallised into a professional inclination and outlook that would later lead her—at first via many detours—to enter that profession in which she found great fulfilment until the end of her life: her work as a Jungian analyst.

According to Julie's curriculum vitae, her professional life first involved several transfers and relocations, as a result of pursuing various occupations: From Easter to October 1922, she worked as a "housemaid" in Lübeck, "where she learned to keep house from top to bottom."[20] Later, she returned to Berlin, where she took an "inhouse examination" at the maternity and infants home at Brunnenstrasse 41 after completing "a six-month apprenticeship." At Easter 1923, she took a job as an assistant nurse for one and a half years at Friedrich Luisen Hospice in Bad Dürrheim, before eventually returning to Berlin, where she worked as a ward nurse in the maternity and infants home at Brunnenstrasse 41. She was 18 years old, yet the age requirement for qualifying as an infant nurse was 21 years.

Her social and psychological interests, as she later wrote, continued to grow as her professional life evolved. She also began working with older children and ran

Figure 2.3 Julie (left) with her friend Susi Cohn while training as an infant nurse in Mannheim

a day nursery in Berlin before returning to Auguststrasse, now as a nurse at the polyclinic. During this period, she also began preparing to sit her school-leaving examinations, which she was eager to take, in order to "pursue scientific, psychological and philosophical work."

Four years had passed since Erich and Julie had last heard from each other. One day, Erich called her. Now aged 20, they resumed their relationship. Soon afterwards, though, Julie left Berlin again, at Easter 1926, in order to take her state examinations as an "infant nurse" at Mannheim General Hospital, "in recognition of her earlier work." She then returned to Berlin and "ran a day nursery" until she married Erich. When Julie graduated in Mannheim in 1926, Erich was enrolled at the University of Erlangen, where he wrote his dissertation and was awarded a doctorate in philosophy on 2 March 1927.

Several passages in his diary reveal how close Julie and him had remained during their separation:

Figure 2.4 Julie, 1925

It dawned on me that we shared the rare conviction that unreserved closeness was indeed possible. And that's why we made it so difficult for ourselves … because it's a very fundamental change that we're demanding of ourselves. Put briefly, we take matters so much more seriously than almost everyone else. … "Hallowing" what for others is "everyday fare" is what I have learned from you in an utterly new way.

(UD)

In his diary, Erich also shared his fears and doubts, among others, the gulf looming within himself:

I still don't feel that you are strong enough to cope with my negativity. It's entirely mine. And if one had understood this negativity, only then would one have understood me completely. I'm quite positive … but my foundation lies in "darkness" (that's what I called it during puberty and I'm sticking with that word).

(UD)

Moreover, he confessed:

When people think all is well with me, it's always the opposite. And as if that weren't bad enough, I'm also accused of not wearing my heart on my sleeve.

(UD)

Nevertheless, he sensed that he could develop his character with Julie by his side:

> In general, people believe I'm egotistical. There's nothing I can say to dispute that. It's possible, except that I believe that my ego isn't limited to myself. It's wider. And there's so much that I need to do.
> You change me a lot, for the better I think.

(UD)

His touching declaration of love for Julie reveals how deeply grateful Erich was that he had met her:

> Please remember: You've made me infinitely rich. What it is, I don't quite know, but sometimes I even believe to be in your debt. The fact that you're alive is reason enough for me to believe that the world makes sense. Wherever such groundedness and purity can exist, there's still a long way to go before all is lost.

(UD)

Erich and Julie were married in September 1928 and moved into an apartment on Weimarer Strasse in Berlin-Wilmersdorf. Erich's parents, who were very affluent, at first expressed little interest in their son's intention to marry, as Julie had

Figure 2.5 The young couple in Berlin

received no dowry. However, they soon succumbed—as her younger sister Ruth reported—to Julie's charm.[21]

At Easter 1929, Julie entered the Pädagogium Thie, where she earned her baccalaureate in 1932. As she wrote in her curriculum vitae, she set herself the goal of "studying psychology and, in particular, to undergo training in special needs education."[22] While Erich had begun studying medicine at Berlin's Friedrich Wilhelm University, with the intention of becoming a psychoanalyst, Julie's inclination towards psychology at first concentrated on the new psycho-chirological method developed by Julius Spier.[23] Spier had opened his first practice in Berlin in 1931 and soon gained a reputation among doctors and psychologists as a chirologist working according to scientific principles.[24] Spier, who had developed chirology into a serious instrument of interpretation, did not live to see the publication of his only book, *The Hands of Children* (1944). In this work, he describes his specific approach to hand analysis, which links Jungian analytical psychology and classical chirology.[25] In his preface to Spier's book, C.G. Jung wrote:

> I have had several opportunities of observing Mr. Julius Spier at work, and must admit that the results he has achieved have made a lasting impression on me ... Spier's chirology is a valuable contribution to character-research in its widest application.[26]

Jung credits Spier's method chiefly for its remarkable, highly intuitive approach. He also believed that only exceptionally intuitive persons were capable of learning this method. Julie, who later felt committed to Jung's typology, recognised herself in the "intuitive type of feeling." Later, after Erich and Julie had emigrated to Palestine, she worked not only as an analyst but also as a chirologist trained in Spier's method. She became widely recognised in the field for her accurate diagnoses.

Micha, the Neumann's first child, was born on 17 June 1932. The young family, however, chose not to stay in Germany much longer. The streets of Berlin were full of hordes roaring at the top of their voices and parading anti-Semitic slogans during Nazi marches. But moving to Palestine required a certain amount of funds, both to pay for the passage and to acquire the assets to be declared to the British authorities in Palestine in order to obtain a settlement permit. Financial support came from the couple's parents, even if neither the Neumanns nor the Blumenfelds shared their children's Zionist convictions and remained sceptical about their intention to emigrate.

In the summer of 1933, Erich (and his friend Gerhard Adler) had participated in a seminar given by C.G. Jung in Berlin. By that time at the latest, the Neumanns must have decided that they would travel to Zurich to undergo analytical training with Jung. In the early autumn of 1933, they left Germany with their little son for good. Their journey first took them to Switzerland. Yet the fate of the Neumann and Blumenfeld families—like that of all other Jewish families in Germany and

Figure 2.6 Erich, Julie and their son Micha in Berlin, Weimarer Strasse

in the territories occupied by German forces—was marked by murder, flight and suffering. Several of Julie's maternal and paternal relatives failed to escape Nazi persecution. Her mother's brother and sister were murdered at Theresienstadt concentration camp, as were several of her father's relatives. Julie's siblings and parents managed to save themselves.

Ruth Goldstone, Julie's youngest sister, was instrumental in their successful emigration to London.[27] Martin, their oldest brother, had emigrated to Australia. Lotte, their eldest sister, received a domestic permit since she could only come to England if she accepted a post as a housemaid. Later she resumed her profession as a piano teacher. Paul, the third of the five Blumenfeld siblings, secured a transit visa to Argentina for Ruth. He had arrived in London with his wife shortly before war erupted. The outbreak of war, however, meant that he could no longer use the visa and was therefore forced to stay in London with his wife. After some time, he found work as a cellist in an orchestra.

Julie's parents arrived in London with ten Reichsmark. Two relatives of Ruth's husband vouched for them, or they would have been denied entry to England. Erich's father had died on 25 March 1937 after a Gestapo interrogation. His sister Lotte, a communist, emigrated to Paris in 1939, while his brother Franz moved to London. Neither was able to continue practising as a doctor for a long time. Erich's mother first lived with Franz in London. She spent the last period of her life, from 1947 until her death in December 1955, with Erich and Julie in Tel Aviv.

Notes

1 Translator's note: Blau-Weiss was the Jewish equivalent of the Wandervogel, the name adopted by a highly popular movement of German youth groups from 1886. The latter translates as "rambler, hiker or wandering bird."

2 In his speech at the unveiling of the commemorative plaque for Erich and Julie Neumann in Berlin in 2007, Micha Neumann observed: "I can hardly imagine that this very serious and intellectual young man really wanted to learn to dance. I rather believe that he frequented this address to meet a nice, pretty and smart Jewish girl and to befriend her."

3 The "Blau-Weiß-Bund" (Blue-White Association) was a Jewish hiking association established in 1913. Its foundation was legitimised in particular by various (recurring) events, including the exclusion of Jewish children and youths from the increasingly anti-Semitic Wandervogel. Famous Blau-Weiss members included intellectuals like Norbert Elias, Leo Löwenthal, Erich Fromm, Hans Jonas and Leo Strauss. The organisation saw itself as spearheading the awakening of a new generation. The two most important figures of this "young Jewish" elite were Kurt Blumenfeld and Felix Rosenblüth. Blumenfeld became its first professional official. Rosenblüth, widely considered the "inventor" of the Jewish youth movement, later became a leading Zionist politician and entered the history of the new state as Pinchas Rosen, Israel's first Minister of Justice; see Jörg Hackeschmidt, *Von Kurt Blumenberg zu Norbert Elias: Die Erfindung einer jüdischen Nation* (Hamburg: Europäische Verlagsanstalt, 1997), p. 7.

4 Hackeschmidt, p. 44.

5 Ibid., p. 52.

6 Ibid., p. 109.

7 Angelica Löwe, "Wir waren eine zufriedene und glückliche Familie: Interview mit Ruth Goldstone, *Analytical Psychology* 39 (1), 2008.

8 Rali Loewenthal-Neumann, "My Father, Dr. Erich Neumann," *Harvest* 52 (2), 2006.

9 Moshe Zimmermann, *Die Deutschen Juden 1914–1945* (Munich: De Gruyter, 1997), pp. 22ff.

10 Shulamit Volkov, "Die Dynamik der Dissimilation: Deutsche Juden und osteuropäische Einwanderer," in Dan Diner and Dirk Blasius (eds.), *Zerbrochene Geschichte: Leben und Selbstverständnis der Juden in Deutschland* (Frankfurt am Main: Fischer, 1991), pp. 64ff.

11 Moral and spiritual support for the Eastern Jews came in particular from Hasidism scholars gathered around Buber. Other Jewish intellectuals, including Albert Einstein and Arnold Zweig, also expressed their solidarity; see further Moshe Zimmermann, *Die Deutschen Juden 1914–1945* (Munich, 1997).

12 Volkov, "Die Dynamik der Dissimilation," p. 77.

13 Ibid., p. 78.

14 Edith Rosenzweig and Ernst Simon (eds.), *Franz Rosenzweig, Briefe* (Berlin: Schocken Verlag, 1935), p. 95; cited in Volkov, "Die Dynamik der Dissimilation," p. 77.

15 Samuel Adler-Rudel, *Ostjuden in Deutschland* (Tübingen: Mohr Siebeck, 1959), pp. 123ff.

16 It was also the home of the "Jüdische Kinderhilfe" (Jewish Children's Relief Agency). Founded by the Zionist paediatrician Hermann Stahl and some other young people, it provided medical care to refugee children as well as Jewish children in northern Berlin. This marked the beginning of Jewish family welfare, which was later provided on a large scale by the Jewish Welfare Office; see Adler-Rudel, *Ostjuden in Deutschland*, p. 124.

17 Ibid., p. 124.

18 Ibid., p. 125.

19 On the "Ahawah," see Ayelet Bargur, *Ahawah heißt Liebe: Die Geschichte des jüdischen Kinderheims in der Berliner Auguststrasse* (Munich: DTV, 2004).

20 Julie Neumann, handwritten curriculum vitae (unpublished). The references in the next few paragraphs are all to this document.

21 Angelica Löwe, "Wir waren ein zufriedene und glückliche Familie: Interview mit Ruth Goldstone," *Analytical Psychology* 39 (1), 2008.

22 See Julie's curriculum vitae.

23 Born in Frankfurt in 1887, Julius Spier began as a staff manager at a metal goods factory. Later he founded a publishing house and also began taking singing lessons. Spier's discovery of his chirological capabilities was a momentous occasion in the life of this highly gifted man, whom women in particular described as a "magical" personality. In the mid-1920s, Spier underwent analysis with C.G. Jung for two years in Zurich. Jung encouraged him to become a professional psycho-chirologist.

24 In 1938, shortly after the *Reichspogromnacht*, Spier emigrated to Amsterdam where he ran a successful practice until he died of cancer shortly before his anticipated deportation to Auschwitz in 1942. Spier had a relationship with Etty Hillesum, who was deported to Auschwitz shortly after his death and murdered there by the Nazis. Her famous diaries also describe their relationship.

25 Spier has received considerable acclaim in the field of innovative chirology, which strives for scholarliness. He intended *The Hands of Children* to be the first part of a trilogy.

26 Julius Spier, *The Hands of Children: An Introduction to Psycho-Chirology* (Abingdon, Oxon: Routledge, 1999; first published in 1944).

27 Ruth had already travelled to London in 1930 to study English. She stayed in London and married her cousin.

"… the wound of isolation beckons"[1]

Neumann's early writings

The dissertation period

For Neumann's generation, rejecting assimilation, and thus aspiring for distinction as a Jew, moreover in an increasingly anti-Semitic Germany, involved more than merely challenging one's background and parents. Nor were these manifestations of Jewishness simply associated with Zionist politicking, even if Neumann's membership in the Berlin Zionist Union seemed to suggest this. His struggle for Jewish identity can be understood first and foremost as an inner psychological and spiritual process, one of selectively exploring while "creating" an intellectual and spiritual Jewish heritage for himself. This development, however, meant taking recourse to a traditional German education and its canonised values. Neumann's doctoral dissertation reflected to what extent and how exactly he felt committed to this heritage.

Let us first briefly consider the academic environment in which Neumann pursued his humanistic studies as a university student. As early as the late 19th century, German academic circles began fiercely opposing "the spectre of soulless modernity."[2] This critical stance towards culture intensified in the next few decades. Characteristic of the 1920s was the widespread conviction that "a serious crisis" was unfolding, one of "education," "values" and "thinking."[3] Both the "growth of relativism and determinism" and the "isolation of the creative individual" were deplored. The "tyranny" of the natural sciences was denounced, as was one-sided, disproportionate intellectualism. The day and age was perceived as a "no man's land between decay and renewal." Inflationary use was made of the word "crisis." In this vein, the crises of the various university disciplines were proclaimed one after another, while excessive specialisation was lamented as positivism increasingly strengthened its grip on scholarship.[4] Hugo von Hofmannsthal referred to this academic movement as a "conservative revolution" in his famous lecture "Das Schrifttum als geistiger Raum der Nation" (Literature as the Spiritual Space of the Nation), delivered in January 1927 at the University of Munich: "The process that I am talking about is nothing more than a conservative revolution on a scale without precedent in European history."[5]

The urge to renew the sciences also manifested itself in the use of powerful catchwords.[6] Most university professors now promoted the quest for *synthesis* and *wholeness*. The need to establish new connections between science, education and worldview was widely approved. Originally a pivotal category of Romantic philosophy, wholeness once more became an astonishingly suggestive concept, while Hegelian synthesis gained currency in popular science.[7] The methodical use of intuition was now once again recommended as "a much needed reaction against the exclusive rule of the intellect, which ... has subjected everything to analysis, dissection, circumscription, mechanisation, and has thus killed ... synthesis: that is creation, analysis, death."[8]

Erich Neumann was awarded his doctoral degree in philosophy by the Faculty of Humanities at Erlangen's Friedrich-Alexander University on 2 March 1927. His dissertation was titled *Johann Arnold Kanne, Ein vergessener Romantiker: Ein Beitrag zur Geschichte der mystischen Sprachphilosophie* ("Johann Arnold Kanne, A Forgotten Romantic: A Contribution to the History of the Mystical Philosophy of Language").[9] On 14 October 1927, Neumann signed a publishing agreement with Reuther and Reichard in Berlin. In keeping with the academic *zeitgeist*, his study was not short of speculative undertones through which he sought to revive Romantic thinking. Neumann contrasted his own scientific position with what he called the "specialist philological orientation of the authoritative historians," who had largely ignored the mystical legacy of Romantic linguistics, and had therefore fallen into oblivion.

During his studies in Erlangen, and meanwhile aged 22, Neumann considered the benefits of earning an academic title in his diary: "Perhaps my doctoral thesis also matters so much to me because this is where one acquires the habitus of stepping out in the world" (UD).

At the same time, however, he was sceptical about pursuing a career in academia or science:

> In essence, my professional opportunities lie in the human sphere, hence my constant resistance to the constraints of scientific tasks, which threaten to devour everything. ... I have the feeling, indeed the awareness, that I am capable, at least to a certain extent. Yet this is not my essence. Only unswerving commitment can take me further. And scientific work never demands my totality.
>
> (UD)

Neumann, in spite of his aversion to academia, nevertheless saw the positive side of his studies, namely in the context of his future development, which he felt was closely linked to his relationship with Julie:

> If ever I had thought that studying philosophy would turn out to be futile, this idea itself turns out to be hugely mistaken. The past year in particular has been hugely important for me in this respect. Studying the history of philosophy has challenged me to confront a myriad of problems, interconnections and perspectives. These, moreover, have barely begun to penetrate my world.

Figure 3.1 Erich Neumann as a university student

I am well aware that they are being laid out within me in a far-reaching manner and will hence gradually expand. Just how exactly this will work, how the theoretical, religious, practical, scientific, human and Jewish measures will engage and become entwined with each other is of course less than conceivable. I am, however, certain that everything will find its place, and that each position will energise the others. … Without knowing anything at all, I am quite sure of this. Incidentally, you have no inkling to which extent you will help me. You have already corrected so much of where my thinking has gone astray.

(UD)

The three authors whose philosophy of language most preoccupied Neumann were Louis Claude de St. Martin, Johann Arnold Kanne and Gotthilf Heinrich Schubert. In the background stands their "forefather" Jakob Böhme, the late-16th century shoemaker and mystic, whom Hegel called "the first German philosopher."[10] Böhme's work, influenced by Paracelsus, yet also by Heinrich Cornelius Agrippa von Nettesheim (1486–1535), contains distinct Kabbalistic elements. These also occupied an important role in the thinking of the three aforementioned authors.[11] It is both astonishing and significant that Neumann's spiritual research in his early academic career stands in the same mystical-alchemical tradition that later became crucially important in C.G. Jung's later work. At this historical interface of German culture, where the Christian-Western heritage in its mystical form had once entered into a fruitful relationship with Jewish mysticism, new scope opened up for Neumann's thinking. Along the fault lines of his own life, he sought to draw fresh inspiration from excavating remote, long-forgotten thought processes.

The theological-philosophical speculations of the three mystical linguists discussed by Neumann in his dissertation focus on losing a "primordial language" (DS, p. 12). In this respect, Hebrew occupies a special role as the "bridal language" (ibid., p. 16). This loss corresponds to the loss of closeness to God, or rather to the Word of God. As we will see, the question of origin, which is bound up with the sense-giving, energising One, preoccupied Neumann all his life.

The mystical-romantic answer to the loss of origin (DS, p. 19; see also Neumann's comment on Buber) expresses itself as a demand for the restitution of the human relationship with God as one of listening to the "inner word" (ibid., p. 89; see also p. 14). In analysing this mystical, acoustically guided "rebirth," Neumann's dissertation arrives at distinctions in the mystical realm that we find later in his first Eranos lecture, delivered in 1948,[12] albeit in far more differentiated form. Crucial in this respect is the respective mystic's "degree of maturity." Neumann classifies Kanne's *unio mystica* (mystical union) as an "end in itself," which corresponds to the "low-level mysticism" discussed in his Eranos lecture (MM, p. 400). Louis Claude de St. Martin, on the other hand, occupies a much higher rank as a mystic of "responsibility" (ibid.). Translated into the language of Neumann's Eranos lecture, this implies the following distinction: "low-level mysticism" sees a pre-worldly, pleromatic state as the only true one, and hence aspires to kill the ego. In this mystical formation appear those with a weak or fragmentary ego and in whom potentially destructive states such as obsession, ecstasy, inflation, depression or psychosis manifest themselves. Now this does not, however, rule out that such states may occur, also in the "high-level mystic," when attempting to integrate such abysmal contents. The Eranos lecture contains no further references to individual mystics; instead, Neumann coins the term "*homo mysticus*" (MM, p. 375; original italics) and refers the mystical element to the anthropological realm. By his own admission, Neumann's notion of the mystical is "very broad" and "vague" (ibid., p. 377). The homo mysticus represents the "creative person" or, as Neumann later repeatedly called him, the "Great Individual."

The last section of Neumann's dissertation, about Gotthilf Heinrich Schubert's philosophy of language, is particularly interesting since it anticipates the field of "language research" or the interpretation of language by psychoanalysts. Neumann closely examines Schubert's *Symbolik des Traums* (Dream Symbolism) (DS, p. 112). The latter assumes that the language of dreams is subject to laws different from those governing verbal language. Its essential characteristic, as he emphasises, is its "hieroglyphics," its pictorial nature. The language of dreams expresses more in a few fleeting moments "than we would be able to discuss over the course of several hours."[13] Thus, according to Schubert, the language of dreams corresponds more to the nature of the soul than verbal language does. Being hieroglyphic, it reflects the original state of language. It is identical among all peoples, also exists in the field of poetry and, in its very highest form, in the language of the prophets.[14]

In one footnote, Neumann writes: "Juxtaposing Schubert's views with Freud's and Jung's, for instance, might be worthwhile for the history of the new psychology," since Schubert focuses on a "psychology of the unconscious" (DS, p. 115). For Schubert, as for Kanne and de St. Martin, the other authors treated in Neumann's dissertation, this involves an act of restoration, of "reconquering" lost capabilities. It is, he adds, synonymous with "speaking the language of love" (ibid., p. 118), by which he means Christian love.

Neumann's reception of mystical-romantic ideas laid the foundation for his later cultural philosophy. Central to this are theological and philosophical questions, returning to (and thus restoring) the lost unity, thinking in terms of origins and establishing links between new, unusual thoughts through defining historical cross-sections. Later, in a letter to Jung dated 21 June 1952, Neumann refers to his writing projects self-ironically as "a highly 'meta-psychological thing,'" between all chairs of all faculties" (JNC, p. 290). In the same letter, he also speaks of designing a "unified model," one that "gives a place to all the phenomena that till now have rattling around at the edge of our world-view" (ibid.).

Neumann's dissertation reveals an important aspect of his later close intellectual relationship with C.G. Jung,[15] whose "being-more-than-European" and "quest through the times and nations" had "helped me very much," as he acknowledged in a letter written in July 1950 on the occasion of Jung's 75th birthday (JNC, p. 267).[16]

Kafka commentary, Kafka studies

Central to Neumann's later major works, in particular *Depth Psychology and a New Ethic* and *The Origins and History of Consciousness*, is his criticism of the psychic and spiritual constitution of Western people. In his Eranos lecture "Mystical Man," he describes this condition as "the rigidity of [his] ego" and "imprisonment in consciousness" (MM, p. 380). He insists that only "the force which mystically changes" them (ibid.) enables human beings to overcome this one-sidedness. He outlines the development of Western consciousness as follows:

> The development toward the ego and consciousness leads in every sense to isolation; it leads to the isolation and suffering of the ego. But in its extreme, it leads also to the isolation and specialization of consciousness, to its complete absorption by the purely individual, to a split, purely egoist existence, which can no longer apprehend the broad contexts of life or its connection with the creative void and is not accessible to mystical experience.
>
> (MM, p. 388)

But what is this mystical element, which changes and transforms the human being?

Early on in "Mystical Man," Neumann defines poetic force and conceptual darkness: He speaks of the "creative unconscious" and, even more obscurely, of the "source of creative nothingness—which is the point of departure for the autonomous, spontaneous, and unconscious activity of the creative, vital psyche" (MM, p. 377).

Autonomy, spontaneity and unconsciousness: These are the three basic manifestations of the mystical process. From this creative nothingness, the centre of the human soul-space, arises a vortex that is capable of directing the individual towards a creative process that assumes diverse forms. All of this occurs "outside of consciousness," which explains why such events can only be approached "by a sort of ritual circling, an approach from many sides" (MM, p. 377).

These introductory remarks lead us from the previous outline to another writing project very dear to Neumann during his time in Berlin and Erlangen: his *Kafka-Kommentar* (Kafka commentary) and other studies on Kafka's work. Neither has been published in its entirety. On the whole, Neumann appropriated Kafka as a "mystical author."[17] In the 1920s and 1930s, Kafka commentaries by Jewish intellectuals were still rare. Thus, it is even more interesting that Neumann not only wrote a three-part *Kommentar*,[18] but also several other studies on Kafka. The latter included a longer, self-contained piece about Kafka's novel *Das Schloss* ("The Castle") as well as interpretations of several short stories, some of which bear precise dates.[19] Aside from some brief remarks on Max Brod and a reference to Martin Buber, Neumann does not refer to the secondary literature that had begun appearing in literary magazines since the publication of Kafka's works.[20]

Neumann provides a late clue as to when he wrote his (undated) commentary, since he apparently intended to publish at least one chapter, an interpretation of the cathedral chapter in *Der Prozess* ("The Trial"). He mentions that he completed his *Kommentar* in 1933, that is, before he met C.G. Jung.[21] The chapter was published in the commemorative volume published in 1958, in honour of Daniel Brody's 75th birthday.[22]

Like other exegetes, Neumann attempted to identify indications of transcendence in Kafka's enigmatic work. According to Neumann, individuals experience transcendence only within themselves. It confronts them as the uncanny, in a psychological experience that makes them experience themselves as strangers; in this way, they sense the alienation to which they have fallen victim. The transcendence experienced by the modern person does not seem to initiate a process of integration but instead is experienced as punitive and judgmental justice. Thus, somewhat exaggeratedly: The human being is made to stand trial.

Neumann concludes his Kafka commentary by characterising the punitive forces as representatives of a deep layer within the human being. These forces are the "representatives of the same deep layer that confronts the individual's ego-consciousness." As human beings, so Neumann, we are forced to grapple with this "forever superior" layer. "It overwhelms the modern person, causing him to flee from what lives inside him and from what he represses." Then, however, "as long as he is still alive and has not frozen or died," it "assails him 'from behind and from above'; it breaks into him, persecutes him." It is striking, he continues, "how strongly the depicted destinies seem to resemble diseases, precisely because people's life always 'happens' to them" (KC, "Epilogue").

This transcendent power is directed with inexorable violence and severity against the alienated lifeworld, against human isolation and "rootlessness," against human beings, who have lost their relationship with themselves and others, whose inner world has "withered" (KC, p. 69) and has "turned to ice."[23] Thus, the dark world of the court, the trials that it sets in motion, the sentences that it passes and the human downfall in Kafka's world all frame Neumann's interpretation. To him, this world is a world of justice precisely on account of its logic of doom, into which merely a weak ray of redemption penetrates and in which grace exists in highly fragmented form.

Neumann describes Kafka's fictional world as "grotesque and eerie" (KC, p. 194), as "ambiguous" and "paradoxical" (p. 176) and as a "double causality" (ibid.). Next to the real world, whose causality concerns the individual ego, exists a sphere for the "trial," in both meanings of the word, where decisions about life and death are taken. Neumann calls this realm a "halfway abode," a sphere connecting the "subjective psyche" and the "objective reality of the tribunal's deep region" (ibid.). This region, which Neumann consistently abbreviates in his Kafka interpretations as the "Trans," is the transpersonal, "interlocated" layer of "forces" that breaks into life. It is the supreme power, the authority that governs the individual's life:

> No mortal can escape the tribunal, which is absolutely superior. Of course the existence of a deep region, a Trans, can be denied, ... but this takes effect beyond all statements. The assertions, attitudes of faith and non-faith, of knowledge and volition, are all "placed on record"; that is, they determine the deep layer's mode of action. It is of crucial importance whether a person is aware of the tribunal or not; this largely determines the way in which the tribunal behaves towards him.
>
> (KC, p. 189f.)

Neumann persistently interprets the individual's guilt, who must answer to this deep region, which in turn afflicts him incessantly, as follows: It means "not hearing," "being severed from the inner and from the outer world," "being unable to look one's fellow humans in the eye, to recognise them as human beings" and possessing "an incorrect attitude, an egotistical, restricted life and horizon of existence" (KC, p. 184). Thus, for Neumann, Kafka's protagonists always bear the stigma of inadequate spiritual development. This may be seen as guilt, as infidelity to one's own inner self. These figures remain locked in a state of "defiance" (ibid.), of "stubbornness, cowardice, insecurity" (p. 178). Or they "obstinately believe they know better against every influence of the Trans" (p. 70).[24]

Since this guilt stems from the individual's lack of development, the process in which subjectivity comes into contact with the authority of the tribunal, which is supposedly objective, can only emanate from the individual. This process, as I have suggested, has both frightening and violent dimensions: While it "undermines ... a fixed attitude of consciousness" (KC, p. 191), in the final instance it amounts to the death of the ego. Paradoxically, this annihilation is simultaneously desired and feared—since it only affects those who are open to being ruled by the transpersonal forces. It affects those who have grown conscious of their narrow horizon, those whom "the wound of isolation beckons" (ibid.):

> The Trans incessantly throws human beings back upon themselves, through fear, doubt, conscience, guilt, dream, disease and death. It takes hold of them when they are in need, and by becoming a need, in the trial. This purported negativity ... seems to lead automatically ... to transformation, that is, to conversion, to a reconnection with the Trans. And yet, this transformation always implies death, dying.
>
> (KC, "Epilogue," p. 69)

Neumann conceives of the negative process at work within the human being as a "confrontation between these two parts," at whose end "stands the self-development, the victory of the transpersonal or the Trans and the demise, or rather the collapse of the ego" (KC, p. 195). Thus, the victory of the transpersonal implies a person's return to their creative origin.

In *The Origins and History of Consciousness*, Neumann explores in-depth the transitional aspect of dying, as well as the life and death of the hero, who represents the respective human levels of consciousness, in the context of the Osiris cult.[25] Since dying or death, as the collapse of the ego, is constitutive of human transformation, Neumann accepts the cruelty of Kafka's verdicts as necessary. These are often, yet mostly, unreflected death sentences: "What, this is meant to be justice?" (KC, p. 195). Or do they perhaps instead reflect a "strange and downright absurd dogmatism?" (p. 190). In Neumann's worldview at that time, this form of justice seemingly provided the only path to radical change. His trust in this form of justice seemed to be fundamental:

> The hard reality of this justice, which is at the same time natural and trans-like, which means that whoever detaches himself from the foundation, dies, withers as a rootless being, is a world-constituting law.
>
> (KC, "Epilogue," p. 69f.)

What form of grace, then, might the human being expect in this process? Does any mercy exist here?

Neumann's Kabbalistic line of interpretation leads him to bracket rigour, justice and grace.[26] Two exemplary figures in this respect are the coal merchant and his wife in Kafka's *Der Kübelreiter*.[27] The "bucket-rider" battles desperately through the wintery cold atop his empty bucket to reach the coal merchant's house, hoping that he will be saved. The merchant's wife, however, dismisses the man's plea outright, whereas her husband considers giving this unfortunate soul some coal. The harsh woman prevails over her yielding husband and thus condemns the bucket-rider to perdition. How might we understand her stance in Neumann's Kabbalistic perspective? He comments:

> Here, too, the magisterial figure of the woman is transcendental ... while the good-natured man is the keeper of coal, that is, of the warmth that makes life possible without freezing or dying. Here, as in the Kabbalah, the masculine principle represents grace, the feminine principle justice. Saying that, we ought not forget that this is also grace in the deepest sense of the word ... Precisely since justice is the law of the world, salvation lies both inside and outside.
>
> (KC, "Epilogue," p. 70)

However, the inexorable logic with which Kafka's work gravitates around the theme of guilt led not only Neumann[28] to understand these stories as a message, or indeed even as instruction. He therefore credits this work for its "comprehensive cultural-philosophical generality" (KC, *Das Urteil*, p. 4). Analogously to the concept of metaphysics, Neumann calls his very personal interpretation a "metapsychology" (KC, "Epilogue," p. 68). Considering that he speaks of "revelation" (KC, *Das Urteil*, p. 1) to denote the region where the Trans becomes visible and audible, this metapsychology may also be understood as a cryptotheology. On balance, Neumann's Kafka commentary attempts to systematise the "experience of transformation," whose semantic configuration is that of a processual figure of psychic experience made under extreme historical circumstances. This reading— or so it seems retrospectively—presents Neumann as a young, radicalised intellectual whose interpretation of Kafka's cosmos of guilt and punishment formed part of his search for an objective authority, such as a world tribunal, amid the ever-more fragile nature of human and humanistic values prevailing in the 1920s. From a present-day perspective—after the cultural break, after Auschwitz—this interpretation is oppressive, or indeed ghostly, as it relentlessly highlights the problem of theodicy.[29]

Here, we may refer to Neumann's letter to Jung of 5 December 1951. Written after reading the latter's *Answer to Job*, it critically examines Jung's work. Neumann hopes that Jung "will not take offense at the bluntness of my objections" (JNC, p. 274). Still, the book "grips me deeply," as he states in his introduction, adding that it is the "finest and deepest of your books" (p. 271). While Neumann mentions its comforting, consolatory aspect, he also points out Jung's one-sided outrage at God:

> In a certain sense it is an argument with God, a concern similar to that of Abraham when he argues with God because of the downfall of Sodom. It

is—for me personally—especially also an argument against God who allowed 6 million of "His" people to be killed, for Job is precisely also Israel, and I don't mean that in a "small" way. I know we are the paradigm for the whole of humanity in whose name you are speaking, protesting, and consoling. And exactly the conscious one-sidedness, yes, often the inaccuracy of what you are saying is, to me, an inner proof of the necessity and justice of your attack—which is, of course, not one, as I well know.

(JNC, p. 271)

Among other objections, Neumann feels that Jung makes things too easy for himself by taking God's omniscience for granted:

When you speak of the omniscience of Yahweh, it sounds always ironic. But what if he really possesses it and only gives himself archaically to the archaic because he can only become comprehensible to it in this way and if everything that you say is correct but necessary at the same time.

(JNC, p. 273)

Another objection concerns Jung's anthropomorphisation of God:

You portray the transformation of humanity in this numinosum as if there were no problem of transference and projection.

(JNC, p. 273)

Furthermore, Neumann finds Jung's assessment too one-sided, since he only hears God's "loud," fearsome voice, but neglects the subtlety of divine revelation:

I am not defending Yahweh but the advocate in heaven whom Job himself calls upon. The analysis of Job is after all only a part, the other side is also present, which, for example, puts this Yahweh on trial in you yourself today. With the manifestation in the storm and thunder, have you not overlooked the one in the rustling of the wind although it has revealed itself as the higher form?[30]

(JNC, p. 274)

Later, after completing his extensive research for *The Great Mother*, Neumann adopted a critical stance towards the position of the feminine in Jewish tradition.[31] He would have considered his Kafka interpretation—or so we might assume—to accurately describe the devouring aspect of the Great Mother, that is, as a deadly, death-bringing mother who sets in motion the archetypal process of psychic transformation. In his Eranos lecture of 1953, "Die Bedeutung des Erdarchetyps in der Neuzeit" (The Meaning of the Earth Archetype for Modern Times) (see Chapter 10), Neumann takes his listeners down into the underworld, into the entangled chthonic powers, from where "downfall," but also "transition" occurs (MM, p. 376).

The inner experience of the "terrible character of the psyche"—as a dark mirror of the frightening Great Mother—is a prerequisite for "transformation" and "break-through." Only after completion of the "journey through the purifying elements" can the "transformation of the negative effects into positive feelings" occur (MMF, p. 152f.). The earth, he adds, can only reveal its maternal, elemental character as a great transformer and great creator to those who are capable of withstanding the terrible aspect of the Great Mother (MEA, p. 188).

Neumann sent his Kafka commentary to Buber, whose opinion, as the mentor of a generation of Jewish intellectuals who remembered their origins and found their spiritual home in Zionism, interested him.[32] It is unclear when exactly Buber received the manuscript: Neumann may have sent it before he left Berlin for Zurich in 1933, or perhaps at a later date, from either Zurich or Tel Aviv. Acknowledging its receipt, Buber wrote: "I received your manuscript at the time" (which suggests an extended lapse between his receipt of the manuscript and his reply). Here is Buber's (unpublished) reply of 13 November 1935:

> Dear Doctor!
>
> I have not written to you so far, since work and travel commitments have made excessive demands on me. I received your manuscript at the time, but have only now found time to read it, as it defies casual reading. I was very interested in your treatment of Kafka. Your clear and precise methodology does remarkable justice to some of the references and contexts. Your commentary seems most successful when it deals with those stories, like "Die Brücke" [The Bridge], whose nature is clearly symbolical.
>
> However, I cannot agree with you quite as unreservedly where—as so very often with Kafka—his stories defy straightforward interpretation on account of their style, and instead demand a more fluid, more musical reading. It also seems to me that sometimes a theological conception, which you understandably avoid out of shyness, would be more fitting than your metaphysical one, as far as this might be conceived at all. In my opinion, for example, a commentary on "Das Ehepaar" [The Married Couple], ought to mention that the figure of the sick son is surrounded by a Christological atmosphere. Of course, this is particularly difficult, since these points reveal most forcefully how Kafka, consciously or unconsciously, opposes his commentator and causes him all sorts of trouble—not only of arbitrariness, but also of fundamental essence.
>
> That is all for the time being. I will, however, be happy to continue to discuss your valuable work with you.
>
> Respectfully yours,
> Buber[33]

For Buber, Neumann's interpretation is too one-sided. Although he praises its "precise methodology," Neumann's reading lacks a "fluid, musical" element.

Nevertheless, his suggestion, that Kafka "sometimes" requires theological interpretation, is surprising. Could a "theological" conception "sometimes" be woven into the fabric? Buber, though, probably means "theological" instead of metaphysical—or what Neumann would call "metapsychological"—concepts. Neumann's concepts, so Buber, are crypto-theological. The overwhelming guilt burdening Kafka's protagonists in Neumann's interpretation strikes him as barely tolerable, the faint consolation of their accepting their downfall too meagre and the workings of the larger forces too cruel. Thus, he cannot avoid introducing a "Christological" aspect, that is, an aspect of grace.

Let us return to the previously mentioned "nothingness of revelation": Neumann assumes that a force, a "primal vortex" (MM, p. 377),[34] inheres in the human being. This, he says, "operates as a differentiating, centralizing force," for which he introduces the term "centroversion." The vital force of centroversion leads to the formation of a new centre, a "center of filiation." This is the ego, which now commands its creative powers (ibid., p. 404).

This nothingness, which Neumann also calls the numinous, as is common in Jungian literature, and later also the Self, appears in many guises: as an epiphany, not least as a revelation, which needs to be understood as an "idea," "inspiration" or "notion" (ibid., p. 381). One unmistakable sign of a mystical process is emerging transformation and personality change, whether as a "well ordered process" or as a change that all of sudden affects the personality structure, or indeed spells its destruction. For Neumann, other mystical events include experiences of love and artistic-creative processes (ibid., p. 405f).

He hypothesises, quite pointedly, that mystical experience is tantamount to transformational experience: All mystical experiences originate from a "revolutionary, dynamic impetus of a psychological event, which takes the ego out of the structure of its consciousness" (MM, p. 381). In a later passage, he comments on this phenomenon even more keenly: "The creative-mystical experience is by nature opposed to the dominant religion and the dominant conscious contents of the cultural canon—that is to say, it is in principle revolutionary and heretical." This leads him to conclude: "The authentic, fundamental experience of the numinous cannot be other than anticonventional, anticollective, and antidogmatic, for the experience of the numinous is always new" (ibid., p. 386).

Der Anfang (The Beginning), A novel

In his unpublished diary, Neumann wrote:

> I have an infinite number of relationships with people and can see into so many fates. Sometimes I am very sad that I am unable to grasp this artistically, but it is impossible. I believe that none of this is pointless in my case, because I will very much need my knowledge of human nature and therefore never feel that there is something wrong with me in this respect.
>
> (UD)

In spite of his artistic ambitions (see Chapter 2), Neumann ruled out turning to writing as profession. Just as he did not contemplate pursuing a scientific career. Instead, he saw writing as an attempt to process his experiences.

Alienation, isolation, death, transformation: Neumann explored these dark regions of human life in his Kafka studies. The inner connection that he must have felt with Kafka's "heroes" surfaced in two chapters of his unpublished novel *Der Anfang* (The Beginning). They offer insight into the inner turmoil and existential needs of their protagonist, Ahareni, Neumann's dark *doppelgänger*, a figure who bears the traits of a negativity most familiar to Neumann.[35]

The anthology *Zwischen den Zelten* ("Between the Tents") was published in 1932 by Die Nachricht ("The News") in Berlin. Its editor, Julius Wassermann, presented 17 young Jewish authors. In spite of their contrasting styles, genres and literary concerns, these writers shared a determination "to present the inner situation of today's Jews."[36] The volume's title—*Zwischen den Zelten*—evokes a stance that resonates with the search for a world of experience in association with others, beyond the isolation of grey urban existence. It also places the volume within the context of its literary audience: the youth culture of that time. Accordingly, Wassermann's preface mentions the "right to existence and development" that the youth movement had been striving to establish since the beginning of the century. He also speaks of a "camp camaraderie," of an "eternal emotional bond between one tent and the next." This support, he asserts, is significant to the extent that the present day and age appears to be "perhaps the most abysmal of all transitional epochs."

The plot of Neumann's novel is straightforward: Its Jewish protagonist, Jakob Ahareni, undergoes a peculiar process of transformation in which he becomes increasingly "self-estranged" (DA, p. 135).[37] He experiences

Figure 3.2 Erich Neumann in his study

consciousness-altering processes, acts as his own shadow, is sapped of confidence and becomes passive. As Neumann explains in a brief commentary accompanying each chapter, Ahareni stands at the beginning of inner transformation. At that very moment, however, he seems to fall into an even deeper crisis, since he feels drawn to a circle of young people—led and seduced by a demonic, gloomy figure named Elia Rubenson, who intends to commit suicide (and does in the end)—"not out of resignation, but to set himself apart from a disintegrated world" (ibid.).

During a dramatic conversation with another member of the group, Klaus Etzlo, who later commits suicide, the contours and backgrounds of this decay (and despair) become ever more apparent:

> We are finished … out of powerlessness, because nothing has any meaning; everything is taken away; we are surrounded by walls and laws … an ancestral line of fools has begotten our world.
>
> (DA, p. 137)

These musings on the utter futility of life are followed by a tirade against the hypocritical bourgeois world: "The foul stench of J.S. Bach and brothels, cultural pride and hunger edema." Such formulations (and various others) suggest a stylistic affinity with the linguistic expressionism of the time. They are also indicative of the sheer contempt of a youth whose adolescence was marred by the catastrophe of World War I, and which was forced to accept the social depression in the aftermath of war as the pivotal experience of early adulthood: "What holds us now? Murdering animals, singing chorales, slaughtering people" (DA, p. 138).

What finds literary expression here, in a sarcastic and resigned portrayal of a yearning for death, is at the same time a clear-sighted expression of a "superfluous generation,"[38] which Neumann couches in the language of sociological theorising. In sharp contrast to the previous "front generation," whose formative experiences were war euphoria and subsequent disaster, the "superfluous generation" plunged into a complex vacuum, as a result of outward impoverishment and rapidly declining social values. All this drove young people to oppose the "Weimar gerontocracy."[39]

Reviewing *Der Anfang*, Erich Neumann's friend Gerhard Adler offers a very vivid account of the "young generation," whose principal challenge in life was to come to emotional terms with World War I. Adler contrasts two groups within that generation:

> On the one hand, those who consciously experienced the war and no longer wish to suffer from it, because they know what this means (or rather because they accept it as experience; in any event, however, they are willing to come to terms with the war experience); on the other, those who did not consciously experience the war and therefore suffer from it without knowing.[40]

Burdened by this legacy, which "cannot simply be rejected," the young generation developed characteristics described by Adler as "its objectivity, its untragic
acceptance of loneliness, its distance, its 'as-if' existence."

For Germany's Jewish population and for young Jews, coming to terms with
disaster involved various other dimensions, among others, even greater "superfluousness." One term that vividly expressed what it meant to be a Jew during the late
19th and early 20th centuries was *Luftmensch* ("an impracticable contemplative
person"). Deriving from Yiddish *luftmentsch* (from *luft*, air and *mentsch*, human
being), this metaphor palpably conveys a "concept of Jewish existence in modernity."[41] It was used by Jews already in the 19th century to ironically describe the
deplorable circumstances of their world, in particular in Eastern Europe. Anti-
Semitism turned it into a swear word, and *luftmentsch* soon became notorious as
a distorting, stereotypical attribution of "superfluousness":

> Within the general world crisis there was a specifically Jewish shock …
> Notably, the previous social definition had now been replaced by a collectivist-
> national one: under the changed political coordinates, all Jews had potentially
> become airmen … To be an airman was now the collective fate of the Jews.[42]

To return to Neumann's novel: *Der Anfang* describes the psychological consequences of Jewish superfluousness, which is perceived as a "world in decay,"
as hopeless loneliness. All existence is now "monological" (DA, p. 140). When
Etzlo, the protagonist, takes his life—out of the blue—Ahareni feels guilty, since
he failed to challenge Etzlo's despair and longing for death with a positive outlook. Deeply confused, Ahareni leaves the city. His overriding sense is that "everywhere death beckons, everyone is caught up in it" (ibid., p. 142).

What follows is a lecture and subsequent discussion about various concerns
preoccupying young Jews at that time. Geyer, the lecturer, is a prototypical "youth
leader." Concerned about life and culture beyond his early adulthood, he strives
to forge an alliance with combative young people. His claims, presented during
his lecture, form the thematic backdrop to a conversation that ensues between
Ahareni, Neumann's dark *doppelgänger* (who has since returned to the city), and
the "Germanic" physician Josua Exter. The debate takes Exter's reflections on his
"Germanic adolescence" as its starting point:

> Unquestionably, heroism has played a major role for me … even more so than
> any Gothic experience. Of course, much is determined by race, and originates
> in the popular sphere. Some matters, however, are also much more general.
> If you ask me, Geyer seems to have gone way too far in equating people,
> puberty and metaphysics. I believe he has exaggerated the exceptional case
> of the Jews. Among you Jews, while the ancestral, the historical and the reli-
> gious are identical, this is a stroke of luck in world history, of which you have
> every right to be proud.
>
> (DA, p. 148)

This view of Judaism—in contrast to stereotypical anti-Semitism—might be considered to positively anticipate the expectations that Neumann secretly harboured about his encounter with C.G. Jung. The latter, as is well known, discussed the subject of "Germanness versus Judaism" on various occasions. He did so in a manner that some may find difficult to understand today, even if his tone was perhaps not as ill-fated as it became later (see Chapters 4–7).

In Neumann's *Der Anfang*, Exter steers his conversation with Ahareni towards the profound "sense of being forlorn and lost," a sentiment widespread at the time (DA, p. 148). In the novel, however, being lost is not equal to feeling lost. It seems, instead, to describe an ongoing transformation resembling the process detected by Neumann in Kafka's protagonists. Transformation goes hand in hand with losing one's previous sense of self, and is thus equivalent to extinction. Exter describes this as follows:

> One lives here and now, even if one has been taken possession of, and everything changes. ... One remains oneself, yet is no longer an option as such; one is taken away from oneself, and yet matters depends upon oneself; one is—meant.
>
> (DA, p. 150)

Ahareni replies:

> As soon as one has placed oneself at the disposal of the unknown, the contract can no longer be terminated, in no way whatsoever. The worst kind of being lost is when you feel your mouth screaming "No," while your hand is already saying "Yes." This is no ordinary dividedness. It is much more and must be called being lost; for one knows that you are the hand; but you are not the one who screams, who suffers pain, who is bent double; whatever defends itself and suffers, that you are not.
>
> (DA, p. 150)

From this epicentre emerge a power and dynamism: "being lost makes us effective ... what unfolds within us takes effect, but we cannot control it" (DA, p. 151). Being lost arises not only from being possessed, but also involves taking possession. Ahareni describes this as follows: "All one knows is that one has taken possession, not when and how. The contract is presented to one with a signature, so to speak, all at once. And one then confirms it" (ibid., p. 152).

During the conversation, the "Germanic" Josua Exter gradually becomes a counterpart with whom Ahareni is able to discuss (his) innermost psychic life. Exter has experienced what "being lost" means. "Everything changes," he says, while Ahareni mentions the writhing pain from which he suffers. His predicament leads him to express his desire to establish a special allegiance with Exter, whose experience of this mysterious process of inner transformation exceeds his own:

I would just like to talk to someone like yourself, in order to change things within myself. I wish to draw closer to myself by taking a detour through you; it often feels as if I were a stranger to myself. This has been a long and serious development, perhaps also a disease. In any event, I endeavour to change this, and I am going to need your help to accomplish this.

(DA, p. 153)

At the end of the second chapter, Ahareni reaffirms his proposed allegiance with Exter by referring to the integrity of his critical and discerning faculty: "I cannot decipher myself, but I will know whether whatever you say applies to me or not" (DA, p. 153).

He also expresses his desire that their relationship be symmetrical:

Exactly the same will happen to you with me, of course. You will be able to reciprocate what I need. A friend could not be what you are supposed to be for me, do you understand? Nevertheless, this will not necessarily mean that we will almost become friends.

(DA, p. 153f.)

Let me conclude with a few remarks on the names of Neumann's characters: "Ahareni" and "Exter." Presumably, Josua Exter represents Jung, which would make Neumann's "The Beginning" a *roman à clef*, a novel in which real persons or actual events figure under a semblance of fiction. Exter's first name, perhaps puzzling at first, recalls a letter written by Freud to Jung on 17 January 1909, in which he referred to himself as Moses, and to Jung as Joshua: "We are certainly getting ahead; if I am Moses, then you are Joshua and will take possession of the promised land of psychiatry, which I shall only be able to glimpse from afar."[43]

If we further assume that this choice of names had spread beyond the confines of Freud's letter, then Jos(h)ua alias Jung represents a wish, as his surname appears to suggest: "Exter" is probably composed of *ex* and *terra*, "out of the land." As we have seen, Erich and Julie Neumann decided to emigrate to Palestine in the very early 1930s—against their parents' wishes. Neumann hoped to receive spiritual support from Jung, which he did (see Chapters 4 and 6). Thus, Exter alias Jung would become the figure whom Neumann would take "out of the land," that is, Germany.

The name "Jakob Ahareni" also invites interpretation. As for Jakob, Neumann devoted one of his early studies to Jacob and Esau, the two unequal brothers.[44] Neumann mentions this study at the end of one of his most important letters to Jung, written on 5 December 1938 (see Chapter 7). Jung was familiar with the biblical story about Jacob and Esau (Genesis 25:19–34). It concerns a crucial event in a son's life: the importance of fatherly recognition, which is conferred upon the firstborn son by birthright and blessing. Jacob, the younger of the twin brothers, knows how to acquire both, aided by his mother and by a ruse. Thereupon he leaves the country out of fear of his father's punishment. Most likely, Jung—rather than his biological father—gave Neumann the blessing that he needed to be able to leave "home."

Ahareni: The first two syllables of this surname, "Ahar," could be short for Ahasver, the controversial figure of the "eternal or wandering Jew." Originating in Christian legends, this figure was misappropriated by the Nazis for propaganda purposes. One hint about the role played by this figure in Neumann's dreams can be found in his previously mentioned letter of 15 November 1939 (in which he recounts a dream in which Jung appears to him as a pilgrim; see also Chapter 7). The next two syllables "eni" are an anagrammatic rearrangement of the German word "ein" (one). The name Ahareni, then, would mean "a wandering Jew."

We can imagine that Neumann, equipped with such ascriptions and hopes, set off for Zurich in 1933, willing "to be deciphered by Jung and to change things about himself on his detour via Jung." And also in order to experience what it means when "everything changes."

Notes

1 The phrase is from Neumann's *Kafka Kommentar*, his unpublished commentary on Franz Kafka (completed in 1933); hereafter cited as KC.
2 Fritz K. Ringer, *Die Gelehrten: Der Niedergang der deutschen Mandarine 1890–1933* (Stuttgart: Klett, 1983), p. 13.
3 Ibid., p. 13.
4 Ibid., p. 345.
5 Hugo von Hofmannsthal, *Das Schrifttum als geistiger Raum der Nation*, p. 31; cited in Ringer, *Die Gelehrten*, p. 355.
6 Ringer, *Die Gelehrten*, p. 349.
7 Ibid., p. 352.
8 Friedrich Schürr, *Sprachwissenschaft und Zeitgeist: eine sprachphilosophische Studie* (Marburg: Elwert, 1922), p. 30; cited in Ringer, *Die Gelehrten*, p. 346.
9 Erich Neumann, *Johann Arnold Kanne, Ein vergessener Romantiker. Ein Beitrag zur Geschichte der mystischen Sprachphilosophie* (Berlin: Reuther and Reichard, 1927), p. 7; unpublished doctoral thesis, hereafter cited as DS.
10 See also Martin Buber's dissertation, *Der Begriff der Individuation bei N. Cusanus und Jakob Böhme* [The Concept of Individuation in N. Cusanus und Jakob Böhme] (Vienna, 1904).
11 So inspired by Böhme was the French philosopher and mystic Louis Claude de Saint-Martin that he learned German (at the age of 50) so he could read his writings in the original. He thus also initiated a Böhmian renaissance in Germany. Neumann's dissertation also contributed to Böhme's reception.
12 The lecture was titled "Der mystische Mensch." It was first published in *Der Mensch* (2), Eranos Yearbook 1948 (Zurich: Rhein-Verlag), pp. 317–374. The English translation appeared as "Mystical Man" in *The Mystic Vision*, ed. Joseph Campbell (Princeton, NJ: Princeton University Press, 1968), pp. 375–415; hereafter cited as MM.
13 Gotthilf Heinrich Schubert, *Symbolik des Traums* (Bamberg: Kunz Verlag, 1814); cited by Neumann in his dissertation, p. 112.
14 Schubert, ibid., p. 10.
15 The final sentence of Neumann's dissertation reads: "Schubert's 'philosophy of language' has again lost every connection with philology and linguistics. And yet, pre-

cisely its psychological turn sheds light, retrospectively, on the foundations of these theories. Taken together, these are not entirely unimportant for Romanticism, neither as a whole nor for its branches, from comparative mythology, linguistics, etc., to the seemingly most remote tendencies for parapsychology, mesmerism, psychopathology and dream life, for the demonic in E.T.A. Hoffmann as well as for Friedrich Schlegel's and his friends' turn to Catholicism" (DS, p. 120).

16 Neumann, according to his son Micha Neumann, "read Freud's works with great interest, but was particularly enthusiastic about Jung's writings. He admired his great culture and his knowledge of the art, myth and roots of Western civilisation"; see *Zur Utopie einer neuen Ethik: 100 Jahre Erich Neumann, 130 Jahre C.G. Jung* (Vienna: ÖGAP, 2005), p. 19.

17 Neumann wrote a number of (unpublished) letters to Olga Fröbe-Kapteyn, the founder of the Eranos conferences; the correspondence is hereafter cited as NOF. In a letter dated 1 January 1950, Neumann wrote to Fröbe-Kapteyn while preparing his forthcoming Eranos lecture on rites and ritual: "As for the topic: would you mind if an essential part of it consisted of an interpretation of Franz Kafka's story 'In the Penal Colony,' and if were entitled 'The Nature of Ritual'?" Neumann, whose Eranos lecture was eventually titled "Zur Psychologischen Bedeutung des Ritus" ("The Psychological Meaning of Ritual") chose not to comment on Kafka. On 18 January 1950, he wrote again to Fröbe-Kapteyn: " I haven't given up Kafka yet, you don't know me very well. The fact that you don't like Kafka is almost a reason to talk about him, since he is one of the great artists and I would be pleased to acquaint you with his works. By the way, my best works are comments, e.g., the "Psyche" and the interpretations of mythology. I do not consider myself to be as creative as you do and believe that my 'obstetric' ability is also my strongest." Neumann refers to Kafka only once during his Eranos lectures, namely, in his first-ever lecture, "Der Mystische Mensch" (Mystical Man).

18 The front page of Neumann's unpublished three-part commentary mentions the following works by Kafka:

  I: *Der Prozess*
  II: Appendix to *Der Prozess: Der Schlag ans Hoftor – Der Nachbar – Der Bau*
  III: Stories: *Das Urteil – Das Ehepaar – Der Kübelreiter – Ein Landarzt – Die Brücke* – Epilogue.

19 Neumann's (unpublished) Kafka studies discussed the following short stories: *Der Jäger Gracchus – In der Strafkolonie – Beim Bau der chinesischen Mauer – Eine Kreuzung/Nachlass: 17–18 August 1932; Die Brücke/Nachlass: 23 August 1932 – Kleine Fabel/Nachlass 1: 1 September 1932 – Die Wahrheit über Sancho Pansa/ Nachlass 1: 1 September 1932 – Das Schweigen der Sirenen/Nachlass 1: 18 September 1932 – Das Ehepaar/Nachlass: 24–25 September 1932.*

20 After Kafka's death in 1924, Max Brod published his novels—against the author's last wishes. They were greeted by the literary establishment with numerous, anthemic reviews: Max Brod, *Die geistige Gestalt Franz Kafkas* (1929); Margarete Susmann, *Das Hiobproblem bei Franz Kafka* (1930); Walter Stumpf, *Das religiöse Problem in der Dichtung Franz Kafkas* (1931); Heinz Politzer, *Franz Kafkas zweifache Heimat* (1934). The correspondence between Gershom Scholem and Walter Benjamin, in which interpreting Kafka's works occupied a prominent place from 1933 to 1940, is still widely recognised as paradigmatic; see *The Correspondence of Walter Benjamin and Gershom Scholem*, edited by Gershom Scholem, translated by Gary Smith and Andre Lefevere (Cambridge, MA: Harvard University Press, 1992; first published in German in 1980).

21 "This section is from a Kafka commentary that I completed in 1933, thus before meeting C.G. Jung. I have left it unchanged except for some minor stylistic changes, although I would have formulated a few things differently today"; see *Geist und Werk, aus der*

Werkstatt unserer Autoren, Zum 75. Geburtstag von Dr. Daniel Brody (Zurich: Rhein-Verlag, 1958), p. 175; the chapter includes pp. 175–196. A second commentary on Kafka's story "Der Kübelreiter" was published by courtesy of Julie Neumann in *Kreativität des Unbewussten: Zum 75. Geburtstag von Erich Neumann (1905–1960)*, eds. Dieckmann, Meier and Wilke; reprint of *Analytische Psychologie* 11 (3–4), Basel, 1980.

22 Brody, who had served as editor of the Rhein-Verlag since 1929, had been publishing the Eranos yearbooks ever since the inaugural conference in August 1933. Publication was interrupted only by World War II, which forced Brody into exile in Mexico. From 1947, the series of yearbooks was once again published under his editorship. Neumann, one of the most important speakers in Ascona every year from 1948 until his early death, took the commemorative publication as an opportunity to reflect on his dabbling in the essayistic genre before meeting C.G. Jung in 1933. The most significant piece for Neumann was probably his Kafka commentary.

23 Here is Walter Benjamin's verdict on Kafka in 1938: "Kafka's work is an ellipse with foci that lie far apart and are determined on the one hand by mystical experience (which is above all the experience of tradition) and on the other by the experience of the modern citydweller": see *Correspondence of Walter Benjamin and Gershom Scholem*, p. 223.

24 Neumann's approach resembles that of Erwin Loewenson's lectures on Kafka, which were delivered in Jerusalem; see Erwin Loewenson, *Der Weg zum Menschen: Philosophische Fragmente*. Selected by Carl Frankenstein (Hildesheim: A. Lax Verlag, 1970).

25 See Neumann's *The Origins and History of Consciousness*: "The situation as we find it in myth and ritual is that, simultaneously with the ego's experience of its death, a revivifying self appears in the form of a god. The hero myth is fulfilled only when the ego identifies with this self … Only in this paradoxical situation, when the personality experiences dying as a simultaneous act of self-reproduction, will the twofold man be reborn as the total man" (p. 255).

26 In this respect, see Hannah Arendt's critical stance in *Die verborgene Tradition: Acht Essays* (1932–1948) (Frankfurt am Main: Suhrkamp, 1976).

27 Published in *Kreativität des Unbewussten*; see earlier footnote 21.

28 Writing to Benjamin on 17 July 1934, Scholem believed that a "*correctly* understood theology" provided the "key to Kafka's world"; *Correspondence of Benjamin and Scholem*, p. 126 (original emphasis).

29 Writing to Scholem on 20 July 1934, Benjamin mentions that Kafka tried "to feel his way toward redemption." However, he preferred not to interpret theological secrets, but to trace their forms, which have been distorted by profanity"; *Correspondence of Benjamin and Scholem*, p. 129.

30 Jung responded to Neumann's questions in his reply of 5 January 1952: "I thank you very much for your kind letter and the way you understand me. This compensates for 1,000 misunderstandings! You have put your finger on the correct spot, one that is painful for me" (JNC, p. 280).

31 Erich Neumann, *The Great Mother: An Analysis of the Archetype*. Translated by Ralph Manheim. With a new foreword by Martin Liebscher (Princeton: Bollingen Series XLVII, Princeton University Press, 1955); orig. *Die Grosse Mutter: Der Archetyp des grossen Weiblichen* (Zurich: Rhein-Verlag, 1956); hereafter cited as GM.

32 Neumann's Kafka commentary includes an explicit reference to Martin Buber: "Although this commentary has deliberately avoided establishing how the basic concepts of Kafka are deeply connected with those of Judaism, from which they originate, at this point a counterpiece to the sketch entitled 'The Neighbour' needs to be pointed out, which, in its strange correspondence, is as exciting as it is revealing. This is '*Das Spiegelbild*' [The Mirror Image], a story published by Martin Buber in his *Tales of the Hasidim*"; see Erich Neumann, *Der Bau, unveröffentlichter Kafka-Kommentar*, p. 12.

33 Unpublished, translated here by Mark Kyburz.
34 The relationship with the Kabbalistic concept of *En Sof* is obvious here. It describes infinity and refers to the extreme reality of God beyond the qualities of the *sefirot*. According to Isaak Luria, the contraction (*tzimtzum*) of the indefinable and indeterminate primordial light of *En Sof* gives rise to the Creation.
35 *Der Anfang* (The Beginning); hereafter cited as DA. Neumann's novel, as he notes in his summary-like introduction, has three parts. Their titles are: I. Danger; II. Death; III. Return.
36 *Zwischen den Zelten, Junge Jüdische Autoren* (Berlin: Verlag die Nachricht, 1932). The anthology also included works by Neumann's childhood friend Carl Frankenstein and his spiritual father Erwin Loewenson.
37 A parallel to Kafka's *Die Verwandlung* ("The Metamorphosis"), published in 1915, cannot be ruled out.
38 Detlev J. K. Peukert has described the generation born around 1900 as "a generation that is superfluous in many ways." This concept describes the fundamental experiences of that generation: among others, economic stagnation, social misery, an overcrowded labour market, a youth depraved by war, the "front generation" and its near-total dejection. Together, these realities gave rise to a widespread sense of powerlessness and superfluousness, while at the same time spurring young people to devise manifold social alternatives; see Peukert, *Die Weimarer Republik: Krisenjahre der Klassischen Moderne* (Darmstadt, 1997), pp. 26ff.
39 Ibid., p. 3.
40 Gerhard Adler, "Junge Generation über sich selbst," in *Die Literarische Welt, Unabhängiges Organ für Deutsches Schrifttum* (19 February 1932).
41 Dan Diner, in Nicolas Berg, *Luftmenschen: Zur Geschichte einer Metapher* (Göttingen: Vandenhoeck & Ruprecht, 2008), p. 8.
42 Ibid., p. 163f.
43 *The Freud/Jung Letters: The Correspondence between Sigmund Freud and C.G. Jung*. Edited by William McGuire. Translated by Ralph Manheim and R.F.C. Hull, Bollingen Series XCIV (Princeton, NJ: Princeton University Press, 1974), pp. 196f.
44 Erich Neumann, *Jacob and Esau: On the Collective Symbolism of the Brother Motif*. Edited by Erel Shalit. Translated by Mark Kyburz (Asheville, NC: Chiron, 2015).

Part II

Zurich; Tel Aviv; Moscia–Ascona, Lago Maggiore

"… the Jews must go to the *tzaddikim*"

C.G. Jung and Neumann's early letters and writings

Carl Gustav Jung, who left the Psychoanalytical Association in 1913, began his self-analysis in the same year. This led him to systematically raise unconscious images, which he preserved in his consciousness through writing and painting, and thus contributed to developing his method of active imagination.[1] In this period of creative isolation, which lasted until 1919, Jung usually received only private patients.

In 1916, a small, yet active Jungian group gathered in Zurich to establish the "Psychological Club." Following his isolation, Jung regained international acclaim in the early 1920s. In 1926, the "Allgemeine ärztliche Gesellschaft für Psychotherapie" (AÄGP; General Medical Society for Psychotherapy) was founded in Germany.[2] Its members were psychotherapists who saw themselves as a "younger generation" and as an alternative to the "heavily outdated" neurological and psychiatric associations.[3]

From the outset, Jung, one of its 399 founding members, played an active role in the AÄGP,[4] which soon became known as the "Internationale allgemeine ärztliche Gesellschaft für Psychotherapie" (IAÄGP; International General Medical Society for Psychotherapy). This name was deliberately chosen in order to distinguish the IAÄGP from other associations, in particular the "Berliner Psychoanalytisches Institut" (Berlin Psychoanalytical Institute), which had become the world's most renowned training centre for psychoanalysts.[5] The new association, whose membership already totaled 575 persons in 1930, sought, among other objectives, to bring the various therapeutic directions closer together. At the numerous congresses held across Europe, Jung almost always appeared as a speaker. He also published articles on a regular basis in the *Zentralblatt für Psychotherapie*, the association's highly respected international journal (published first by Robert Sommer, later by Ernst Kretschmer).[6] His lecturing and publishing activities made Jung considerably better known in Germany in the early 1930s. In 1931, he co-chaired the IAÄGP with Kretschmer.[7] At the end of the same year, the C.G. Jung Gesellschaft was founded in Berlin on 24 December 1931.[8]

Jung's followers in Germany also included German Jews. Antonia Sussmann, née Borchardt (1883–1967), who lived in Berlin at the time, became one of Jung's students in Zurich as early as 1916. When she emigrated to England in 1937, she wrote to Jung to tell him that all her patients in Berlin were Jews.[9] Käthe Bügler (1898–1977), a "half-Jew" under the Nuremberg Racial Laws, studied with Jung in Zurich in 1927. Her account of Jung as her training analyst further illumines his provocative approach to analysis:

> In 1927, I undertook training analysis with Jung. We were soon forced to admit that studying books and empiricism alone did not suffice. … In Küsnacht, sitting opposite Jung, I suffered several mental shocks. His first question was: "Can you tolerate things that have a false bottom?" I vividly recall my dismay. Next: "Where is God, inside or outside?" … On another occasion, after I had relaxed somewhat: "Do you also know that—if you touch God—the devil is sitting in the next corner?[10]

Among Käthe Bügler's patients in Berlin were James Kirsch, Heinz Westmann, Max Zeller (Ernst Bernhard's cousin)—and Erich Neumann.[11] Ernst Bernhard (1896–1965), who had first pursued Freudian training in Berlin under the supervision of Sandor Rado and Otto Fenichel, continued having Jungian analysis with Antonia Sussmann, and possibly also with Käthe Bügler, whom he certainly knew very well before travelling to consult Jung in Zurich.[12] Like Neumann, Bernhard, nine years Neumann's senior, was fascinated by Hasidism, which soon brought him under the spell of Buber's work.

Most likely, Neumann and Ernst Bernhard had already met in Berlin. Their paths crossed again later, at the Eranos conferences in Ascona and Rome; moreover, Neumann and his wife Julie were on amicable and good professional terms with the Bernhards. Neumann's other friends at that time included his student-friend Gerhard Adler, another important Jewish student of Jung's. Neumann was grateful to Adler for introducing him to Olga Fröbe-Kapteyn, the founder of the Eranos conferences.

After earning his doctorate in philosophy, Neumann entered medical school in Berlin in 1928, quite simply because he wanted to become a psychoanalyst. His intellectual orientation, already evident in his dissertation and his literary experiments, and firmly based on his strong Zionist convictions, attracted him to Jungian theory from the outset. As Micha Neumann has observed: "He [Neumann] read Freud's works with great interest, yet was particularly enthusiastic about Jung's writings. He admired his great culture and his knowledge of the art, myth and roots of Western civilisation."[13]

In 1933, after the Nazis seized power, Neumann left Berlin with his wife and his little son. They travelled to Zurich, where they stayed with Jung for a while. Already in the same year, Julie emigrated to Palestine, and Erich followed her in 1934.

The year 1933 marked an incisive historical caesura. It highlighted the fact that emancipation was reversible, in that a "cultural nation was prepared to adopt a system characterised by a lack of freedom."[14] After Hitler's appointment as German chancellor on 30 January 1933, the so-called *Ermächtigungsgesetz* ("The Enabling

Act, Law to Remedy the Distress of the People and the State") came into force a mere seven weeks later, on 26 March 1933. The new legislation abolished all constitutional safeguards against the state's monopoly on the use of force. On 1 April 1933, the National Socialists called for a boycott of businesses owned by German citizens of Jewish faith and descent.[15] A few days later, "non-Aryan" civil servants were forced into early retirement. On 10 May, cheering crowds gathered outside Berlin Opera House to witness the barbaric burning of books by members of the paramilitary *Sturmabteilung* (SA) and by students loyal to the Nazis. Sigmund Freud's works also fell victim to the systematic purging of intellectual achievements.

Jung's affinity with seemingly anti-Semitic language makes it difficult, at least at first, to understand what might have attracted Jewish intellectuals of Neumann's stature to Jung or to consult him for treatment. Thus far, however, no systematic investigation exists into the obvious parallels between Buber's and Jung's reflections on the "current Jewish situation." In other words, Neumann—who was familiar with Buber's polarising language, as well as with that of his followers and the Zionists—had no good enough reason to consider Jung's talk (I am paraphrasing) of the domesticated Jew, who lacks groundedness, and must therefore counterbalance the threatening preponderance of his two cultures by returning to a primal source (see Chapter 5), to be anti-Semitic invective. It was instead a psychologist's diagnostic assessment based on most welcome differentiation.

Written in 1934, Neumann's first (undated) letter to Jung from Palestine suggests how crucial the idea of the people and the earth was for him at the time:

> The fact that Jews here as a people, as a not-yet-people, seemed so extremely needy was a shock at first. On the other hand, though, the landscape gripped me in such a compelling way that I couldn't ever have thought possible. Precisely from the place I hadn't expected it, a vantage point emerged. I haven't fully made sense of this. Anyhow, as you prophesied, the anima has gone to ground. She made an appearance all nice and brown, strikingly African, even more impenetrable to me, domineering—with a sisterly relationship—to many animals ... this gives me strength, however, I feel strongly. Even dreams are confirming it.
>
> (JNC, p. 16)

After settling in Palestine, Neumann realised that he had not met the "people" he had been seeking as a Zionist. Nor had the anticipated sense of belonging established itself. And yet, the "landscape" and "soil" soon took effect on him, evoking deep inner images and dreams and thus making him feel "in the right place." The subject of the "earth," which he conceived of in very concrete, physical terms, preoccupied him intensely in the years to come.

Neumann's work with Jung must have been extremely fruitful. When they first met, Neumann was 28 years old, Jung 58. As Micha Neumann has remarked: "Neumann developed strong feelings of respect, admiration and gratitude towards Jung, who offered his student and colleague much support, encouragement and appreciation. The years 1933–1934 laid a solid foundation for their long-standing cooperation and friendship."[16]

As Neumann told Jung in his second (undated) letter from Palestine, he had found a special designation for him—"Zaddik":

> Before I came to you, I was rather sad that I was not able to go to a Jewish authority because I wanted to go to a "teacher" and I found it typified precisely the decline of Judaism that it had no such authoritative personality in its ranks. With you, I became aware of what was prototypical in my situation. According to Jewish tradition, there are Zaddikim of the nations, and that is why the Jews have to go to the Zaddikim of the nations—perhaps that is why they do not have any of their own left.
>
> (JNC, pp. 34–35; written sometime in 1935)

Hasidism, as we will see, assumed great importance for Neumann (Chapter 10). The *tzaddik*, its "righteous man," possesses extraordinary spiritual charisma. His divine possession attracts disciples and believers beyond his mere knowledge of the Torah. "He is," as Gershom Scholem noted, "the living incarnation of the Torah," and therefore embodies a new religious ideal.[17] Hasidism, and thus also the *tzaddik*, appeals to an original feeling in the Jew.

Beyond this idealisation, Neumann's letter contains his thought-provoking cultural assessment of contemporary Judaism, which had lost its capacity for spiritual self-regeneration. The letter also suggests that Neumann was not looking for a psychoanalyst in the traditional, therapeutic sense and had no intention of resolving any personal difficulties through analysis. He was, instead, searching for psychological ways and means of reconnecting with collective Jewish roots. Until then, this profound longing had found its most concise articulation in Buber's "Jewish Renaissance."

Jung seemed to be the right "teacher," for which Neumann was immensely grateful. Thus, he concludes his first, undated letter from Palestine (cited above) with the following words of gratitude:

> Dear Dr. Jung, it still seems too crass simply to thank you for what I have received from you; I am ambitious enough to say that I hope to be able to give something to you in return too. I don't think it is that I cannot say thank you—this is just not enough. This is connected to the fact that I did not know what to do when you gave me the gift of the *The Sermons*.[18]
>
> (JNC, pp. 21–22)

Neumann must have experienced Jung's "gift" as a sort of "initiation": He was among the very few people whom Jung allowed to read the manuscript of *The Sermones*—in what amounted to a strong vote of confidence. Other than Jung's wife, only a handful of people had read the text.[19] The *Sermones* was a "key text" with regard to Jung's technique of active imagination. As observed, he had withdrawn into self-analysis as early as 1913. Contemplating the genesis of the *Septem Sermones ad Mortuos*, during the year 1916, Jung later wrote:

> In 1916 I felt an urge to give shape to something … The whole house was filled as if there were a crowd present, crammed full of spirits … As for myself, I was all a-quiver with the question: "For God's sake, what in the world is this?" Then they cried out in chorus, "We have come back from Jerusalem where we found not what sought" … Then it began to flow out of me, and in the course of three evenings the thing was written. As soon as I took up the pen, the whole ghostly assemblage evaporated.
>
> (MDR, p. 183)

In the same passage, Jung also recalls an earlier fantasy: His soul had flown away, which he interpreted as meaning that it had withdrawn "into the unconscious or into the land of the dead" (MDR, p. 183). In this sphere, the soul became effective in a very particular way: "There it produces a mysterious animation and gives visible form to the ancestral traces, the collective contents. Like a medium, it gives the dead a chance to manifest themselves" (ibid.).

The *Septem Sermones ad Mortuos* is a psychological cosmology written in the form of a "gnostic creation myth."[20] For Jung, the imaginary figure of Abraxas represented the symbolic union of the Christian God with Satan, and thus the transformation of the Western image of God. And yet, it was not until 1952, in *Answer to Job*, that he presented this complex topic to a wider audience.[21]

The tone of the *Sermones*, which are divided into seven sections, is visionary and prophetic.[22] Structurally, the principle of opposites is particularly striking: "Sermo I" is arranged in terms of eleven "pairs of opposites." The first three are "The Effective and the Ineffective, Fullness and Emptiness, Living and Dead."[23] These pairs of opposites are the properties of the "Pleroma." The Pleroma is "nothingness or fullness." It represents the "undivided" and stands opposed to the "CREATURE," even if the Pleroma "passes through" the creature. The creature's task is to "distinguish." It is important to distinguish, in order to avoid dissolution into nothingness. This would spell "the death of the creature": "Hence the natural striving of the creature goeth towards distinctiveness, fighteth against primeval, perilous sameness. This is called the PRINCIPIUM INDIVIDUATIONIS. This principle is the essence of the creature."[24]

How did reading this seemingly impenetrable text affect Neumann? We have seen that Neumann's early work, in particular his Kafka studies and his novel *Der Anfang* (based on our little knowledge about its emergence), had become embroiled in an agonising and supposedly indissoluble tension between mutually exclusive opposites. This explains why Neumann also set out in search of a "third" dimension. Thus, in *Der Anfang*, he observed:

> The worst kind of being lost is when you feel your mouth screaming "No," while your hand is already saying "Yes." This is no ordinary dividedness.

> It is much more and must be called being lost; for one knows that you are
> the hand; but you are not the one who screams, who suffers pain, who is bent
> double; whatever defends itself and suffers, that you are not.
>
> (DA, p. 150; see also Chapter 3)

The protagonist (Neumann's alter ego) hopes to escape from this extreme turmoil.
And yet, this will only happen if he forges a discursive alliance with a counterpart
as familiar with this forlornness as he is.

The wicked world in which—according to Neumann's interpretation—
Kafka's figures lived was irreconcilably separated from the world of the "Trans."
This force, representing higher justice, eventually leads to the extinction of the
individual. The "solution" that Jung offered Neumann was paradoxical. Whereas
Neumann, most of all in his Kafka studies, attempted to overcome separation and
disunity through holding a tribunal, Jung did not suggest that his students reconcile opposites, but instead ought to endure the tension between opposing forces as
fundamental to the human condition. He also introduced them to the "Principium
Individuationis." In *Memories, Dreams and Reflections*, Jung offered a somewhat
"dark" explanation:

> Since we ourselves are the Pleroma, we also have these qualities [e.g. life and
> death—Angelica Löwe] present within us; inasmuch as the foundation of our
> being is differentiation, we possess these qualities in the name and under the
> sign of differentiation, which means: First—that the qualities are in us dif-
> ferentiated from each other, and they are separated from each other, and thus
> they do not cancel each other out, rather they are in action. It is thus that we
> are the victims of the pairs of opposites. For in us the Pleroma is rent in two.[25]

Presumably, Jung's gift to Neumann (a copy of the *Sermones*) contributed significantly to establishing the desired allegiance; moreover, the *Sermones*, by introducing the method of active imagination, now became the locus where Neumann
could encounter his tormenting thoughts and questions. The fact that he had previously entered the realm of the imagination as an adolescent transpires from his
letter to Jung of 18 February 1959. There, he reacts approvingly and joyfully to
the publication of Jung's *Memories, Dreams, Reflections*. He also observes how
closely related he feels to Jung about being contained in a myth:

> And you know well how closely the "myth" I wrote when I was 16 led to all
> of this, and if I survey my development as I get older and trace its stages, I
> have a very similar experience of life as the one that speaks out of this book.
>
> (JNC, p. 343)

Writing to Jung from Tel Aviv on 5 December 1938, thus a little over 20 years
earlier, Neumann had described the form and gratification of active imagination
that he had experienced:

I slid into these things [i.e. his preoccupation with the Jewish situation—A.L.] … in my engagement with images from the unconscious that I paint at longer and shorter intervals. A large part of my thoughts originates in the effort of capturing these images conceptually.[26]

(JNC, p. 142)

These contents, in Neumann's thinking, seem to connect "the most individual and the ancient" in an experience that has "something strong and almost joyful about it" (JNC, p. 143). Thus, writing was meant to establish connections "from within" in the torn world in which he found himself.

Neumann's entire correspondence with Jung offers insight into the wide-ranging topics the two men had discussed during Neumann's stay in Zurich in 1934: Judaism, the psychic and spiritual situation of assimilated Jews and, of course, National Socialism. The latter became the subject of controversial debate between them, as Micha Neumann has observed:

Neumann, who had experienced the Nazis's malicious, poisonous anti-Semitism in Germany, attempted to convince Jung of the terrible threat posed by the National Socialist movement and its brutal inhumanity. He advised Jung to speak out openly and clearly against its ideology, most of all against its poisonous anti-Semitism. He admitted to me that he had failed to alter Jung's stance. My father warned Jung that if he remained silent in such an evil time for Jews, this would be remembered forever and he would never be forgiven.[27]

Jung's assertions on National Socialism and Judaism proved quite calamitous. On 26 June 1933, he gave an interview (to Adolf Weizäcker) on Radio Berlin. He spoke of the "reconstruction of the German community" and of "a necessary course of events," which would make it possible to cast off the shackles of "the false intellectualism that characterized the whole nineteenth century." The "widespread splintering of opinions," he argued, ought to be replaced by a "*Weltanschauung* [worldview]," "a unitary view of things" that places the "collective movement" and the "idea of leadership" at its centre. Its teaching, appropriate to the "German mind," corresponded to "the whole of creation." However, the divergence from Freudian and Adlerian psychoanalysis—in which "a part of the phenomenon [he mentions sexuality or the striving for power—A.L.] is isolated from the whole and broken down into ever smaller fragments, until the sense that dwells only in the whole is distorted into nonsense, and the beauty that is proper only to the whole is reduced to absurdity"—was unbridgeable.[28]

Jung's most momentous, and almost calamitous, assertion came a few months later, in an article titled "Zur gegenwärtigen Lage der Psychotherapie" ("The State of Psychotherapy Today"). This was published in the March 1934 edition of the *Zentralblatt für Psychotherapie und ihre Grenzgebiete*, whose editor Jung was serving as at the time. Jung wrote:

> The still youthful Germanic peoples are fully capable of creating new cultural forms that still lie dormant in the darkness of the unconscious of every individual—seeds bursting with energy and capable of mighty expansion. The Jew, who is something of a nomad, has never yet created a cultural form of his own and as far as we can see never will, since all his instincts and talents require a more or less civilized nation to act as host for their development.

Further:

> The "Aryan" unconscious has a higher potential than the Jewish; that is both the advantage and the disadvantage of a youthfulness not yet fully weaned from barbarism. In my opinion it has been a grave error in medical psychology up till now to apply Jewish categories—which are not even binding on all Jews—indiscriminately to Germanic and Slavic Christendom ... Freud ... did not understand the Germanic psyche any more than did his Germanic followers. Has the formidable phenomenon of National Socialism, on which the whole world gazes with astonished eyes, taught them better? Where was that unparalleled tension and energy while as yet no National Socialism existed?

> (CW 10, §353–354)

This article caused widespread consternation and outrage among experts and was criticised for being Nazi-friendly and anti-Semitic. Neumann, too, was indignant. In a scathing (undated) letter to Jung, he distanced himself clearly from the latter's views:

> I know I don't have to tell you what you mean to me, and how hard it is for me to disagree with you, but I feel I simply must take issue with you on a matter that goes far beyond any merely personal concerns. I will refrain from commenting on whether the reverberations that your words are bound to have were indeed what you intended, and I will be silent about whether it is truly a Goethe-inspired perspective to view the emergence of National Socialism in all its human-lashing, bloodthirsty barbarianism as a "mighty presence" in the Germanic unconscious ... As a Jew, I do not feel I have any licence to intervene in a controversy that no German can avoid today when they encounter this Germanic unconscious, but as it is certainly correct that we Jews are accustomed to recognizing the shadow-side, then I cannot comprehend why a person like you cannot see what is all too cruelly obvious to everyone these days—that it is also in the Germanic psychic ... that a mind-numbing cloud of filth, blood and rottenness is brewing.
>   ... It is precisely my conviction about the uniqueness of your own nature that causes me now—(not only in my own interest)—to ask you if this easy affirmation, this throwing yourself into the frenzy of Germanic exuberance—is this your true position or do I misunderstand you on this point?

... Believe me, as a Jew, I quite love the Germanic potential as far as I am able to see it and get a sense of it, but to equate National Socialism with the Aryan-Germanic is perhaps ominously incorrect and I cannot understand how you reach this conclusion and whether you must reach it.

Earlier in the same letter, Neumann tries to explain Jung's mistaken sense of judgment:

May your error of judgment perhaps be conditioned (in part) by the general ignorance of things Jewish and the secret and medieval abhorrence of them that thus leads to knowing everything about the India of 2000 years ago and nothing about the Hasidism of 150 years ago?

He closes with the following assessment:

I fear that you are confusing Freud—whom you have classified sociologically as European by the way—with the Jew, and therefore the use of Nazi ter-minology—simply to identify Freud's categories as "Jewish categories"—is doubly puzzling coming from your pen. ...

I do not wish to change anything in this letter. It will remain as it is writ-ten. Hopefully you will appreciate how it is intended. It seems to me that it is precisely my gratitude toward you that obliges me to be candid.

(JNC, pp. 11–15)

Another of Jung's students, James Kirsch, who was also from Berlin and prac-tising as a Jungian analyst in Jerusalem, discussed Jung's article in a reader's letter to the *Jüdische Rundschau*, the weekly magazine of the German Zionists (published in Berlin). Kirsch's letter was published in issue 43 on 29 May 1934 as "Die Judenfrage in der Psychotherapie: Einige Bemerkungen zu einem Aufsatz von C.G. Jung" ("The Jewish Question in Psychotherapy: Some remarks about an essay by C.G. Jung").

Kirsch called Jung's article "significant." He shared his attitude towards Freud and Adler, whom he also accused of one-sidedness, since they turned one aspect "into the main pillar of their psychological edifice," which "only takes into account the human shadow side." Instead of arousing fear and harbouring "perverse sexual infantile fantasies," Jung's understanding of the unconscious refers, so Kirsch, "to the creative psychic ground from which all human greatness comes."[29] Moreover, Kirsch hails Jung as the doctor of the "sick Jewish soul." "The great Zurich psychologist," "who has often been treated with hostility and as if he did not exist by Jews in the past," could become "an excellent healer" in restoring the "living connection with the primordial powers." This was possi-ble, Kirsch believed, since Jung's personality, his psychology and psychotherapy contained what "appeals to the sick Jewish soul in its depths and can lead to its liberation."[30]

Upon this lavish praise followed criticism. Among others, Kirsch believed that Jung's view of Judaism was too narrow:[31] Based on his image of Freud, Jung inferred a Judaism that was "characteristic of the *galut* psychology ... but far from the final word on Jewish psychology." Finally, he accuses Jung of associating a historical fact, the Jewish diaspora, with the "essence of Judaism." This, he finds, amounts to creating a "distorted image of the Jews." A typical Jewish trait, in Jung's eyes, was to "negate the roots of one's creativity, which inevitably led to intellectualism":

> It seems as if all that has remained with Jung, through his decades-long struggle with Freud, is the *galut* image. He has not moved on from the phenotype of the Jew living in exile from the *Shekhinah* to the genotype of the real Jew.

However, Kirsch was most critical of Jung's speculations about the relationship between the Jews and their unconscious. Apparently, Jung believed that "it was less dangerous for the Jew to negatively assess his unconscious." Precisely because the loss of the "creative primal ground" was so "characteristic" of the Jews living in "exile"—according to Kirsch—it was no less dangerous for them to neglect unconscious contents. On the contrary: It was particularly hazardous for them to destroy the "connection with the creative primal ground of the soul."

Next, Kirsch objects to Jung's insinuation that Judaism possesses no cultural form of its own. He also corrects Jung's claim that the Jews are "relative nomads" by pointing to the historical circumstances. The Jews, so Kirsch, are "a restless people, a people with a collective neurosis that has never since found a permanent home, because they have lost this connection." The most visible expression of the revision of this tragedy is the "return to one's own soil. Surely a new type has already emerged here in the old-new country, which affirms both itself and its peculiarity, and all the forces of life."

Writing to the editor of the *Jüdische Rundschau*, Neumann's fiercely contests Kirsch's central reservation about Jung,[32] namely, that "it is less dangerous for the Jew to negatively assess his unconscious." He writes:

> Jung claims that the Jew has a special tendency and capacity to recognize the negative, the shadow, and he even thinks that while the Aryan needs more illusions, the Jew is more capable of living with negative knowledge.[33]

Instead of considering this an anti-Semitic stereotype, Neumann substantiates his claim with examples supporting his view that "Jewish psychology" is able to endure the negative with open eyes:

> At the highest level, this trait shapes the historical consciousness of the Jews. Already in the Bible, the Jewish people know that their history is one of experiencing guilt in ever new ways. It is in the prophets, who were truly connected with the primal cause, that this motif reaches its creative incarnation.

Time and again, they have raised the negative, dark side into people's consciousness. If one misunderstands this basic attitude as a feature of *galut* psychology, then one is doing Judaism no favour, since this deprives it of its basic moral instinct, which still reaches into the one-sidedness of Freudian psychology.[34]

Neumann's letter to the editor of the *Jüdische Rundschau* reflects his systematic disillusionment with a positive image of the Jewish person. This, moreover, also explains his attack on Kirsch's idea that a (good) genotype of the Jew lies behind the phenotype of the present-day Jew. "We have no need," Neumann asserts, "to flee into the image of a non-existent 'real,' 'actual' Jew." On the contrary, Jung's diagnosis is quite apt and correct, insofar as his work on "contemporary Jewish people" detects and identifies the "fatal tendency" towards repressing the "greater aspect of the human soul." Neumann also commends Jung's intuitive capacity in this respect:

> In 1918, when Judaism had barely taken note of Zionism, Jung wrote: "The Jew is greatly embarrassed about that aspect in man that touches the earth and that receives new strength from below ... where does he touch his earth?"[35]

Neumann considers Jung's formulation to be fundamentally Zionist. He thus concludes that Jung is "more Zionist than the Jews and the Zionists, who wish to gloss over things." Neumann is convinced of the radicalism of Jung's assessment of the Jewish situation, and thus also emphasizes the need for conscious realisation in the Jews, in a process that, in his eyes, challenges every individual:

> Zionism must also take the difficult path of making the negative conscious. Only then will a definitive and profound construction of Eretz-Israel and a rebirth of the Jewish person be possible based on his creative foundation.[36]

In this respect, Neumann seems to err in Jung's favour: "passive, half-hearted German Zionism" already began changing after 1909. He continues:

> The principal spokesmen of this new direction were Richard Lichtheim and Kurt Blumenfeld. ... For Blumenfeld, Zionism was almost entirely a matter of character ... He sensed the coming catastrophe ... Blumenfeld observed a complete lack of "Jewish" substance in his generation ... In his eyes, Zionism was the catalyst for a personal development towards true Jewish identity ... In 1909, Blumenfeld was elected president of the Zionist Association of Germany, first and foremost by young Jews rebelling against their bourgeois parents.[37]

In spite of their differences, Kirsch's and Neumann's reactions to Jung's article have one essential aspect in common: Both are keen to "rescue" Jung, due to their significant professional and human debt to the only depth psychologist whose theoretical approach in their eyes does justice to the psyche as a whole. Compared to Kirsch, Neumann's response reflects his greater identification with Jung's position, as is evident from his agreement with Jung's claim about the "negativity" of the Jewish person. On the one hand, this may be understood in light of the self-critical manner in which the inner-Jewish discourse on "*galut* Judaism" evolved in the Zionist press (even if Neumann leaves this fact unmentioned in his afore-cited letter). In line with this tradition, Neumann formulates his stance towards Jewish self-criticism as follows:

> The constant fear that evidence of the negative aspects of the Jews could be abused by the enemies of Judaism has influenced and prevented the Jew from any movement toward consciousness.
>
> (Roots I, p. 9)

On the other hand, Neumann, in his Kafka studies, had already described how negativity, the "basic fact of moral instinct," invaded the individual as a relentless, punishing authority, in whose hopeless cycle of guilt Neumann hence became entrapped. On balance, while Neumann recognised Jung's disastrous tendency to idealise National Socialism as an important movement, he did not deny his far-sightedness and profound insight, in particular with regard to the Jewish situation.

Neumann considered the "spiritual revolution" of Hasidism to be an important source, moreover one independent of Jung's thinking, to seek the renewal of deeply entrenched Jewish positions (Roots II, p. 4). For him, Hasidism was paradigmatic of a genuine possibility for initiating a new beginning. In this respect, Neumann grounds himself firmly in Buber's thinking. He has high hopes for the revival of what once distinguished the Hasidist movement:

> This spiritual movement forms a subterranean current that invisibly nurtures living Judaism—invisibly, because the inner face of Judaism has become disguised by a rigid and lifeless orthodoxy. This current comes to light again as a secret rivulet in the individual, but perhaps also as the gushing source of a beginning.
>
> (Roots II, p. 4)

Notes

1 See C.G. Jung, *Memories, Dreams, Reflections*, recorded and edited by Aniela Jaffé, translated by Richard and Clara Winston (New York: Pantheon Books, 1962), see esp. "Confrontation with the Unconscious," pp. 165ff. For further details on Jung's technique of active imagination, see "The Transcendent Function" (1916; CW 8); "Animus and Anima" (1928; CW 7); "The Psychological Aspects of the Kore" (1941; CW 9/1); see also his introduction to Richard Wilhelm's *The Secret of the Golden Flower*; see also C.G. Jung, *Letters*, vol. 1 (Princeton: Princeton University Press, 1973), pp. 459f. and 561.

2 C.G. Jung and James Kirsch, *The Jung-Kirsch Letters*, ed. Ann Conrad Lammers (London; New York: Routledge, 2011), p. xxiii.
3 Regine Lockot, *Erinnern und Durcharbeiten: Zur Geschichte der Psychoanalyse und Psychotherapie im Nationalsozialismus* (Frankfurt am Main: Fischer, 1985), p. 54.
4 Deirdre Bair, *Jung: A Biography* (New York: Back Bay Books, 2004), p. 432.
5 Ibid., p. 433.
6 Ibid., p. 433f.
7 Lockot, *Erinnern und Durcharbeiten*, p. 57.
8 Ibid., p. 51; JNC, "Introduction," pp. xiv ff.
9 Giovanni Sorge, *1934–1959 Lettere Ernst Bernhard-Carl Gustav Jung* (Roma: Vivarium, 2001; Supplement to *Rivista di Psicologia analitica*, 32, No. 64/2001, new series No. 12).
10 Ibid.
11 Ibid.
12 See Bernhard's letter to Jung of 15 October 1934 (collected in Giovanni Sorge, *1934–1959 Lettere Ernst Bernhard-Carl Gustav Jung*).
13 Micha Neumann, "Die Beziehung zwischen C.G. Jung und Erich Neumann auf Grund ihrer Korrespondenz," in *Zur Utopie einer neuen Ethik* (Vienna: Mandelbaum, 2005), p. 19.
14 Wanda Kampmann, *Deutsche und Juden: Die Geschichte der Juden in Deutschland vom Mittelalter bis zum Beginn des Ersten Weltkrieges* (Frankfurt am Main: Fischer, 1979), p. 447.
15 Bill Rebiger, *Das jüdische Berlin* (Berlin: Jaron, 2002), p. 27. When the National Socialists seized power in 1933, Berlin had 160,000 Jewish inhabitants, which corresponded roughly to about 4 per cent of the city's population and to about one third of all German Jews.
16 Micha Neumann, "Die Beziehung zwischen C.G. Jung und Erich Neumann," p. 22.
17 Gershom Scholem, *Major Trends in Jewish Mysticism* (New York: Schocken Books, 1961), p. 344.
18 Jung's *Sermones* is a highly, baffling, indeed mysterious text, which "sprang spontaneously ... from his imagination." The process resulting in this text began in 1913 and ended in 1916; it is an extraordinarily dark text, so that Jung did not show it to anyone except some very few friends. Only at the end of his life did he agree to publish the *Sermones* (see the appendix to the German edition of *Memories, Dreams, Reflections*); see also Bair, *Jung: A Biography*, p. 290.
19 According to Deidre Bair (*Jung: A Biography*, p. 295), these were Alphonse Maeder, Hermann Sigg, Adolf and Tina Keller; see further *The Jung-Kirsch Letters*, p. 80.
20 C.G. Jung, *The Red Book: Liber Novus*. Edited by Sonu Shamdasani. Translated by Mark Kyburz, John Peck and Sonu Shamdasani (New York: W.W. Norton, 2009), p. 205. Writing on Gnosis, Gilles Quispel remarks: "Gnosis is the third component of Western culture, which I could formulate as follows: Faith was born in Jerusalem, and still the churches ask for faith. Logos, reason, was invented in Athens ... Especially Thomas Aquinas honors reason and ever since the middle ages philosophy is reason. Alexandria is the cradle of gnosis, which is imaginative thinking, that is, imagination. Gnosis is the permanent third component next to faith and reason of Western civilization. And Jung saw this." See Lyn Cowan, ed. *Barcelona 04: Edges of Experience: Memory and Emergence* (Proceedings of the 16th International Congress for Analytical Psychology) (Einsiedeln: Daimon, 2006), p. 150; see further *The Red Book: Reflections on C.G. Jung's Liber Novus*, ed. by Thomas Kirsch and George Hogenson (London & New York: Routledge, 2014).
21 In his introduction to the *Red Book*, Sonu Shamdasani writes: "After writing the *Septem Sermones* in the *Black Books*, Jung recopied it in a calligraphic script into a

separate book, slightly rearranging the sequence. He added the following inscription under the title: 'The seven instructions of the dead. Written by Basilides in Alexandria, the city where the East touches the West.' He then had this privately printed, adding to the inscription: 'Translated from the Greek original into German'" (p. 206).

22 Bair, *Jung: A Biography*, p. 290ff. In 1914, Jung re-read Nietzsche's *Zarathustra*, which had exercised his thinking since his youth. Nietzsche's stylistic influences are evident, especially in "Liber Novus," in which not God's death is depicted, but rather his rebirth in the human soul; see also Shamdasani, Introduction to *The Red Book*, pp. 204ff.

23 www.gnosis.org/library/7Sermons.htm (last accessed 1 October 2018).

24 Ibid.

25 C.G. Jung, *Septem Sermones ad Mortuous*, cited here from the translation by Stephan A. Hoeller, first published in his *The Gnostic Jung and the Seven Sermons to the Dead* (Wheaton, IL: Quest Books, 1982). The passage appears in Section I.

26 Neumann kept a little booklet of imaginations, which he called "Initiations." The volume was sold at an auction at Sotheby's in 2006; see JNC, p. 162, n. 368.

27 Micha Neumann, "Die Beziehung zwischen C.G. Jung und Erich Neumann auf Grund ihrer Korrespondenz," in *Zur Utopie einer neuen Ethik*, p. 20.

28 *C.G. Jung Speaking: Interviews and Encounters*. Edited by William McGuire and R.F.C. Hull, Bollingen Series XCVII (Princeton, NJ: Princeton University Press, 1977), pp. 61ff.

29 Jung attributes this one-sidedness to Freud's Jewishness.

30 *Jüdische Rundschau* no. 43, 29 May 1934, p. 11.

31 How exactly he could thus be a healer of the "sick Jewish soul" is somewhat difficult to understand.

32 *Jüdische Rundschau*, no. 48, 15 June 1934, p. 5.

33 Ibid.

34 Ibid.

35 Ibid

36 Ibid.

37 Amos Elon, *Zu einer anderen Zeit* (Munich: dtv, 2002), pp. 283ff.

Chapter 5

Excursus: "Motherly Soil" and "Renewal"

Martin Buber's and C.G. Jung's metaphors of cultural criticism

"The Jew": This collective singular was widespread in turn-of-the-century Germany. It served as a projection screen for an array of pejorative and distorting attributions, whether by Jews themselves or by others. Early 20th-century Jewish self-consciousness, that is, critical reflection on one's specific plight, employed—particularly in Zionist circles—"various semantic dichotomies, for instance, *uprooting* versus *rootedness* or *earth, land, soil*; these gave rise to further dichotomous images bearing racial, ethical and psychological implications and conclusions."[1]

In Eastern Europe, *uprooting*, as a result of mass poverty and repeated pogroms, contributed to widely disseminating this metaphor. In Western Europe, it came to symbolise the negative aspects of modern urban life. Also known as "alienation" at the time, it denoted the loss of faith, due to increasing secularisation.[2] In this logic, the Jewish diaspora represented an alienated, false life that soon became subject to ever-greater intra-Jewish and anti-Semitic criticism. Thus, defending this way of life had already become the exception by 1900.[3]

In contrast, terms like *earth* and *soil* attained idealistic and mystical value, for instance, in the works of Martin Buber, but also in Tolstoy's, although in a different context. A new cultural theory emerged and established "the epigeal axiom"—that is, an affiliation with the earth and a closeness to the soil—as the norm.[4] In economic terms, however, *earth* became a "cipher for primordial production and proper economic activity," while *air*, attributed to the Jews, became a "symbol of the abstract value of goods, trade, false economy."[5] Calamitously, this criticism affected both those (predominantly Eastern) Jews who had little to no income and all those who enjoyed economic and financial success.

Anti-Semitism had deployed the topos of the unrooted, floating and homeless Jew already during the age of Jewish emancipation, so as to stigmatise the alleged anomalies of the Jewish world.[6] Various phenomena of modern life such as migration, urbanisation, multilingualism and professionalisation, meanwhile divorced from pre-modern primary production, seemed to be particularly appropriate examples of alienated Jewish lifestyles in the emergence of anti-Semitic stereotypes.

And yet, Zionist theorising took up theories of the anti-Jewish tradition by branding characteristic Jewish social and professional structures as unnatural or even as pathological.[7] Various Jewish periodicals, including *Palästina, Ost und West* or *Der Jude* (edited by Buber), began publishing debates in which political values shifted increasingly from the model of emancipation and acculturation towards that of land, the people, combativeness and work. The line of argumentation in these debates followed a consistent pattern: The diaspora had forced the Jews to earn their living not through agriculture, handicrafts and livestock farming—the "natural forms of human employment"—from which arose a certain type of human being, from which the Jews were compelled to detach themselves, in favour of a "new human being," who was now meant to pursue "creative work."[8]

This Zionist discourse had established great interpretive power by the early 20th century. One illustrative example is the life and work of Martin Buber.[9] It is contrasted here with excerpts from the writings of C.G. Jung in order to reveal the surprising similarities between their seemingly distinct argumentations. Obviously, the motivations driving Buber's and Jung's thinking require careful and strict differentiation: On the one hand stands the Jewish talk of uprooting and earth (as a "remedy" against alienation), which applies especially to Zionist self-awareness; on the other are pejorative-distorting ascriptions and anti-Semitic stereotypes, to which Jung, like many others, succumbed. These different motivations correspond to "two opposing axes of evaluation": On the one hand, the intra-Jewish, which sprang from a precarious social status; on the other, the anti-Semitic, brought forth by the Jews seemingly adopting modernity and its values too quickly, in a line of argumentation consistent with the discursive impetus of conservative cultural criticism.[10]

As we have seen (Chapter 1), Martin Buber was widely considered the father of the "Jewish Renaissance." Buber, who often speaks of the "uprooted Jewish people,"[11] paints a gloomy picture of the "*galut* Jew" (i.e. the Jew living in exile), who often and indeed confusingly resembles anti-Semitic stereotypes. Buber depicted the life of the assimilated Jew as an unstable, torn existence, whose alienation must be overcome. Thus, in the second of his three fiery addresses on Judaism, delivered in Prague at the invitation of *Bar Kochba*, the Jewish student association, he leaves no doubt about his strict condemnation of the diaspora, on account of its destructive effect on the Jewish people. This explains his distinction, in "Judaism and Mankind," between "men with goals and men with objectives; between the creative and the corroding—between elemental Jews (*Urjuden*) and *galut* Jews."[12]

Fuelling Buber was his inner mission to contribute to the (re-)creation of Judaism, which he believed was undergoing large-scale spiritual upheaval: "If Judaism is not to continue its sham existence, if it is to be resurrected to true life, its spirit must be renewed and its spiritual process start anew."[13]

Buber regarded the Jewish diasporic tradition merely as "official Judaism." This, he asserted, needed to be contrasted with *true* Judaism, which was only just beginning to emerge. What Buber also called "subterranean Judaism" could not be attained by "polishing up old values, but only by radically overthrowing tradition":[14]

> The great creative epoch was followed by that long span of years which one can truly call the Age of Exile, for it expelled us from the very core of our existence. It was the era of barren intellectuality, an intellectuality that, far removed from life and from a living striving for unity, fed on bookish words, on interpretations of interpretations; poverty-stricken, distorted, an sickly, it subsisted in a climate of idea-less abstraction. Once the natural unity of land and well-rooted community, the sustaining unity of the soil, had prevented the inner duality from degenerating into ambivalence and instability.[15]

Buber uses two central, dichotomous metaphors: *golus* or *galut* versus *earth, soil* or *home*.[16] His diagnosis of the current diasporic situation of Judaism opposes two sets of concepts: *dissension, distortion, abstractness, unstableness* and *disintegration* versus the ideal, *primordial essence of Judaism*, which includes *down-to-earthness* and the *unity of the earth*. His "Das Land der Juden" (1910) reveals the close linkage between his vision of a new Judaism and a specific place:[17]

> The renewal of Judaism, which must begin in Golus [i.e. exile], will not be able to complete itself in Golus ... it can only come from a certain soil: from the soil of the homeland. It has created our special kind, our peculiar energies ... it alone will be able to renew them ... Let us not believe that it is enough to come out of the outer Golus! What we need more than anything is that we cleanse ourselves from the inner Golus ... But this inner liberation from the Golus must also be striven for with all strength by the individual, for the people it must remain piecemeal: for the people it can only succeed in *one* place in the world ... Only there can we truly come to ourselves. Here we are a wedge that Asia drove into the fabric of Europe ... Let us return to Asia's bosom ... and we shall return to the meaning of our existence.[18]
>
> (Original emphasis)

Buber here draws on a central topos of Zionist discourse, which was convinced "that a special relationship existed or had to be newly established between the Jewish people and the Jewish land, and that both had to redeem themselves through mutual transformation."[19] Thus, at the time, numerous Zionist travelogues emerged in programmatic defiance of the stereotype of the rootless Jewish diaspora. Their titles reflected this stance: *Neue Menschen auf alter Erde* ("New People on Old Soil") or *Eine werdene Welt* ("An Emerging World").[20]

The concept of *groundlessness*, shaped by the German religious philosopher and historian Bruno Bauer (1809–1882), became a sweeping accusation against Jewish existence and occupied a central place in the arsenal of anti-Semitic stereotypes.[21] Bauer's concept of *bodenlose Existenz* ("baseless existence") took aim both at the diaspora as actual Jewish life and at the resulting questions about the legal equality of the Jews. His scathing criticism of early 19th century Judaism was widely acclaimed. Moreover, it significantly reinforced the tendency to evaluate Jews within the meanwhile prevalent dichotomous logic: soil versus air, earth versus spirit, root versus "uprooting."[22]

The soil metaphor was also widely deployed in the field of economics. In *Die Juden und das Wirtschaftsleben* ("The Jews and Economic Life"), his critical study of capitalism, the German economist and sociologist Werner Sombart (1863–1941)[23] described the Jews as a wandering people who had never forged close ties with the earth, but instead an increasingly intense bond with the abstract value of money. Essentially, so Sombart, Judaism had only striven for goal-driven, rational relationships, thereby acquiring a capacity for capitalism that a settled people could never have developed.

The third example of the interpretive power attributed to the metaphor of the soil in the field of science is the historian Heinrich von Treitschke (1834–1896).[24] His key image for German culture was that of a widespread tree whose roots symbolised the use of the past layers of the earth as a source of strength and life for present welfare and growth. While the ethnification of such neo-romantic images became increasingly common, among others, in art and literary history, it also radicalised the anti-Semitic impetus.[25]

We also find evidence of dichotomous thinking within the aforementioned conceptual framework in C.G. Jung's writings. For instance, Jung dedicated his lecture "Seele und Erde" ("Mind and Earth"), delivered in 1927 to the "Gesellschaft für freie Philosophie" in Darmstadt, to the earth metaphor. Hermann Graf Keyserling, chair of the society, collected Jung's essay and others in an anthology titled *Mensch und Erde* ("Man and Earth"), published in 1927. In his lecture, Jung associates the earth with the archetypes:

> They [the archetypes—A.L.] are thus, essentially the chthonic portion of the psyche, if we may use such an expression—that portion through which the psyche is attached to nature, or in which its link with the earth and the world appears at its most tangible. The psychic influence of the earth and its laws is seen most clearly in these primordial images.
>
> (CW 10, §53)

Jung chthonicises the archetypes, yet without further explanation. He thus draws on the metaphorology common at the time, which aligned permanence, value and substance semantically with earth and soil. What is striking is his blurred concept of earth, which equates the earth with the world.[26] At the end of his lecture, Jung combines a cultural-conservative, anti-modernist position with a psychological location of the unconscious, through which we are bound to "our earth." Jung places this concept within the interpretive framework of "historical contingency." This, in turn, guarantees duration, security and psychic health:

Our contact with the unconscious chains us to the earth and makes it hard for us to move, and this is certainly no advantage when it comes to progressiveness and all the other desirable motions of the mind. Nevertheless I would not speak ill of our relation to good Mother Earth. Plurimi pertransibunt—but he who is rooted in the soil endures. Alienation from the unconscious and from its historical conditions spells rootlessness. That is the danger that lies in wait for the conqueror of foreign lands, and for every individual who, through one-sided allegiance to any kind of -ism, loses touch with the dark, maternal, earthy ground of his being.[27]

(CW 10, §103)

In this perspective, modernity and the associated progressiveness—at whose forefront the Jews were said to stand—came dangerously close to losing contact with the unconscious. The specific type of contact with the unconscious is characterised by gravity and stasis. Metaphorically, earth means a connection with tradition and the past, and more broadly a commitment to one's own culture and continuity. And yet, at the same time, it also implies a warning against rupture and discontinuity. Finally, as the previous passage suggests, earth for Jung is situated within the maternal sphere.

A further variant of earth appears in Jung's *Zarathustra* seminar: In May 1933, Jung gave a seminar on Nietzsche's *Zarathustra* at the Zurich Psychological Club. Further seminars followed (the cycle ended in 1939). They were conducted in English, as a reading course on Nietzsche's text. Here, for instance, is Jung's interpretation of Nietzsche's dictum, "Let your will say: The Superman shall be the meaning of the earth!" (*Zarathustra* I, p. 42):

Here he begins with his real philosophy, interpreting the Superman as the meaning of the earth.

"Let your will say: The superman shall be the meaning of the earth."

He makes it imperative—you shall make him so. For the earth of course could have other meanings; that the superman is the meaning of the earth is not the most obvious conclusion to draw. ... Yes, instead of calling it flesh or animal he calls it the earth, and the earth is the body. So the body is the mediator. ... As you know from dream symbols, the meaning of the earth is essentially the body. ... All the people who claim to be spiritual try to get away from the fact of the body; they want to destroy it in order to be something imaginary, but they never will be that, because the body denies them. ... They think they can live without sex or feeding, without the ordinary human conditions; and it is a mistake, a lie, and the body denies their convictions. That is what Nietzsche means here. The superman, the self is the meaning of the earth; it consists of the fact that we are made of earth.

Therefore when you study symbols of individuation, you always find that no individuation can take place – I mean symbolically – without the animal, a very dark animal, coming up from primordial slime enters the region of the spirit; that one black spot, which is the earth, is absolutely indispensable on the bright shield of spirituality. ... The essences of the body then constitute the self. ...

It is the essential metaphysical meaning of the earth that it gives specification to things that it makes things distinct.[28]

The interpretative framework established here by Jung's reading of Zarathustra has far-reaching ideological implications: Nietzsche's earth metaphor interprets the superhuman—which for Jung represents the self—as his very own condition and destiny. He attaches considerable importance to the human body as a representation of earth. Jung interprets the concept of the earth here symbolically, in terms of its significance in dream and individuation images. Not only the individual, but also collectives must possess "earth" or "soil" if they are to escape "rootlessness." Jung formulated this idea as early as 1918. Considering the distinction between "the Jew" and the Germanic peoples in the context of World War I, he observes:

> Christianity split the Germanic barbarian into an upper and a lower half, and enabled him, by repressing the dark side, to domesticate the brighter half and fit it for civilization. But the lower, darker half still awaits redemption and a second spell of domestication. Until then, it will remain associated with the vestiges of the prehistoric age, with the collective unconscious, which is subject to a peculiar and ever-increasing activation. As the Christian view of the world loses its authority, the more menacingly will the "blond beast" be heard prowling about in its underground prison, ready at any moment to burst out with devastating consequences. When this happens in the individual it brings about a psychological revolution, but it can also take a social form.[29]
>
> (CW 10, §17)

He continues:

> In my opinion this problem does not exist for the Jews. The Jew already had the culture of the ancient world and on top of that has taken over the culture of the nations amongst whom he dwells. He has two cultures, paradoxical as that may sound. He is domesticated to a higher degree than we are, but he is badly at a loss for that quality in man which roots him to the earth and draws new strength from below. This chthonic quality is found in dangerous concentration in the Germanic peoples. Naturally the Aryan Europeans has not noticed any signs of this for a very long time, but perhaps he is beginning to notice it in the present war; and again, perhaps not. The Jew has too little of this quality—where has he his own earth underfoot? The mystery of earth is no joke and no paradox.
>
> (CW 10, §18)

Here, too, earth is connoted as a necessary and salubrious "new force." The positive effect of the earth "from below" seems sufficient to explain the text in Jung's thinking. In actual fact, however, it remains open. Closer scrutiny reveals that the text contains an analogy between Germans and Jews. First, Germanic fragmentation is treated, then the corresponding Jewish one. In a superficial reading, this makes the text appear "fair," that is, symmetrical, since both Germans and Jews are subjected to depth psychological criticism. But the text withholds further explanation of the collective unconscious of "the Jew." For in a clear analogy to the "Germanic barbarian," whose religious division was described by Christianity in terms of upper and lower, the subsequent discussion of "the Jew" should logically address the problem of religion. Jung, however, merely states that "the Jew" possesses "two cultures," without commenting on their internal and external tensions. Rather, he suddenly introduces a notion of the earth that is no longer symbolic but concrete. This is directed against the diasporic situation of the Jews, which suggests that Jung employs a highly charged anti-Semitic stereotype in the tradition of Bruno Bauer's concept of "groundlessness" to explain depth-psychological facts, even if his account lacks consistent argumentation. Seen in this light, earth serves Jung as a "multi-functional metaphor." It represents the archetypes, the maternal, duration, continuity and safeguarding against one-sidedness. It is a "Nietzschean imperative," through which the human body experiences a vitalistic charge and becomes the basis of individuation.

The "Germanic barbarian" has individuated to a considerable extent, whereas the "more domesticated Jew," to his disadvantage, entirely lacks this quality. As soon as Jung steps onto political terrain, the symbolic content of the concept of earth quickly becomes concrete and polemical. Moreover, it lacks any interpretive effort. The ideological framework of Buber's and Jung's political discourse[30] rests on the following argumentation: It first concerns the cultural autonomy of peoples and their collective identity, and second emphasises the right or duty of peoples to become aware of their cultural differences. Further, Buber and Jung both entertained the notion that "soil" and "earth" possess healing, centering and even renewing powers.

Taken together, in Jung's thinking these claims amount to an argumentation consistent with racial psychology. For Jews like Erich Neumann, who embraced Buber's ideas and Zionism, this thinking was not primarily anti-Semitic but anti-racist, since it insisted on cultural difference, so that the core of the respective culture would be enhanced.[31] This stance was perhaps also considered less anti-Semitic because Jung was not sparing with his criticism of the "Germanic barbarian." He could therefore also be seen as attempting to grasp the deep structure of the unconscious in diverse cultures. In this respect, the claim about the incompatibility of collective-unconscious positions was legitimised by the diversity of religious traditions and their beliefs.

Notes

1 Nicholas Berg, *Luftmenschen: Zur Geschichte einer Metapher* (Göttingen: Vandenhoeck & Ruprecht, 2008), p. 8.
2 Ibid., p. 34f.

3 Ibid., p. 60.
4 Ibid., p. 146.
5 Ibid., p. 90f.
6 Ibid., p. 23.
7 Ibid., p. 101.
8 Ibid., pp. 101ff.
9 Ernst Simon has assessed Buber's influence on the Jews, not least through his journal *Der Jude*, as follows: "The influence of the monthly *Der Jude* among German and Central European Jews was immense from the outset, comparable only to that of the *Jüdische Rundschau* since 1933." Simon pays tribute to Buber, "who knew how to let almost all living Jewish spirits of the time have their say and to allow all the urgent questions to be treated, without blurring the journal's human-national direction … The thinking German Jew of the First World War generation, who tried to find inner direction and orientation, sought, unless he belonged to the strictly orthodox minority, to orient himself in a spiritual force field determined by the ideas and aspirations of Herzel, Hermann Cohen and Buber"; see Eugen Simon, "Martin Buber und das deutsche Judentum," in Robert Weltsch, ed., *Deutsches Judentum. Aufstieg und Krise. Gestalten, Ideen, Werke* (Stuttgart: Deutsche Verlagsanstalt, 1963), pp. 59ff. The ideological influence of Kurt Blumenfeld, who was elected chairman of the German Zionist Association in 1909, in forming the opinions of young Zionists should not be underestimated.
10 Berg, *Luftmenschen*, p. 24.
11 Ibid., p. 98.
12 Martin Buber, *On Judaism*, edited by Nahum N. Glatzer, translated by Eva Jospe (New York: Schocken Books, 1967), p. 31.
13 Ibid., p. 52f.
14 See Klaus S. Davidowicz, *Gershom Scholem und Martin Buber: Die Geschichte eines Missverständnisses* (Neukirchener Theologie, 1995).
15 Buber, *On Judaism*, p. 29f.
16 Other terms central to Buber's thinking include *blood* and *people*.
17 Martin Buber, "Das Land der Juden" (1910), in *Die jüdische Bewegung*, vol. 1, *Gesammelte Aufsätze und Ansprachen 1900–1915* (Berlin: Jüdischer Verlag, 1916), pp. 192–195, cited in Paul R. Mendes-Flohr, *Von der Mystik zum Dialog: Martin Bubers geistige Entwicklung bis hin zu Ich und Du* (Königstein/Taunus: Jüdischer Verlag, 1978), p. 104.
18 See also the following remarks by Buber: "In the detachment and dissolution of his occidental existence, of course, it [Judaism—A.L.] can only be piecemeal; … a great creation that … resumes the continuity of Jewish becoming … will only be able to emerge if the continuity of Palestinian life is resumed, from which once the great conceptions of this unitarian instinct arose … if it (the soul of the Jew) touches its motherly soil, it will again be creative"; Martin Buber, *Der Geist des Orients und das Judentum*, p. 44f.; cited in Mendes-Flohr, *Von der Mystik zum Dialog*, p. 104.
19 Berg, *Luftmenschen*, p. 99.
20 Ibid.
21 Bauer blended religious resentment with racist and ethnic elements and thus anticipated the racist anti-Semitism that only emerged later.
22 Berg, *Luftmenschen*, p. 23.
23 Ibid.
24 Ibid.
25 Ibid., p. 42.
26 See CW 10, §64: "Mother Germania is for the Germans, like la douce France for the French, a figure of the utmost importance behind the political scene, who could

be overlooked only by blinkered intellectuals. The all-embracing womb of Mother Church is anything but a metaphor, and the same is true of Mother Earth, Mother Nature, and 'matter' in general."

27 See also: " Just as, in the process of evolution, the mind has been moulded by earthly conditions, so the same process repeats itself under our eyes today. Imagine a large section of some European nation transplanted to a strange soil and another climate. We can confidently expect this human group to undergo certain psychic and perhaps also physical changes in the course of a few generations, even without the admixture of foreign blood. We can observe in the Jews of the various European countries marked differences which can only be explained by the peculiarities of the people they live amongst. It is not difficult to tell a Spanish Jew from a North African Jew, a German Jew from a Russian Jew" (CW 10, §93).

28 *Jung's Seminar on Nietzsche's Zarathustra*, edited and abridged by James L. Jarrett, Bollingen Series XCIX (Princeton, NJ: Princeton University Press, 1998), pp. 45ff.

29 Originally published in *Schweizerland. Monatshefte für Schweizer Art und Arbeit* IV/ 9 and 11/12 (Zurich, 1918).

30 Pierre-André Taguieff observes that this discourse exemplifies a "differentialist and culturalist racism"; see his "Die Metamorphose des Rassismus und die Krise des Antirassismus" (1991), in Ulrich Bielefeld, ed., *Das Eigene und das Fremde: Neuer Rassismus in der Alten Welt?* (Hamburg: Hamburger Edition, 1998).

31 Less shocking than the fact that Jung, as a depth psychologist, used this "cultural code" (Shamulit Volkov) is that he later, from 1933, instrumentalised it in vitriolic attacks against Freud and "Jewish psychology."

Chapter 6

"I must learn to distinguish myself"[1]

Neumann's correspondence with C.G. Jung on the collective unconscious and individuation

Neumann wrote nearly 60 letters to C.G. Jung, some of which were quite extensive. Taken together, they provide insight into their discussions during Neumann's stay in Zurich in the early 1930s. Some of these letters, particularly the first nine, which were written between 1934 and 1940, deal explicitly with the subject of "Jewish identity." They do so in different "registers," and with an important shift in substance, as Neumann's letter of 15 November 1939 reveals.

Neumann's letters to Jung capture a dramatic tension, which needs to be understood in terms of both the difficult circumstances of living in Palestine and the drastic escalation of Jewish life in Germany after Hitler's rise to power. Aside from this tension, the Jung–Neumann correspondence also casts light on the two men's relationship.

With the passage of time, Neumann's profound trust in Jung prevailed in spite of adverse circumstances: the sense of fragility caused by the repeatedly interrupted postal service between Zurich and Tel Aviv and the large geographical distance. Perhaps even more strikingly, their close working relationship was not disrupted by various conflicts that might have been more damaging: Jung's implicit or even outright anti-Semitic remarks, his revoking of previously articulated positions and his lack of consistency towards the recently established Zurich Institute. Over the course of a correspondence spanning 25 years, Neumann's voice, however, did not always remain calm or admiring, but at times became critical,[2] disappointed,[3] oppositional,[4] or demanding.[5]

Neumann's examination of the "Jewish question" reflected a deep existential struggle, since he considered this subject—however collectively he understood it—as a personal mission. In this process, Neumann at first saw Jung as a teacher (Chapter 4), whose task was to guide his student from a narrow, constricted vantage point to a universal, overarching one. Or, as Neumann wrote to Jung on 19 July 1934:

> I have the firm intention not to give you any peace about the Jewish problem and, if necessary, I will earn again the lost tenacity and stubbornness of my race in order to be taken into the depths of these problems by you so that I no longer see them from a blinkered standpoint.
>
> (JNC, p. 35)

The fact that Neumann views his own perspective as "blinkered" springs from his disappointed expectations about his "country" and his "people," both having turned out to be illusory ideals. He had complained about the "poor" Jews already in his first letter to Jung, sent from Palestine in 1934, in which he shared his experiences of coping with a difficult, dangerous, improvised and chaotic reality:

> I did not, by any means, come here with any illusions, but what I have found extraordinary was that I haven't found a "people" here with whom I fundamentally feel I belong. I might have known that before, of course, but it was not the case, and the fact that the Jews here as a people, as a not-yet-people, seemed so extremely needy was a shock at first ... As a people, the Jews are infinitely more stupid than I expected ... Please don't misunderstand me—I am not reproaching the Jew[s]. How could it be any different? We come, as individuals, from who knows where and are then supposed to be one people.
>
> (JNC, pp. 17–18)

One of Neumann's next letters (undated, but written in 1935) begins by describing the Jews as the "most disappointing people of world history" (JNC, p. 77).[6] In the same letter, he writes:

> I got far too caught up in "praise of the Jews" and did not take into account nearly enough the fact that, at the same time, the Jews are always the most disappointing people of world history. And indeed not only that—all too many are willing to pay for the attitude toward the future with an impoverishment of the present ...
>
> We are not only living off the interest of old capital but now that this has been largely devalued by the inflation of emancipation, we are inclined to live on credit, while hoping for an upturn or even invoking one. This won't do, of course.[7]
>
> (JNC, pp. 77–78)

Neumann's criticism acknowledges the Jews' lack of authenticity, their failure to examine their own heritage and a lack of critical distance to the emancipatory developments brought about by the *Haskalah* (i.e. Jewish Enlightenment). The current and highly significant upheaval—the emergence of a new state and the formation of a "people"—provides a unique opportunity to create something new:

> I see quite factually the Jews are in a quite peculiar situation that is calculated to force them to find new and groundbreaking solutions, but one should not be awarding them laurels in advance, while it is still so terribly questionable whether they will succeed or whether they won't just fail as they nearly always do. No real disappointment in the failure of the Jews could dissuade me from believing in them because, out of the making conscious of

their failure, a step forward has always emerged, but I wouldn't want to be a "gushing enthusiast in Israel"—that is not my role but rather my danger.

(JNC, p. 78)

The reality of Jewish life in Palestine challenges Neumann to engage with his people's "shadow," which has now been "liberated" (JNC, p. 18). Nevertheless, this confrontation dampens any high hopes of harmonious change occurring in the near future:

> The Jews are coming to a—terrible—civilization. It cannot be changed. The traditionlessness of this struggle that has no core gives everything a rather ghostly demeanor.

(JNC, pp. 17–18)

In this context, Neumann points to an important asymmetry between Jung and himself:

> I am really no "legitimate" representative of Judaism, although you are absolutely a legitimate representative of the Occidental World; I know therefore how unevenly the weights are distributed.

(JNC, p. 36)

This passage, from his letter dated 19 July 1934, resonates with Neumann's self-evaluation as a Jew: Being Jewish, in his eyes, means belonging to an "emerging" people,[8] one that must first reflect on its very own primordialism on account of its profound self-alienation. Western people, he believes, suffered no such loss. Here, Neumann reverses one of Jung's basic claims: Whereas the latter's notorious essay of March 1934 ("The State of Psychotherapy Today," CW 10) had maintained the ability of the young Germanic peoples to create new forms of culture" (in contrast to the nomadic Jews), Neumann claims the position of the "emerging people" for his own Jewish reality.

Neumann's reference to unequal distribution further emphasises the position he had previously articulated in his letter to the editor of the *Jüdische Rundschau* in 1934. As is well known, he took issue with the views of James Kirsch: "We have no need ... to flee into the image of a non-existent 'real,' 'actual' Jew" (Chapter 4). This also reflects how critically Neumann saw himself in particular, and the Jews in general: as traditionless, "rootless" and unconnected to their own collective unconscious. His diagnosis refers to Jung's fundamental distinction between the Western and the Jewish collective unconscious.

Jung did not interpret historical circumstances as the consequences of political contingencies having considerable, even catastrophic effects, but instead as manifestations of a collective unconscious that from time to time manifested itself in a manner specific to a particular culture or people. In Jung's thinking, the idea that the "earth," the soil of Palestine, is crucial for the Jewish path of development, and the basic assumption of a people-specific collective unconscious, enter into an intimate connection and coalesce as it were.

The theorem of the collective unconscious makes it possible to reject the power of contingency, that is, to uphold the idea of development and to reduce complexity. For the Jews, the assumption that unconscious collective forces were escalating their situation could provide considerable respite, since they felt under constant pressure to legitimise themselves and to "identify themselves psychically."[9]

Jung's theorem, moreover, added a further dimension to the subject of "the collective and the individual," which was being debated above all among Zionists:[10] It connects the religious foundation, the covenant once entered into by God with his people, with the modern Jew's loss of faith in and experience of the spiritual dimension by accepting an indestructible psychological containment. The legacy of what was once revealed can be stored in a deep psychological layer, from where it can be summoned by the individual. Thus, the correspondence between the individual and the lost collective tradition, which Orthodox Judaism no longer believed capable of preserving, seems to be salvaged, moreover sustainably. For Neumann, his agreement with Jung on the basic assumptions about the collective unconscious formed the basis of his self-assurance—and also the inescapable precondition for achieving individuation.

The collective unconscious became Neumann's guiding assumption through providing—beyond all rupture and discontinuity—constant inner orientation:

1. Historical events can be regarded as a vehicle of painful, yet necessary or meaningful development from a distanced, archetypal viewpoint.
2. Crises can be understood as "imperative" upheavals and can therefore be regarded as an inner mission serving reorientation.

The idea of the collective unconscious forms the basis of a two-volume manuscript whose first part Neumann sent Jung in the late 1930s.[11] Although Neumann described the work as a contribution to "radical self-contemplation" (Roots I, p. 9), he could not decide in favour of publication.[12]

His introduction unmistakably announces Neumann's interest in the collective unconscious of the Jewish person:

> Judaism, then, is facing a crisis that threatens its very existence. Not because economic or political expulsion is at stake—this, of course, is the Jewish fate, although previously it never spelled an existential crisis—but because Jewish religion is no longer an effective force in the world, just as little as, or even less than, Protestantism. This situation affects modern Jews and modern Western Christians alike, because currently emerging developments in their unconscious will prompt new philosophical and religious influences.
>
> (Roots I, p. 6)

Here, Zionist ideas, particularly Buber's crisis thinking, and Jung's conviction that the situation of Western humanity needs to be interpreted as one of upheaval, are combined into an overall thesis. The dialectical interweaving pervading Neumann's account—turning to the Jewish tradition while critically distancing himself from it and reinterpreting it—points to a historical method of interpretation aptly described by David Biale as "counter-history."[13] Neumann brushes traditional Jewish ideas against the grain, so to speak, above all the idea of continuity, the idea of a "consistent Judaism." Essentially, he attacks the eschatological view of the history of the Jews, at whose centre stands the chosen people. Neumann refutes the theological notion that the catastrophe of the *galut* (exile) began after the second destruction of the Temple. Instead, he seeks to identify the symptoms of internal alienation, which, in his eyes, is not linked to an external historical catastrophe. He blames this hollowing out on a rigid theological edifice:

> Alongside the famous affirmation of Judaism, a productive negation of Judaism is needed as well, by those who assume that the individual's plight is inextricably bound up with the community's. Beyond the paralysis of dogmatic Judaism, innumerable hidden creative tensions exist within the Jew. These tensions must be identified and kindled, so that the old sources of living water will once again flow from the seemingly lifeless stone.
>
> (Roots I, p. 6)

These "sources of living water" are primarily the Hasidic tradition and Kabbalistic ideas, whose publication helped Buber reach a broad audience. If, however, this was more than a well-established Eastern Jewish cult that lasted several years, in which sentimental-romantic transfiguration and the idealisation of an original and authentic way of life were at best reflected, and if the talk of the renewal of Judaism from within contained an element of truth, then the question of the forces inherent in the psyche and its transformational power inevitably needed to be raised.

The concept of revelation suggests how Neumann associates the central themes of the theological debates at that time[14] with a depth-psychological perspective. It also reveals how he argues "from the unconscious problem of the modern Jew" (Roots I, p. 7). He reinterprets the key theological concept of revelation as "the rise of new and normative contents from the unconscious into consciousness" (ibid.).[15]

Neumann's guiding interest is to find a depth-psychological explanation for the "breaking point" responsible for the "inner transformation of the ancient Jew into a galut Jew" (Roots I, p. 8). He is searching for pivotal psychosocial situations capable of explaining why Judaism had fallen into such a threatening and precarious situation. Like Jung, he speaks of a "parasitic" form of existence. Jung's concept of individuation was particularly fruitful for the project of rediscovering buried, once living contents: The search for an authentic form of existence in the present took shape as an initiatory return to the collective unconscious.

For Neumann, as he wrote on 29 October 1935, this authentic form could only be attained in Palestine:

> As has become clearly evident to me though, individuation does not belong to the category of confession but that of growth … The relationship of the Jews to the "earth" … can be resolved neither by a simple return to the soil (political Zionism) nor by only a psychical return to the soil (the Galut Jew[16] with analytical psychology). Both of these must be achieved together. The environment of the Jew in Europe is the collective unconscious of the non-Jews, and with this, his individuation is impossible. Only among Jews was it and is it possible, for only there does he encounter his archetypal foundation in the world and only in collision with this, can he—at best—achieve individuation.
>
> (JNC, pp. 116–117)

It was—as he complains in the same letter—"always characteristic of the tendency of the Jews to avoid the bitter path of individuation through the path of being a parasite" (JNC, p. 115). His emphasis on the religious questions of Judaism, while paying slightly less heed to external political factors (e.g. anti-Semitism), is linked to the notion of guilt. This, he argues, should be sought out in the unconscious. This guilt concerns neglecting the unconscious. On a collective level, Neumann locates this guilt in extraversion. It is, as he wrote to Jung on 5 December 1938, the "enormous extraversion of Judaism that had led it the brink of its grave" (JNC, p. 140).

"The non-self-evident way in which Jews are Jews": Neumann diagnoses the psychological aspects of the Jewish lack of authenticity as resulting from various factors: alienation through assimilation, excessive extraversion, reservations towards the unconscious, which had once addressed the Jewish collective as revelation, and a lack of inwardness. He identifies several remedies on the path of individuation: introversion, returning to tradition without any fixation on theological dogmatics and openness towards the contents of the unconscious. All of these stages manifest themselves primarily in dreams and the imagination.

This self-critical perspective, which claims that the Jews have long pursued a path that has rendered individuation impossible, lends Neumann a position of sovereignty. Although Jewishness is a pervasive subject in his letters to Jung, only the first ones emphasise the laborious nature of his search, for instance, when he observes that "the work on the Jewish material … is slow and difficult" (JNC, p. 114; 29 October 1935). His main endeavour, at least until 1939, was to combine the individual and the collective, that is, to make a personal contribution to reintegrating the collective contents, as he told Jung in his letter of 5 December 1938:

> Thus, the full uncertainty about any future and yet still having the feeling of being in the right place gives me—at least now and again—a remarkably paradoxical inner confidence, from which I believe that there could be a new, lively beginning in the individual and in the collective. And exactly because

what has been experienced collectively and repeatedly with what has been historically effective, this connection between the most individual and the ancient has something strong and almost joyful about it.

(JNC, p. 143)

One problem, however, arose from how he could be inspired by Jung without mimicking his teacher's theories. His letter of 29 October 1935 (cited variously in previous chapters) reflects his struggle to "distinguish" himself in spite of adopting Jung's concepts of the collective unconscious and individuation. The letter assesses, both programmatically and summarily, the spiritual situation of Judaism as well as the possibilities, aided by analytical psychology in Palestine, to strike out—as a Jew—on a path of individuation. This, in Neumann's view, must differ from the Western path of individuation. And yet, he could not prevent himself from taking sideswipes at his Jewish colleagues, who seemed to be taking matters too lightly:

> Gropingly I feel for contours, difficult because I am myself only gradually starting to grasp where analytical psychology cannot fully be the ground on which I stand. That does not mean that I am not standing on the ground of analytical psychology, more than ever I believe I sense its central significance for me. What is self-evident is becoming clearer to me—that analytical psychology itself has a foundation that is in part so self-evident that it can only become conscious of itself in part. Switzerland—Germany, the West, Christianity. Not a discovery, and yet it is one after all. I must learn to distinguish myself. It is difficult when so much weight lies on the other side, it is certainly easier to do as "your Jews" do and to assimilate, such as Westmann, Kirsch,[17] but this would only mean avoiding one own's individuation that must be achieved, despite everything, on the collective-archetypally different foundation.

(JNC, pp. 114–115)

In the same letter, dated 29 October 1935, he adds:

> The final problem in Judaism cannot be affected, it seems to me, and not theorized. I for one must realize it in a Jewish reality, as filthy and as beautiful as it is and will be. A theoretical occupation of the earth is really Jewish, intellectual with goodwill. I am beginning to understand what it means that you said to me that I needed to get into the collective.

(JNC, p. 116)

We can understand the initial condition of his Jewish individuation, as Neumann describes it, as an inevitable "collision" with the complex reality he encountered in Palestine. For this represented a situation of departure and upheaval, in which no reliable recourse to existing strategies was possible, from coping with daily life to the highly explosive political situation. This, he observed, left the individual no scope for cherishing preconceptions:

> As has been clearly evident to me though, individuation does not belong to the category of confession but to that of growth. Of course I [know] this and everyone "knows" it, but the elemental fact of Jewish soil equating to Jewish reality is only just dawning on me.
>
> (JNC, p. 116; translation corrected)

On 22 December 1935, Jung replied as follows:

> What the European Jews are doing I already know, but what the Jews are doing on archetypal soil—that interests me extraordinarily... The "Culture Jews" are always en route to being "non-Jews"; you are completely right, the route does not go from the good to the better, but first downhill to historical actuality. I routinely draw the attention of most of my Jewish patients to the fact that they are self-evidently Jews. I would not do this if I had not so frequently seen Jews who imagined that they were something else. To such as these being "Jewish" is a form of personal insult.
>   ... Your disparaging assessment is valuable to me as it is your very positive conviction that the Palestinian soil is essential to Jewish individuation. How does the fact that the Jew in general has lived in other countries than in Palestine for *much longer* relate to this? ... Is it then that the Jew is so accustomed to being a non-Jew that he requires the Palestinian soil *in concreto* in order to be reminded of his being Jewish? I find it hard to comprehend a soul that has grown up in no soil.[18]
>
> (JNC, p. 119; original emphases)

Neumann concludes that he "must learn to distinguish myself." This insight arises from contemplating that form of individuation he considers possible under the circumstances. This form contains neither any imitation nor any profession of faith that would distinguish him from the existence of a "Culture Jew" (JNC, p. 119).

The preceding letter reveals several intentions and relational aspects: It indicates Neumann's serious intention to travel a very special Jewish path aided by analytical psychology. Notably, no paradigm (or template) existed for this path. Thus, Neumann's individuation began with a radical change in his life, one approved solely by Jung, yet not by his family. Now, in a second step, "the bitter path of individuation" (JNC, p. 119) meant distancing himself from the West and its traditional values, and to avoid succumbing to the threat of becoming entrapped in psychological adventures not one's own. So deeply entrenched in Neumann was the sting of alienation created by overadjustment.

Neumann's sense of having to distinguish himself also involved a sense of rivalry, as his relationship with James Kirsch suggests. This rivalry was fuelled by the desire to be the "better" son, the one who more profoundly understood the father's message, and who was therefore more consistent and more conscientious than an "average" son ever would be in his endeavour to fulfil his filial duties.

This father's message is the mission of individuation (Neumann, as we have seen, looked up to Jung like a disciple to a *tzaddik*; see Chapter 4). This mission, however, proves to be ambiguous: The "good" son tends to imitate the father, to please him so as to gain acceptance. And yet, by pledging allegiance to the father and his values, the son denies himself and his innermost essence. This is how Neumann's comment in his letter of 29 October 1935—"individuation does not belong to the category of confession"—might be understood. Thus, Neumann seeks recognition as the son who truly understands the father, which, should any doubt arise, might also imply that he must first of all forsake instant gratification, that is, immediate recognition: "Analytical psychology, not yet fully realized, also holds this danger—that of the betrayal of one's own foundation in favor of a 'nicer,' 'more advanced' and 'modern one'" (JNC, p. 115).

How, then, ought we imagine this father–son relationship? In an early, undated letter to Jung, Neumann quotes a Hasidic story about a father and a son that aptly illustrates this special relationship:

> After a Sabbath meal at which many Jewish fathers were present, Yehudi speaks: "Well, people, if any of you are asked what is your purpose on earth, each one of you answers, 'to raise my son to learn and to serve God.'" And when the son has grown up, he forgets his father's purpose on earth, and strives for exactly the same thing himself. And if you ask him the point of all this strife, he will tell you: "I have to raise my son in the doctrine and for good works." And thus it is, your people, from generation to generation. But when, finally, will we get to see the rightful child.
>
> (JNC, p. 77)

Neumann's account of Jacob and Esau further illumines his concept of individuality. The story concerns the opposition between the hostile twin brothers. With reference to Bin Gorion's *Die Sagen der Juden*, Neumann describes their "polarity" as follows:[19]

Jacob: the moon, inside, the other world
Esau: the sun, outside, this world.

(JE, p. 5)

He observes:

> The hallmark of Esau's world is visibility, and it includes the outer, the ordinary, the unholy world.
>
> Jacob is neither like Esau nor like the peoples of the world, but instead he is turned toward that world which not only proves to be the coming world, the otherworld, but also the inner and invisible world. Jacob, the Jew, looks

inward, toward YHWH and his inner demand. But this does not mean that YHWH reveals himself only within. Unlike the gods, however, he never manifests himself in images or in the man-made, nor does he become concretized in any part of the outer world where he can be worshipped.

(JE, p. 6)

According to Neumann, this inner world, towards which Jacob turns, "casts light on a decisive feature of Judaism":

The radical prophetic demand for an orientation within the human heart toward the inner voice, toward the voice of God, toward the law that is placed within him, needs to be mentioned in this respect.

(JE, p. 6)

This connects the inner world with being "chosen" and "sacred." In Jung's typology, Jacob, inward-looking and sacred, is an introvert, just as Esau is an extravert. For Neumann, this typology was invaluable because "the attitude of the Jew is introverted" (JE, p. 6). His thinking now reached the point where what Scholem called the "possible spiritual, cultural, and, above all, social rebirth" of Judaism would only become possible based on Jung's concept of introversion. Thus, Jacob's connection with the "inner world" and the "sacred" makes him the "true" son and the legitimate heir.

Hasidism and the Kabbalah, which reached a wider audience especially through Buber's publications, were the spiritual ground that Neumann recognised and acknowledged as the inner foundation. His need for radical distinction lasted only briefly, three years to be precise, until actual historical events inexorably came to the fore in form of the massive civilisational rupture in Germany. How the pogroms in November 1938 led Neumann to revise Jung's concept of the collective unconscious as specific to a culture and people, and what this reversal meant for him, is the subject of the next chapter.

Notes

1 JNC, p. 115. Translator's note: The existing English translation has been corrected to more accurately reflect the meaning of the German ("Ich muss lernen, mich zu unterscheiden," *Jung-Neumann Briefe*, p. 167).

2 For instance, in the previously cited letter: "The way in which your being Swiss, Christian, and a Western man is self-evident differentiates you centrally, and not only you, from the way in which it is not self-evident that Jews are Jews. Do you, in fact, [not] underestimate the significance of this point in the analysis of the Jews? … Please do not misunderstand this to be impudence" (JNC, p. 116; translation corrected).

3 See, for instance, his letter of 15 November 1939 (JNC, pp. 148ff.).

4 See, among others, this passage from an undated letter written in 1935: "I believe my opposition to some of your objections or alleged underestimations led me to overcompensate rather" (JNC, p. 78).

5 See JNC, pp. 35–36 (19 July 1934), pp. 60–61 (undated, but written before 17 November 1934) and p. 96f. (undated, 1935).

6 In fact, this is a variation on Nietzsche's dictum that "the Jews are the most remarkable people in the history of the world"; see also his assertion that the Jews are also "the most *fateful* people in the history of the world"; see *The Antichrist*, No. 24.

7 See further the following passage from a letter written in 1934: "Indeed, the ongoing development of the Jews failed precisely because, on the one hand, they were united in a collective-religious bond and, on the other, they were under pressure from other nations as individuals. After the emancipation they caught up unnaturally quickly and powerfully with the Western trend toward the individual (secularization, rationalization, extraversion, the break with the continuity of the past)" (JNC, p. 18; undated).

8 In his letter of 5 December 1938, Neumann writes about the November pogroms: "It is both as clear to me that we will not be wiped out, as it is also that immeasurable numbers of us must perish in the process. And to watch this from the sidelines is a terrible torture" (JNC, p. 140).

9 Nicholas Berg, *Luftmenschen: Zur Geschichte einer Metapher* (Göttingen: Vandenhoeck & Ruprecht, 2008), p. 115f.

10 Ibid.

11 The volumes were titled *Beiträge zur Tiefenpsychologie des jüdischen Menschen und zum Problem der Offenbarung* ("Contributions to the Depth Psychology of the Jewish Person and to the Problem of Revelation") and *Der Chassidismus und seine psychologische Bedeutung für das Judentum* ("Hasidism and Its Psychological Meaning for Judaism"). Long unpublished, they have recently appeared as *The Roots of Jewish Consciousness.* 2 vols. Edited by Ann C. Lammers. Translated by Mark Kyburz and Ann Conrad Lammers (Routledge, 2019); hereafter cited as Roots I and II.

12 Gershom Scholem's correspondence with Gustav Dreifuss reveals that Neumann visited Scholem in 1934 to convince him of the value of Jung's theory of archetypes for his Kabbalistic research. Scholem, however, rejected this idea. Neumann never mentioned these manuscripts to Scholem later; see Gershom Scholem, *Briefe*, vol. III, ed. Itta Shedletzky (Munich: Beck, 1999); the corresponding letter is dated 24 April 1981, p. 233f.

13 See David Biale, *Gershom Scholem, Kabbalah and Counter-History* (Cambridge, MA: Harvard University Press, 1979); Biale also mentions Buber's "anarchist chain of tradition."

14 See Jörg Hackeschmidt, *Von Kurt Blumenfeld zu Norbert Elias: Die Erfindung einer jüdischen Nation* (Hamburg: Europäische Verlagsanstalt, 1997), p. 93ff.

15 In this context, there is also mention of Buber's "view" of the Bible.

16 Neumann uses the terms *galut Jew* and *golus Jew* to refer to Jews living in exile.

17 Heinz Westmann and James Kirsch were also among Jung's German-Jewish students.

18 See also C.G. Jung, *Letters*, vol. 1, pp. 206–207.

19 Micha Josef Berdyczewski, *Die Sagen der Juden, gesammelt von Micha Josef Bin Gorion*, 5 vols. (Frankfurt am Main: Rütten & Loening, 1913–1927).

"... a general and identical revolution of minds"[1]

The pogroms of November 1938 and the Jung–Neumann correspondence

An unusual synthesis

During Neumann's training analysis with Jung from autumn 1933 to June 1934, the two men agreed that their future correspondence would discuss questions about Judaism and Zionism, or what they both regarded as " the Jewish problem and questions of Judaism and Zionism."[2] This arrangement gave rise to an important exchange of letters, which provides insight into their views and discourse. We may imagine the impetus of their working relationship as an interpretation of the "signs of the times," in an attempt to explore the meaning hidden behind the brutal facts of actual history, to re-establish a connection with the lost threads of tradition and to create a fabric of meaning that would constitute a sustainable cultural-philosophical view of Western history or a vision of future developments. During the 1930s, Neumann developed an approach to culture and history based on three principal sources: Zionism, Jungian depth psychology and Hasidism. In a letter to Jung dated 15 November 1939, he described this unusual synthesis as "revolutionary" (JNC, p. 149) and later (11 May 1940) as "very incomprehensible and untimely even for Jews" (p. 157). Essentially, he intended this synthesis to be identity-forming at a time of severe upheaval and acute threat for the Jewish people.

Briefly put, these three strands of discourse were related as follows: Jewish periodicals such as *Palästina*, *Ost und West* or *Der Jude* (the latter was edited by Buber) served as platforms for Zionist debates in which political values were shifting increasingly from the established model of emancipation and assimilation to one focused on land, nation, valour and work.[3] There was now talk of a "new, young type of Jewish person."[4] Buber, as is well known, spoke of "an uprooted Jewish people"[5] and painted an image of the "galut Jew" that bore a striking resemblance with the prevailing anti-Semitic stereotypes. The life of assimilated Jews was an unstable, torn existence whose alienation needed to be eradicated. Buber saw his spiritual mission in contributing to the "recreation" of Judaism, whose fundamental spiritual upheaval he diagnosed in numerous writings.[6] Zionist circles were contemplating how to achieve a "possible spiritual, cultural, and, above all, social rebirth."[7] Realising the latent potential of Judaism seemed possible only if the "Jew would encounter himself, his people, and his roots."[8] This required returning to tradition. Once again, Buber set the decisive course. His publication of the Hasidic tales nurtured the longing for a return to "wholeness" and "originality." It was believed that these qualities could be found in Eastern European Judaism, above all among the Hasidim, whose mystical depth exerted a profound fascination on Zionists.[9]

In seeking ways out of their inner turmoil, which they interpreted ideologically along Buberian lines, particularly those Jews interested in psychotherapy turned to C.G. Jung, in the hope that his thinking would enable them to unearth the many treasures documented by Buber as "underground Judaism." Jung's cultural conservatism, anti-modernist stance, sympathy for traditional spiritual values and theory of the unconscious, as the source and origin of creative life, made him a beacon of hope for a new spiritual beginning.[10]

Neumann's first letters to Jung share his many impressions of and mostly critical reflections on his new life in Tel Aviv. They are pervaded by a sense of gratitude towards his revered teacher and reflect his profound affinity with Jung. And yet, the pogroms of November 1938, which culminated dramatically in the *Reichskristallnacht*, the devastating pogrom on 9 and 10 November, not only foreshadowed the subsequent genocide but also seriously affected the trust between Neumann and Jung.

The November pogroms

In 1938, the political situation of Germany's Jewish population worsened significantly. The November pogroms, planned and executed by the Nazi regime, occurred between 7 and 13 November 1938. About 400 people were murdered or driven to commit suicide. Over 1,400 synagogues, prayer rooms and other places of assembly, as well as countless shops, apartments and Jewish cemeteries, were pillaged. From 10 November, about 30,000 Jews were imprisoned in concentration camps. Hundreds were murdered or died from the consequences of incarceration.[11] Historians Saul Friedländer and Orna Kenan have described the consequences of the pogroms as follows: "In the decisive weeks from November 1938 to January 1939, the measures adopted by Hitler, Göring and their cronies completely destroyed any remaining possibility of Jewish life in Germany."[12]

Could their cultural theorising, which had forged a close tie between Jung and Neumann, withstand the onslaught of actual historical events? Or would they need to abandon their shared intellectual venture? Their discussion about the "Jewish path," and how it differed from the European one, now seemed irrelevant in view of the existential threat to the Jews. Was a "Jewish path" still conceivable under the dramatic circumstances unfolding in the 1930s? Had these not rendered such a path impossible? The premeditated attacks on Germany's Jewish population constituted an unprecedented abuse of state power. All that now mattered for Jewish people was survival.

The shockwaves of this massive civilisational rupture are reflected in four letters written by Neumann and Jung over a period of one year: two letters by Neumann—which appealed for help—and Jung's replies. After a lapse of over a year, Neumann wrote to Jung on 5 December 1938, with Jung replying on 12 December 1938. A year later, on 15 November 1939—yet another year had passed—Neumann again wrote to Jung. This second letter marks a major turning point in Neumann's conception of Jewish identity. A month later, on 16 December 1939, Jung sent a brief reply to his student.

"Uprooting" and "inner revelation"

The long letter that Neumann wrote to Jung on 5 December 1938, in the wake of the November pogroms, expresses a profound yet disguised sense of abandonment (JNC, pp. 139–144). It begins with Neumann's observation that he had written Jung "such a large number of unwritten letters," a remark that implies his inhibitions and difficulties. None of these feelings, however, was evident in his earlier letters. Now, however, under the impression of actual history, his emotions range from reproaching Jung to apologising to him. Neumann's letters also convey his sense of inferiority. In the end, he admits that he is in a "state of confusion."

In the first section, which takes up almost one quarter of his letter, Neumann tries to explain that he is struggling to maintain his inner connection with Jung, since he doubts whether Jung actually cares. He believes that "someone like you has inevitably been touched at best only once by the events that are affecting us Jews" (JNC, p. 139). However, to avoid directly insinuating that Jung lacks empathy and solidarity, with him personally or with the Jewish people, Neumann transposes Jung to another sphere of life, one far removed from the Jews' desperate struggle for survival in the late 1930s: "It is fully obvious and natural to me to know that you live on a completely different plane from ours" (JNC, p. 139). Eager to conceal his implicit reproach, Neumann relativises his earlier comment: "Yes, I must say, it is almost a comfort to me to know that your age, if one might put it this way, has removed you some degrees from these horrific world events" (ibid.). This suggests that Jung, aged 63 at the time, could be excused given his advanced age. Nevertheless, Neumann's disappointment about Jung's silence is unmistakable. He feels abandoned, although not only by Jung, his spiritual father, whom he once called his "tzaddik," his spiritual master (see JNC, pp. 16ff. and 51ff.). He also mentions his father's death, just as implicitly as he criticises Jung, and notes that he was "always happy" that his father had died before the November pogroms.

Neumann's father, like most German Jews, was adamant that the civil rights arduously acquired in the process of assimilation were inviolable. He clung to this deceptive belief until his death. On 25 March 1937, Neumann's father died as a result of a Gestapo interrogation. We know (from conversations with his children) that Neumann's father rejected his youngest son's Zionist ideas. His untimely death spared Eduard Neumann further confrontation with his disillusioned, Zionist son. At the same time, however, his father's death denied Neumann the opportunity to make the case for what he considered his superior political views. The unclosable wound of abandonment felt by Neumann stemmed from the disruption of the dialogue between Jewish fathers and sons caused by the inescapable political events in Germany. The theme of the father appears a third time—now biblically veiled—towards the end of Neumann's letter, where he refers to his book about Jacob and Esau, which Jung already knew about (Chapter 6).

The central theme of the biblical story about Jacob and Esau is the importance of fatherly recognition, gained by birthright and by the blessing of the first-born (1 Moses 25, 30f.). Jacob, the younger of the twin brothers, knows how to obtain both. The reference to the story of Jacob and Esau suggests that Neumann, not unanxiously, is wondering whether he can still be assured of his spiritual father's blessing. His acute fear—of having to live without the personal blessing of his biological father, and perhaps even without Jung's—perhaps best captures Neumann's profound sense of abandonment. He is unable to reproach his fathers (spiritual and biological) for their lack of understanding. Nor is he able to accuse the Germans of being barbaric, since he feels, "despite all this, I have too great a debt of gratitude to this [i.e. German] nation to be able to identify this simply as the symptoms of its schizophrenic episode" (JNC, p. 140).

His letters palpably convey how forcefully "the reports that crowd in on one on a daily or hourly basis, and sadly, the reports of eyewitnesses" (JNC, p. 140) threw Neumann off balance. In the meantime, he directed a helpless anger against his own people, which would suggest a sense of profound shame. For Neumann, the "enormous extraversion of Judaism" is the collective stigma that "the inexorable consistency of our destiny" subjects to correction. Not knowing whether he "will be among the survivors of this upheaval or not," he assumes "that immeasurable numbers of us must perish … And to watch this from the sidelines is a terrible torture" (ibid.). Based on his particular concept of religious history, he seeks to wring a redemptive, life-saving idea from his vision of doom.

Neumann developed this idea in Zurich during his analysis with Jung in 1933–1934. In the years that followed, it evolved into a critical theory of culture, which he now discusses in his letter.[13] Central to his thinking is the problem of religious alienation. For Neumann, the Jewish religion, in its original form, constituted an intact dialogue between God and his people. Before their exile, the people of Israel still "stood in productive dialogue" with "direct revelation." That is to say, there existed a public discourse with the Father and his religion. But the "traumatic experience of exile" had shifted this discourse into the individual's inner world. Now it was only possible to speak of "inner revelation," that is, no divine voice could be heard collectively anymore. The Talmudic law, and in the final instance "assimilation and emancipation," had led to "uprooting and the loss of memory" (JNC, p. 141), two terms crucial in Neumann's critical self-diagnosis. The redemptive idea capable of countering impending doom is the concept of "inner revelation," whose religious precursor Neumann discovered in the mystical and in the Hasidic tradition. He endeavours to trace this "inner revelation" in the "dream and fantasy material" of his clients, and eventually in himself.

The fact that every individual can reconnect with the former revelation, and thus with a divine-fatherly voice, leads Neumann to believe that a meaningful development of Judaism is possible. In his view, this "inner revelation" is, in terms of depth psychology, based on Jung's distinction between ethno-specific formations of the unconscious. For Neumann, this background of the "Jewish unconscious" also constituted a valid framework (within which lay his spiritual father's, that is, Jung's hidden blessing). After all, this had empowered him to strike out on his own path, to expect his parents to accept his decision to emigrate to Palestine and to feel confident about his political views. For Neumann, Jung's talk of the "Jewish unconscious" enabled a return to the "inner world of the father." This corresponded to his idea that the "inner revelation" manifested itself within the individual. Jung's distinction and his depth-psychological methodology made it possible to once again access the lost, yet invigorating elements of tradition. It provided the support that was needed to defy "infernal reality" (JNC, p. 142), since everything could be "a lot worse … when a large group of relatives must be provided for and, on top of that, the economy is declining along with the practice." At the end of his letter, Neumann speaks of

> a remarkably paradoxical inner confidence, from which I believe that there could be a new, lively beginning in the individual and in the collective. And exactly because what has been experienced by the individual has such a strong connection with that experienced collectively and repeatedly with what has been historically effective, this connection between the most individual and the ancient has something strong and almost joyful about it.
>
> (JNC, p. 143)

C.G. Jung's theoretical self-correction

Neumann's letter of 5 December 1938 closes with the words: "With best wishes, I am your ever grateful E. Neumann" (JNC, p. 143). Two weeks later, Jung's reply began thus: "You must not imagine that I have retreated to the snow-clad heights, enthroned high above world events. I am right in the thick of it and am following the Palestinian question on a daily basis in the newspapers, and think often of my acquaintances there who have to live in this chaos" (ibid., p. 145). He added: "I have a great deal to do with [Jewish] refugees and am constantly occupied with accommodating all my Jewish acquaintances in England and America. In this way I am in constant contact with contemporary events" (ibid.; translation corrected). In attempting to mitigate Neumann's reproach, of abandoning him, Jung sidesteps this thorny issue, and thus moves out of reach:

> When I was in Palestine in 1933, I was unfortunately able to see what was coming all too clearly. I also foresaw great misfortune for Germany, even

quite terrible things, but when it then [happens], it still seems unbeliev-
able. Everyone is shocked to their core as it were by what is happening in
Germany.

(JNC, p. 145; translation corrected)

The relationship that Jung offers Neumann refers to his clear-sighted prediction
of impending disaster. Thus, he elevates himself to a prophetic authority that saw
(and perhaps would see) the irreversible events ahead. In the prophet's clothes,
Jung remains unassailable for Neumann. The fact that the "fate" foreseen by Jung
now took its course made him the mouthpiece of a deity that was avenging itself
violently on humanity. Importantly, however, Jung remained distant as a human
counterpart, in whose presence Neumann could have expressed his anxiety and
concerns. While Jung expresses his interest in Neumann's religious-philosophical project, he flatly rejects his previous distinction between a "Jewish" and an
"Aryan unconscious":

I think you must be very careful when evaluating your specifically Jewish
experiences. While there are, for sure, specific Jewish traits in this development, it is at the same time a general one that is also happening among
Christians. It is a question of a general and identical revolution of minds. The
specifically Christian or Jewish traits have only a secondary meaning.

(JNC, p. 146)

We can only conjecture as to what changed Jung's mind. One possible explanation is that the catastrophic events compelled him to abstain from making any
remarks that might have been considered racist. His previously strong convictions had since become a "merely subjective impression." This reserve now also
included a restrictive assumption: "All the same, I can imagine very well that
among Jews who live in Palestine the immediate impact of the environment
brings the chthonic and old-Jewish into view" (JNC, p. 146).

A dream

On 15 November 1939, as if to commemorate the pogroms (World War II had
since erupted), Neumann wrote another long letter to Jung, in which he explained
his long silence as follows:

To some degree, I have also been absent to myself and have not come back to
myself fully even now [...], but am more or less swallowed up by the work
with individuals and the private work on the Jewish [material]. At the same
time neither the one thing nor the other any longer seems as important as it
did, say, a year ago.

(JNC, p. 148)

What does he mean by "absent" and "swallowed up"? Neumann's handwritten postscriptum relativises his earlier, rather categorical observation:

> I am not as completely swallowed up as this somehow rather inhuman letter strikes me at this time. Please believe me about the personal matters. It is almost unhealthy to almost only have oneself to check things out with, so that this letter is a bit too much like an "analytic session".
>
> (JNC, p. 153)

Thus, Neumann's letter conveys a cognitive and emotional process, an "analytic session," in which he manages to grasp, express and reflect on his "state of being swallowed up." Nevertheless, his message to Jung is ambiguous. The "inhuman," impersonal aspect of this letter stems from the fact that Neumann, taking into account the shift in Jung's theory of culture, had "abandoned" certain views:

> In the meantime, I have also recognized that Jewish symbolism—at least that of Western Jews—is consistent with that of European people, that here something secular is taking place. Of course, I knew this before, but the problem of the singularity of the Jews would have been simpler if a specific symbolism could have been demonstrated. I have abandoned this and stand without preconceptions before something that is incomprehensible to me.
>
> (JNC, p. 149)

Jung's unexpected secularisation thesis shook Neumann's belief in his own deeply rooted psychological fate, since his previous depth-psychological assumptions about the specific, or at least different, foundation of the Jewish psyche, verifiable in the unconscious, had afforded him both the strength and a sense of justification to start afresh in Palestine. It might be objected that Jung's actual view of the political situation in Nazi Germany, considering its catastrophic escalation, had fortunately lost its ideological charge and given way to long overdue revision. The fact that Jung, whose predictions had made him unassailable, now wheeled around, deprived Neumann of fatherly blessing amid the precarious circumstances. To assure himself of his spiritual father's goodwill, Neumann indicates his willingness to abandon his belief that his situation, and its basis, is unique. After all, Jung had taught him to see his personal problems in terms of the "Jewish question," that is, as part of a collective question. In light of Jung's secularisation thesis, searching for singularity and drawing on one's own unconscious now seemed ridiculous. Neumann begins entertaining self-critical thoughts about the prospect of self-heroisation: "[…] but I always have the feeling that I am playing a role as a Jew, mindful of the Gods, while a quiet ironic feeling—battle of Thermopylae—resonates at the same time" (JNC, p. 148).[14] At the same time, though, he does not intend to completely abandon his previous position, which he had developed based on Buber and Jung, as well as on his personal experiences:

But, you see, my position toward Judaism is extremely revolutionary and even my attempt to create the continuity through to the modern Jewish person from the openness of revelation to antiquity via the inner Hasidic revolution is, as I of course will know myself, a new interpretation—how can I help myself in this paradox?

(JNC, p. 149)

Neumann, who had meanwhile grown "so tired of the Jews and the Jewish" (JNC, p. 149), comes to his own rescue by providing a detailed account of a dream (in June 1939). It went like this: Neumann sees himself as a pilgrim, wearing a wide-brimmed hat and holding a staff, in an inn, presumably in Nazi Germany. Although he feels threatened, he shows some of the other guests, to whom he "half belonged," several small pictures. He considers this "something revolution-ary." Next, he rips up the pictures, which the innkeeper had looked at silently moments ago, in front of the man and his son. The innkeeper now transforms into an old taunting prince, who condemns the pilgrim and commands him to leave—without allowing him to bid farewell to his son. The latter protests, yet to no avail. In the end, the prince murders the pilgrim, while a ship, which could have saved the pilgrim, passes by. Here, the dream takes a surprising turn, since a large army disembarks from the ship and kills the prince, thus ending his reign and ushering in a new era. The dream ends with the words: "The dying pilgrim rising above the prince in the dialogue, he in an ascending curve, the prince in a descending and sinking curve" (ibid., p. 150). Neumann comments on this dream as follows:

On the whole I would be able to say much about the dream. [...] Especially the "sacral" killing of my pilgrim soul by the prince is rather sinister, just as the pilgrimage is all in all rather surprising. [...] This seems to be most tragic.

(JNC, p. 151)

Through the charged imagery of his dream, Neumann tells Jung something that his implicit accusations in his previous letter had anticipated: the double murder of two adversaries whose encounter is marked by scorn and revenge. The innkeeper-cum-prince represents profane or secular power.[15] This authority demonstrates its superiority with a "judgment scene," "with a mocking smile," before dealing a deadly blow to the wandering Jew, who represents the "sacral viewpoint." The tragic aspect of this account is its description of the son, who protests in vain against the pilgrim's condemnation and is denied a last farewell.

The dream presents Neumann's two roles vis-à-vis Jung: son and pilgrim. The son's protest remains unheard; nor is he granted the opportunity to take leave of his "sonship." The father–son relationship is beyond repair. The pilgrim repre-sents the authority that still insists on the sacral source of the pictures (despite tearing them up) towards Jung, who makes belief that he has shifted to secu-larisation (the sacral bond between the student and his *tzaddik* is also severed).

Another, new motif now appears in the discourse between Neumann and Jung: the desire to take political action, for higher justice to be served by an external human agent, for justice to be administered by the "civilised world," as represented by a high court and by the army that kills the prince.

"PaRDeS"

Let me briefly comment on one of the most obscure parts of Neumann's dream, the passage about the *pardes*:

> At the foot of the castle the prince asked (something like): So you think I am letting the *pardes* be worked on incorrectly? He, the pilgrim, said humbly, as if excusing himself: No, only I have learned to do it in a different way, you should clear the weeds.
>
> (JNC, p. 150)

Prince and pilgrim, as we have seen, are locked in an ultimately fatal conflict. In this brief scene, they are arguing about exegesis and interpretation. Their disagreement concerns the "PaRDeS," the Jewish version of the "doctrine of the fourfold meaning of scripture."[16] Before 1290, Moses de Leon had written a (meanwhile lost) book titled *Pardes* (Paradise). He "employed this highly suggestive term, so rich in shades of meaning, as a cipher for the four levels of interpretation. Each consonant of the word PaRDeS denotes one of the levels: P stands for *peshat*, the literal meaning, R for *remez*, the allegorical meaning, D for *derasha*, the Talmudic and Aggadic interpretation, S for *sod*, the mystical meaning."[17] Thus, "incorrectly" tending the *pardes* might imply not doing proper interpretive justice to the source texts or, more seriously, introducing a method of interpretation that deviates from the classical, that is, "correct" method.

Might Neumann's dream sequence be related to his doubts about Jung's "exegetic competence"? The pilgrim, although humble and apologetic, contradicts the prince. The weeds, he says, need to be cleared. In the symbolism of *PaRDeS*, this would mean that paradise must be freed from rank growth. Thus, the understanding of the "holy" scripture needs to be cleared of useless, rampant interpretations. For a while, Neumann seems to have believed that Jung and him had entered an exegetical paradise of sorts, yet from which he now saw himself banished. Which weeds, though, have grown in the meantime that need removing? Can we read Neumann's dream as a form of self-criticism, as an admission that people (himself included) had allowed interpretations to grow rampant like weeds?

Or does his dream instead draw a line between Jewish and (meanwhile) secular exegesis? The Jewish doctrine of the fourfold meaning of scripture concerns an "initiation ... into the revelation of eternity in the midst of time."[18] This theme occupies a central place in Neumann's *Roots of Jewish Consciousness* (see Chapter 10). While in the Jewish tetralogy the secret of scripture must be preserved,[19] Jung's secular interpretative efforts threaten to desecrate the secrets enclosed within the walls of Eden. By way of anticipation: Jung's reply will mention Wotan, the Germanic wind god, in response to Neumann's self-interpretation of wearing Wotan's soft pilgrim hat. Does Jung's reference to the "pagan" god (Wotan) perhaps raise Neumann's suspicion about sprawling, weed-like growth?

The dream, as we have seen, ends tragically. The pilgrim, Neumann's alter ego, dies. The dream, moreover, overturns Neumann's system of interpretation and values, because thus far he had been convinced that the "upheaval" would serve the "salvation of Judaism." Moreover, "the terrible state of emergency that has gripped the entire people and will continue to do so will inevitably force the inner source energies to be called either into action or to their peril" (JNC, p. 140).

A "spiritual wind" across Europe

Jung replied within a month, on 16 December 1939 (JNC, pp. 154f.). He attributes the extreme density of Neumann's letter to the latter waiting too long to write. Jung chooses not to elaborate on the "secrets" of the dream (and even less on the depicted dominant–submissive relationships). His reference to Wotan, however, once again takes up his secularisation thesis, although this time it is mythically charged. Neumann, angry at himself, had interpreted the pilgrim's soft hat as Wotan's "wide-brimmed" one. Jung replies:

> The Wotan association does not refer to the Germanic regression in Germany, but is a symbol for a spiritual development that involves the entire cultural world (Wotan as the wind God = Pneuma).
>
> (JNC, p. 154)

In Jung's thinking, "the spiritual wind that blows over Europe or probably over the whole world, for even in the far East all of these things are in a rapid flux" (JNC, p. 155), symbolises the origin of those events commonly referred to by modern historians as a "break in civilization." This, in turn, raises the question whether the metaphor of the "spiritual wind" (that is, "Wotan") represents Jung's attempt to play down his previous, explosive cultural and theoretical delibera-tions, in order to evade any questions about moral responsibility.

Another long silence ensued after Jung's reply. It lasted almost half a year, until Neumann's letter of 11 May 1940. In it, he enclosed a lecture, in actual fact a chapter from his *Tiefenpsychologie des jüdischen Menschen* (the later *Roots of Jewish Consciousness*) to indicate that he had not "abandoned" this project after all. On the contrary, he tells Jung that he would soon be sending the entire manu-script and adds: "It would be important for me to know whether you could identify at least to some degree with its formulations, or whether this way seeing things is foreign to you" (JNC, p. 156).[20] Thus, that part of Neumann that was seeking to "distinguish" itself (see Chapter 6) had meanwhile gained the upper hand.

"A sign of solidarity"

The correspondence between Jung and Neumann breaks off at this point. A second hiatus—most likely due to the havoc wreaked by World War II—follows the one discussed earlier, which had sprung from diverging opinions and disappointment. Neumann did not write to Jung again until 1 October 1945.[21] The content and tone of his letters to Jung after 1946 differ markedly from his earlier correspondence. The later letters clearly reflect an independent, mature personality. Neumann had in the meantime written two important books (*Depth Psychology and a New Ethic* and *The Origins and History of Consciousness*). Now, in 1945, he wrote to request Jung's support in securing publication of both works by Rascher Verlag: "I think it is now [time] to come out" (JNC, p. 166; translation corrected).

A new dialogue now ensued: The former teacher–student relationship had turned into a friendship between two men who, as authors in their own right, approached one another with praise and criticism. This mutual respect lasted until Neumann's sudden death in 1960. With the passage of time, the tensions during World War II seemed to have dissipated and in their place an indissoluble bond had grown. When the Sinai War (between Israel and Egypt) broke out in October 1956, Jung sent Neumann a worried telegram. Neumann replied on 12 November: "Your telegram moved and comforted me, a thousand thanks for it, it arrived quickly and reached us at a time when such a sign of solidarity was more necessary and affected us more deeply than at any other time" (JNC, p. 322).

Concluding remarks

From today's perspective, barely any passages in the Jung–Neumann letters invite identification or are related to present-day thinking. Their theoretical constructs, devised before the mid-20th century, now seem unwieldy, indeed almost impenetrable. On the one side we have Jung, who adapted to circumstances in the 1930s; on the other is Neumann, who survived the chaos that engulfed Europe as a Jewish émigré in Palestine. And yet, the pain expressed in Neumann's letters is deeply moving. Pain speaks many languages: that of dreams, theory, the rejection of one's own thinking, groping towards a new beginning, silence.

Neumann preserved carbon copies of his letters to Jung. That part of him intent on remembering prevailed over that determined to "abandon." Moreover, several unpublished manuscripts have also survived decades of oblivion and may yet stand a chance of publication. They bear unique testimony to "thinking without a banister," as Hannah Arendt described what theorising against the grain, at odds with official thinking, involved.[22] Even later, after he had become an acclaimed author and speaker, first and foremost at the annual Eranos conferences in Ascona, Neumann never forsook references to "the Jewish heritage to which he felt connected and committed." These were the words that Gershom Scholem wrote in his obituary of his greatly esteemed counterpart after the latter's unexpected death.[23]

The friendship between C.G. Jung and Erich Neumann reflects—however tension-laden, dejected and fragile it was during the persecution and annihilation of the Jews—a facet of a lost spiritual world that also represents part of the history of psychoanalysis. Looking back, we must remind ourselves that understanding and remembering cannot ultimately be brought into line. Recollection presupposes openness, a determination to understand in order to move to the edges of what presents itself to the unmediated gaze as a terrain mined by ideologies. Understanding, on the other hand, follows the desire to remember, as an obscure awareness of what is missing. Although this gap will never be closed, it will become smaller in the process of rapprochement.

Notes

1 Jung to Neumann, 19 December 1938; see JNC, p. 145.
2 Micha Neumann, "Die Beziehung zwischen C.G. Jung und Erich Neumann auf Grund ihrer Korrespondenz," in *Zur Utopie einer neuen Ethik: 100 Jahre Erich Neumann-130 Jahre C.G. Jung* (Vienna: Mandelbaum, 2005), p. 23.
3 Nicolas Berg, *Luftmenschen. Zur Geschichte einer Metapher*, p. 8.
4 Ibid., p. 109.
5 Ibid., p. 98.
6 Martin Buber, *Drei Reden über das Judentum* (Frankfurt am Main, 1916); published in English as *On Judaism*, edited by Nathum N. Glatzer, translated by Eva Jospe (New York: Schocken Books, 1967).
7 Gershom Scholem, *From Berlin to Jerusalem*, p. 54.
8 Ibid.
9 Martin Buber, *Die Geschichten des Rabbi Nachman* (Frankfurt am Main: Rütte und Loening, 1906) and *Die Legende des Baal-Schem* (Frankfurt am Main: Rütte und Loening, 1908).
10 Thomas Kirsch, *C.G. Jung und seine Nachfolger* (Giessen: Psychosozial Verlag, 2000), p. 201.
11 Saul Friedländer and Orna Kenan, *Das Dritte Reich und die Juden 1933–1945* (Munich: Beck, 2010), pp. 133ff.
12 Ibid., p. 147.
13 This is the previously mentioned *Tiefenpsychologie des jüdischen Menschen.*
14 The Battle of Thermopylae has repeatedly been cited as an example of heroic sacrifice; see Anuschka Albertz, *Exemplarisches Heldentum: Die Rezeptionsgeschichte der Schlacht an den Thermopylen von der Antike bis zur Gegenwart* (Munich: Oldenbourg Verlag, 2006).
15 Translator's note: The German word *Wirt*, "host," implies that the Germans are a *Wirtsvolk*, "host people," an expression that Jung, like many others, used at the time.
16 Daniel Krochmalnik, "Vierfacher Schriftsinn in Judentum und Christentum," in Uwe Gerber and Rudolf Hoberg (eds.), *Sprache und Religion* (Darmstadt: Wissenschaftliche Buchgesellschaft, 2009).
17 Gershom Scholem, *On Kabbalah and its Symbolism*, translated by Ralph Manheim (New York: Schocken Books, 1969), p. 57.
18 Krochmalnik, "Vierfacher Schriftsinn in Judentum und Christentum," p. 78.
19 Ibid., p. 79.
20 See Neumann's letters of 11 May 1940 and 1 October 1945. In the latter, he qualifies Part One of his *Tiefenpsychologie des jüdischen Menschen* as "now obsolete and only useable as source material." He adds, however, that "I still stand by" Part Two.

21 Micha Neumann, "Die Beziehung zwischen C.G. Jung und Erich Neumann auf Grund ihrer Korrespondenz," p. 28.

22 Heidi Bohnet and Klaus Stadler, *Hannah Arendt, Denken ohne Geländer: Texte und Briefe* (Munich: Piper, 2010); published in English as *Thinking without a Banister: Essays in Understanding 1953–1975*, ed. Jerome Kohn (New York: Schocken Books, 2018).

23 Gershom Scholem, "Erich Neumann, Nachruf November 1960," *Mitteilungsblatt. Wochenzeitung des Irgun Olej Merkas Europa* 28, 47 (18 November 1960), p. 4; also published in *Das neue Israel* 13 (1960/61), p. 313.

"... yet still have the feeling of being in the right place"[1]

Life in Tel Aviv

Theodor Herzl articulated his (urban) vision of the Jewish state in his utopian novel *Altneuland* (1902): "A thousand white villas appeared, glowing out of the green of lush gardens. From Akko to Carmel there seemed to be a large garden, and the mountain itself was crowned with shimmering buildings."[2]

Seven years later, on 11 April 1909, a group of Russian and Polish immigrants drew lots in the sand dunes outside the village of Jaffa to decide where the first houses would be built. What was initially planned as a garden settlement of sorts expanded swiftly and sprawlingly in a northerly direction towards the sea. The emerging city was called "Tel Aviv" (Spring Hill). It took its name from the Hebrew translation of Theodor Herzl's *Altneuland*. Tel Aviv symbolised the dream of a city capable of being shaped by self-determined Jewish life in the new homeland, as opposed to the strictures of the European ghetto. The various waves of immigration in the 1930s—caused by the Nazi's rise to power in early 1933 and the threat this posed to Germany's neighbouring countries—almost doubled Palestine's Jewish population within the space of three years.

Palestine's three main cities—Tel Aviv, Haifa and Jerusalem—underwent rapid expansion.[3] Practicable architectural solutions were called for. During this period, the central districts of Tel Aviv were built consistently in the Bauhaus style brought to Palestine by German immigrants, making "Spring Hill" one of the most modern cities in the world before World War II.[4] Before the outbreak of war, over 130 architects living in Palestine at the time had completed their training at a German university. In the 1920s, the Bauhaus in Dessau had developed a modern architecture that, characterised by the doctrine of functionalism, had generated a completely new way of thinking. Its *Neue Sachlichkeit* (New Objectivity), whose typical features included horizontal ribbon windows, strictly geometric forms, glass and terrace roofs, were adapted to the climatic conditions of Palestine, where the Bauhaus style soon began expressing its own formal language.

By 1933, roughly 2,000 German Jews had emigrated to Palestine, while another 55,000 took refuge there between 1933 and 1939.[5] *Hitachdut Olej Germania*, the institution overseeing the admission of German immigrants on behalf of the British authorities, had little to offer the new arrivals.[6] They were more or less left to fend for themselves. Finding accommodation proved particularly difficult. The difference between Palestine and the comfortable cities of Western Europe could hardly have been greater in terms of living standards.[7]

Julie and Erich Neumann were among the more alert immigrants and refused to believe that the political situation back home would "calm down." The rise of the Nazis marked a turning point for the Neumanns, who realised that they no longer wanted to live in Germany under the prevailing conditions. Julie and Erich found respite in their Zionist affiliation: The Zionist Union tried tirelessly, although not very successfully to begin with, to strengthen the willingness of its members to emigrate to Palestine. Their stay in Switzerland encouraged the Neumanns to emigrate, since C.G. Jung expressly welcomed their plan to search for "Jewish roots in the former homeland." These corresponded to the Zionist ideal of the Jewish settlement of Palestine, although for other reasons.

Julie had left for Palestine already in February 1934 with Micha, their son, after completing six months of analytical training with Toni Wolff in Zurich. Erich followed in May 1934. Establishing a psychoanalytic practice in a country whose political and social future was uncertain involved a considerable risk. Neumann, whom political upheaval in Germany had denied the internship required to obtain his doctorate in medicine, wrote to the Department of Health in Jaffa to obtain permission to practise as a therapist in Palestine.[8] He also wrote to Jung, to request confirmation of their professional association.[9] On the whole, he must have possessed considerable courage, self-confidence and perseverance, as nothing deterred his plan to enter private practice as an analyst in Palestine. Thus, in his first letter from Tel Aviv to Jung in 1934, he writes:

Figure 8.1 Tel Aviv, 1934

Of course, I have very little to do, although there is still something, but I am not worried as I had reckoned with an extended lead-in time. I am preparing a great deal, am absolutely not unproductive, and now—and this is new—and for this, along with infinitely more, I thank the work with you—it is no longer work "for me"; on the contrary it wants to [enter] reality.

(JNC, p. 19; translation corrected)

Shortly after his arrival, Neumann began delivering a series of lectures in Jerusalem and Tel Aviv.[10] Each series consisted of 12 units, each lasting one and a half hours. The audience consisted of about 20, sometimes as many as 30 people. The talks, given in German, covered a wide range of topics: the psychology of C.G. Jung, the collective unconscious, the work of Martin Buber, the Hasidic movement, Jewish mysticism, Franz Kafka, the fairy tales of the Brothers Grimm, child psychology and pedagogical questions. Very soon, however, Neumann managed to secure a livelihood in Tel Aviv through his psychotherapeutic work, even if the number of patients was small to begin with. Julie wanted another child and did not intend to work as a therapist. It took a while until she became pregnant with their second child, and so she also decided to start practising as a Jungian analyst. At the same time, she carried out chirological analyses based on the methodology developed by Julius Spier (see Chapter 2). When Rali, their long-awaited second child, was finally born on 8 May 1938, Julie was already a widely recognised chirologist and analyst. Neumann believed that Julie was better suited to analytical work than himself. While she was an intuitive feeling type, he saw himself as an intuitive thinker.

The financial support of their parents, who were still living in Berlin, eased the Neumanns' difficult transition into their new surroundings. They could not have entered Palestine without sufficient funds, since the British authorities only granted settlement rights to a limited number of immigrants. Britain recognised two types of immigrants: so-called capitalists, who brought at least 1,000 British pounds, and farm workers.[11] From the outside, the young couple's situation was not untypical of German-Jewish immigrants or *yekkes*, as they were also called. The *yekkes* (Jews of German-speaking descent) brought urban European culture to Palestine: heavy mahogany furniture, pianos, modern household goods and extensive stocks of German literature and works of art.[12] The Neumanns also shipped items of great personal value to their new home: furniture, a large library, many records and a gramophone, an object of inestimable value, above all for Erich. His luggage also included his special passion: a collection of *netsuke*, miniature ivory figures invented in 17th-century Japan. Later, during his travels to Europe, he added many fine and valuable specimens to his expanding collection. Regarded as a connoisseur, he gained admission to the "holy of holies" of important traders, where he could admire valuable pieces, which gave him great pleasure.

Notwithstanding the confidence he gained from his decision to emigrate to Palestine, Neumann painted an extremely critical and drastic picture of the prevailing circumstances, for instance, in a letter to C.G. Jung (cited earlier) written sometime between 15 June and 19 July 1934:

> The situation here is exceedingly serious, as I see it. The original spiritual, idealistic forces who established the country, the core of the working class and of the land settlements are being repressed by a growing wave of undifferentiated, egotistic, short-sighted, entrepreneurial Jews, flooding here because of the economic opportunities.
>
> (JNC, p. 17)

His tone then becomes even more sombre:

> As a people, the Jews are infinitely more stupid than I expected, while only a concerted effort could overcome the difficult situation of being sandwiched between the Arabs and the English. [...] Everywhere the economy is booming, it's all hard work and speculation. There is little interest in intellectual things except among the workers and almost none in things Jewish. A newly prospering petit bourgeois middle class is evident everywhere, not only in Tel Aviv. All of this is quite natural. We find ourselves in a strongly extraverted phase—how else could be Palestine be developed? The Jews are coming to a—terrible—civilization. It cannot be changed. The traditionlessness of this struggle that has no core gives everything a rather ghostly demeanor. It is a people of infinite opposites. What orthodoxy does exist here is so immeasurably foreign to me that I'm shaken by it. Alongside this are the unprincipled speculators and then the hordes of people who, by the investment of their [existence], have constructed the prettiest villages and landscapes out of deserts and swamps.
>
> (JNC, pp. 17–18)

In the end, however, Neumann's lengthy assessment strikes a more positive note:

> Overall, there are many individuals who are not yet visible, but who are there and whose time will eventually come, individuals for whom it be worth it.
>
> (JNC, p. 18)

As unmistakable as Neumann's voice may sound, his lamenting the lack of spiritual and intellectual stimulation in Palestine reveals parallels with the way in which German Jews in general coped with their new surroundings. The *yekkes* were known to struggle with adapting to changes in circumstances. They were widely regarded as the only group of immigrants to Palestine during the 1930s that adamantly clung to their own culture and identity, and not just that. They attempted, in actual fact quite successfully, to impress their own, unmistakable stamp on their new surroundings.[13]

Figure 8.2 Erich with Rali, age five

To begin with, the Neumanns found temporary accommodation, a small apartment at 37 Sirkin Street. In 1936, however, they managed to move into an apartment with a balcony, generously proportioned for the time, at 1 Gordon Street, and overlooking the sea. Like some other streets in Tel Aviv (for instance, Ben-Jehuda Street, Jarkon Street or Frischman Street), Gordon Street was considered "German."[14] In the local shops, mostly German was spoken. The area around Gordon Street was full of emigrants from Nazi Germany and Austria. In the cafés, on the streets, in the shops almost only German was spoken. The Neumanns bought from Miss Krause, who was employed in Mr. Kohn's shop. Julie struggled to learn modern Hebrew ("Ivrit"). But under the favourable circumstances—a predominantly German-speaking environment—this was no disadvantage. Her language teacher was Alice Jacob, a pianist and the wife of Erwin Loewenson, who had emigrated to Palestine in 1933.

The Neumanns' four-room apartment was luxurious by the standard of living at the time, even if rainwater sometimes leaked into the apartment in winter and protecting oneself against cold weather was not always straightforward. For the Neumanns, the apartment remained the centre of their everyday life and work until the end of their lives. Their psychotherapeutic practice was integrated into the apartment, which meant that patient appointments formed an integral part of the family's daily life.

The rooms served various purposes. The "green room," lined with shelves brought along from Germany and reaching up to the ceiling, served as Neumann's study. Here stood his desk with a photo of C.G. Jung smoking a pipe; it was also where he received his patients. The family room doubled as a dining room. Julie saw her patients in the "blue room," which also served as the Neumann's bedroom. Divided by a curtain, part of the children's room was the waiting room. Behind the curtain, the children either played or did their homework. When Neumann's mother came to Palestine in 1947, she lived in the fourth room, which also served as a reception room during daytime.[15] Julie's patients waited for their appointments in the children's room. When the "waiting rooms" were occupied, virtually every corner of the apartment, including the kitchen, served as a waiting area for patients until they were called for their session.

A telephone was not installed until after Neumann's death. He believed that not having a telephone prevented patients from cancelling consultations and going to the hairdresser or beauty salon instead. In the mornings, the Neumanns received their patients at the door, in the afternoons the children took over. Erich received his clients on the hour while Julie began her sessions half an hour later. A knock on the front door announced a patient's arrival. Another knock, accompanied by the words "One moment, please," meant that something important had to be announced, or that someone had arrived to cancel their session. When the children did "door duty," they sometimes needed to decide whether a matter justified interrupting their parents' work. Little Rali gave the patients names and sometimes sat on their laps.

The lunch break lasted from 1:30 to 4 p.m. The Neumanns employed a cook, since Erich was reluctant for Julie to spend her time in the kitchen. The apartment soon developed into a small, yet well-known cultural centre, an institution that first served German emigrants and later also other circles. Neumann gave his lectures here in the evening. For this purpose, the door between the two workrooms was opened and folding chairs, stored in the shower, were set up. Up to 30 people, including patients, gathered here. In the front row sat someone who furnished a transcript, which was later typed up. One met once a week at the Neumanns to listen to classical music. Miss Simonson operated the gramophone. Music by Bach, Mozart, Beethoven, Schubert, Brahms and Mahler was played. The repertoire also included opera.

Family life was a central part of daily routine. Great importance was attached to keeping regular mealtimes: They were filled with extensive conversations, mostly congenial and interesting, even if Neumann could become quite irascible at times. During the children's adolescence there were fierce debates, mostly between father and son, in which Julie sometimes intervened as a mediator to calm down the two "agitated men." On the whole, the Neumanns' pedagogical attitude was very generous. This struck their children's classmates, who, like the Neumanns, were also emigrants (and went by names like Gundesheimer, Weinschenk, Steinitz, Frenzdorf or Klopfer). They also admired the beautiful apartment and its large library. The children naturally took note of the Neumanns' lifestyle, which differed from that of other families: Neumann, who was out on his own as a researcher and practitioner in the field developed by Jung, was unlike other fathers: He did not go to the beach with his children like other fathers. He spent his life in his chosen retreat between his practice and his writing. Julie's professional activities could be explained almost even less than Erich's psychotherapy: What did the mysterious handprints of her patients mean? In the evenings, the Neumanns took time for their children. Julie sang them German lullabies, picture books in German were read and fairy tales of the Brothers Grimm recited. Sometimes the children played board games like Checkers, Monopoly or *Mensch ärgere Dich nicht* ("Don't get angry") with their father—yet not for long, since he would soon return to work.

For his children's birthdays, Erich would often illustrate a fairy tale or a biblical story. One particularly beautiful example of his drawing skills is his rendition of the Old Testament story of Joseph. He invented fairy tales that were suited to his children's imagination. Another shared passion was painting. Friday evenings were special: Candles were lit, and the family held (secular) celebrations; Seder evenings, to which guests were invited, were also celebrated. The Haggadah and Torah were read. Biblical stories were told to introduce the children to the Jewish religious tradition.

When the children were older, Goethe's work became popular family reading. Micha and Rali learned *Fraktur* ("Gothic type") in order to read the Goethe edition brought along from Germany. Micha recalls visiting Jona Sternberg at Ben-Jehuda Street to take lessons in "reading Gothic." They practised by reading *Götz von Berlichingen*. Julie loved Rilke and Hölderlin most, so these poets

Figure 8.3 The Neumann family on the balcony at 1 Gordon Street with Selma Neumann, Erich's mother, 1947

also entered the children's educational canon. When Micha left Israel to study medicine in Zurich, his father gave him a copy of Goethe's *West-Östlicher Divan*.

While Neumann was convinced that his children would integrate into their new homeland, he felt part of a transitional, "interim" generation.[16] He was clear-sighted and was under no illusions in light of the political tensions, whose cause he identified in his compatriots' spiritual chasms. Thus, in his previously cited letter to Jung in the summer of 1934, he wrote:

> It is strange to recognize that my generation will only be an interim generation here—our children will be the first ones to form the basis of a nation. We are Germans, Russians, Poles, Americans etc. What an opportunity it will be when all the cultural wealth that we bring with us is really assimilated into Judaism.
>
> (JNC, p. 18)

And yet, these developments would not unfold untroubled:

> The way forward, as I see it, is certainly as hard as it is dangerous. I actually fear that all our repressed instincts, all our desires for power and revenge, all our mindlessness and hidden brutality will be realized here. Indeed the ongoing development of the Jews failed precisely because, on the one hand, they were united in a collective-religious bond and, on the other, they were under pressure from other nations as individuals. After the emancipation they caught up unnaturally quickly and powerfully with the Western trend toward the individual (secularization, rationalization, extraversion, the break with the continuity of the past).
>
> (JNC, p. 18)

Neumann describes the overall consequence as follows:

> Thereby the shadow was finally "liberated," and here in Palestine it can reveal itself for the first time as, here, there is no external pressure. This will not be pleasant—perhaps we will all be killed, but it's no use—it simply must be out in the open at least and worked through.
>
> (JNC, p. 18)

Nor were the personal consequences unequivocal:

> In the face of this apparently historic necessity, the chaos here becomes not only bearable to me but I also feel myself to be infinitely closely bound up with it; I emerge out of this to my own "people." I must, though, confess that I am quite often afraid at the same time. I feel myself here to be quite account-able and I still know that my place is here, quite independently from whether the Jews will grant me this place one day or not.
>
> (JNC, pp. 18–19)

As a married couple, the Neumanns were very well suited to each other. This allowed Erich to theorise the feminine as positively complementing the masculine, a central idea of some of his later works. According to Micha Neumann, his mother was his father's true muse and source of inspiration. "I taught Erich to enjoy," Julie once said, and Erich agreed. Marriage carried the Neumanns through a life that was devoted to intense concentration on essential topics and therapeutic practice. While Julie maintained contact with the outside world, friends and the pleasurable aspects of life, Erich mostly withdrew to his study to think and write. The outcome was a prolific number of books and lectures.

The apartment was Neumann's world. He seldom left it unless he was travelling, since his sessions with patients lasted until late at night. The apartment, as observed, also served as a cultural venue in the evenings. Neumann took to the "green room" to pursue his inner urge to write. He placed himself under considerable pressure and rarely went out to concerts or the theatre. He wrote. Writing, for Neumann, was like giving birth. It was an extraordinarily creative, yet exhausting process. He would pour tirelessly over his manuscripts during the holidays.

Neumann described his approach to writing, and its significance in his life, in a letter to Jung dated 28 March 1953:

> It is truly a type of compulsion and addiction—I have been writing almost continuously since my twelfth, certainly since my sixteenth year—and while I also know that this is definitely part of my nature and, I hope, of my authentic life task, it sometimes seems to be a true paper hell. […] Are you familiar with anything like this yourself, or does this belong to my individual idiosyncrasies?
>
> (JNC, p. 301)

He often listened to music when writing. The gramophone was put into operation and Neumann's study became filled with the inspiring sounds of his favourite classical works. He once remarked that if he were ever born again, he would become a conductor. Writing was a passion, a life's work, a desire to express his innermost feelings. "Writing bores me, tires me, is difficult," he sometimes complained to Julie. Approaching his "innermost" core mattered immensely to Neumann and made him feel close to Jung.

Circumstances, however, made devoting enough time to writing far from easy. Maintaining his practice took up most of Neumann's time and energy. He took the burden of many hours of therapy upon himself largely for financial reasons. On 5 December 1938, shortly after the November pogroms, he wrote to Jung:

> Only infernal reality makes it extremely difficult to formulate things because I need time to do it and an occasional half day simply is not enough. In future, when a large group of relatives must be provided for and, on top of that, the economy is declining along with the practice, it will be a lot worse for sure. But on the other hand one's concentration increases because of it and a

certain despairing—joyful will to come to terms with reality precisely as an introvert and, what is more, as an intuitive.

Nevertheless, he concluded:

> Thus, the full uncertainty about any future and yet still having the feeling of being in the right place gives me—at least now and again—a remarkably paradoxical inner confidence, from which I believe that there could be a new, lively beginning in the individual and in the collective.
>
> (JNC, pp. 142–143)

"Infernal reality": By this, Neumann first and foremost means the November pogroms of 1938, in which Jewish shops and apartments were systematically pillaged and destroyed, fires were started in almost all synagogues across Germany, over 90 Jews were murdered, and tens of thousands of Jews were arrested and deported to concentration camps, mostly to Buchenwald, but also Sachsenhausen and Dachau.[17] These events made even those Jews who remained optimistic until the very end realise that their days in Germany were numbered. Newly introduced legislation, including "Die Verordnung zur Ausschaltung der Juden aus dem deutschen Wirtschaftsleben" ("The Ordinance on the Elimination of Jews from German Economic Life") of 12 November 1938, eventually drove German Jews into abject poverty.[18]

Neumann's father had died in Berlin on 25 March 1937 after a Gestapo interrogation. In 1936, he had visited Erich and Julie in Palestine with his wife, amid great tensions with the Arab population. Far from Berlin, life in this new country seemed utterly foreign and highly threatening to Neumann's parents. They tried to persuade their son to return to his homeland, or at least to allow them to take Micha, their grandson, back to Germany, "where he belongs."[19]

The events of November 1938, however, left no doubt in anyone's mind that the Nazis were serious. In 1939, Erich's sister Lotte managed to emigrate to Paris, while his brother Franz secured passage to London, where their mother also sought refuge a little later. Neumann's siblings first lived in extremely modest circumstances, since they were not allowed to pursue their profession as medical doctors. Julie's siblings and parents emigrated to England with the assistance of Salo Goldstone, their English son-in-law, before warfare erupted. Her oldest brother Martin emigrated to Australia. Obviously, those family members who had emigrated, above all their parents, had to be financially supported.[20]

In the early summer of 1936, Erich and Julie travelled to Europe for the first time since settling in Palestine. They spent two months in Switzerland, to continue analysis with Jung. They did not return to Europe again until 1947. This second visit to Switzerland enabled Neumann to continue his analytical discussions with Jung and to make the acquaintance of Olga Fröbe-Kapteyn, the organiser of the Eranos conferences, which had been taking place in Moscia near Ascona since 1933. Neumann met Fröbe-Kapteyn at Gerhard Adler's summer residence in southern Switzerland (Adler was a friend of Neumann's from his student days in Berlin and a later Jungian analyst). Adler vividly recalled the words he used to introduce Neumann: "Mrs Fröbe-Kapteyn, may I introduce you to your future speaker?"[21] Writing to Fröbe-Kapteyn in 1960, after Neumann's death, Julie Neumann also remembered the beginning of a long and deep friendship:

> Summer 1947 is still as clear to me as Erich was in your archive, completely fascinated by the pictures of the Great Mother; you came along in your own way and told us to stay for lunch. I refused only because we were expected somewhere else, but Bänzinger whispered to me: "We" should accept, since it was a great honour to be invited so spontaneously by you; from then onwards, we belonged, and you and Eranos became a spiritual home.[22]

Neumann gave his first Eranos lecture, "Der mystische Mensch" (later published in English as "Mystical Man"), in 1948. He quickly became one of the leading figures at the conferences, where he delivered lectures every year until his death in November 1960 (Chapter 9). Meeting Fröbe-Kapteyn proved fruitful also in other respects: She introduced Neumann to the large image archive she had been compiling for years and whose world "enchanted and gripped him."[23] The archive contained a wealth of pictures and documents dealing with the Great Mother (Chapter 9). Neumann was invited to write an introduction about this topic, from which one of his most important works, *The Great Mother*, emerged a few years later. In addition, a lifelong, cordial friendship developed between the Neumanns and Olga Fröbe-Kapteyn, as is reflected in their lively exchange of letters. Aside from mutual affection, the correspondence was based on Olga's extraordinary willingness to provide various sorts of assistance. The Israeli–Palestine civil war, which erupted only a day after the announcement of the UN partition plan in November 1947, escalated into a full-scale war on 15 May 1948[24]—shortly after Israel's declaration of independence. Neumann's comments on these events were sparse.[25] Fröbe-Kapteyn offered the Neumanns to live with her in Switzerland. Neumann responded to this offer on 18 June 1948:

> Your generous offer to welcome me and my whole family in Ascona deeply touched me and my wife. Thank you very much for that! Especially in these difficult and often disappointing times, the sheer fact that you have made this proposal is encouraging and almost comforting. Once more, thank you very much, although making this prospect materialise seems inconceivable to us. So far, the bombing of Tel-Aviv has been a minor, yet disturbing matter (for those affected, it is of course terrible, even if the numbers aren't large.) Hopefully, there will soon be peace, and they won't sell us again.
>
> (NOF)

Time and again, Olga Fröbe-Kapteyn proved to be a motherly and most supportive friend to the Neumanns. Among others, she sent regular food parcels.

In his letter of 8 November 1951, Neumann acknowledged the receipt of this vital source of help:

> The day after I sent you my manuscript, your two packages arrived. The joy was very great, and was clouded only by the quiet worry that you will soon have to be locked up for your wastefulness. Didn't we specifically say you shouldn't send us such gorgeous packages? Gluttonous as man is, you have plunged us into serious internal conflicts, in which the joy of good things quarrels with our concerns about your wastefulness.
>
> (NOF)

Fröbe-Kapteyn supported Neumann's application for a Bollingen Fellowship, which would enable him to pursue his work on *The Great Mother*. To begin with, Neumann was disappointed at the lack of funding, discussion and diplomatic skills on Fröbe-Kapteyn's part.

In Moscia, the Neumanns stayed with Fröbe-Kapteyn. Her house had a "wonderful room" (NOF, 14 May 1949), which Neumann asked to use as a study. Aside from hosting the Neumanns, Fröbe-Kapteyn made various arrangements on their behalf (obtaining visas and airline tickets, raising funds for stays and publications, enabling Julie to teach chirology and securing a scholarship for Micha's medical studies in Zurich). She was so discreet that she caused the Neumanns no embarrassment and enabled them to express requests also on behalf of friends and acquaintances.[26] In a letter dated 14 April 1950, for instance, Neumann asked Fröbe-Kapteyn for funds to invite Gershom Scholem, who had been lecturing at the Eranos conferences since 1949, to Switzerland: "Please ensure that you raise the money for Scholem, it would be very nice and important. Perhaps the folks in Zurich can organise a well-paid seminar for him if the rich people can't afford to" (NOF).

The letters soon became more familiar: "Dear Mrs. Fröbe-Kapteyn" became "Very Dear Olga" or "Dearest Olga." The intimate tone allowed both sides to mention more serious concerns, to share problems and to offer one another advice or comfort.[27] Thus—on Neumann's side—we find some sideswipes at Jung, yet also at the Zurich Institute, with which he had been on extremely bad terms ever since the outrage caused by the publication of his *Depth Psychology and a New Ethic* in 1949 (see Chapter 12). Neumann had strong reservations in particular about Carl Alfred Meier, one of the institute's co-founders (it had been established in April 1948). Although he lectured there, and was even offered the post of director (which he turned down) after the end of the war, the tensions persisted. Neumann was envied in Zurich, where he was widely felt to be promoted too strongly by Jung. His work was often dismissed as not Jungian (enough). Neumann, in turn, repeatedly made ironic remarks about the servile attitude of some Jungians.

From 1934 to 1947, Neumann pursued his work and research almost in complete isolation. The most important spiritual connection with Europe was his exchange of letters and manuscripts with C.G. Jung. During this period (1934–1940), as we have seen, he produced two comprehensive manuscripts: *Beiträge zur Tiefenpsychologie des jüdischen Menschen und zum Problem der Offenbarung* and *Der Chassidismus und seine psychologische Bedeutung für das Judentum* (see Chapters 10 and 11). Neumann wished neither work to be published during his lifetime, as he considered his knowledge of Judaism to be insufficient.

After her husband's death, Julie Neumann sought Gershom Scholem's advice about the manuscripts; he cautioned against publication, since Neumann's account of Hasidism was too one-sidedly oriented towards Buber's thinking.[28] Two other important works followed: *Ursprungsgeschichte des Bewusstseins* ("The Origins and History of Consciousness") and *Tiefenpsychologie und Neue Ethik* ("Depth Psychology and a New Ethic"). In 1946, Neumann asked Jung for assistance with the publication of these two works, which he completed between 1945 and 1948. Although Jung put in a good word for him at Rascher Verlag, Neumann was aggrieved when he retracted his first, enthusiastic preface to *Ursprungsgeschichte des Bewusstseins*, his "big book," as Neumann called it, and instead contributed a complimentary, yet more reserved version. In a letter to Olga Fröbe-Kapteyn dated 19 May 1949, he remarked:

> By the way, Jung, who is obviously under pressure from the institute, has decided to amend his short preface for the worse. Very well. Please could you

Figure 8.4 On the balcony at 1 Gordon Street with a sea view

tell Frau von Keller that her "prophetic" words, that I must now go my own way like a rhino, comfort me time and again (Jung is still very nice to me, even touchingly so, yet he is clearly not reliable—an old man).

(NOF)

Only three days later, Neumann again described Jung and his entourage, this time however in drastic, even relentless and disillusioned terms:

Jung is very touching towards me, and making an effort in a way that really perturbs me. Of course this ought to matter more to me than the fact that he is weak on details and, as I believe, not always right. Nevertheless, the whole thing has a tragic importance for me, because it reveals that Europe is becoming reactionary and is taking control of Jung. Catholicism, individualism—well, these are values, but also forces, and it all rhymes so sadly and so smoothly with fascism and National Socialism. Jung's carelessness has already made it tremendously difficult to extricate him and his work from this not only embarrassing but also disastrous proximity. I fear that the folks in Zurich, including Kranefeldt with his "Archetypus sinaiticus" of 1933, who has been reintegrated into the club, will not improve the world's situation. And nothing exists here without the greatest danger. Anyway, all the best to you.[29]

(NOF, 22 May 1949)

In his letter of 13 December 1950, Neumann observed that the "Züricher are agitating, and it has gotten under my skin." He felt distracted and unable to work properly (NOF). He managed by isolating himself, a ploy that often proved successful due to his geographical distance to Zurich. This also kindled his resistance, which he described as follows:

I don't, however, intend to beat a retreat, but instead feel obliged to supply new material over and over again, as a stumbling block so to speak. In a certain sense, I am now "through": One can do me harm, although little more than barely, and so what anyway. I made it quite clear from the outset that I was not expected to be orthodox, and they accepted that.

(NOF, 27 May 1951)

On 10 December 1955, on the occasion of Emma Jung's death (27 November 1955), which almost coincided with his mother's, Neumann wrote to Jung. His letter of condolence also reflects on his strained relationship with the Zurich Institute:

For me all this belongs together, as different as it is.

Although I only got to know your wife in the last years, from 1948, I think, for me Zurich has been curiously changed without her. She was the conscience, something one could rely on in gloomy Zurich, something solid and full of interest and understanding, with all due distance. (You, yourself, by the way, so that you do not misunderstand, belong for me to Bollingen and Küsnacht, not to Zurich. [...] It was painful to me as seldom before to be so far away, for my gratitude toward your wife is great.

(JNC, p. 315)

His annual Eranos lectures provided Neumann's daily chores with an additional temporal framework. He likened Eranos to a new "era." In an undated letter to Olga Fröbe-Kapteyn, he added the following (handwritten) note:

My Eranos calendar has shifted considerably; previously, the "pre-Eranos" era began roughly in spring, now it begins as soon as we reach home, and I can already start looking forward [to the next conference].

(NOF)

Eranos, the "friendly island" (NOF, 29 January 1951), had become his new centre—geographically and humanly. Although the Neumanns continued to see Jung in Zurich, in order to continue their analytical work with the Jungs, it was no longer their emotional focus. Every year, they spent two to three months in Europe. Other than Neumann's lecturing commitments, they visited friends and relatives,[30] took cultural trips and sought relaxation in the Swiss mountains.

Julie Neumann also told Olga Fröbe-Kapteyn how strongly the annual meetings influenced the family's time structure. In one letter, she describes Erich's return from giving his first Eranos lecture in 1948:

[He] returned thrilled from Eranos, not only from the conference, but also from the human atmosphere. Afterwards a new era began. Eranos, after Eranos, before Eranos, and I was always allowed to be present and to experience how your topic for the coming year did not let go of Erich and occupied him until he began writing.[31]

Julie's words capture one of her husband's most characteristic traits: He allowed himself to be gripped by a topic or an idea, insofar as it was in some way related to what had been exercising his mind ever since his school and university days. In this respect, he was "possessed," as Scholem's obituary phrased it.[32] Neumann, who consistently referred to himself as an "introvert," was pregnant with ideas. He often used metaphors of creation and birth to describe the genesis, execution and completion of his works. Thus, several letters speak of "precipitate labour" or "difficult birth." While his intellectual ventures inspired and protected him, they also demanded extraordinary amounts of energy. His ambition was to share his ideas, most of all in writing. Publishing his work (and ensuring its translation) mattered deeply to him. They were both a source of pride and greatest vulnerability.[33] His work came at a high price, namely, the isolation he repeatedly referred to. His favourite phrase for this predicament was living "on the edge." In his peripheral existence, he needed the comfort that Olga Fröbe-Kapteyn knew how to give him. Thus, one of his typewritten letters to her ends with a touching handwritten note:

> The good contact with you, as well as with the Bänzigers, for example, is very comforting. Even if you overestimate my role for Eranos, it has become a friendly island to which I belong, unlike Zurich, unfortunately, after recent experiences. Nevertheless, I also have made many positive experiences there. They comfort me. Oddly, I seem to need that. How strange. This, however, has to do with the fact that we are of course living on the very edge and, apart from our practice, we barely ever have anyone round or see people.
>
> (NOF, 29 May 1951)

It was more than understandable that his wounded pride, which sought amends, fuelled Neumann's efforts to have his doctorate in medicine recognised, which political turmoil in Germany had denied him in the 1930s. On 6 November 1956, he submitted an application to Hamburg Medical Faculty, in which he described his request as an "act of cultural restitution"; he filed another application on 23 December 1957. On 18 November 1958, his doctorate was officially recognised by the Hamburg Faculty: *Ursprungsgeschichte des Bewusstseins* was approved as a doctoral dissertation, while the oral examination was waived. The award was preceded by several events:

> At one Eranos conference, Professor Arthur Jores from Hamburg asked Neumann why he was only "Dr. phil." but not "Dr. med." although he had studied medicine. After Neumann had explained matters, Dr. Jores arranged for Neumann to receive the degree of Medical Doctor; his *Ursprungsgeschichte des Bewusstseins* was approved as a doctoral thesis.[34]

Neumann was not interested in public office even if this would have earned him acclaim and prestige. In 1957, for instance, he declined a request from Tel Aviv University to serve as director of its newly opened Institute of Psychology.

Gradual relief in the last years of his life came from working one day less a week with patients; soon afterwards he reduced his practice by another day, which enabled him to devote more time to writing and to preparing his lectures and seminars, which he continued to deliver on a regular basis in Zurich and Basel.

His Eranos contacts also secured invitations to lecture in the Netherlands.[35] Thus, Neumann was honoured at a reception hosted by Queen Juliane of the Netherlands, who was interested in the work of C.G. Jung. He also appeared as a speaker at the inaugural International Association for Analytical Psychology (IAAP) Congress, which was held in 1958.

In 1960, the last year of his life, Neumann set foot on German soil for the first time since 1933. His visit, while attending a conference, was accompanied by

Figure 8.5 Julie at the IAAP Congress in 1958 (foreground); with Dvora Kutzinski (left)

"difficult feelings," since his love for Germany had been wounded too deeply. His children recall that there was never any mention in Israel of life being beautiful in Berlin. Nor did their parents ever express any longing for Germany.

Few friendships survived Neumann's trajectory from Berlin to Tel Aviv. The longest was undoubtedly that with Carl Frankenstein, his classmate in Berlin, who remained a lifelong confidant. Frankenstein recalls that Neumann and him often "skived" classes to take part in discussions about philosophy and Jewish history outside school.[36] Frankenstein, later appointed chair of education studies in Jerusalem, had written his doctoral thesis in Germany about Franz Joseph Molitor, whose four-volume study on Kabbalistic thought Neumann frequently cited in his studies on Jewish mysticism.[37] A student of Schelling and Baader, Molitor's work even wrested a positive comment from Gershom Scholem, who observed that its author "did know more about the subject than Judaic authorities of his time."[38] Frankenstein's name also appeared alongside Neumann's in *Zwischen den Zelten*, an anthology of young Jewish authors (see Chapter 3), which suggests that they shared not only theoretical but also poetic interests.[39]

Personal documents about Neumann are rare: They include Carl Frankenstein's commemorative speech after Neumann's death.[40] This mentions Neumann's "unique dedication to his life's task," as well as "his calm obsession that drove him from one work to the next."[41] Frankenstein adds how astonished many of Neumann's readers and listeners are "at the wealth and diversity of his knowledge, which he employed in a sovereign manner to substantiate his claims."[42]

Moreover, he captures "the man behind the work" with two of Neumann's out-standing traits: his "love of poetry, artwork and music" and his "optimistic belief in the healing power of the transpersonal."[43]

In his obituary, Gershom Scholem described Neumann as "a man of high rank, of great integrity of character and astonishingly comprehensive interests"; he "possessed great human freedom and dignity" and a "moral compass" that guided him "unswervingly through many difficult situations." Scholem ranked Neumann among "the world's most respected and talented representatives of Jungian psy-chology." Above all, he praised Neumann as an Eranos speaker: "His speeches were an event and one of the main attractions of these conferences." Scholem repeatedly emphasised the significance that Neumann attached to his Jewish her-itage, "to which he felt bound and committed."[44] He stressed Neumann's inde-pendent thinking and that, as he observed, Neumann was the "logician of the Jungians."

A noteworthy, yet entirely different source of information in this regard is an interview conducted by Henry Abramovitch with Dvora Kutzinski, Julie's analy-sand and Erich's supervisee.[45] When they first met, in 1948, Dvora was 22 years old, Neumann age 43. Neumann impressed Dvora deeply. She first thought he was an elderly man of around 70. He radiated serenity, barely spoke and had very warm eyes. He struck her as very introverted. His hair was long, a veritable mane, and his slender, beautiful fingers held an elegant cigarette holder.[46]

She made no secret of her initial surprise when Neumann referred her to his wife. She suspected charlatanry. Matters worsened when he told her to take a chi-rological test with Julie. She was convinced that she had fallen into the hands of gypsies. Nevertheless, she decided to consult Julie. When Julie asked her why she had come, she answered truthfully: "Your husband told me to." Dvora was inter-ested in psychology, yet decided not to reveal this. Instead she said, "I have no idea." Julie made a handprint and said, "Let me see." Then she continued: "You have many possibilities, but you are well suited to the field of psychology." Dvora asked what kind of psychology she meant, and Julie replied: "You could become an analyst."[47] Julie did not want to hear about the financial or language problems besetting the young uniformed soldier sitting before her. Rather, she told Dvora to go to university, to study psychology and to earn at least a "Master's degree." She added: "You will make it." As with Neumann, her encounter with Julie had given Dvora a special sense of elation.[48]

Dvora, an Auschwitz survivor, travelled with her remaining funds from Tel Aviv to Jerusalem, where she enrolled at the latest possible matriculation date. When the university discovered her financial hardship, she was awarded a ref-ugee scholarship. She studied psychology and became Julie's analysand. After qualifying, Dvora had her first analysand at the age of 30; Neumann became her supervisor.

She describes him as someone who gave her complete independence, yet whose presence she felt. He was never patronising, nor did he stylise himself as a parental figure who believed that he needed to support his child. When she told him, "I don't understand this dream," he replied, "He is *your* patient," thus leaving her to find her own interpretation. Neumann, she says, believed in her. He saw her as the person she was in her process of becoming; that confidence helped her immensely.

Although he spoke very little, Neumann had an incredible sense of humour. His clarity of mind impressed her most. From him, she learned to express herself directly. He did not mince his words. If he had anything negative to say, he did. He took difficult issues in hand and refused to sugar-coat his patients. He adopted the same approach in their professional relationship, revealing her blind spots at every juncture. He taught her to serve the self and the soul, not the ego. Through her work with Neumann, Dvora learned to have courage without hurting others. Transference was never discussed. Neumann was primarily intuitive, and she later understood that his empathy was key to his professional success.

She also vividly recalled Neumann's evening seminars, which were lectures more than anything else. He would ask his audience what they made of his deliberations, yet nobody dared answer.[49] He did not realise how intimidating he was, even if he never identified with the role of the "great man." He was very modest.

The Neumanns later became friends with Dvora and her husband. One evening, the two couples listened to classical music into the early hours. At one o'clock in the morning, Neumann suddenly recalled that he owned a recording that Dvora's husband did not have, so he dashed home, a few houses along the same street, to fetch it: Haydn's *Quartet 72, No. 3*. She once asked him: "As far as music goes, you discuss it with my husband as if you were the great expert, but you're so modest in psychology!" He replied: "What do we really know about the psyche? If we know 10 per cent, that's a lot. We know nothing about the other 90 per cent."[50]

Dvora remembers one occasion when a petal fell from one of the roses that were standing in a vase on the table. She picked it up and began rolling the leaf between her fingers. Neumann took the petal away from her, smoothed it again, laid it back to the rose and said, "It's alive!"[51]—She admired him deeply, not only as a psychologist, but also as a human being, most of all for his compassion for the living. He was deeply religious, although not in the sense of organised religion, but out of a profound respect for the self, the numinous. Dvora Kutzinski considered Erich Neumann to be the most developed person she had ever met.

In 1960, Neumann returned to Israel after visiting London. He was fatally ill. His son Micha and Dvora received him. Sitting in a wheelchair, he was so emaciated that he was barely recognisable. He died on 5 November 1960. A mere three weeks after her husband's death, Julie Neumann wrote a touching letter to her friend and close confidante Olga Fröbe-Kapteyn (NOF, 24 November 1960). She was the first person whom Julie notified in writing of Neumann's death. The kidney cancer that had so ravaged her husband lasted a mere three weeks. He suffered no pain, but grew increasingly weaker. Until the end, he refused to believe that he would die. He died peacefully in his sleep, in the presence of his wife.

A month later, Gerhard Adler also wrote to Olga Fröbe-Kapteyn. Shortly before Erich's death, the Neumanns had travelled to London to visit relatives and friends, when his condition began deteriorating rapidly. Adler mentions the "hopeless diagnosis" that Neumann had received in London. Thereupon, Neumann—as so often at crucial junctures—consulted the *I Ching*. In "Possession in Great Measure. Supreme success" (no. 14), the oracle answered: "Possession in great measure is determined by fate and accords with time … The time is favorable—a time of strength within, clarity and culture without."[52]

Illness had wrenched Neumann brutally from his intellectual and spiritual endeavours. When he died, he had been working on a book about the psychology of the child, which Julie published posthumously as *Das Kind* (1963).[53] Other projects dear to him were a study on creativity (*Wesen der Kreativität*) and another on the psychology of the creative person (*Psychologie des kreativen Menschen*). In her (previously cited) letter of 24 November 1960 to Olga Fröbe-Kapteyn, Julie also discusses Neumann's work and its nature:

> Time and again, he told me, "why *must I always* write about the 'final things,' why can't I do case discussions like so many others, and also expect myself to do likewise. But it bores me, and I *must* write like this, even if it goes beyond me"; Eranos was the forum where he could talk about these final things. Now I know, since he had to die so early, not only why he had to write, but also why he did with such intensity.
>
> (NOF; original emphases)

In a letter to Olga Fröbe-Kapteyn dated 30 May 1961, Julie mentions that after Erich's death she "simply does not exist," but works. She ruled out a trip to Switzerland that year, preferring instead to arrange Erich's manuscripts with a view to publication. She did, however, explicitly state that she would be participating in further Eranos conferences in the future.[54]

On 23 January 1961. C.G. Jung sent Julie Neumann a letter of condolence:

> I regretted very much that I did not see Dr. Neumann once again last autumn. […] Following on from the death of my son-in-law I was particularly shattered by the unexpected and, for me, sudden death of my friend and [fellow traveller] in whose fate I participated in tranquility and from a distance.
>
> (JNC, p. 354; translation corrected)

Dvora Kutzinski was devastated by Neumann's death. For her, he symbolised a barrier against the terrible psychological consequences of the Holocaust, which, as an Auschwitz survivor, she had experienced first-hand. Neumann was convinced that there existed the prospect of renewal from the depths of hell. To her, he represented salvation. She feared that without him, she would fall back into the suicidal mood besetting her on arriving in Israel from Auschwitz. A dream came to her aid:

Figure 8.6 Julie Neumann in 1985

I am in an amphitheater, not a half but a full circular one. There are people sitting all around. On the stage is a gigantic lion, three meters tall, who opens its mouth. The lion faces me and inside his maw, I see the gate of Auschwitz, "Arbeit Macht Frei." He wants to swallow me. I turn around and see outside the circle fields of gold, golden wheat that came nearly shoulder high, moving in the wind. Suddenly, I see Neumann, only his head above the golden wheat, his hair blowing in the wind. I turn to my friend who is there and say, "Look! Look! He is alive. He is only walking in other fields!"[55]

Hannah Arendt tenderly recalled her encounter with Erich Neumann. In her diary, she wrote:

31 November 1960
On the death of Erich Neumann

What was left of you?
No more than a hand,

no more than your quivering fingers,
which closed firmly to bid the time of day

For this grip remained as a trace
In my hand, which did not forget,
Which continued to feel even after
Your mouth and your eyes had long failed.[56]

Notes

1 Neumann to Jung, Tel Aviv, 5 December 1938; see JNC, p. 143.
2 Myra Warhaftig, *Sie legten den Grundstein: Leben und wirken deutschsprachiger jüdischer Architekten in Palästina 1918–1948* (Tübingen: Wasmuth, 1996), p. 24.
3 Michael Brenner, *Geschichte des Zionismus* (Munich: Beck, 2005), p. 105 (immigration figures were as follows: 1933: 37,000; 1934: 45,000; 1935: 66,000).
4 Ralf Balke, *Tel Aviv, das Open Air Museum des Bauhauses*, website of the Deutsch-Israelisches Gesellschaft E.V., 2003.
5 Gideon Greif, Colin McPherson and Laurence Weinbaum (eds.), *Die Jeckes: Deutsche Juden aus Israel erzählen* (Cologne, Weimar, Vienna: Böhlau, 2000), p. 30.
6 Ibid.
7 Ibid., p. 32.
8 According to this letter, Neumann had attended the lectures until the summer semester of 1932. On 24 April 1933, he passed his medical state examination, yet without receiving certification of his internship.
9 Rali Loewenthal-Neumann, "My Father Dr. Erich Neumann," *Harvest,* Special Edition on Erich Neumann, 52(2), 2006, pp. 148–156.
10 Unless otherwise stated, the sources for the following details are personal conversations with Professor Micha Neumann and Rali Loewenthal-Neumann; Micha Neumann's "Erinnerung an Erich und Julie Neumann," *Analytische Psychologie* 39(1), 2008, pp. 35–38; and Loewenthal-Neumann, "My Father Dr. Erich Neumann."
11 Greif et al., *Die Jeckes*, p. 23.
12 Ibid., p. 3.
13 Ibid., p. 3; see also the following passage: "They were, as it were, the inner other from whom it was necessary to distance oneself. In this respect, the German Jews were exposed to collective expectations in Israel to rid themselves of their German parts. And yet, the Hebrew language alone seemed more burdensome to them than to other immigrants. Not because they were less eager to learn than others, but because the German language as a language of culture had become the basis of their self-image in Germany. In linguistic and cultural terms, the German Jews had been German. In addition, most of them had been forced to emigrate from Germany and had been driven out of occupations that required great linguistic proficiency. Hebrew, far less developed, on the other hand seemed to impose upon them a downgrading of civilization"; see Dan Diner, "Vorwort," in Greif et al., *Die Jeckes*, p. VII.
14 Ibid., p. 39.
15 She died on 8 December 1955. On this occasion, Neumann's siblings Lotte and Franz travelled to Israel for the first time.
16 This impression was confirmed by Micha Neumann in his speech at the unveiling of the commemorative plaque for Julie and Erich Neumann on 6 May 2007 in Berlin.
17 Greif et al., *Die Jeckes*, p. 28; see also Brenner, *Geschichte des Zionismus*, p. 110.
18 Greif et al., *Die Jeckes*, p. 29. The rise of terror in Germany made Western democracies vigorously oppose "the spreading Nazi poison" or "throwback to barbarity." However,

no decisive measures were taken even then. President Roosevelt summoned his ambassador in Berlin "to report" to the White House. Chamberlain declared that England would immediately grant Jews without any means permission to settle in Tanganyika; see Guido Knopp and Ralf Piechowiak (eds.), *Heimkehr in die Fremde: Die Gründung des Staates Israel 1896–1948* (Mainz: Gaasterland, 1992), p. 80f. Palestine's Jewish population was determined to save the European Jews towards the end of 1938. Thus, the *Yishuv* (the Jewish residents in Israel prior to the establishment of the State of Israel) harnessed all possible means to organise an illegal *Aliyah* (i.e. the immigration of Jews from the diaspora to Israel). The plan was to steer the immigrants passed the blockades erected by the British along the coasts; see Knopp and Piechowiak, *Heimkehr in die Fremde*, p. 81. It is against this background that severe political tensions persisted in Palestine: Thus, the "Great Revolt" of the Palestinian Arabs, which lasted until 1939, began as early as 1936; see Brenner, *Geschichte des Zionismus*, p. 126.

19 Loewenthal-Neumann, "My Father Dr. Erich Neumann."

20 Angelica Löwe, "Wir waren eine zufriedene und glückliche Familie: Interview mit Ruth Goldstone," *Analytische Psychologie*, 39(1), 2008, pp. 41–49.

21 Gerhard Adler, "Erich Neumann," in *Kreativität des Unbewussten*, eds. H. Dieckmann, C.A. Meier and H.J. Wilke (Basel: S. Karger Verlag, 1980), p. 183.

22 Julie Neumann to Olga Fröbe-Kapteyn, 24 November 1960. Collected in the unpublished letters of Erich Neumann to Olga Fröbe-Kapteyn; cited hereafter as NOF.

23 Neumann to Olga Fröbe-Kapteyn, August 1951; published in Dieckmann, Meier and Wilke, *Kreativität des Unbewussten*, p. 187.

24 It was not, however, until February 1949 that Israel and the Arab war parties signed separate ceasefire treaties.

25 On 12 March 1948, Neumann wrote to Olga Fröbe-Kapteyn: "As you can see, I am trying to pretend that everything here is at peace and that nothing could come between us, even if our situation in Palestine and the world as a whole make this seem far from certain. In any event, all that remains for us to do is to continue working and, if possible, to do what is possible when one has the time."

26 The Neumanns also expressed their concerns about Olga Fröbe-Kapteyn's welfare. On 24 April 1958, Neumann wrote: "It's terrible about your flu. We are worried, but hope that you are already feeling better. Who's looking after you? Do you have good medical care? … It's sad that we are so far away and can't do anything than wish you all the best." Julie added: "Only now that you're ill do I realise the long distance between Tel-Aviv and Moscia. It's really awful not to be able to help you in any way. We can only extend our very heartfelt wishes for a good recovery. To be a little closer to you, I was looking at your last handprints. I have rarely seen such an ever-increasing liveliness as in your hand."

27 The correspondence also includes several references to health issues. Neumann complains about the serious colics from which he had been suffering for many years, and which he was trying to cope with by exercising. He also mentions his daughter's asthma. Scholem acted as an intermediary for information about Fröbe-Kapteyn's eye operation.

28 On Scholem and Buber, see, among others, Klaus Samuel Davidowicz, *Gershom Scholem und Martin Buber: Die Geschichte eines Missverständnisses* (Neukirchener Theologie, 1995).

29 In another letter, however, Neumann strongly defends Jung against Olga Fröbe-Kapteyn's assumptions: "What you wrote about Jung is so outrageously wrong that I was downright shocked. Don't you know him? He never regards the artist as sick, but always as creative. That, in contrast to Freud, is the main thing … His essay about Joyce is particularly ingenious, and the one about Picasso is nice" (NOF, 29 January 1951).

30 For instance, they received regular invitations to visit Gerhard Adler in London; they also met Ernst Bernhard in Rome.

31 Julie Neumann to Olga Fröbe-Kapteyn, published in *Analytische Psychologie* 39(1), 2008, pp. 39–40.
32 Gershom Scholem, "Erich Neumann, Nachruf November 1960," *Mitteilungsblatt. Wochenzeitung des Irgun Olej Merkas Europa* 28, 47 (18 November 1960), p. 4; also published in *Das neue Israel* 13 (1960–1961), p. 313.
33 See, for instance, his letter to Olga Fröbe-Kapteyn of 4 February (no year, yet probably written in 1949): "The course and with it the book [i.e. *The Great Mother*— A.L.] will be quite nice. It's strange that something always comes to mind, but it's the most rewarding thing about this existence, although it means that one never gets away from working, nor from a sense of falling short."
34 Aniela Jaffé to Werner Steltzer, Inter Nationes, Bonn, September 1977 (unpublished letter).
35 Neumann told Olga Fröbe-Kapteyn: "Prof. Mennicke has asked me to lecture for a week at his International School for Wijsbegeerte ... I am of course very willing" (NOF, 11 December, no year, presumably 1952). Neumann was also invited to Amersfoort by van Waveren. Other lectures followed in Amsterdam, Arnheim, Leiden and The Hague.
36 Loewenthal-Neumann, "My Father Dr. Erich Neumann."
37 Carl Frankenstein, "Gedenkrede nach dem Tode Erich Neumanns 1960," *Analytische Psychologie* 11(3), 1980, pp. 297–311; reprinted in H. Dieckmann, C.A. Meier and H.J. Wilke (eds.), *Kreativität des Unbewussten,* pp. 382–386.
38 Gershom Scholem, *From Berlin to Jerusalem,* p. 113.
39 Carl Frankenstein, "Gleichnisse," *Zwischen den Zelten,* pp. 156ff.
40 Frankenstein, "Gedenkrede nach dem Tode Erich Neumanns 1960."
41 Ibid., p. 382.
42 Ibid., p. 383.
43 Ibid., 385f.
44 Gershom Scholem, "Erich Neumann, Nachruf November 1960," *Mitteilungsblatt. Wochenzeitung des Irgun Olej Merkas Europa* 28, 47 (18 November 1960), p. 4.
45 Dvora Kutzinski, "Neumann as my Supervisor: An Interview with Dvora Kutzinski," by Henry Abramovitch, *Harvest* 52(2), 2006; interview held on 23 October 2005; cited here from http://henry-a.com/jungian/neumann-as-my-supervisor-interview-with-dvora-kutzinski; see also e-jungian.com (Jungian Online Magazine).
46 Ibid.
47 Ibid.
48 Ibid.: "I went out in the clouds. After I met for the first time with Julia I was also in the clouds."
49 However, reading the minutes of these seminars does not give one the impression that nobody dared to ask questions. On the contrary, the atmosphere seemed to be lively and stimulating.
50 Kutzinski, "Neumann as my Supervisor."
51 Ibid.
52 Richard Wilhelm, *I Ching,* with a foreword by C.G. Jung (London: Penguin, 2003), p. 60.
53 Erich Neumann, *Das Kind: Struktur und Dynamik der werdenden Persönlichkeit* (Zurich: Rascher, 1963; published posthumously); published in English as *The Child,* trans. Ralph Manheim (Boulder: Shambhala, 1990).
54 Julie Neumann survived her husband by 25 years. She died in 1985 after a car accident.
55 Kutzinski, "Neumann as my Supervisor."
56 Hannah Arendt, *Denktagebuch,* vol. 1 (Munich: Piper, 2002), p. 613. Translator's note: No English translation has appeared to date, hence the translation is mine.

"...belonging to this island as if to a plot of land"[1]

Olga Fröbe-Kapteyn and Eranos

Walter Robert Corti, the editor of *Du*, the renowned Swiss monthly, dedicated its April 1955 issue to Eranos. In response to his invitation, he had received texts from renowned speakers at the Eranos conferences, held in Moscia near Ascona since 1933. He also received a reply from Olga Fröbe Kapteyn, the "creatrix spiritus of Eranos."[2] In answering Cortis's question "What is Eranos?" she conjures up the atmosphere of those memorable occasions:

> I have always failed in my attempts to answer this question. There is no rational formula. However simple the Eranos event might be, it is so complex and so connected with deep springs … Let's stroll through the garden, across to the hall. Have a look around … We start from the large terrace, where the round table awaits us for dinner. This table is the centre of Eranos, its heart and soul, where its many discussion take place. Here, dinner really means "to receive," in both senses of the word … Let us pass this table and head out into the garden … On the narrow path, we have now reached the lecture hall, whose doors and windows are open. Do you see the speaker, who, gripped by his subject, lays aside his manuscript and speaks freely? … The audience listens attentively, only the waves beat quietly, rhythmically, down on the shore.

Her account continued as follows:

> Hanging in the hall are images of large religious symbols, taken from old manuscripts housed at the Vatican Library, the British Museum or the Morgan Library in New York. As much as Eranos seems to rest in silence, it spans the world, is connected with and contained in the world. The images belong to the archive and seize our attention like the lectures, the garden, the audacious conversations around the round table. … All of this is the garden of Eranos, a simple, flourishing place that serves the meeting of minds. That it has become the mighty, sustaining garden of intellectual and spiritual pursuit will forever remain its secret.[3]

Olga Fröbe-Kapteyn, the founder of Eranos, was born in London in 1881 to Dutch parents. Her father worked as an inventor, engineer and general manager for the

Figure 9.1 Neumann at Eranos

British Westinghouse Brake and Signal Company.[4] Olga's mother had supported the women's and life reform (*Lebensreform*) movement.[5]

Young Olga attended art school in Zurich. Shortly after graduation, she married Iwan Fröbe, an Austrian adventurer, flutist, aviation pioneer and inventor, who died in a plane crash in 1915, leaving his wife, who had just given birth to twin daughters, unprovided for. In 1919, Olga relocated to Ticino, the southernmost canton of Switzerland, with her father and two daughters. The following year, her father bought a house in Ascona-Moscia, directly on the shore of Lake Maggiore: This was Casa Gabriella,[6] once described by Erika Mann, after visiting there, as a "sophisticated, crazy villa."[7] Olga Fröbe soon decided that she would turn the house into "A Meeting Place for East and West."[8] For this reason, she had a guest house, the Casa Shanti, and a large building erected on the lakeside property in 1928. The latter later served as a lecture hall for the legendary Eranos conferences.[9] It was no coincidence that the villa was not far from Monte Verità, the famous meeting place of many utopian communities (Olga Fröbe-Kapteyn's ties with the local alternative scene are well documented). Since 1900, Monte Verità ("Hill of Truth") provided an experimental field for new forms of life: "Vegetarians, natural healers, anarchists, theosophists and other seekers of truth, as well as poets, prophets and artists of all kinds occupied the mountain, making it a sanctuary for alternative lifestyles."[10]

In her search for interreligious, inner truth, Olga Fröbe was inspired by theosophical ideas that had previously sought to bridge Eastern and Western cultures. She corresponded with Martin Buber, whom she had met at a seminar about Lao-Tse at Monte Verità in 1924.[11] Already before meeting Buber, she maintained a friendly relationship with the Munich eccentric Ludwig Derleth, who was close to

Stefan George and his circle. Derleth, the author of *Der Fränkische Koran* (1933), and a proponent of early Christianity, also moved to Monte Verità in the 1930s.[12]

Derleth's wife remembers Olga Fröbe-Kapteyn:

> When Olga met Ludwig Derleth, she had been an excellent circus rider and one of the first people to climb Mont Blanc, but the thoughts occupying Ludwig's mind were new to her. Her eyes sparkling, she sat opposite Ludwig on Marienplatz and absorbed the abundance of mythological ideas being discussed at table. These thoughts and concepts expanded her inner life and transformed Olga into what she became a decade later: the founder of Eranos.[13]

Arguably, the most momentous encounter in her life occurred in 1930, when Fröbe-Kapteyn met C.G. Jung in Darmstadt at Count Keyserling's "Schule der Weisheit" (School of Wisdom).[14] Another important figure she met in the early 1930s (in Heidelberg in 1932) was Rudolf Otto, the eminent religious scholar. They openly discussed her project to establish a spiritual meeting place. She invited Otto to the inaugural event. He called the conference, held for the first time the following year, "Eranos," the Greek word for a festive banquet.[15]

Ever since the summer of 1933, the Eranos meetings, each lasting ten days, have been held every year—not even interrupted by World War II. Their initial focus was the encounter between East and West, but from 1938 the emphasis shifted to mythological, religious-philosophical and anthropological topics. A decisive innovation was introduced in 1946, when the dialogue between the humanities and the natural sciences was initiated with a conference titled "Spirit and Nature." C.G. Jung's lectures attracted large audiences from the outset until 1951[16] when ill health forced him to stop his lecturing activities. "Some of the most important concerns of Jung's psychic research became the focus of discussion at Eranos."[17]

Jolande Jacobi has provided a vivid account of the atmosphere at the conferences:

> Those gathered in the lecture hall, surrounded by that magical garden, for about 550 hours, sitting silently on the hard, woven chairs common in Ticino, and seeking to escape the quiet or loud murmuring of the lake to devote themselves entirely to the words of the speaker, know about the tension that one had to endure there ... A tree with golden fruits happened upon them and struck root within each of them, of which they were unaware; a new, promising "tree of knowledge," which stands outside the "paradise of unconsciousness".

She also explains the reasons for attending the Eranos conferences:

> At the very beginning, in 1933, a certain curiosity attracted one, of course, a certain pioneering spirit. It was said that famous men and some less famous

Figure 9.2 Heading to the Eranos conference

ones, but no less skilled and knowledgeable, would make eastern and western knowledge fertilise each other, in the notorious Ascona, at the "Great Mother's," in her unique lecture hall, built especially for this purpose ... In the first years, the conferences had a decidedly cheerful note.

She describes the audience as follows:

The bright, whitewashed lecture hall, shaded by deep blue curtains, teemed with all sorts. Quiet souls, true scholars, mystics, snobs, enthusiasts, starry-eyed idealists, prophets, wannabe members of the in-crowd and many anonymous, contemplative and knowledge-hungry people filled the hall to the last seat. The vast majority of women, young and old, fair and arid, fearful of suffering and artificially prepared, stuck out a mile ... From the outset, C.G. Jung, an experienced guide to the labyrinth of the human soul and an interpretive mediator of its manifestations, occupied a central position.[18]

In addition to the lectures, discussions were held at the "round table," and, first introduced by Jung, "events out on the terraced wall." Immediately after a lecture or during an interval, Jung would gather by the stone wall out on the terrace with friends and colleagues to discuss the psychological significance of what they had just heard.[19]

In 1933, the Munich analyst Gustav Richard Heyer sent an enthusiastic report about the first Eranos conference to Daniel Brody, the publishing manager at Rhein-Verlag. Brody immediately caught fire and wrote to Fröbe-Kapteyn. "The Eranos idea has seized me." He continued:

> At the time, I predicted that if it were possible to hold three meetings, we could expect to reach the seventh year, and if this moment of crisis were also overcome, then a permanent stock would be assured. And I have not regretted my decision to publish the yearbooks for one minute, because over the years the Eranos corpus has emerged, which today is a mainstay of [our] publishing house while it pays tribute to my friendship with the creatrix spiritus of Eranos, Mrs. Olga Fröbe. Eranos and its penetrating power are indebted entirely to this unusual woman's intellectual openness and organisational energy.[20]

The careful publication of the yearbooks served as a strong multiplier: Eranos soon staked its claim as a first-rate site of scientific exchange—thanks to the publications of highly renowned scholars. And yet, just what exactly distinguished the Eranos conferences from other venues and institutions hosting important intellectual and spiritual exchanges? Gershom Scholem, a distinguished Eranos speaker for 28 years, put it as follows:

> Eranos meant two things for us. It placed great scientific demands upon speakers, not least on account of its requirement to speak for two hours. I am sure that I speak for many of the speakers I have met here over the last 30 years in emphasising what it means to be invited to deliver lectures not lasting the usual fifty to sixty minutes. Rather, at Eranos, a topic could and should be developed, not merely aphoristically, but also *ad extensum*. This enables speakers to demonstrate real knowledge of their subject. It is, after all, true that the often seemingly abstruse or profound matters treated at the Eranos conferences cannot be dealt with in a single hour … The two hours allocated to lectures at Eranos contribute greatly to fettering people like myself to this conference … At Eranos, serious attempts are made to provide comprehensive perspectives and to establish interconnections that demonstrate the unity of scientific thought.[21]

Mircea Eliade, who lectured at Eranos from 1950 to 1967, described his experience thus: "The originality of Eranos lies primarily in the fact that speakers are able to rid themselves both of their timidities and of their superiority complexes."[22]

Olga Fröbe, dressed in flowing, Indian-looking robes, seemed to float "through life an inch or two off the ground" and "to be in the business of merchandising Higher Things."[23] Even so, her approach to reality was neither dreamy nor detached. Rather, her critical attitude towards the dramatic political developments in the 1930s had become entwined with her personal fate: Her daughter Inge was born with brain damage, and Fröbe had placed her in a German institution in the 1920s. When she learned, during a visit in 1937, that her daughter had been murdered, Fröbe spoke out openly against the Nazis. After the Nazi occupation of Holland, she stopped protesting, as the Nazis had threatened to arrest her second daughter Bettina, who was living in the country at the time.[24]

C.G. Jung's behaviour also displeased her at times, even if he was her "star attraction" and provided the Eranos meetings with decisive impetus through his lectures (which he delivered until 1951, bar some occasional interruptions).[25] Jung defended her against criticism, among others, on account of her "tremendous energy and organisational skills." He also explicitly welcomed the funding of Fröbe's trip to the USA,[26] during which she intended to expand her collection of pictorial symbols—the famous Eranos Archive—by visiting a number of museums. In a letter of 1938, Fröbe thanked Mary Mellon and her husband for supporting her "winter research trips." In the 1930s and 1940s, at Jung's suggestion,[27] Olga Fröbe travelled to various European and American libraries and museums with a view of establishing a collection of archetypal images. From this collection emerged a research archive for archetypal symbolism, which later played a central role in Neumann's life and work.[28] Fröbe had invested her entire fortune in the Eranos idea, and yet was increasingly reliant on external funds. Mary Mellon, who had remained loyal to Jung since 1934 and had funded the translations of his works into English, was doubtless Fröbe's most important benefactor. Fröbe had met Mary Mellon and her husband Paul in 1938.[29] Even before they left Olga's estate in Moscia, the Mellons arranged to partly fund the forthcoming conference on the "Great Mother,"[30] as well as Fröbe's publications and study trips to Italy and Greece, where she wanted to purchase images to further expand her collection.[31]

Jolande Jacobi, in reviewing 22 years of Eranos in 1955, described the 1938 conference on the "Great Mother" as a "counterspell," since only 3 of the roughly 75 speakers—Rhys-Davids, Collum and Baynes—were female.[32] At this conference, photographs of the images collected by Fröbe were displayed for the first time, in order to raise financial support for the lectures.[33]

The Mellons attended the 1939 and 1940 Eranos conferences. Their support enabled Fröbe to travel to the USA, where she gave a number of talks about the Eranos conferences. The outbreak of war, however, halted payments as well as postal services, and thus seriously threatened the future existence of the conferences. Mellon's lawyers had advised the couple to dissolve the first Bollingen Foundation.[34] From 1943, however, new funds were sought in America to revive the project. Heinrich Zimmer had suggested Kurt Wolff as the new publisher, which turned out to be a stroke of luck.[35] On 1 January 1946, the Bollingen

Foundation[36] officially began operating again. It was dedicated to promoting the Eranos idea in manifold ways.[37]

Let us return to Olga Fröbe's image archive: As observed, she conducted an intense search for symbolic representations in the years 1935 to 1938.[38] At first, she stowed the images in her bedroom, which caused her quite some distress. Jung wrote to tell her that this would threaten both her "personal existence and the Eranos archive." He considered her strong identification with Eranos detrimental and advised her to reassume her former identity as Mrs Fröbe.[39] But she struggled to distance herself from the project, since it played a major role on her path towards individuation. In 1951, she wrote to Ximena de Angulo Roelli, who had done some editorial work during the early days of the Bollingen Foundation:

> Eranos is my individuation. That was so when it began, has remained the case throughout its further development, and so it is today with the greatest intensity. It seems to be my destiny to make my way to individuation in this way. And I had to do it alone.[40]

Reviewing "the last three decades" of Eranos in 1979, Gershom Scholem wrote both critically and appreciatively about Olga Fröbe, who was "commonly known as the 'great mother' behind her back":

Figure 9.3 Neumann in conversation with Gershom Scholem, with Adolf Portmann (right) and Olga Fröbe-Kapteyn (left, from behind)

Olga Fröbe was unforgettable for anyone who stayed here more often or for a longer period. I was never a great Jungian and cannot claim to speak in Jungian categories, but I must say that for us Olga Fröbe was the living representation of what Jungian psychology calls anima and animus. ... It was almost crucial that she sought speakers who identified with her subject. She called this "emotion." She wanted emotional, inspired speakers, not professors. ... And yet, it was the tension between distance and identification, which became so palpable for all of us at Eranos, which shaped my own work at these conferences for many years, for example.[41]

In the summer of 1947, the Neumanns returned to Europe for the first time in 11 years. Between these visits lay the devastating event of World War II. Erich and Julie had attended a conference and were visiting Gerhard Adler, their childhood friend and his wife in Ticino, where they were introduced to Olga Fröbe. This meeting contributed to healing the Erich and Julie's relationship with Europe (Chapter 8).

In August 1951, Neumann wrote a touching letter to Olga Fröbe-Kapteyn on the occasion of her 70th birthday. He expressed his congratulations and gratitude and recalled the significance of this unusual woman, her image archive and his participation at the annual Eranos meetings. He had meanwhile attended the event as a speaker for the fourth time, accompanied by Julie on each occasion:[42]

Figure 9.4 The Round Table: C.G. Jung in conversation with Erich Neumann and Mircea Eliade; to their left Julie Neumann in conversation with Gershom Scholem

When I returned to Europe for the first time, in 1947, after the Second World War, after eleven years, I was sure that after everything that had happened, Europe would seem strange and uncanny. Time had not stood still for me either, and it seemed more than questionable whether I would manage to reconnect with the past. Living far away and on the periphery, I felt as I did everywhere else, also in Ascona at the conference. In one place, however, I find firm ground, for myself, as well as for my existence and work, and that was at the Eranos archive, whose pictorial world both delighted and seized me. Afterwards … I was completely surprised when I was invited to talk about the "mystical man" at the next conference and to write a book about the visual representations of the "Great Mother," which you had collected in the archive.[43]

Thus, at Eranos, that part of Neumann that felt "essentially homeless" now found "firm ground," in particular during the discussions at the "large round table on the terrace overlooking the lake." Most of all, however, Olga Fröbe's hospitality offered the homeless Neumann a spiritual home: "as Eranos in your heart."

Olga Fröbe's energy, as well as her ability to imagine and bring into existence spiritual contexts, enabled Neumann to sense—although melancholically—that the "reality of the occidental spirit is alive."[44]

Neumann, Olga Fröbe's closest confidant, significantly fostered her inner development. She sent him her paintings, mandalas and texts. He wrote to encourage her creativity, and probably did so explicitly whenever he was in Moscia. In his letter of 31 December 1952, he added a dose of irony to his encouragement:

Figure 9.5 Neumann with Daisetz Suzuki

Why don't you fantasise about Hermes with music and relax on your bed so that it can "go through"? It's nice to assume the air of a long-distance healer, isn't it?

(NOF)

A month later, on 21 January 1953, he again expressed his encouragement:

It is clear that Eranos always places you at risk of gorging yourself on archetypes. Presumably, you always need to work on the archetypal, which is not so much relevant to Eranos as it is to yourself. Please continue to work on detachment! This is very important. It is terrific how you keep making progress with yourself!

(NOF)

His reply to her letter of 25 May 1958 was enthusiastic:

Dearest Olga! What a pleasant surprise! How wonderful that you have succeeded in doing just that. And how miraculous that you have managed to create a representation, one that is so clear, so forceful and so completely new. One senses from how much you have thus freed yourself, and also how much we may hope is still to come. I can very well imagine how much effort this has involved, and yet how wonderful it must be for you to have accomplished all of this from within yourself. Just how worthwhile has the great suffering of your loneliness been for you personally, and which has always received wonderful affirmation at Eranos as a transpersonal achievement. ... In any event, you have now grounded the story of Eranos in its most personal foundation. Congratulations to all of us.[45]

In the same letter, Neumann responded to possible topics for the next Eranos conference. True to her character, while Fröbe's approach was purely intuitive, she corresponded with Neumann about the matter. She had sent him several proposals for 1959, including "Der Mensch und die Wende der Zeit" ("Man and the Turning of Time") and "Die Erneuerung des Menschen" ("The Renewal of Man"). Neumann carefully queried both suggestions, pointing out that they were too closely related to the topics for 1951 ("Man and Time") and 1954 ("Man and Change").

The 1959 Eranos conference was indeed titled "Die Erneuerung des Menschen" ("The Renewal of Man"). Even if Fröbe had disregarded Neumann's concerns on this occasion, he continued to play a major role in her decisions. Much earlier, in the early summer of 1948 (they had only known each other for a year), she confronted him with her plan to comprehensively expand the Eranos gatherings. By then, he had already begun tempering her energy by letter; she trusted his advice, since he was close enough to C.G. Jung on the one hand and independent enough to welcome independent developments on the other. Fröbe's thinking was

Figure 9.6 Olga Fröbe-Kapteyn with Erich Neumann and Julie Neumann

Figure 9.7 Neumann in conversation with Gerhard Adler and Gilles Quispel, 1951

also tactical. C.G. Jung was a crowd-puller, but he was already quite elderly. He gave up lecturing in 1951 for health reasons. Fröbe saw Neumann as a possible legitimate successor, an opinion that he refuted as "excessive overestimation." However, his letter of 18 June 1948, a mixture of approval and criticism, seemed to have had its intended positive effect with regard to the dimensions of the Eranos project:

> Let me come to an important point: your Eranos project. Of course you have to talk about it, since it can't be done in writing. It is very interesting, although your plans are far too ambitious. Also, you must be careful not to compete against the Jung Institute in Zurich. This must be avoided at all costs from the start; otherwise, there will be nothing but trouble. Ascona can only be advertised as a specialised workplace affiliated with the Institute. The city libraries required to perform such work are irreplaceable. Nevertheless! Your idea is very appealing and hugely important. Nevertheless, I believe it will require significant funding.
>
> (NOF)

It is important to remember that the C.G. Jung Institute had been founded in Zurich on 24 April 1948. At the time, Neumann had no reason to be at odds with it, since his *Origins and History of Consciousness* and *Depth Psychology and a New Ethic* had not been published, and thus had not yet caused any offence in Zurich (see Chapters 8 and 12). Still, his letter to Fröbe of 14 March 1949 already struck a different note, not only about the Jung Institute, but also about Jung:

Figure 9.8 In the Swiss Alps, 1958

I am very curious to hear about your meeting with Jung. Unfortunately, our relationship is quite tense at present. As you may have heard, the Jung Institute, or rather its board of trustees, presided over by C.G., has found it necessary not to publish my *Origins and History* itself, so as to avoid compromising itself with me, the author of such church- and state-endangering ethics. A delightful letter that arrived from C.G. prior to this decision, in which he distanced himself most ironically from these concerns, has not done anything to persuade me that this matter is nothing but a disgraceful mess ... I sent an indignant and sharp letter to Jung, to complain that it is truly outrageous that he has conceded his position. I have not yet heard from him. Thus, I don't know whether I have been "ditched" or whether I may expect to receive an answer, which I very much hope I will. However, I received some consolation in the same post as Meier's indecent and clumsy letter: Routledge and Kegan Paul will be publishing the English edition of my *New Ethic*. Nevertheless, I'm sad all the same. This is how cowardly and opportunistic circumstances were in Nazi Germany. Mind you, while it was really dangerous there, it is simply business in Z.—and completely misunderstood for that matter, but that is no consolation.

(NOF)

Neumann and Fröbe now seemed to be closing ranks as far as the Jung Institute and Jung himself were concerned. Their letters also discussed critical reviews of Neumann's publications. Neumann, who was certain that Fröbe's approved of his work, did not hide his disappointment about the reactions to his *New Ethic*:

Rascher sent me a pile of reviews that are all stupid and depressing. Nobody notices what matters. Only one of them, most certainly a Jew, a Michael Grünwald, has at least noticed something of moral seriousness, while the rest are horrified Christians or fools ... if, however, I have to stomach the fact that the book is "too conscious, too intellectual, too cold," I would at least have wished that someone had grasped the urgency of its problem; none of this is the case, though.

(NOF, 14 May 1949)

Characteristic of the correspondence between Neumann and Fröbe is its confidential tone. They openly shared hurt feelings and discussed conflicts, thus lending each other moral support whenever possible: Neumann felt ill-treated, by the Jung Institute, but also by Jung himself. Fröbe comforted him, just as he counterbalanced her occasional mood swings about Jung. Their letters also discussed a variety of other matters. On one occasion, Neumann advised Fröbe not to expect too much from Jung anymore: "You can no longer ask him to be polite or pretend to be kind." On another, Neumann suggested that her "Eranos obsession" was about to sacrifice a long-standing friendship, a stance that he did not approve of. In his letter of 15 April 1955, he mentions relocating the image archive from Fröbe's private rooms to publicly accessible premises:"I find it very sad that the archive is gone, but I understand that it was the right decision and am glad that your room has been "humanised" as a result" (NOF).

Neumann's communication with Daniel Brody at Rascher Verlag appears to have been sluggish, which Neumann also complained about in several letters to Fröbe. As early as 25 March 1950, he wrote:

> I wrote to Brody a long time ago and sent him a request from Jerusalem University to consider sending them a copy of the Eranos series as a gift, to agree to a purchase at a reduced price, or whatever. I also asked him, of course, since we really have no funds in Israel. Naturally, I also mentioned that I could very well understand if he declined the request on principle. Since I have not heard from him, I would like to know if my letter arrived or if B. has taken offence; saying that, I wouldn't know why; in short, I would like to know what is going on.
>
> (NOF)

Unquestionably, Fröbe must have been both surprised and shocked by Neumann's unexpected death on 5 November 1960. In the same month, Julie Neumann wrote a long letter to her in which she looked back at the past 13 years, which, she emphasised, had been greatly enriched by meeting Olga and by attending the annual Eranos conferences. Gershom Scholem sent his obituary with "sad greetings." Gerhard Adler reported that the last *I Ching* received by Neumann in London had been no. 14, "Possession in great measure" (see Chapter 8).

Neumann gave his last lecture, "Die Psyche als Ort der Gestaltung" ("The Psyche as a Place of Creation"), at the 1960 Eranos conference (17–25 August). Olga Fröbe dedicated the preface of the Eranos yearbook, published a year later, to her dear friend:

> We hardly realise that he has departed from us. Since 1947, Eranos had been his spiritual home, which he found nowhere else. In his humanity lay such a rich experience of the inner world, about which he spoke to us, constantly, that we gradually went hand in hand with him, so to speak.[46]

A commemorative piece by the zoologist Adolf Portmann,[47] who played a major role in 20th-century philosophical anthropology (along with Arnold Gehlen, Hellmuth Plessner and Max Scheler), remembered Neumann as a long-standing friend and Eranos companion. While Neumann's lecture had opened the conference for over a decade, Portmann's had closed proceedings. As Portmann observed, Neumann and him had complemented each other in a special manner. Together, as he observed, they had provided the "Eranos vessel" with a solid framework:

> We seldom discussed. In essence, the give-and-take that defined our cooperation took place during times of physical separation, across great

geographical distance—for each of us, in our very different fields of activity, although always in the knowledge that we were thinking of each other, with a view to our beautiful shared task. Thus, on several occasions, Neumann had already considered the contribution of life research in his introduction to the conference in such a way that anticipated many of the ideas that I had considered including in my final review. The rearrangements that our agreement gave rise to during the conferences helped us to clarify some of the interrelations between the psychological and biological aspects of the unknown reality of life. I have in mind the silent, yet persistent effort to resolve the mystery that Neumann described as "extraneous knowledge," as transpersonal and apersonal at the same time, which my deliberations regarded as a "prepared relationship with the world," and which others described as a "specific intelligence" (A. Vondel): the mystery of archetypes and instincts that Neumann's thinking has struggled with for a lifetime.[48]

Figure 9.9 The Neumanns in Sils Maria, 1958

Notes

1 Neumann's birthday letter to Olga Fröbe-Kapteyn, August 1951; included in *Kreativität des Unbewussten*, p. 187.
2 Daniel Brody, "Das Eranos–Jahrbuch," *Du, Schweizerische Monatszeitschrift* (Zurich, April 1955), p. 51.
3 Olga Fröbe-Kapteyn, "Brief an Walter Robert Corti," *Du, Schweizerische Monatsschrift* (Zurich, April 1955), p. 10.
4 Deirdre Bair, *Jung: A Biography*, p. 412. See also "Walking in the Footsteps of Eranos mit Beiträgen von Robert Hinshaw, Paul Kugler, H. Kawai, D. Miller, Gilles Quispel," in *Barcelona 04, Edges of Experience: Memory and Emergence, Proceedings of the Sixteenth International Congress for Analytical Psychology*, edited by Lyn Cowan (Einsiedeln: Daimon Verlag, 2006), pp. 93–155.
5 Ulrike Vosswinckel, *Freie Liebe und Anarchie: Schwabing-Monte Verità. Entwürfe gegen das etablierte Leben* (Munich: Allitera Verlag, 2009), p. 163.
6 Bair, *Jung: A Biography*, p. 412.
7 Vosswinckel, *Freie Liebe und Anarchie*, p. 161.
8 Bair, *Jung: A Biography*, p. 412.
9 Ibid., p. 412; see also Paul Kugler in "Walking in the Footsteps of Eranos," *Barcelona 04*, p. 100.
10 Erik Hornung, *Das Abenteuer Eranos* (see www.eranos-ascona.ch). On Eranos, see also "Walking in the Footsteps of Eranos," pp. 93–155.
11 Sybille Rosenbaum-Kroeber, "Was ist Eranos und wer war Olga Fröbe-Kapteyn?" in Harald Szeemann (ed.), *Monte Verità: Der Berg der Wahrheit* (Milan, 1978), p. 117.
12 Vosswinckel, *Freie Liebe und Anarchie*, p. 163; Thomas Mann variously portrayed Derleth in his work, for instance, as a poet and prophet in *Doctor Faustus*.
13 Christine Derleth, *Das Fleischlich-Geistige: Meine Erinnerungen an Ludwig Derleth* (Bellnhausen über Gladenbach: Hinder und Deelmann, 1973); see also Vosswinckel, *Freie Liebe und Anarchie*, p. 163.
14 Sybille Rosenbaum-Kroeber, "Was ist Eranos und wer war Olga Fröbe-Kapteyn?" p. 117. Jung had met Leo Baeck, the Berlin rabbi, at Keyserling's *Schule der Weisheit* ("School of Wisdom"). Baeck gave a talk at the 1947 Eranos conference. See also Kugler, "Walking in the Footsteps of Eranos," p. 105. In the same year, Olga Fröbe-Kapteyn invited Alice Bailey, who headed a movement in New York called the Arcane School, to start a "School for Spiritual Research" with her, for which she wanted to make her land available. This plan never materialised, however. Two years later, the two women went their separate ways; see Bair, *Jung: A Biography*, p. 412.
15 Otto was taken ill and could not accept Fröbe's invitation, leaving his colleague Friedrich Heiler to stand in for him.
16 Jung's first lecture was titled "Der psychologische Prozess der Individuation" ("The Psychological Process of Individuation"), his last one "Über Synchronizität" ("On Synchronicity").
17 Adolf Portmann, "Eranos," *Du, Schweizerische Monatszeitschrift* (Zurich, April 1955), p. 8.
18 Jolande Jacobi, "Eranos – vom Zuhörer aus gesehen," *Du, Schweizerische Monatszeitschrift* (Zurich, April 1955), p. 51ff.
19 Aniela Jaffé, *Jung and Eranos* (Zurich: Spring Publications, 1977), p. 202.
20 Brody, "Das Eranos-Jahrbuch," *Du, Schweizerische Monatszeitschrift* (Zurich, April 1955), p. 51.
21 Gershom Scholem, "Identifizierung und Distanz: ein Rückblick," *Eranos-Jahrbuch 1979*, vol. 48, eds. Adolf Portmann and Rudolf Ritsema (Frankfurt am Main, 1981), p. 463f.

22 Mircea Eliade, "Encounters at Eranos," in Joseph Campbell (ed.), *Spiritual Disciplines: Papers from the Eranos Yearbooks*, Bollingen Series XXX, vol. 4 (Princeton, NJ: Princeton University Press, 1960), p. xvii.

23 Ximena de Angulo Roelli, Letter to William McGuire, 5 March 1979, cited in Bair, *Jung: A Biography*, p. 413.

24 William McGuire, *Bollingen: An Adventure in Collecting the Past*, Bollingen Series (Princeton, NJ: Princeton University Press, 1982), p. 21; see also Bair, *Jung: A Biography*, p. 799, n. 146.

25 For example, she helped the former lawyer Vladimir Rosenbaum out of a serious existential crisis after his cold-blooded rejection by Jung. In 1934, Jung had consulted Rosenbaum as a legal counsel, in order to incorporate some legal "loopholes" into a document that would mitigate, if not prevent, the "Nazification of the Statutes" of the forthcoming meeting of the International Society for Psychotherapy in Bad Nauheim. Rosenbaum worked on the statutes, which even "outwitted their authors." Rosenbaum's revision meant that Jewish psychoanalysts were able to maintain their professional status by becoming members of the international organisation. However grateful Jung was to Rosenbaum for his excellent legal services, he turned his back on him when Rosenbaum found himself in a legal predicament a few years later. In 1937, after spending several months in prison, Rosenbaum visited Jung to ask whether he could attend the meetings of the Psychological Club in Zurich. Jung, who had originally agreed, allowed the other members to change his mind. In the end, Rosenbaum fell victim to Jung's infamous assertion: "Auch das verwundete Tier verkriecht sich, um zu verenden" (Even the wounded animal hides to die). Rosenbaum later settled in Ascona, where he regained a foothold in life, not least with the financial support of Olga Fröbe, who made no secret about her indignation at Jung's insensitivity. She subtly exacted "retribution": Rosenbaum was always a guest at the Eranos conferences, and she placed him either next to Jung or in his field of vision. See Bair, *Jung: A Biography*, pp. 261ff.; see further Bair, pp. 448–451; see also nn. 95 and 96 in chapter 29, pp 796f. See also Peter Kamber, *Geschichte zweier Leben: Wladimir Rosenbaum und Aline Valangin* (Zurich: Limmat Verlag, 1990).

26 Bair, *Jung: A Biography*, p. 470.

27 Hans Thomas Hakl, *Der verborgene Geist von Eranos: Eine alternative Geistesgeschichte des 20. Jahrhunderts* (Bretten: Scientia Nova, Verlag Neue Wissenschaft, 2001), p. 181.

28 See esp. www.eranosfoundation.org/history; see also Robert Hinshaw in *Barcelona 04, Edges of Experience: Memory and Emergence, Proceedings of the Sixteenth International Congress for Analytical Psychology*, p. 94.

29 Hakl, *Der verborgene Geist von Eranos*, p. 179.

30 The full title of the 1938 conference was "Gestalt und Kult der Großen Mutter" ("The Form and Cult of the Great Mother").

31 Fröbe told Mary Mellon that she had made "the greatest psychological experience of my life" in Crete, where she had been overwhelmed by panic and fever because she identified with the "Great Mother." The experience, she reported, had provided her with essential insights; see Hakl, *Der verborgene Geist von Eranos*, p. 182,

32 Jolande Jacobi in *Du, Schweizerische Monatszeitschrift* (Zurich, April 1955), p. 52.

33 Hakl, *Der verborgene Geist von Eranos*, p. 184.

34 An unfortunate circumstance arose in connection with Fröbe's research: She was investigated by the FBI in 1941 and suspected of being a German agent since she travelled on a German passport; she had already attracted negative attention in 1939 for carrying "folders filled with mysterious pictures." When questioned, she stated that she had travelled to the USA to pursue "iconographic activities." When the Mellons declined further support, Fröbe contacted the Rockefeller Foundation, the American

Council of Learned Societies, as well as several professors at Princeton and Yale, to fund her "Eranos-USA" project. Above all, she needed funds to pay for the numerous pictures she had purchased on credit. In 1942, the FBI's "Fröbe file" thwarted the first attempt to establish the Bollingen Foundation; see Bair, *Jung: A Biography*, p. 479f.

35 See Bair, *Jung: A Biography*, p. 575. Now began a fruitful cooperation, spanning 25 years, between the Bollingen Foundation and Pantheon Books; the latter was run by Kurt Wolff.

36 Ibid., p. 577.

37 Paul Mellon (whose wife Mary had already died in 1946) decided to discontinue the foundation in 1967. Its long-standing president, John Barrett, retired. Although some of its publications were successful, they had always relied on Mellon's funding.

38 Since her collection was not given enough attention, except by Erich Neumann, Mircea Eliade and Alfons Rosenberg, Fröbe first handed over the originals to the Warburg Institute in London and left only duplicates to the C.G. Jung Institute in Zurich and the Bollingen Foundation in New York. Eventually, the C.G. Jung Foundation in New York acquired the entire collection, which was expanded further by Olga Fröbe, C.G. Jung, Jolande Jacobi and Jesse E. Fraser. See Hakl, *Der verborgene Geist von Eranos*, p. 372. Today, the *Encyclopedia of Archetypal Symbolism* makes the archive accessible to the wider public. See *Encyclopedia of Archetypal Symbolism*, ed. Beverly Moon (Boston: Shambhala, 1991) and George R. Elder, *The Body: An Encyclopedia of Archetypal Symbolism* (Boston: Shambhala, 1996).

39 C.G. Jung, Letter to Olga Fröbe, 18 September 1942; see Hakl, *Der verborgene Geist von Eranos*, p. 372.

40 Olga Fröbe, Letter to Ximena de Angulo, 7 September 1951; see Hakl, *Der verborgene Geist von Eranos*, p. 285.

41 Gershom Scholem, "Identifizierung und Distanz: ein Rückblick," *Eranos-Jahrbuch 1979*, vol. 48, eds. Adolf Portmann and Rudolf Ritsema (Frankfurt am Main: Insel Verlag, 1981), p. 463.

42 The titles of Neumann's lectures from 1948 to 1951 were "Der mystische Mensch" (1948), "Die mythische Welt und der Einzelne" (1949), "Zur psychologischen Bedeutung des Ritus" (1950) and "Kunst und Zeit" (1951).

43 Erich Neumann, Letter to Olga Fröbe-Kapteyn; see *Kreativität des Unbewussten*, p. 188f.

44 Ibid., p. 188f.

45 It was actually a larger collection of papers, a kind of biography, as I learned from Rali Loewenthal-Neumann in conversation.

46 Olga Fröbe-Kapteyn, *Eranos-Jahrbuch 1960*, vol. XXIX, *Mensch und Gestaltung* (Zurich: Rhein-Verlag, 1961), p. 7.

47 When Olga Fröbe-Kapteyn died on 25 April 1962, Adolf Portmann took over as director of the Eranos conferencee (her last will had appointed him as her heir and successor). Ill health prevented him from attending the conferences after 1980. He died in 1982.

48 Adolf Portmann, "Zum Gedenken an Erich Neumann," *Eranos Jahrbuch 1960*, *Mensch und Gestaltung*, p. 10.

Part III

Reading Neumann's works

Chapter 10

"The Transparency and Transcendence of the Earth"[1]

Spiritualising a problematic concept

Neumann's discourse proceeds in pairs of opposites. It is quite possible that C.G. Jung's *Septem Sermones ad Mortuous*, also structured in terms of strict polarities, influenced Neumann's analytical thinking (Neumann was among a select group of readers to receive a copy of the manuscript for review; see Chapter 4). He provides a cogent explanation of his approach and methodology in his 1953 Eranos lecture, "The Meaning of the Earth Archetype for Modern Times":

> To our conscious minds the archetypal realm appears in terms of the differentiation of groups or symbolic opposites … It is in terms of opposites and of the multiplicity of qualities that we experience what really exists in the form of a unity of opposites beyond all qualities.
>
> (MEA, p. 165–166)

Neumann's *The Origins and History of Consciousness* (published in German in 1949) traces the basic pairs of opposites to their original unity: His starting point is the unity of the intertwined "World Parents" (*Ureltern*), who are separated by discerning consciousness (OHC, p. 31). As consciousness develops, heaven and earth are separated, as are above and below. Heaven is associated with certain characteristics (e.g. "light, bright, male, active"), earth with others (e.g. "below, heavy, dark, feminine and passive") (MEA, p. 180).

The following oppositions, derived from the "primordial couple" (*Urpaar*), are fundamental to Neumann's thinking:

Mother (maternal) – father (paternal)
Woman – man
Nature, body – spirit, mind
Bassar, Sarx, flesh – Ruach, Pneuma, spirit
Unconscious – consciousness
Introversion – extraversion
Moon – sun
Affect, instinct – reason

Several attributes belong to the symbolism of the earth archetype: this-worldly, substance-based, material and immovable, silent. The symbolism of heaven also includes the following attributes: the hereafter, unbodily, immaterial, spiritual, moving, loud (MEA, p. 178).

Another pair of opposites central to Neumann's thinking from the outset is the polarity between heaven and earth. This chapter traces his prolonged fascination with these opposing concepts. It also considers how this polarity evolved in his theory of culture, which rested on various theological motifs, and to what extent this fundamental polarity formed the basis of his ethical deliberations on good and evil (e.g. in *Depth Psychology and a New Ethic*, also published in 1949 like *The Origins and History of Consciousness*).

Heaven – earth: This pair of symbols is located entirely in the mythological-archetypal realm. In keeping with Neumann's intellectual reorientation in 1938, it underwent a significant transformation: His core themes, originally focusing on Jewish questions, now became more generalised and more secularised. As I have explained in previous chapters, the concept of "earth" for Neumann was located in a context highly charged with anti-Semitic stereotypes, imperialist power aspirations and Zionist plans for the future. Jung's theory of the collective unconscious, while providing his Jewish students with orientation, also proved an obstacle: In 1938, Jung retracted his theorem of an inalienable connection between the unconscious and the earth, soil and homeland (see Chapter 7).

After arriving in Tel Aviv, Neumann wrote to Jung sometime in June or July 1934. His (undated) letter is strongly tinged by his impressions of his new surroundings and by his unguarded response to them. It also reveals just how powerfully psychic images had taken hold of him since his arrival:

> I did not, by any means, come here with any illusions, but what I have found extraordinary was that I haven't found a "people" here with whom I fundamentally feel I belong … On the other hand, though, the landscape gripped me in such a compelling way that I couldn't ever have thought possible. Precisely from the place I hadn't expected it, a vantage point emerged. I haven't fully made sense of this. Anyhow, as you prophesied, the anima has gone to ground. She made an appearance all nice and brown, strikingly African, even more impenetrable in me, domineering—with a sisterly relationship to many animals … That this gives me strength, however, I feel strongly. Even dreams are confirming it.
>
> (JNC, p. 16)

In remarking that "the anima has gone to ground … brown … a relationship to many animals," Neumann echoes Jung's comments on Nietzsche's *Zarathustra* (Chapter 6). After coming to Zurich in 1933, to pursue his training analysis with Jung, Neumann had attended Jung's seminar on Zarathustra until May 1934.

In line with Jung's position (expressed as early as 1918) that a difference existed between the Western and the Jewish unconscious (see Chapters 4, 5 and

7), Neumann now turned his attention to the unconscious contents of Jewish culture. Thus, in 1934, he began working on a two-volume manuscript titled *Tiefenpsychologie des jüdischen Menschen* ("The Depth Psychology of the Jewish Person"), whose completion occupied him until 1938. He never consented to publication during his lifetime. This work has, however, since been published as *The Roots of Jewish Consciousness* (2019). Closer scrutiny reveals obvious connections between this early work and Neumann's later major work. *Roots* served him as a "quarry" for his later cultural theory and metapsychology. Only a single statement by Neumann about his reasons for not publishing the manuscript has survived: It occurs in an essay by Gustav Dreifuss, who had emigrated to Israel in 1959 and had worked with Neumann on his dreams:

> At that time, I criticised him [Neumann—A.L.] in a dream for not intending to publish his manuscript on Jewish material, which I considered important. In the dream, he replied: "I'm an engineer, I can't publish that." When we discussed the dream, his attitude was that publishing these thoughts would be possible solely if he was completely sure of the Jewish sources. Being sure meant not only knowing the language of the original text completely, but also being closer to the way of life of the Jewish ancestors than would ever be possible for someone (like himself) raised in German culture. He had neither the strength nor the possibility to immerse himself in the Jewish material and the Hebrew language in the manner required for many years.[2]

In the first part of *Roots*, titled *Beiträge zur Tiefenpsychologie des jüdischen Menschen und zum Problem der Offenbarung* ("Contributions to the Depth Psychology of the Jewish Person and the Problem of Revelation"),[3] Neumann pursues the basic claim that the Jewish experience of exile, the so-called galut, is a story about losing the productive correspondence between consciousness and the unconscious. "The paralysis of dogmatic Judaism," as well as inner alienation, stifled the creative forces: The manuscript may also be read as a depth-psychological examination of various stereotypes common in both Zionist and anti-Semitic political discourse at the time: the "rootless and homeless Jew," the "rational Jew," the "Jews alienated from nature and earth," the "instinctless Jew" and the "nomadicising Jew."

Already early on Neumann believed that the political situation in Germany posed a considerable threat for the country's Jewish population. Further assimilation seemed impossible—which, he observed, had once been different. Thus, the "western world, for the assimilating Jew, meant humanism in the sense of a universal human consciousness. It meant transnationalism and internationalism" (Roots I, p. 5). He speaks of the "surging hatred of the Jews." This was "isolating the Jewish people … and eliminating them from western communal life, to the point where Balaam's long-forgotten sentence is once again true: 'Here, a people, alone-in-security it dwells, among the nations it does not need to come-to-reckoning'" (ibid., p. 9).[4]

Neumann's assessment of Germany's political reality during the early 1930s placed him on maximum alert: His *Beiträge zur Tiefenpsychologie des jüdischen Menschen* (i.e. *Roots*) sought to counter the impending annihilation of his people, from a vantage point that measures historical developments on a scale of centuries. This view might be indebted to Neumann's orientation towards various works of cultural philosophy that he held in high regard.[5] It might, however, also stem from his perspective on his own Jewish tradition, namely as someone who knew—to adapt a phrase coined by Moritz Goldstein—"that the Jewish people had lived on the thin ground of Scripture for 2,000 years."[6]

Shifting to Jung's perspective, Neumann observes that a full-scale Western process is directed against the Jews:

> Tragically, however, the process in which the western world finds itself presupposes a reconnection with the pre-Christian, that is, the pagan collective unconscious ... The western world must become conscious of its pre-Christianized layers.
>
> (Roots I, p. 6)

He feared that this could "lead to an elimination of the Jewish element" (Roots I, p. 6) and believed that the chances for the regeneration of the Jewish people were very slim:

> Whereas all other peoples continue to exist, and have time to undergo such developments, the rootless and homeless Jew faces the danger of not surviving this age. And there is a danger that Judaism will perish as a result.
>
> (Roots I, p. 6)

Neumann's remedy for Judaism is "radical self-contemplation." He considers this the weapon needed most urgently by the Jewish people in its struggle against anti-Semitism:

> And yet the poisonous wave of these other peoples' hatred of the Jews, which threatens to corrode the psychic structure of the Jew, can be averted only if Judaism places itself on maximum alert, and only if it establishes, through radical self-contemplation, a meaningful connection with its deepest levels.
>
> (Roots I, p. 9)

Only individuals, not collectives, can achieve "self-contemplation." For Neumann, only the individual is able to counteract the threatening destruction of the spiritual and psychic identity of the Jewish people, by engaging in a process of inner transformation. And yet, according to Neumann's theory (see later), this also depends on the individual, insofar as he is a "Great Individual," that is, functions as a precursor and as a pioneer of later collective transformations.

The process of transformation, in Neumann's eyes, begins by accounting for the lifelessness of the Jewish people due to centuries of exile. This had alienated the Jews from natural processes while never-ending persecution and centuries-long ghettoisation in foreign countries had impoverished their instincts.[7] Exile had severed the Jewish people from its deep layers, which he considered closely related to the Mosaic religion. Therefore, "radical self-contemplation" goes along with the search for the religious foundations of Judaism, beyond "dogmatic Judaism" (Roots I, p. 6), which no longer promised any invigoration. The reasons for this "paralysis" of Jewish theology—here, Neumann's own approach becomes evident—include the splitting of consciousness, in which the male principle predominates, from the collective unconscious, which he attributes to the maternal-feminine principle. The "banished" feminine archetype becomes malignant, and thus impedes creativity and causes unproductiveness and weakening:

> With the destruction of the Second Temple and the expulsion of Israel into the galut, it is said that the *Shekhinah*, the indwelling presence of God in Israel, the personified feminine aspect of the deity, also goes into the galut and wails for reunion. This symbol seems to contain the key problem of all Jewish existence. For this separation of the lamenting and banished *Shekhinah* from the divine, this separation of the lamenting and banished Israel from YHWH, symbolizes and expresses the disastrous fact that galut-Judaism is disconnected from its creative primal ground.
>
> (Roots I, p. 133)

Neumann addresses this "key problem of all Jewish existence" historically: He returns to the psyche of the ancient Jewish world, to "self-contemplation" and to the origin of the unfolding YHWH–human relationship. This return seeks to "reveal basic psychological attitudes" and to "work out forms of psychic behavior and outlooks on life" that are "related to the unconscious problem of the modern Jew" (Roots I, p. 10).

Quite surprisingly, Neumann depicts the ancient Jewish person as lacking any aspiration to transcendence and, instead, as being endowed with an evident "Dionysian tendency" (Roots I, p. 16). He describes the Jewish tribes' "attachment to the earth and the hereafter" as follows:

> Greatly simplified, this psychology reveals a highly belligerent, cruel, and primitive group, whose defining characteristic is that it is powerfully possessed by the earth. Quite possibly, this hunger for land corresponds to the transition from nomadic life to a settled, agricultural life.
>
> (Roots I, p. 15)

Neumann finds evidence for this assumption in a biblical metaphor:

> A fanatical attachment to the land is evident in all ancient accounts, a determination to claw oneself into the earth and cling to its fertility. Several fundamental motifs emerge repeatedly in these narratives: fertility of the soil, the

land of milk and honey, fertility of the herds, fertility of the tribes, becoming like the dust of the earth, like the stars of heaven, like the ocean sand.

(Roots I, pp. 15–16)

For Neumann, the Bible provides unique information about the worldliness of the Jewish people, a characteristic for which he coined the term "earth axis." Thus:

It has always been the incomparable charm and awe-inspiring greatness of the Bible—disregarding its determinative religious content for a moment— that it is governed by a powerful closeness to the earth, an undistorted view of good and evil, which no other people or time in the world knows.

(Roots I, p. 36)

Based on the "modern research" available to him at the time, Neumann questions the affinity of the Jewish tribes with this world in depth-psychological terms. He cites Baudissin's *Kyrios als Gottesname im Judentum und seine Stelle in der Religionsgeschichte* (1929), which observes that "for all Semites, with the sole exception of the Hebrews, male and female deities appear next to each other" (Roots I, p. 40).

The elimination of the feminine principle from the cult, that is, the absence of a female deity, led to its unconscious projection onto earth. This subsequently became the Holy Land, in which *Eretz Israel* ("Land of Israel") now occupies that place and importance in the Jewish soul that the Mother Goddess has for other peoples. The immense significance of the Holy Land and its incarnation— Zion—in Jewish history and in the history of ideas is well known. According to Neumann, however, the actual meaning of the Holy Land for the psychology of the Jewish people had never received appropriate consideration. "For better or worse, the earth and the Holy Land become a highly active and destiny-determining partner of the Jew, who owes his vitality to the projection of the archetypal mother-image onto the earth" (Roots I, p. 41).

This aspect of the Jewish people, which belongs to this side of the world on the one hand, yet lacks a Mother Goddess on the other, experiences its compensatory corrective through the "charismatic individual," the Jewish prophet, whose "prototype" is Moses.[8] In this regard, Neumann considers the dynamics of the "YHWH–earth tension" to be extremely creative. These now unfold between the Dionysian, nature-oriented affirmation of the people's life and the ascetic, admonishing figure of the lonely prophet, who criticises the people's moral constitution. Historically, these dynamics are first documented by the "Revelation on Sinai," which, "like all forms of revelation, must be seen as an irruption of the collective unconscious" (Roots I, p. 19).

What appears in prophecy as a salubrious tendency to limit the "supremacy of the earth" is nothing other than the compensatory function of the unconscious, in what constitutes an attempt to abolish the regressive "*participation mystique* with earth" (Roots I, p. 41). The prophet is the mediator of YHWH's *ruach* (spirit).[9]

Here, Neumann follows Rudolf Otto's concept of the numinous. In doing so, he emphasises that Otto's "basic idea of the numinous is the final word on the matter in all religious scholarship." He adds that "after emphasizing the numinous character of the *ruach*, Otto agrees entirely with our view when he writes":

> The intuition of the contrast between *ruach* and *bassar, pneuma* and *sarx*— "spirit and flesh"—is the basic intuition. It underlies the entire biblical world of feeling and is its universal condition, its primary *a priori*.
>
> (Roots I, p. 39)

This *ruach* now follows the prophet's "unconditional willingness to follow the call of God's inner voice." This, he adds, "always includes the willingness to abandon all natural, worldly, earthly ties" (Roots I, p. 45). Neumann describes this willingness as an "existential form of an eschatology that is ready for the call" (ibid.). Now this considerably heightens the tension between a rootedness in nature and transcendence in Jewish existence. Another effect of YHWH's numinous call is that, contrary to a neurotic "escapism" (ibid., p. 46), which may also be found in mysticism, it grows from "primary introversion" and strives to "*enter the world*" (ibid.; original emphasis). The "ensuing flooding of consciousness leaves no room for any doubt whatsoever, that is, for any autonomous activity of consciousness" (ibid.).

Here, at the very latest, arises the question about the distinction between "true" and "false prophecy" (Roots I, pp. 47ff.). Neumann draws attention to the "harsh rejection of all soothsaying, divination" already in biblical times, when an awareness of this problem of discernment became manifest. He characterises a prophet's "authenticity" by referring to the psychologically significant phenomenon of the "strange fusion of inner revelation, as the revelation of YHWH, and the simultaneous emphasis on consciousness" (ibid., p. 47). One example is Moses, whose reaches the highest level of distinction as a prophet, since he receives "the revelation while fully conscious and by day" (ibid., p. 48).

Other than a highly alert consciousness, the prophet's announcement of impending doom is another measure of his authenticity. The fact that a prophet must proclaim misfortune to his people—against his own wishes and also theirs— is sufficient evidence for Neumann that "the revelation compensates for the prophet's conscious situation, and especially for the people's" (Roots I, p. 47):

> A true prophet is only someone to whom are whispered the contents of the collective unconscious, the inherent activity of which determines the historical process. This is the deepest foundation for the idea of YHWH as the God who determines history.
>
> (Roots I, p. 47)

Neumann's *Roots of Jewish Consciousness* conceptualises a history of religious decline, which leads him to describe the once-so-vibrant YHWH–earth tension as infertile. This, in other words, means that the originally intact relationship between earth and spirit, earth and God, earth and heaven, or, symbolically, between the female and male principles has become dysfunctional. The associative linkage between the feminine, introversion and silence is significant here as the psychological basis for developing inwardness:

> Of particular importance in this respect is the loss of the feminine side of consciousness in favor of radical masculinization, an extreme emphasis on active and rational components. This is particularly evident with regard to introversion. Originally, Judaism had consciously emphasized an inner, feminine stance toward the irradiating impulse and the word of God. This stance had been symbolized most strongly in the image of the people as the bride of God. This attitude of stillness, maintaining silence and preparing oneself for inner experience, poses no contradiction to the active assimilation and realization that are then demanded, but this attitude now began to disappear. Even introversion became active, speculative, and rational, geared toward working through what was found, rather than being expanded by a new thing breaking in.
>
> (Roots I, p. 129)

In his foreword to *The Origins and History of Consciousness*, Jung wrote that Neumann "arrives at conclusions and insights which are among the most important ever to be reached in this field" (OHC, p. xiv). Here, in one of his early major works from the 1940s, Neumann further develops the insights gained from examining his own Jewish tradition on a general anthropological, that is, religious-psychological and cultural-theoretical basis. Jung, in turn, identifies the juncture at which Neumann's fundamental theoretical orientation begins as "where I unwittingly made landfall on the new continent long ago, namely the realm of *matriarchal symbolism*" (p. xiii; original emphasis).

In *Origins and History*, Neumann develops the "YHWH–earth tension" previously explored in *The Roots of Jewish Consciousness* into the following principles of opposites: masculinity, father, heaven, spirit, consciousness versus Great Mother, femininity, fertility, earth, intuition, emotion, the unconscious. Consciousness is what distinguishes below from above, inside from outside. Its progressive development is represented symbolically by the hero myth: "Thus the hero is the archetypal forerunner of mankind in general. His fate is the pattern in accordance with which the masses of humanity must live" (OHC, p. 131).

Neumann describes the "hero's journey" as a path of consciousness that emancipates itself in equal measure from the maternal and the paternal principle. The hero acts as an intermediary between these two principles. Emancipation, for the hero, means liberating himself from attachment, entanglement and containment. In mythological language, this involves fighting a dragon, in a test the hero must pass if he is to succeed.[10] Unless the transpersonal forces constellate themselves, cultural-historical progress, which needs to be considered in terms of discontinuity and stems from the "irruption of irrationality," and which overcomes tradition and looks to the future, remains inconceivable. The hero archetype manifests itself in the form of the "Great Individual," who appears in various guises: a founder of religion, a culture hero, a reformer and an artist. He manages to travel the archetypal heroic path and thus contributes to renewing or surmounting a rigidified system. The Great Individual, however, is also endangered, since he is

> always and pre-eminently the man with immediate inner experience who, as seer, artist, prophet, or revolutionary, sees, formulates, sets forth, and realizes the new values, the "new images." His orientation comes from the "voice," from the unique, inner utterance of the self, which has all the immediacy of a "dictate." Herein lies the extraordinary orientation of this type of individual … The important thing … is that the archetypal canon is always created and brought to birth by "eccentric" individuals.
>
> (OHC, pp. 375–376)

Paradigmatically, behind the Great Individual stands Moses, the prophet; behind the mission fulfilled by that Great Individual stands the "existential form of an eschatology that is ready for the call" (Roots I, p. 45). This significant transposition—of the prophetic figure into the secular world—clearly suggests that his earlier *Roots of Jewish Consciousness* served Neumann as a "quarry" for his later work. Thus, some passages and footnotes in *Origins and History* explicitly refer to the Jewish path of development, for instance, when Neumann refers to "patriarchal castration" and the "Isaac complex" (OHC, p. 189). His corresponding footnote reads as follows:

> Isaac's father-son psychology is characteristic for the Jew, in whom it is still found to this day as the Isaac complex. For him the law and the old serve as a refuge from the demands of reality. The law becomes "Abraham's bosom," and the Torah a sort of masculine spiritual womb from whose clutches nothing new can be born.
>
> (OHC, p. 189)

Patriarchal castration occurs when the father—a transpersonal figure in Neumann's thinking—"captures and destroys the son's consciousness" from beyond and above (OHC, p. 187). This father is represented as "the binding force of the old law, the old religion, the old morality, the old order; as conscience, convention, tradition, or any other spiritual phenomenon that seizes hold of the son and obstructs his progress into the future" (ibid.).

Neumann carefully distinguishes patriarchal from matriarchal castration. The latter stems from the emotional side, as the "paralyzing grip of inertia or an invasion by instinct," whereas that which castrates the father is directed against "all contents capable of conscious realization, a value, an idea, a moral canon" (OHC,

p. 187). Thus, "whereas matriarchal castration is orgiastic, the other tends toward asceticism" (ibid., p. 189).

While Neumann identified patriarchal castration (without, however, employing the term itself) in *The Roots of Jewish Consciousness* as symptomatic of the Jewish person, whom he considered severed from the living source of the unconscious, he generalises this problem in *The Origins and History of Consciousness*, where it becomes the basic problem of modern Western people (see Chapter 14).

Thus, the radical self-questioning evident in his earlier work has given way to an extensive cultural critique of the psychological problems of modern people. Interestingly, many anti-Semitic stereotypes aimed at Jews now emerge in this cultural critique as signatures of modernity. Neumann's treatment of anti-Semitism might arise from his realisation that anti-Semitism had projected the shadow of modernity onto the Jews. Some of these stereotypes, now appearing as symptoms, include the "possessed character of our financial and industrial magnates" (OHC, p. 391), as well as the overemphasis on consciousness, the ego and reason, the loss of instinct, the rigidity of consciousness, the identification of the spirit with the intellect and the impoverishment of the feminine aspect. Neumann's substantiates the central shadow motif—the symptom of "losing one's feet under the ground"—by referring to the "heavenly journey," a thoroughly ambiguous metaphor, which recalls the anti-Semitic stereotype of the "air man" on the one hand, while representing a heretical allusion to Christian beliefs on the other (ibid., p. 382).

Transformation and renewal, however, come from the "Great Individual." Neumann's entire cultural theory and its developmental dynamics hinge on this figure. He conceives of the creative hero's non-adaptation to the cultural canon transmitted by the fathers in terms of discontinuity. The future dimension breaks open, and the hero, through his actions, prepares "to change the face of the world" (OHC, p. 220). In Neumann's final analysis, the hero

> is one who brings the new and shatters the fabric of old values, namely the father-dragon which, backed by the whole weight of tradition and the power of the collective, ever strives to obstruct the birth of the new.[11]
>
> (OHC, p. 377)

Neumann's later writings, especially his Eranos lectures, are characterised by him not contenting himself with a negative assessment of modern living conditions. Instead, he prefers to contemplate the possibility of human transformation and redemption. He is deeply convinced that potential inner transformation resides as a force within the individual. Concurring with Jung, Neumann believes that this potential is linked to the productive, synthesising effect of the *transcendent function* (MEA, p. 223).[12] This mediates between "bright" consciousness and the unconscious, which lies hidden in mystery and "darkness." The third symbol to appear in each case refers pictorially to the absence of the collective, which may correct or unhinge a previous cultural canon (*Kultur und Erneuerung*, p. 75f.).[13]

This becomes possible through images and symbols, as he already suggested in *The Origins and History of Consciousness*:

> Images and symbols, being creative products of the unconscious, are so many formulations of the spiritual side of the human psyche ... The inside "expresses" itself by way of the symbol ... Myth, art, religion, and language are all symbolic expressions of the creative spirit in man; in them this spirit takes on objective, perceptible form, becoming conscious of itself *through* man's consciousness of it.
>
> (OHC, p. 369)

In *Krise und Erneuerung* ("Crisis and Renewal"), his last completed work, Neumann develops his basic ideas into a panoramic view, which may be described as an anthropology of the *homo religiosus*. The prerequisite for the creative spirit about which Neumann speaks is "an essential basic structure of the human being ... the ego-self structure of the psyche" (KUE, p. 60). This structure forms a unity in which the "numinous underground" connects with the ego, and thereby produces a fruitful tension between the creative unconscious and active, shaping consciousness. Only here is a creative process able to develop. Neumann formulates this ego-self structure as a religious-numinous dialogue:

> The personal human-creative spirit experiences itself as that upon which the divine gaze has fallen and as that which is instituted by the transpersonal-creative spirit. Man knows that in his own transformation that which is transforming him is also transforming and that through his openness he opens up new paths into the world for the creative spirit. Thus, the ego not only experiences itself as being "meant" by the self, but also understands that it, too, is part of the ego-self unity. This basic dialogical structure of the human psyche, as a mythical image of godlikeness and of the dialogue between the human and the divine, belongs to the basic religious experiences of mankind.
>
> (KUE, p. 65)

In 1953, Neumann opened the Eranos conference with a lecture on *Die Bedeutung des Erdarchetyps für die Neuzeit* ("The Meaning of the Earth Archetype for Modern Times").[14] Exploring one of the major turning points in Western cultural development, the Renaissance, he demonstrates how the creative impetus for change, which could have dissolved the prevailing one-sidedness, became effective. He had attributed a fundamental "revolutionary ingredient" to the Western cultural canon already in *Origins and History* (p. 382).[15] The rise of the Renaissance, and with it the onset of modernity, marks a significant paradigm shift in Western history, which Neumann interprets culturally, psychologically and archetypally. He identifies a compensatory movement of the earth archetype already at the end of the Middle Ages, which, he asserts, were fettered to the patriarchal, spiritual "world of Heaven and of the values of the conscious mind" (MEA, p. 173). This dominance, which affects everything earthly, expressed itself in the "devaluation of the Earth, hostility towards the Earth, fear of the Earth"; it also turned women into the bearers of this negative projection (ibid., p. 171). This incipient compensatory process, emerging "from the unconscious of Western man" (ibid., p. 177),[16] runs parallel to a "decline in the dominance of the archetype of Heaven," which once formed "the backbone of western patriarchal culture" (ibid., p. 180).

Neumann begins his lecture by briefly listing various historical facts part and parcel of the cultural canon. These, he adds, document the newly developed worldview and legitimise the concept of modernity. The Renaissance brought the Copernican turn, through which humankind lost the earth as the centre of the world. Once again, by way of compensation, the earth archetype grew stronger and the human being became the "Son of the Earth" (MEA, p. 180). The Renaissance, moreover, marked the beginning of scientific thought while the discovery of uncharted territories was also an expression of this process of transformation.

The earth now appeared as "the richness of a living creature, which no longer stands opposed to a hostile Spirit-Heaven of the deity, but in which the divine essence actually manifests itself" (MEA, p. 177). In this respect, both Leonardo da Vinci's artistic and scientific work presents "the beauty of the earth." Its spiritualisation becomes apparent, and the earth reveals "its creative and psychospiritual countenance (p. 174).

Neumann's Eranos lecture is a highly complex condensate of his previous publications. Thus, we come across the hero archetype, the main theme of *Origins and History*; the problem of evil, his central concern in *Depth Psychology and a New Ethic* (which emerged at the same time); and the Great Mother, the key figure of matriarchy, who had featured prominently already in *Origins*, and to whom Neumann dedicated his comprehensive *The Great Mother*.

It would, however, be mistaken to assume that Neumann simply rehashed his previous thinking in his Eranos lecture. On the contrary, its topics were of central concern, not to mention that the venue—Olga Fröbe-Kaptyn's house in Moscia—played a considerable role. As I have shown (Chapter 9), proceedings at Eranos were presided over by Fröbe-Kaptyn, "generally known behind her back as 'the great mother.'"[17] Daniel Brody, the editor of the Eranos yearbooks, called her "the creatrix spiritus of Eranos."[18] It mattered greatly to Neumann that he could develop an issue central to his encounter with this remarkable woman in the house of "the great mother." Olga Fröbe-Kaptyn, after all, had entrusted him with the project of the "Great Mother," on which she had been working for many years (Chapter 9).

Neumann's lecture combines several intentions: On one level, he criticises modern culture. On another, deeper level, he stages an initiation, which is ultimately followed by a vision of transformation. In this deep layer, the lecture opens a sacred realm for an epistemological and transformational process. In keeping with the allocated two-hour slot, Neumann divided his lecture into two parts. At the end of the first part, which was followed by an interval, Neumann cites a heretical, 17th-century Kabbalistic myth by Nathan of Gaza, a student of Sabbatai Zevi:

> In the beginning of the cosmic process, *En-Sof* withdrew His light into Himself, and there arose that primal space in the center of *En-Sof* in which the worlds take birth. This primal space is full of formless, hylic forces, the *Kelipoth*. The process of the world consists in giving shape to these formless forces, in making something out of them. As long as this has not been done, the primal space, and in particular its lower part, is the stronghold of darkness and evil. It is the "depth of the great abyss" in which the demonic powers have their abode. When, following the Breaking of the Vessels, some sparks of the divine light, radiating from *En-Sof* in order to create forms and shapes in the primal space, fell into the abyss, there also fell the soul of the Messiah, which was embedded in that original divine light. Since the beginning of Creation, this soul has dwelt in the depth of the great abyss, held in the prison of the Kelipoth, the realm of darkness. Together with this most holy soul at the bottom of the abyss there dwell the "serpents" which torment it and try to seduce it. To these "serpents" the "holy serpent" is given over which is the Messiah—for has not the Hebrew word for Messiah, *Nahash*, the same numerical value as the word for Messiah, *Mashiah*? Only in the measure in which the process of the *Tikkun* of all the world brings about the selection of good and evil in the depth of the primal space, is the soul of the Messiah freed of its bondage. When the process of perfection, on which this soul is at work in its "prison" and for which it struggles with the "serpents" or "dragons," is completed—which, however, will not be the case before the end of the *Tikkun* generally—the soul of the Messiah will leave its prison and reveal itself to the world in an earthly incarnation.[19]

This "fate of the Redeemer's soul," as a fettered messiah who leads the life of a "holy serpent" in the "'great abyss' in which the demonic powers have their abode" among the other serpents, is truly a counter-image to the resurrected one, who has overcome death.[20] This "holiest soul" has not yet completed its path of purification, but must instead struggle, against serpents and dragons, for its liberation in a "process of perfection." For Neumann, the "redeemer serpent," and the serpents of evil besetting it, represent "two aspects of the same thing." "The emergence of the Earth archetype of the Great Mother brings with it the emergence of her companion, the Great Serpent" (MEA, p. 197). Neumann here refers to Jung and the importance of the *serpens Mercurii* ("the ambiguous serpent") in the "magnum opus" of alchemy. "The serpent," he adds, "is a primeval symbol of the Spirit, as primeval and ambiguous as the Spirit itself" (ibid.). In the Christian context, it represents the devil, the *Lord of the world*, the redeemer's antagonist. As such, it marks the schism that runs between above and below, good and evil, heaven and hell. For the Christian members of his audience, Neumann's lecture was certainly provocative, not least because he emphasised the "not-yet" of redemption by referring to this particular Kabbalistic text. The "holiest serpent" represents the hero archetype of modernity that has been banished from the world of the Great Mother. Like all previous epoch-making hero archetypes, it leads the work of redemption and liberation, and is thus, as the "forerunner of mankind," "the pattern in accordance with which the masses of humanity must live" (OHC, p. 131). From an iconographic standpoint, placing one's "foot on the head" of this serpent is a sign of victory (MEA, p. 194).

Neumann associates the symbolic reversal of power relations—from heaven down into the interior of the earth, from patriarchy to matriarchy, from redemption to imprisonment and struggle—with an ethical premise that articulated one of his fundamental concerns in *Depth Psychology and a New Ethic*: "the true goal seems to be not the conquest of evil but its redemption, not a patriarchal victory, but a transformation of the lower worlds" (MEA, p. 195).

Placing a Kabbalistic text at the centre of his deliberations, moreover one that was pivotal to further understanding his concerns, is typical of Neumann's Eranos lectures. In this way, he "rescued" Jewish theologoumena, while enabling a secular cultural-philosophical methodology to shape his work ever since *Depth Psychology and a New Ethic* and *The Origins and History of Consciousness*. Or as Scholem observed in his obituary of November 1960:

> Together with his great works, "The Origins and History of Consciousness" and "The Great Mother," his extensive contributions to the Eranos yearbooks form his noblest spiritual legacy … The proud Jew that he was, in his talks, if memory of our work there [Eranos] serves me well, he never forgot to refer to his Jewish heritage, to which he felt bound and committed.[21]

Neumann incorporated the kabbalistic-heretical text (see earlier) into his own work as a "backbone" contrasting with Western, patriarchal heaven. Nathan of Gaza's myth is Neumann's cornerstone. In his lecture on Mozart's *Magic Flute*, Neumann indicated that this myth could be understood as an initiation project into the world of the Great Mother. The purpose of initiation, so Neumann, is "the extension of the personality, that, since it implies illumination, also includes an extension of consciousness" (MMF, p. 124).[22]

As a student of Jung's, Neumann was very familiar with the "hero's night sea voyage."[23] As the heroic path of masculine consciousness, this journey connoted the feminine as a contrasting principle, from which Neumann was about to depart. In essence, the orientation of initiation mysteries was patriarchal, insofar as this involved overcoming the dark principle of the unconscious. Women, as symbol bearers of darkness and negativity, were excluded from initiations.

> The best-known example of such a mystery rite is the initiation into the Isis mysteries, set forth in the novel of Apuleius, in which the initiate reappears "solidified," that is, "illuminated" and illuminating, after he has traveled

through the underworld and survived the ordeal that led him on a path through the four elements.

(MMF, pp. 123–124)

Analogously to his insights in "On Mozart's Magic Flute," Neumann now seeks to break through this basic principle of "solification" in a three-step process and to introduce a new mystery, "in which the *coniunctio*, the union of the Masculine with the Feminine, occupies the highest level of symbolism, beyond a one-sided matriarchal or patriarchal identification" (MMF, p. 146; italics added).

The *coniunctio* plays a significant role in the history of alchemy. Neumann devotes himself in-depth to this principle in his commentary on Apuleius's tale of *Amor and Psyche* (see Chapter 15). Central to this story is two people's love for one another; their strength and resolve is tested, and after both have experienced death while passing through the mystery, their love culminates in their union. In his Eranos lecture, Neumann transposes this unification or principle of *coniunctio*, which derives from the myth of the two lovers, into the archetypal situation of modernity: Neumann synthesises the tension between heaven and earth, in which the human being is suspended, in a graded sequence of three insights.

The first stage of the mystery, according to Neumann, involves descending into the underworld to the chthonic powers. He speaks of a "descent," which also leads to "transformation" (MEA, p. 200):

Having to descend into the earth really means to fall into hell, and many dreams, images, and fantasies of modern man show the witch-like character of the earth and the devilish nature of its spirit.

(MEA, pp. 201–202)

These chthonic images, he adds, constitute a collective imagery at which the individual must slave away:

Whoever refuses to accept consciously the problem of the earth that burns in us and of the deus *absconditus* that burns in it, ends up in the same abyss through the collective "earthing" of modern man. It is just that he plunges as a lamb in the flock or as a wolf in the pack into the precipitous slide towards collective human catastrophe that characterizes our age.[24]

(MEA, p. 202; original emphasis)

The "terrible character of the psyche," experienced within as a dark mirror of the terrible Great Mother, is quintessential for "transformation" and "breakthrough." For it is only once the "journey through the purifying elements" has been completed that the "transformation of negative affects into positive feelings" can occur (MMF, pp. 154–155). Moreover, only those who are capable of withstanding the terrible side of the Great Mother are able to see the earth in its maternal, elemental character, as a "Great transformer" and "Great creatrix" (MEA, p. 203f.).

The second step is initiation. Here, the Blessed Sacrament, the symbol that allows grasping the struggle between light and darkness in its depth and necessity, reveals itself to the initiates. This symbol is the imprisoned soul of the Redeemer, who fights in the depths against serpents and dragons and thus, figuratively speaking, strives to render them perfect. This is the messiah who is held captive in the depths and who appears in the kabbalistic-heretical text cited by Neumann.

In the third and final stage of the "new mystery," the masculine and feminine are united, whereby the latter principle takes the lead (MMF, p. 153). Assisted by active imagination and a dream, Neumann suggests what this *coniunctio* might look like under the leadership of the feminine principle. Symbolically, stars and sources of light in the earth are crucial here. Already Jung had spoken of *scintillae* (sparks in the earth), while Paracelsus referred to the "inner firmament" (MEA, p. 206): "It is an issue of the recognition of an inner light in the unconscious that becomes distinct in the course of the process of psychic transformation and leads to illumination of the individuality by the lumen naturae" (ibid.).

Importantly, Neumann adds:

> Modern man's outlook has withdrawn from a heaven that no longer casts light on him and has returned to earth and to himself, and precisely because of this light that shines from below out of darkness and depth is becoming more and more valuable and significant to him. If we now consider the emerging, numinous images with the appropriate religious care, this light is a female light from the earth, a light of Sophia. But this light of Sophia is identical with a newly emerging "Spirit of the Earth".
>
> (MEA, p. 207)

For Neumann, the "Sophia" represents the highest realisation of the feminine; he offers a detailed account of this theme in *The Great Mother* (pp. 325–336; see also Chapter 15). In this last stage of the "new mystery," he contrasts the abysmal, destructive drama of the Great Mother (in *Origins and History*, he describes her as the earth archetype and as "the birthplace of consciousness") with the Sophia, the "bearer of light" (MEA, p. 226). She might also be called the hero's "anima," that hero who has descended into the depths. She illumines the darkness, thus eliminating the principle of above and below, which was previously defined by light and darkness. The heavenly light (the illuminating, spiritual principle contrasted previously with the earth's devouring, dark abyss) now becomes the light that is projected into heaven and originates in the spirit of the Sophia (ibid.). Her archetype is the *Shekhinah* ("the dwelling or settling of the divine presence of God"). In *The Roots of Jewish Consciousness*, this "lamenting and banished" figure psychologically symbolises exiled Judaism, which has been severed from its creative origin (Roots I, p. 133). In the "Meaning of the Earth Archetype," Neumann writes:

> Inwardly the psyche, just as outwardly as physis, the reality of the earth, now appears to us as the *coniunctio* of the visible earth with an invisible heaven

… Thus the earth that is transfigured and becomes transparent is not only experienced inwardly and psychically, but just as much as in the actuality of external reality. It seems to me that a significant portion of the new religiosity of modern man consists precisely in this experience of the transparence and transcendence of the earth.

(MEA, p. 216)

The experience of descent, which, as in every mystery, is also an experience of death, is followed by the mystery of birth. The child bears the name "Holy Spirit of the Earth."[25] Here, Neumann establishes—once again in contrast to Christianity—a counter-trinity. This comprises the Great Mother, who appears as Sophia, although in altered guise, a "Spirit-Progenitor as an invisible, transpersonal masculinity" (MEA, p. 222) and the child born of the transparent Sophia-Earth. The messianic serpent fighting in the chthonic abyss could be regarded as its dark twin brother.[26]

Neumann considers interpreting the feminine matrix of consciousness, which originates wholly in creative consciousness, to be one of the "fundamental, future-oriented tasks of individual and cultural therapy in our time."[27] The work of the creative person strikes him as a living example of this new synthesis, a *matriarchal turn* as it were:

"Matriarchal consciousness," a "birth-giving consciousness" in a very specific sense, forms the bridge between the woman and the creative individual—for example, the male artist, in whom the anima, his female side (and with the anima also the matriarchal consciousness), is more strongly accentuated than in the average patriarchal man.

(FF, p. xii)

Poets and writers—as creative individuals—often have the final say in Neumann's writings. They are often assigned particular interpretive authority, as his numerous references to the works of Blake, Goethe, Hölderlin, Gide, Tolstoy, Kafka, Trakl, Hofmannsthal, Benn and Rilke attest. In his 1953 Eranos lecture, Neumann summons Rainer Maria Rilke,[28] whose interpretive remarks on the *Duino Elegies* he cites from the poet's famous letter of 13 November 1925 to his close friend, the Polish translator Witold Hulewicz. Since this letter and Rilke's elegies are doubtless an important source of inspiration for Neumann's thinking, I cite a short passage in conclusion:

Hence, not everything in these parts ought to be maligned and disparaged. And yet, for the sake of its provisional nature, which it shares with us, these phenomena and things need to be understood and transformed by us through our most intimate understanding. Transformed? Yes, indeed, since it is our task to imprint this temporary, frail earth upon ourselves so deeply, so sufferingly and so passionately that its essence will arise invisibly within us.[29]

Notes

1 "The Meaning of the Earth Archetype for Modern Times," trans. Eugene Rolfe and Michael Cullingworth, *Harvest: International Journal for Jungian Studies* 27 (1980) and 29 (1982); cited hereafter as MEA from *The Fear of the Feminine and Other Essays on Feminine Psychology*, ed. William McGuire, Bollingen Series LXI/4 (Princeton, NJ: Princeton University Press, 1994), pp. 165–226.

2 Gustav Dreifuss, "Erich Neumanns jüdisches Bewusstsein," *Analytische Psychologie* 11, no. 3 (1980), pp. 239–247; here esp. p. 240. Dvora Kutzinski has also revealed that Neumann, who regularly gave seminars, raised his work-in-progress for discussion; see Dvora Kutzinski, "Neumann as my Supervisor: An Interview with Dvora Kutzinski," by Henry Abramovitch, *Harvest* 52(2), 2006.

3 From a depth-psychological perspective, revelation is the relationship to the unconscious.

4 The reference is to Numbers 23:9.

5 Epochal concepts denoting the rise and decay of cultures and civilisations were commonplace in the canon of cultural philosophy in the 1920s (i.e. during Neumann's student days). At the time, young intellectuals could acquire the theoretical tools for a non-positivist view of culture focused on larger cultural, historical or philosophical phenomena from many different sources. Three philosophers and historians cited by Neumann may serve as examples: Ernst Cassirer, whose major work in cultural philosophy, *Philosophy of Symbolic Forms*, was published between 1923 and 1929. Jakob Burckhardt, whose highly significant piece of historiography, *The Culture of the Renaissance in Italy*, published as early as 1860, provided a completely new perspective on the Renaissance. Finally, Johan Huizinga, whose momentous *The Waning of the Middle Ages* was published in 1919. Characteristic of Huizinga's historiography was his groundbreaking pictorial-intuitive approach to mentality and cultural history.

6 Moritz Goldstein, "Deutsch-jüdischer Parnass," *Kunstwart*, 25, no. 11 (1 March 1912), cited in Nicolas Berg, *Luftmenschen: Zur Geschichte einer Metapher*, p. 50.

7 Ibid., pp. 170f. and 180.

8 Neumann characterises the figure of Moses as follows: "His prophetic traits are depicted as immeasurably strong, whereas his organizational, law-giving traits are strikingly weak. He is described as an extremely passionate and extraordinarily large-souled man, whose inner span extends from his deadly blow (Ex. 2:12) to his vision of grace (Ex. 33:12–23), from his shyness at being unable to speak (Ex. 4:10) to his claim to out-argue God (Ex. 32:10f.) … is obviously a man of introspection. This trait, as we know, is thoroughly compatible with his role as a leader, indeed as *the* leader of the people" (Roots I, p. 29; original emphasis).

9 At this point, Neumann criticises the Christian theology of his time, which challenged YHWH's spiritual nature. In contrast to reducing the Jewish-theological content by an often anti-Semitic Christian theology, he makes a decisive correction: "The theological concept of the 'Holy Spirit' makes it seem highly desirable to eliminate the principle of the 'spirit of God,' the *ruach* of YHWH, from the Old Testament, although many passages still reveal the primitive notion of being possessed by the *ruach* of God" (Roots I, p. 39). In *The Origins and History of Consciousness*, Neumann criticises "Wotanism": "Thus, with its ecstatic abandon and berserker frenzies of emotion, Wotanism, in its orgiastic as well as its mantic form, lacks the clear eye of the higher knowledge, which was lost through the 'upper castration' performed by Erda. The dark Wotan type of savage huntsman and of Flying Dutchman belong to the retinue of the Great Mother. Behind their spiritual incest there is the old longing for uroboric incest, the death wish that seems so deeply engrained in the Germanic soul" (OHC, pp. 379–380; see further his subsequent discussion of patriarchal and matriarchal castration).

10 For a more extensive discussion of the hero's path, see Chapter 14.

11 Neumann's martial language refers to "Jewish Nietzscheanism" (see Chapter 12).

12 Translator's note: Neumann's footnote refers to Jung's *Psychological Types*, CW 6, § 825–828.

13 Translator's note: Neumann's *Krise und Erneuerung* (Zurich: Rhein Verlag, 1961) has not been translated into English; the translations from this work are therefore mine; cited hereafter as KUE.

14 Cited hereafter as MEA.

15 For Neumann, the secularisation of the individual soul in the Renaissance, for example, bears witness to this.

16 See also his essay "Leonardo da Vinci and the Mother Archetype," collected in Erich Neumann, *Art and the Creative Unconscious: Four Essays*, trans. Ralph Manheim, Bollingen Series LXI (Princeton, NJ: Princeton University Press, 1959), pp. 3–80.

17 Gershom Scholem, "Identifizierung und Distanz, ein Rückblick," *Eranos Yearbook* 48 (1979), eds. Adolf Portmann and Rudolf Ritsema (Frankfurt am Main: Insel Verlag, 1981), p. 463.

18 Daniel Brody, "Das Eranos–Jahrbuch," *Du, Schweizerische Monatszeitschrift* (Zurich, April 1955), p. 51.

19 Gershom Scholem, *Major Trends in Jewish Mysticism* (New York: Schocken Books, 1946), p. 297; see also Neumann's "The Meaning of the Earth Archetype for Modern Times," collected in *The Fear of the Feminine and Other Essays on Feminine Psychology*, pp. 195–196; cited by Neumann with some minor omissions.

20 It is also a counter-image to the previously mentioned symptoms of the "heavenly journey."

21 Gershom Scholem, "Erich Neumann (Nachruf)," *Mitteilungsblatt. Wochenzeitung des Irgun Olej Merkas Europa* 28, 47 (18 November 1960), p. 4; see also *Das neue Israel* 13 (1960/61), p. 313.

22 "On Mozart's Magic Flute," trans. Esther Doughty, *Quadrant* 11, no. 2 (1978), pp. 5–32; cited hereafter as MMF from the revised translation by Boris Matthew in Erich Neumann, *The Fear of the Feminine*, pp. 119–164.

23 Leo Frobenius, *Das Zeitalter des Sonnengottes* (Berlin: Reimer, 1904); C.G. Jung, *Symbole der Wandlung* (1912), revised ed. 1951, CW 5; Helton Godwin Baynes, *Mythology of the Soul, A Research into the Unconscious from Schizophrenic Dreams and Drawings* (London: Baillière, Tindall and Cox, 1940); Joseph Campbell, *The Hero with a Thousand Faces* (Bollingen Foundation, 1949); Neumann, *The Origins and History of Consciousness*.

24 Obviously, the lamb in the herd refers to the Jewish people, while the wolf in the pack denotes the Nazi regime, its followers and executors.

25 Neumann is referring to Jung's studies on the child archetype (CW 9/1).

26 The twin motif also plays an important role in *The Origins and History of Consciousness*.

27 Erich Neumann, *The Fear of the Feminine and Other Essays on Feminine Psychology*, translated by Boris Matthews, Esther Doughty, Eugene Rolfe and Michael Cullingworth, Bollingen Series LXI/4 (Princeton, NJ: Princeton University Press, 1994), p. xii; cited hereafter as FF. The German text was published in 1952. Neumann had referred to the need for "collective and cultural therapy" already in his preface to *The Origins and History of Consciousness*, p. xxiv.

28 Neumann quotes Rilke's late work (*The Duino Elegies* and *The Sonnets to Orpheus*) on various occasions in his writings.

29 Rainer Maria Rilke, *Briefe aus Muzot 1921–1926*, eds. Ruth Sieber-Rilke and Carl Sieber (Leipzig: Insel Verlag, 1935), p. 334f.—Trans.

Chapter 11

"Actualised messianism"

The theological conceptualisation of crisis, identity and transformation

In his last letter to Jung, dated 18 February 1959, Neumann wrote:

> For me in any case, it is a fact that the Jewish historical "development" in this mortal world is becoming ever more problematic for me, the "actualization of messianism" in individuation is becoming ever more crucial.
>
> (JNC, p. 345)

Based on their earlier correspondence, Jung knew what undergirded Neumann's concept of "actualised messianism." Its first extensive treatment formed Part Two of *Tiefenpsychologie des jüdischen Menschen* and was titled "Hasidism and Its Psychological Significance for Judaism" (*Der Chassidismus und seine psychologische Bedeutung für das Judentum*). After completing Part Two in the late 1930s, Neumann sent the manuscript to Jung along with Part One (*Beiträge zur Tiefenpsychologie des jüdischen Menschen und zum Problem der Offenbarung*; "Contributions to the Depth Psychology of the Jewish Person and the Problem of Revelation").

Together with his Kafka studies, his Kafka commentary and his brief discussion of the story of Jacob and Esau, Neumann's two-part manuscript is his only explicitly Jewish work. His thinking at the time was fuelled by a fundamental concern:

> The plight of modern Jews—who like all modern humans lack direction, yet find themselves caught up in an age shaken to its foundations by catastrophes, lacking historical continuity, and plunged into a bottomless sociological pit—compels us to try to reconnect with the past in our own way.
>
> (Roots I, p. 9)

The two volumes cover a range of Jewish themes, including the "founding act of Jewish religion," the revelation on Sinai and the revival movement of Eastern Jewish (Polish and Ukrainian) Hasidism in the 18th and 19th centuries. This chapter considers Neumann's interpretation of the Hasidic movement.

His account—in what constitutes a deliberate countermovement to what he considers to be the sterile forms of Orthodox Judaism—focuses on contents that are accessible through the unconscious and originate in an "intellectual revolution" (Roots I, p. 5). This bears the signature of Hasidism, which "was able to break up the old form of Jewish existence." Its primary goal was to search for a path leading out of the "paralysis of dogmatic Judaism" towards the

> innumerable hidden creative tensions … within the Jew. These tensions must be identified and kindled, so that the old sources of living water will once again flow from the seemingly lifeless stone.
>
> (Roots I, p. 6)

Neumann acknowledges that his approach departs from previous interpretations of Hasidism (Roots I, pp. 1ff.). His intention is threefold: First, to establish whether a genuine historical Jewish source exists and, if it does, whether it might serve as evidence of Jewish inwardness, based on which transformation and thus renewal might be hoped for. Second, Neumann—who is still mindful of running the gauntlet through a thicket of anti-Semitic stereotypes, which, in the distorted images of modernity, depicted the Jewish existence as alienated *par excellence*, and above all as rational, analytical, disintegrating, driven and definitely lacking inwardness—is searching for evidence to the contrary. Thus, his quest is one for the inner Jew. Third, Neumann felt that he needed to perform an act of spiritual reconciliation: He therefore considered establishing an argumentative link between Hasidism and early Christianity in another manuscript (which remained unwritten, however):

> Elsewhere, we shall demonstrate to what extent Hasidism, after almost 2,000 years, involves a delayed ripening of essential aspects of early Christianity within Judaism.
>
> (Roots II, p. 18)

While the prophet was once the recipient and the mediator of the revelation, in Hasidism it is now the *tzaddik* who mediates between God and humankind:

> The history of Hasidism is the history of the *tzaddikim*, the righteous men, and of their disciples. Leadership—in the proto-Hasidism of the beginning— means the circle-forming, disciple-making power of the "perfect man," whose central radiance surrounds him with force fields of followers.
>
> (Roots II, pp. 7–8)

From a depth-psychological perspective, the *tzaddik* mediates between conscious and unconscious contents. For Neumann, he represented the moral authority he had sought as a young man and which he believed to have found in C.G. Jung. Thus, one of Neumann's first letters to Jung from Palestine remarks:

> Before I came to you, I was rather sad that I was not able to go to a Jewish authority because I wanted to go to a "teacher" and I found it typified

precisely the decline of Judaism that it had no such authoritative personality in its ranks. With you, I became aware of what was prototypical in my situation. According to Jewish tradition, there are Zaddikim of the nations, and that is why the Jews have to go to the Zaddikim of the nations—perhaps that is why they do not have any of their own left. This Jewish situation, the beginning of an exchange, of an understanding *sub specie die* ["under the sight of God"]—this is what makes this "letter exchange" so important to me.

(JNC, pp. 35–36; 19 July 1934)

Neumann's description of Hasidism envisages—besides providing evidence of a historically guaranteed turn to Jewish inwardness, which he considers important for the reasons mentioned earlier—an interpretation of Jewish traditions that makes it possible to associate them with depth-psychological reflections. He even considers it possible to demonstrate that depth psychology is nurtured by the (preceding) spirit of Hasidism, in that the Hasidic writings represent a kind of "mystical psychology," or what Gershom Scholem described as the Hasidic appropriation of Kabbalistic ideas:

It is by descending into the depths of his own self that man wanders through all the dimensions of the world; in his own self he lifts the barriers which separate one sphere from the other ... With every one of the endless stages of the theosophical world corresponding to a given state of the soul—actual or potential, but at any rate capable of being felt and perceived—Kabbalism becomes an instrument of psychological analysis and self-knowledge.[1]

The secret centre of the two parts of Neumann's Jewish manuscript marks an important turning point: Part One describes the slow decline of Judaism as a collective force, due to its loss of a living tradition of revelation; Part Two exemplifies the renaissance of a tradition that, rather than inhibiting the individual's creative forces, promotes these as a "subterranean current that invisibly nurtures living Judaism" and that re-emerges "as a secret rivulet in the individual," that is, in the "dreams, visions, and psychic experiences of the anonymous modern Jew" (Roots II, p. 4).

Neumann's two-part manuscript also delineates his understanding of religious decadence, and of the possibilities of making a new and creative beginning. He aims to approach the unconscious factors which, on a psychological level, mark the rupture through which the ancient Jewish person became a "*galut* Jew," a Jew living in exile, in whom Neumann recognises the onset of the Jewish history of alienation. In view of the extremely threatening historical circumstances prevailing in the 1930s, he regards "radical self-contemplation" as the Jews' contribution amid their plight. His diagnosis of the Jewish person therefore bears witness to his profoundest concerns and self-criticism.

On this note, let me return to my initial question: What does Neumann mean by the "actualisation of messianism." This complex train of thought, behind which stands a philosophy or rather a theology gaining traction in Neumann's day and age, requires closer investigation. Closely linked to this thinking is the role of the individual in Hasidism. For Neumann, Hasidism counteracted, in its own way, the Jewish "stepping out of history" (Roots II, p. 18). The loss of land and nation meant that the course of history had become irrelevant for Judaism. Individual and collective life were now both considered in terms of "provisionality," in the expectation of the arrival of the last days, which would reverse the losses suffered. The ensuing apocalyptic expectation projected a theocratic ideal into the future, along with the idea of judgment, thus rendering meaningless the present as a form of life and experience:

> Upon the past, upon the Fathers, Zion, and the Kingdom, lay the splendor of perfection, fulfillment, and closeness to God. Upon the future, the time of the Messiah, the future Zion, and the coming rule of God, lay the splendor of hope and justification. The present, however, every present, lay in the shadow of intrusive provisionality and the inauthenticity of exile. In the best and highest case, it amounted to expectation and preparation.
>
> (Roots II, p. 18)

Hasidism, on the other hand, no longer thrives on the looming end of present existence, nor on its provisional nature. Rather, it turns from the future to the present, in a movement that corresponds to internalising messianism. The messianic element represents "a stage of the individual that needs to be fulfilled" (Roots II, p. 18). This, however, also means that redemption is no longer an external event. It is, instead, said to depend on whether individuals fulfil "the messianic stage of their soul" (ibid., p. 19) in the present. Neumann calls this internalising of the redemptive process into present human existence and action "the actualisation of messianism."

For Neumann, unearthing "the historical foundation of Jewish inwardness" (Roots II, p. 4) provides answers to the questions of modern Judaism. He therefore offers an extensive account of the Kabbalistic foundations of Hasidism. Significant in this respect is the Kabbalistic teaching of the *tzimtzum* (the contraction of God). This *tzimtzum*, to which the world owes its origination from infinity, first needs to be understood as a gradual restriction of divine light, which extends across different levels of the world to the most restricted world, the world of things, our material world. Creation in *tzimtzum* means that all the world's contents are individualised forms, from the human being to the greatest diversity. This idea of restriction implies the contraction of God, who—similar to what occurs in vessels or receptacles—withdraws into every individual being and thing in the world, and thus exists within them.

The divine *tzimtzum* enables the individual's and the world's life, and is therefore seen as evidence of God's love. Creation, then, underlines the importance and significance of the individualised, limited form compared to unformed infinity, which lies in the pre-creative realm. The human being represents the zenith of this process of creation (Roots II, pp. 6–7).[2]

Beings and creatures now correspond among each other, while things and people are mysteriously constellated. These constellations correspond to the need for redemption. Everything is secretly awaiting redemption. The divine sparks slumber in all things, and in every single particle, hoping and waiting for their salvation. This referentiality, which needs to be understood in terms of the need for redemption, forms a mysterious, shining cosmos within life, which remains unrecognised and unknown to the extent that human perception is limited. Thus, redemption is linked to the utopian idea of successive, "unified" perception projecting into the future, which is made possible by an infinite number of individualities.[3]

The present comes towards humankind from anonymous, unshaped eternity— as a level of realisation of which it must take hold. No present point in time can be replaced by another. Every moment is defined by its uniqueness.

Neumann associates the idea of "actualised messianism" with the process of individuation. This is particularly evident in the Jewish idea of the "Elijah soul":

> In this connection, I should like to refer to a Hasidic story which has occupied my mind for very many years. It is a story told by a rabbi about a simple Jew, to whom the prophet Elijah had appeared. But the appearance of Elijah "signifies the real initiation of the individual into the secret of the doctrine." The rabbi was asked how this could possibly be true, since the appearance of the prophet had never been vouchsafed to Master Ibn Esra, a man who was spiritually on an altogether higher plane. The rabbi replied that a larger or smaller part of the "allsoul" of Elijah enters into every soul, according to his temperament and inheritance. And if the person concerned, when he is growing up, trains his part of the soul of Elijah, then Elijah will appear to him. The simple man to whom Elijah had appeared had realized his small part of the soul of Elijah, whereas Ibn Esra has not realized his much larger part.[4]

This mystical and at the same time depth-psychological approach leads us back to the historical milieu within which Neumann's understanding of an "actualisation of messianism" finds its theoretical place. Later, I discuss two historically significant formations of thought in more detail, even if this involves abbreviating what are complex facts. In brief, these formations concern the appropriation of tradition on the one hand and the rupture in time on the other.

As we have seen, Neumann belonged to the generation born around the turn of the century. He witnessed a historical era in which social and political transformation occurred on an unprecedented scale. The most striking experiences of upheaval among young people at that time were undoubtedly World War I, the widespread poverty and high unemployment during the post-war years and re-emerging anti-Semitism.[5] While the generation of (Neumann's) parents, raised and moving in assimilated Jewish circles, tended to play down anti-Semitism, and continued to have confidence in the future, intellectual youths in particular reacted more sceptically and hesitantly, often rejecting their parents' life and adaptation strategies.

Since Jewish homes now only seldom exhibited outward characteristics of remembered Jewish identity,[6] the younger generation of Jews began searching for a new definition of Judaism: Under the prevailing historical circumstances, they refuted their available identity in the sense of self-denying adaptation. Key concepts of popular philosophy at the time included wholeness and originality, that is, symbolic counter-metaphors of a modern life that was characterised largely by cultural conformity and the loss of tradition. Even before World War I, it was widely believed that these values could be found in Eastern European Judaism, in particular among the Hasidim, whose mystical depth exerted a profound fascination on younger Jewish intellectuals.[7]

The Eastern Jew became a counter-myth.[8] He was, as Steven Aschheim, has aptly observed

> the embodiment of archetypal Jewish characteristics, the living link in an uninterrupted historical chain of tradition … The charm of the Eastern Jew consisted in his "authenticity" … "Ostjuden" could symbolize premodern, unfragmented "wholeness."[9]

During World War I, the image of the Eastern Jew, previously glorified from afar, now drew relentlessly closer in the shape of Eastern Jewish refugees pouring by the thousands into Germany. This influx dramatised and polarised the struggle over the identificatory status of the Eastern Jew. Neumann, who was still a grammar school student during the war, became a Zionist in 1923, his year of graduation. When war erupted, the Zionists proclaimed that the historic opportunity to reverse the self-imposed assimilatory isolation separating Western Jews from their Eastern Jewish brothers had (finally) arrived.[10]

The cult of the Eastern Jew was an important expression of the rebellion of German-Jewish youth against the German-Jewish bourgeois "establishment," even among moderate Zionists. At times, their opposition was identical to rejecting their fathers. Thus, the Eastern Jews became a kind of surrogate family.[11] Franz Kafka's *Letter to his Father* (1919) is probably the most famous document in this respect, in that these two superimposed problems convey a vivid image of the Jewish search for identity in those years.[12] Another work worth mentioning here is Arnold Zweig's *Das ostjüdische Antlitz* ("The Face of Eastern European Jewry," 1919),[13] in which the Eastern Jew epitomises spirituality in an otherwise mechanised, materialistic world.

The perception of European decadence and the search for saviour figures, in an innocent and authentic sphere, became part of this cult. "The Jew is eternal, for spiritualized Man is eternal," as Arnold Zweig puts it.[14] This view, however, was not limited to Zionists;[15] rather, it provided important identificatory anchoring from which so many young people's search for authenticity advanced, hesitantly, in what Martin Buber hailed as the "Jewish Renaissance" as early as 1900.[16]

The driving forces behind this "Jewish Renaissance" included numerous Zionist and non-Zionist figures committed to modernising and reformulating Jewish tradition and culture. They contemplated ways in which the Jews, through reflecting on themselves and their history, could enable "a possible rebirth of a spiritual and cultural, but also social nature" and how this project might be realised. Neumann's reception of Hasidism is largely indebted to Buber's notion of the Jewish Renaissance.[17]

Thus, this first strand sought to achieve renewal and recollection through a quasi-romantic understanding of Eastern Jewish wisdom in the sphere of individual experience, with which the concept of individuation can be associated as an "independent development from within," one that is structurally adjacent to the classical ideal of education in its belief in the totality and gradual evolution of humanity as progress.

There was also a second strand.[18] In the Weimar Republic, many Jewish intellectuals believed that Buber's position was not only too limited but also too closely related to the linearity inherent in the classical concept of education. And yet, linearity seemed to be exactly what was at stake. While the year 1918 had already been widely perceived as a fault line within history, and had as such severely shaken the idea of linear historical progression, events in the following years, which announced themselves in the ultimate failure of German–Jewish integration and in an increasingly intolerant society, destroyed any remaining belief in reason and in historical progress.

This rupture in historical-philosophical consciousness, whose signs had appeared already before the war, initiated a quest for models of time and history that were meant to enable adopting a position critical of the immanence of history as a developmental category. This consciousness expressed itself first and foremost in the theorem of ruptured time, a caesura, "in the impetus of interruption propagated by the theory of modernity" as a revolt against the rule of instrumental reason.[19] In addition, this theme was dressed in religious garb. Its conceptual counterparts were the apocalypse and redemption, both in right- and in left-wing politics.

The discourse of the Jewish Renaissance—and that of the right-wing thinkers of the Weimar Republic (Jünger, Heidegger, Spengler)—was embedded in post-Nietzschean concepts.[20] Nihilistic categories were deployed and their simultaneously destructive and liberating potential was contemplated. These thinkers were animated by a neo-eschatological spirit, a messianic thinking in which a radical uncoupling of history and redemption was sought.[21]

In the early 20th century, however, no unsevered connection with this source existed if it was based on the Jewish tradition:

> Lukacs, Benjamin, Scholem, the later sociologist of knowledge Karl Mannheim, the revolutionary theorist Gustav Landauer, but also Kafka, Döblin or German Expressionist authors first needed to reacquire, through education, what had long ceased to be easily citable.[22]

For these thinkers, and we might add Bloch and Rosenzweig, the rationally conceivable process of self-development was no longer what could be hoped for as salvation. Instead, these were epiphanic, suddenly illuminating moments that could intimate salvation through interrupting the course of history. Bloch and Benjamin, both Marxists, no longer viewed revolution as the culmination of a progressive process, but rather as the sudden outbreak of a deeper truth capable of prying open the historical continuum.[23]

For Franz Rosenzweig, the most conservative of these thinkers,[24] whose *Stern der Erlösung* ("Star of Redemption") is perhaps the most remarkable attempt in modernity to systematically establish a philosophy of faith, in particular for Jews, redemption lies completely beyond history.[25] Rosenzweig, for instance, replaced the conventional Enlightenment concept of time with the eternal Jewish cycle of time. He combined the latter with "the here and now," and thus rendered redemption not only conceivable but also possible at any time.

These questions were addressed differently by Gershom Scholem, a staunch Zionist and outstanding scholar working in the hitherto neglected field of Jewish mysticism. Scholem, Walter Benjamin's closest friend, was critical of Rosenzweig's approach, in spite of praising his *Stern der Erlösung*. Scholem's appreciation expresses his own relationship with the redemptive figure of the messiah:

> Apocalypticism, which, as an unquestionably anarchic element, has ventilated the house of Judaism; the realisation of the catastrophic nature of all historical order in an unredeemed world, has, in a way of thinking deeply anxious to establish order, undergone a metamorphosis in which the destructive power of salvation appears only as unrest in the clockwork of life in the light of revelation.[26]

Scholem did not consider Rosenzweig's thinking radical enough. It lacked the destructive aspect of apocalyptic upheaval, a stance that Scholem, however, no longer voiced as a personal credo in his 1959 Eranos lecture—"Zum Verständnis der messianischen Idee im Judentum" ("On Understanding the Messianic Idea in Judaism")—in this shape or form.

According to Jewish tradition, God's relationship with humankind and the world manifests itself in three themes: revelation, creation and redemption.[27] These were the themes that Neumann discussed systematically for the first time in his inaugural Eranos lecture *Der mystische Mensch* ("Mystical Man"), delivered in 1948. While this lecture marks a turning point in his work, this is not the only reason why it merits closer attention. On the one hand, the lecture marked Neumann's first public appearance in Europe since emigrating to Palestine in 1934. For 12 years—until his untimely death—Neumann was one of the keynote speakers at the annual Eranos conferences. Aside from introducing a biographical accent, which freed Neumann at least partly from his isolation (see Chapter 9), which he often complained about in his letters to C.G. Jung and Olga

Fröbe-Kapteyn, the lecture represents a shift in his thinking, a change in direction that had been evident since 1939. Concretely, it involved turning away from his previous depth-psychological interpretation of Jewish history, which was another reason why Neumann did not release the manuscript for publication. This shift was preceded by a dramatic exchange of letters with C.G. Jung (on the occasion of the November 1938 pogroms in Germany), during which Jung abandoned his position on the fundamental cultural differences between Jews and Christians, an approach informed by depth-psychological concepts (see Chapter 7). To begin with, Jung's self-correction plunged Neumann into a crisis of orientation, from which he freed himself by incorporating the knowledge and convictions that he had acquired through his intensive studies on Judaism as a "secret structure" into his own depth-psychological work. From this emerged its clear distinction to Jung's approach.

"Mystical Man" marks an intermediate stage in this development; it is a "transitional text" so to speak.[28] Forming its backbone are various central and systematically anthropologised Kabbalistic ideas. These substantiate the claim that coming to terms with Jung's self-correction allowed Neumann to expand and integrate contents instead of distancing himself and insisting on a special historical role. He preserved this special role inasmuch as his careful selection of Kabbalistic and Hasidic passages in his lectures are centrally important to their overall context.

This was characterised not just by Neumann's pride and commitment towards his Jewish heritage, but also by a deep inner conviction pervading his entire work. At the end of the first part of *Origins and History*, which emerged in the 1940s and appeared in 1949, Neumann emphasised the "synthetic path" taken by Hasidism along with alchemy and the Kabbalah, which explains his preference for it over "Christianity [which] grew up under Gnostic influences" (OHC, p. 255). Here, "synthetic" means that ritual and sacred actions "gradually turn inward, becoming first the sacred experience of the initiate, and finally processes within the individualized psyche" (ibid.).

Neumann's *homo mysticus*, the subject of his Eranos lecture, establishes a "mystical anthropology" on the basis of Kabbalistic and Hasidic principles. Human development, especially of the individual personality, depends on creativity. Neumann defines this as follows:

> the spontaneity of the nonego, which manifests itself in the creative process and is by nature numinous. The encounter with the numinous constitutes the "other side" of the development of consciousness and is by nature "mystical".
>
> (MM, p. 380)

His outline of a mystical anthropology may be seen as Neumann's contribution to correcting modernity's one-sided, rational concept of consciousness through recourse to Jewish theology. Neumann finds evidence for the modern person's one-sidedness in "the rigidity of his ego" and in "his imprisonment in consciousness" (MM, p. 380). At the centre of this anthropology stands "man's experience of the creative void" (ibid., p. 383). The creative void or "creative nothingness" is a concept already developed by Neumann in his comprehensive treatment of Hasidism in *The Roots of Jewish Consciousness*. There he writes:

> The world of Hasidism rests on the deity's creative nothingness. Its dynamics not only secretly animates every creature and thing in this world, but also can be attained by the human being at every moment, if he breaks through the world's foreground into this nothingness. It is as if the structure of the world becomes transparent to the seeing eye, which now sees the great lifelines through which divine nothingness, always and everywhere, flows in and pervades the world. The inconstancy of what is given, the non-static, incessantly changing, undetermined nature of the world, is the one major, basic religious concept of Hasidism. Life in this world is only possible, so to speak, if one realizes the reality of this inconstancy and adjusts to it.

Moreover:

> The world lives by continuous repetition of the divine act of creation, creation out of nothingness. This nothingness is the source and regeneration point of all life.
>
> (Roots II, p. 35)

In Neumann's Eranos lecture, "creation from nothingness"—in contrast to *The Roots of Jewish Consciousness*—is a Judeo-Christian theologoumenon that can be understood as a projection of what was originally an inner process (MM, p. 383). The creative nothingness within the human being forms the centre, the core of the human personality, which analytical psychology calls the self (ibid.). In religious history, the concept of the self can be assigned various mythological and pictorial equivalents, including the "temple, *temenos*, the source and paradise." It is also the centre of the "mandala," that is, "an area where mystical theology and mystical anthropology coincide" (ibid.).

Thus, theology, is indispensable when considering the self. For Neumann, it is a "paradoxical truth," which expresses itself in the fact that "God and man are one image, for the ego is not the self; in its individuation the personality no longer experiences itself as ego, or solely as ego, but at the same time as nonego, as ego-self" (MM, p. 384). Following Jung, Neumann refers to the creative process as "individuation," which may have very different consequences, among others, a permanent change in personality or a "momentary trance" (ibid.). The personality structure may transform, even as if it were being destroyed by a "sudden flash" or by "irruption." Being seized or taken possession of may manifest itself as religious experience, as love, as an artistic process, as inspiration or as knowledge. When a numinous experience is made, the once-robust ego structure is broken through, "and the dynamically changed and changing world behind the world is revealed" (ibid.). A central criterion of numinous experience is that it brings the human being into conflict with prevailing consciousness. Numinous experience contrasts with the ruling morals, culture and religion. Its main characteristics are revolution and heresy, discontinuity and interruption (ibid., p. 383). In this act, revelation, creation and redemption become intertwined.

With regard to the concept of revelation: As an element breaking into the human soul, the numinous reveals and is revealed; the self as the centre is the place of nothingness of this revelation. The numinous is—as Neumann had explained in *Roots*—"hidden in all the contents of this world," "from profane, everyday situations to prayer, and to every single letter in the words of a prayer" (Roots II, p. 47). He also uses the concept of "voice" to capture the process of revelation (MM, p. 386).

Voice is among those terms used by Neumann that have repeatedly baffled his readers. This is largely due to his lack of explanation, first and foremost in *Depth Psychology and a New Ethic*. His emphatic use of the word is based on the fact that experiences either desiring or substantiating the acoustic sphere possess the greatest religious authority in Judaism. Gershom Scholem explains the religious power of the word as follows:

> For Judaism, revelation was the Word of God, and tradition understood the entire Torah as such. In which sense one can speak of a word is a question that remains pressing even beyond the Orthodox view.[29]

The word as the bearer of the voice, as "verbal inspiration,"[30] was reinvigorated and expanded in an unsuspected way by the Kabbalists, for whom every word, even every letter, was divinely revealed, by virtue of the creative aspect of God, as his name suggests:

> The Word of God, if there is one, represents an absolute authority, about which one might just as well say that it rests in itself and is moved in itself. ... The Torah appears in this context as a fabric woven from the name of God. It represents a mysterious unity whose primary purpose is not to transmit a specific meaning, to "mean" something, but rather to express the creative force concentrated in the name of God and which is present in all that is created as his secret signature in some variation or another ... The Word of God must possess an infinite fullness, which is conveyed through it. And yet, this communication, and this is the essence of the kabbalistic view of revelation, is incomprehensible. Its aim is not communication, which is also incomprehensible. ... Thus, the key to revelation lies in the diverse views of what the Word of God, and at the same time that of man, means. No single definable context of meaning appears therein, but an infinite abundance of such contexts, in which this word spreads out for us.[31]

About the concept of creation: Scholem, who greatly esteemed Neumann, even if he "often did not understand his ... things,"[32] has handed down the following assertion by Neumann:

Wherefore the creation? The answer that shines in infinite variety, that which shines unreflected only in itself, is ancient, and yet it satisfies me.[33]

For Neumann, the process of revelation, as an act of creation, originates in the "creative nothingness in man" and incessantly provides altering, renewing impulses (MM, p. 380). Therefore, human development, figuratively speaking, resembles an ellipse with two focal points: One must be assigned to the expansion of consciousness and the strengthening of the self; the other to the "creative process inherent in the transforming encounter between the ego and the nonego" (ibid., p. 385).

The concept of redemption, finally, is joined by a more secularised one, that of transformation. At the same time, the understanding of messianic time, which is directed towards an endpoint, that is, redemption, is shifted into the present, in which actualised messianism manifests itself. As such, it takes the sting out of the notion that the last days will be final:

> Originally, Messianism was bound up with a historical process ending in the emergence of a savior who, after the transformation crisis of the apocalypse, ushers in the eschatological age of redemption. This conception can easily be shown to be a projection of an individuation process, the subject of which, however, is the people, the chosen collectivity, and not the individual.
>
> (MM, p. 408)

The human being can be seized—and transformed—by every encounter and event in the world, because "every place, every thing, every situation, and every living creature … are all potential bearers of 'sparks,' as the Hasidim said, capable of kindling and illumining the human personality" (MM, p. 385).

Thus, at the end of his lecture, Neumann returns to a term that he had first used in his earlier account of Hasidism: the "actualisation of messianism." Not least here, and also somewhat hauntingly, it becomes evident how internalising fundamental Hasidic ideas enabled Neumann to place the path of the individual, his individuation, his creative process of transformation, at the centre of his thinking. Messianic time, insofar as it is perceptible to individuals as the numinous taking effect within them, is always present. Thus, "messianic activity" determines individual action. Neumann returns to the Kabbalah one last time in his lecture "Mystical Man" in mentioning the "mystical re-creation of the disrupted world," that is, "the striving for tikkun" (MM, p. 409). In *tikkun*, the human being must "make … the godhead and the world bound up with it 'whole and complete' again" (ibid.). This work is the work of redemption. Every person redeems the "sacred sparks" in their here and now:

> Redemption of the sacred sparks in every Now, in every Here, that is the essential task. And this task confronts not only the world, with its general need of redemption, but every individual, for each individual soul has its own particular sparks that demand to be redeemed.
>
> (MM, p. 409)

What was true of Benjamin, Bloch, Rosenzweig, Scholem and other distinguished Jewish thinkers of the civilisational break, and also of their metaphysical-escha-tological conceptualisation of the bursting asunder of the time continuum, which involved positioning oneself in the reinvigorated discourse of messianism, also applied to Neumann, who nevertheless followed his own, depth-psychological path. His final three Eranos lectures further developed his approach to the crisis of modernity, with a view to critiquing society and contemporary philosophy, especially existentialism in its nihilistic form.

Neumann replaced the term "messianism" with "eschatology" and spoke of "actualised eschatology." Presumably, he substituted one word for the other in an attempt to avoid misunderstandings. Thus, in describing Neumann's conceptual language in *Origins and History*, Jung observed: "You still have to gain experience for yourself as far as being misunderstood goes. The possibilities exceed all terminology" (JNC, p. 202).

The notion of "actualised eschatology" can be understood as Neumann's "legacy" in terms of a body of thought that is based on Judaic sources while summarising his essential assumptions about the crisis of modernity. It is also represents a specific form of transcendental experience. Even if the political sphere seems to stand in the background with Neumann, the political contents of his theoretical intentions can hardly be disregarded. Of course, he draws his political impetus from an inwardness that strives to ignore religious and political boundaries. In Neumann's sense, transformation occurs from the sphere of inwardness—and from it alone. This emphasis—above all its radicalness—can only be understood in terms of the critical distance that Neumann takes from everything that happens and has happened to individuals in the name of collectives and their morals. Thus, in "Man and Meaning," he wrote:

> The ego in its isolation is floundering in despair. It is overwhelmed by the process of collectivisation which fragments the individual into collectively serviceable but otherwise irrelevant segments; and when, in the knowledge of his own impotence, the individual silently accepts this violence, he becomes a victim of terror, not only in Russia or Nazi Germany, but everywhere. Everywhere Western Reason has triumphed, and as it continues on its triumphant march, a consciousness shaped in its image effects the transformation and domination of the world; these changes bring with them industrialization and collectivization, which atomize and rape the individual.[34]

To this diagnosis we might add a passage from a letter that Neumann wrote to Jung on 5 December 1938, a few weeks after the *Reichspogromnacht*:

> And the terrible state of emergency that has gripped the entire people and will continue to do so will inevitably force the inner source energies to be called either into action or to their peril. It is both as clear to me that we will not be wiped out, as it is also that immeasurable numbers of us must perish

in the process. And to watch this from the sidelines is a terrible torture. The reports that crowd in on one on a daily or hourly basis, and, sadly, the reports of eyewitnesses, make one glad to experience firsthand the terrible propensity of human beings to dissociate themselves from overwhelmingly bad feelings.

(JNC, p. 140)

While this passage marks his reaction to the terror inflicted on the Jewish people, Neumann's Eranos lecture talks about the collective traumatisation of the war generation:

Modern man experiences much suffering, has seen too much suffering; his eyes are filled with horror. The death of masses of human beings, the torturing to death of millions, has broken his psychic endurance.

("Man and Meaning," p. 206)

In response to this "too-muchness,"[35] Neumann turns towards revelation as an invasion into symbolic orders. It is precisely the experience of discontinuity, of *too much*, that befalls the individual. Being thrown back upon ourselves enables transformation, in a process through which a new (structural) relationship with the self is evoked. Thus, Neumann is interested in the process through which "it becomes possible for the individual to hear the calling of the voice, his calling of the voice, the calling of the voice that is meant for him."[36]

How did Neumann develop this concept? Here, it is useful to return to his letter (to Jung) of 1938, in which he describes his personal experiences as a therapist:

Reemergence of direct revelation but now in the individual, in direct connection firstly with individuation and secondly with the collective problem of revelation in Judaism … Highly apparent is the strong presence of the religious problem in the first half of life in a strongly collective-toned manifestation, more or less unconnected with one's private problems into which it grows in the course of the work.

Commenting on this work, he adds:

You can well imagine how interesting this work is on the one hand, but how ill equipped I am for it on the other.[37]

(JNC, pp. 142–143)

However, the prerequisite for this experience is "openness."[38] At the same time, this openness, as we will see, marks a turning away. This aversion creates a vacuum, an emptiness in which only an encounter, although one that escapes symbolic representation, becomes visible. For Neumann, as he writes in *Krise und Erneuerung* ("Crisis and Renewal"), what we encounter represents wholeness:

Only this openness towards the underground, this tragic and narrowly over-
powering avoidance of self-exposure opens up the wholeness of psychic
existence.

(KUE, p. 127)

One aspect is of interest with regard to religious philosophy: In 1917, the
Marburg theologian Rudolf Otto elevated perfect negativity as a precondition
for the occurrence of the "Wholly Other" to a mystical "theologia negativa."[39]
The idea of a "tabula rasa" as a prerequisite for "truth," or the productive force
of negativity in the imaginary world of negative theology, is a theme common to
the great religions. It is prevalent both in the Jewish Kabbalah and in Christian
mysticism.[40]

In this respect, Neumann also speaks of experiencing the "Wholly Other": "But
that which intrudes, itself stems from a reality which for the experiencing human
being is 'wholly other,' and thus cannot be classified in terms of the continuity of
his existence up to that point" (KUE, p. 122). The Wholly Other manifests itself
epiphanically, as "the unexpected, revelation as lightning, as a sudden and discon-
tinuous event" (ibid.). Neumann, firmly oriented towards the idea of wholeness,
links the theme of continuity with a new one: discontinuity. He conceives of this
relationship in terms of opposites: "During inner development something wholly
other occurs, which stands in paradoxical contrast to this … continuity. This is the
phenomenon of discontinuity, which comes from a deep layer of the psyche and
of being" (ibid., p. 121).

This discrepancy, that is, the clash of the inner continuum with a sudden,
epiphanic event, is what brings about transformation. Continuity is a rational figure, while discontinuity is at home in the numinous and marks the breaking point
from which newness can be opened up and experienced. "The Other"—according to Neumann—enables us to experience ourselves as an ego-self. It contrasts
with the continuum of our individual system and its development: "The numinous
freedom of our existence, in which we experience ourselves as ego-selves and in
our uniqueness are creatively open to the infinite, or at least can be open to it, is
the Other" (KUE, p. 124).

The experience of irruption, of suddenness, now lends the epiphanic moment
a surplus of meaning, whose structural nature is linked to a specific experience
of time:

As this Other, however, we are discontinuously new in every moment in an
ahistorical reality, which, like us, is new in every moment. It is … a core
event that actually forms the basis of our experience of existence, as far as we
do not dismantle it as a reflecting ego-consciousness.

(KUE, p. 124)

This experience eludes rational debate. It takes place, unnoticed, in the individual
and borders on mystical experience:

Not the slightest external affirmation exists for this experience. It is based entirely and solely on the *religio* in which the ego has found its way back to the self as its self, which at the same time is the self … in which man emerges as a creative man and at the same time as a mystical man.

(KUE, p. 118; original italics)

Their experience makes individuals bearers of redemption—in that they are at odds with the world and become unassailable: "That is why today the individual matters, who, due to his psychological development, is able to oppose the negative collective pressure, inside and outside, actively or passively" (KUE, p. 109).

The concept of discontinuity is not only a figure of redemption, but also one of protest. Discontinuity means "shattering the world's and life's old husks" (KUE, p. 124), that is, following "the call to break the old tablets, the old values" (ibid., p. 126). This explains why Neumann also opposes the subsequent appropriation of discontinuity by a continuum based on interpretation. The extraordinary must retain the significance of the "miraculous" in order to remain assured of its power (ibid., p. 124).

In light of his personal experience of the Jewish name for God, Neumann does not doubt that this experience is religious. Thus, his "Mensch und Sinn" ("Man and Meaning"), which extends his 1957 Eranos lecture "Die Sinnfrage und das Individuum" ("The Question of Meaning and the Individual"), contains a surprisingly open confession:

I fear I am not a good Jew, although I am not quite certain, but on my path through life I have learned to experience and to venerate the divine as something formless and creative. This path in life has perhaps brought me closer to an understanding of the self-revelations of YHWH, in whose sign the Exodus from Egypt took place and every exodus from Egypt takes place, namely the strange divine name *Ehyeh asher ehyeh*: I am who I am. Since every human being can speak only of his own experience when the question of meaning arises, I, too, can speak only of my personal experience and say what this *Ehyeh* means to me.

The passage continues thus:

But I am convinced that the point of consciousness with which I as an ego am endowed springs directly from this *Ehyeh asher ehyeh*, I am who I am, which is the name of God. This numinous I-point of consciousness which has me, which engenders me in every moment as an ego, is the actual self-ego-structure of my imperishable being.[41]

From the perspective of discontinuity, Neumann adopted a threefold opposition to prevailing political, philosophical and religious opinion: First, as a Zionist, for whom the symbolic systems of classification, which were losing legitimacy to a disastrous extent, became the signature and dilemma of modernity; second, as the dilettante as which he saw himself, who immersed himself in Hasidic and Kabbalistic wisdom;[42] and third, as a depth psychologist, who couched the equation of his life, fraught by discontinuity, and whose language already belongs to another world, in philosophical-theological terms.[43]

Let us add to these positions the assessment of one of Neumann's supervisees, Dvora Kutzinski, who came to Israel as an Auschwitz survivor and later became an analyst herself. Asked about Neumann in an interview in 2005, she observed:

> For me Neumann symbolized a wall against the terrible psychological effects of the holocaust, which I went through. He deeply believed that there is renewal out of the hell. He meant salvation for me.[44]

Thus, if biographical memory-work is to constitute more than merely remedying past failures, it is essential to establish correspondences with what has been said in order to enable further questions to be asked.

Let me conclude with three points, one philosophical, one historical, one poetic: Neumann's inner experience corresponds to a special concept of time, one that he described as actualised messianism in his letter to Jung of 5 December 1938. The concept stems from suppressing what might be called a conventional experience of time as chronological sequence: "As this other, however, we are discontinuously new in every moment, in an ahistorical reality, which, like us, is new in every moment" (KUE, p. 145).

In the late 1990s, the Italian philosopher Giorgio Agamben, who is perhaps best known for his "Homo Sacer" project (the third part of his *Remnants of Auschwitz*), gave a series of seminars in France, America and Italy on the Letter to the Romans by the Apostle Paul. Agamben's purpose was to "restore the significance of Paul's Letters to the status of the fundamental messianic text for the Western tradition."[45] This leads him to raise three central questions: "What does it mean to live in the Messiah, and what is the messianic life? What is the structure of messianic time?"[46]

Agamben intends these questions to contribute to redefining political philosophy at the beginning of the 21st century. Considering the difference between chronological and messianic time, he states:

> Whereas our representation of chronological time, as the time *in which* we are, separates us from ourselves and transforms us into impotent spectators of ourselves—spectators who look at the time that flies without any time left, continually missing ourselves—messianic time, an operational time in which we take hold of and achieve our representation of time, is the time that we ourselves are, and for this very reason, is the only real time, the only time we have.[47]

This passage reflects how closely Agamben approaches Neumann's position. More common than *messianic time* is the concept of *kairos*. Agamben quotes the following definition of *kairos* from the *Corpus Hippocraticum*: "chronos is that in which there is kairos, and kairos is that in which there is little chronos."[48]

Neumann himself leaves no doubt that his position is a counterposition, not least since he belongs to "a dying people" (JNC, p. 148), and also since witnessing the horrors inflicted by some humans upon others has exceeded our emotional capacities (KUE, p. 152). Neumann's position incorporates traumatisation as an effective agent of inner events. The speechlessness of trauma, and trauma itself, may be followed by silence on the outside, yet not on the inside. According to Neumann, something new and incomprehensible happens inside, about which nothing remains to be said in rational discourse.

The subject of silence, and the reference to another sphere, recalls an event at the trial of Adolf Eichmann. Yehiel Dinoor (also spelt De-Nur), one of the main trial witnesses, published a series of writings about the death camps under the pseudonym Kazetnick (also spelt Ka-Tsetnik). His testimony was essential to convicting Eichmann. However, when Dinoor was asked to answer the court's questions in his own name, he fainted and lay in a coma for several days. This significant event revealed the limits of the truth-finding methods used in legal proceedings to articulate historical truth. Thus, the court records stated:

> If these are the sufferings of the individual, then the total sum of the sufferings of millions exceeds ... human understanding, and who are we to express it adequately? This is a task for the great poets and men of literature.[49]

Neumann's position is an inner conversation with the "Wholly Other"—an experience that he considers paradigmatic for the creative person, even if it should not be tinted religiously. Let me therefore close with the poet Paul Celan, who found an unmistakable language in which to articulate the suffering of his (that is, the Jewish) people. In "The Meridian," his 1960 speech on the occasion of receiving the Georg Büchner Prize, Celan remarked that the process of creating a poem becomes a meticulous self-examination, which is itself poetological:

> Poetry is perhaps this: an *Atemwende*, a turning of our breath. Who knows, perhaps poetry goes its way—the way of art—for the sake of just such a turn? And since the strange, the abyss *and* Medusa's head, the abyss *and* the automaton, all seem to lie in the same direction—it is perhaps this turn, this Atemwende, which can sort the strange from the strange? ... Perhaps, along with the I, estranged *and* freed here, *in this manner*, some other thing is also set free? ... the poem has always hoped ... to speak also on behalf of the strange ... *on behalf of the other*, who knows, perhaps of an *altogether other*.[50]

Notes

1 Gershom Scholem, *Major Trends in Jewish Mysticism* (New York: Schocken Books, 1946), p. 341.
2 Neumann cites the following Hasidic passage (whose origin is unclear) from Buber's *Tales of the Hasidim*: "Everyone should know and bear in mind that his nature is unique in the world, and no one on earth was ever like him; for if anyone had ever been like him, he would not have needed to be. In reality, however, everyone is a new

thing in the world, and he should bring his character to perfection. For because it is not perfect, the coming of the Messiah is delayed" (Roots II, p. 7).

3 See also the following passage: "An infinite radiant world of revelation lies hidden in created reality. No perceiving subject, however, corresponds to the brilliance of this world diamond, with its inexpressible myriad of facets. It is still concealed, and only a larger or smaller number of the luminous facets of this diamond will become visible to the fulfilled individuality of the individual. Only if a single eye of humanity could be formed from the immense number of human individualities, in their endlessly varied capacity for experience, might that unified eye alone recognize the hidden light of the world diamond. Only such a unified humanity would be the partner for a self-revealing world" (Roots II, p. 16).

4 Martin Buber, *Die chassidischen Bücher* (Hellerau: Jakob Hegner, 1928), p. 690. Cited in Renée Brand, William McGuire and Julie Neumann (eds.), *The Place of Creation, Essays of Erich Neumann*, vol. 3 (Princeton, NJ: Princeton University Press, 2017), pp. 3–62; esp. p. 374.

5 See Chapter 1; see also Detlev J. K Peukert, *Die Weimarer Republik: Krisenjahre der Klassischen Moderne* (Frankfurt am Main: Suhrkamp, 1987).

6 Gershom Scholem, *From Berlin to Jerusalem* (Philadelphia, PA: Paul Dry Books, 2012); Richard Lichtheim, *Rückkehr: Lebenserinnerungen aus der Frühzeit des deutschen Zionismus* (Stuttgart: DVA, 1970).

7 Steven Aschheim, *Brothers and Strangers: The East European Jew in German and German Jewish Consciousness, 1800–1923* (Madison: University of Wisconsin Press, 1982), p. 98f.

8 Ibid., p. 98f.

9 Ibid., 185ff.

10 Ibid., p. 189.

11 Ibid., p. 191.

12 Franz Kafka (1919), *Brief an den Vater* (Frankfurt am Main: Fischer Verlag, 1999).

13 Arnold Zweig (1919), *Das ostjüdische Antlitz. Zu zweiundfünfzig Zeichnungen von H. Struck* (Wiesbaden: Fourier Verlag, 1992).

14 Cited in Steven Aschheim, *Brothers and Strangers*, p. 202.

15 Ibid., p. 203.

16 Martin Buber, *Jüdische Renaissance*. First published in Ost-West. Reprinted in *Die jüdische Bewegung: Gesammelte Aufsätze und Ansprachen (1900–1914)*, Erste Folge (Berlin, 1920), pp. 7ff.

17 Gustav Dreifuss, "Erich Neumanns jüdisches Bewusstsein," *Analytische Psychologie* 11 (1980), p. 240: "Neumann also mentioned that he based his manuscripts primarily on Buber and his treatment of the Hasidic material. However, it now seemed to him that this material was not sufficiently competent, since Buber had adapted his selection and translations very much to common European thinking"—Trans.

18 Steven Aschheim, "German Jews beyond Bildung and Liberalism: The Radical Jewish Revival in the Weimar Republic," in K.L. Berghahn (ed.), *The German-Jewish Dialogue Reconsidered*, A Symposium In Honor Of George L. Mosse (New York, Washington D.C., Baltimore, Bern, Frankfurt am Main, Berlin, Vienna, Paris: Peter Lang Verlag, 1996), p. 125ff.

19 Klaus L. Scherpe, "Dramatisierung und Entdramatisierung des Untergangs: Zum ästhetischen Bewußtsein von Moderne und Postmoderne," in Andreas Huyssen and Klaus L. Scherpe (eds.), *Postmoderne, Zeichen eines kulturellen Wandels* (Reinbek bei Hamburg: Rowohlt, 1986), p. 284.

20 Werner Stegmeier and Daniel Krochmalnik (eds.), *Jüdischer Nietzscheanismus* (Berlin and New York: De Gruyter, 1997).

21 Max Weber (1919), *Politik als Beruf*, 7th ed. (Stuttgart: Reclam, 1982), p. 59. The relevance of such neo-messianic thinking was observed not only by Max Weber, whose

speeches ("Science as a Profession" and "Politics as a Profession") before Munich students in the revolutionary winter of 1919 characterised this thinking as that of ethicists, who "did not tolerate the ethical irrationality of the world." Weber was levelling his criticism at revolutionaries and their thinking, especially their willingness to use violence.

22 Gert Mattenklott, "Mythologie, Messianismus, Macht," in *Messianismus zwischen Mythos und Macht: Jüdisches Denken in der europäischen Geistesgeschichte*, eds. E. Goodman-Thau and W. Schmied-Kowarzik (Berlin: Akademie Verlag, 1994), p. 185.

23 Steven Aschheim, "German Jews beyond Bildung and Liberalism: The Radical Jewish Revival in the Weimar Republic," in Berghahn (ed.), *The German-Jewish Dialogue Reconsidered*; see also Anson Rabinbach, *In the Shadow of Catastrophe: German Intellectuals between Apocalypse and Enlightenment* (Berkeley: University of California Press, 1997).

24 W. Schmied-Kowarzik, "Franz Rosenzweig, Der Stern der Erlösung," in Joachim Valentin and Saskia Wendel (eds.), *Jüdische Traditionen in der Philosophie des 20. Jahrhunderts* (Darmstadt: Primus Verlag, 2000), p. 32. Contemplating the future reception of his *Stern der Erlösung* (1921), Rosenzweig observed: "And the *Stern* will probably once and rightly be regarded as a gift that the German spirit owes to its Jewish enclave"—Trans.

25 Franz Rosenzweig, *Der Stern Der Erlosung* (*The Star of Redemption*). Trans. William W. Hallo (New York: Holt, Rinehart and Winston, 1971).

26 Gershom Scholem, "Zur Neuauflage des Stern der Erlösung," *Frankfurter Israelitisches Gemeindeblatt*, September 1931, p. 15ff.

27 Gershom Scholem, "*Es gibt ein Geheimnis in der Welt*": *Tradition und Säkularisation*, ed. Itta Shedletzky (Frankfurt am Main: Jüdischer Verlag im Suhrkamp Verlag, 2002), p. 24.

28 Neumann's text is mentioned, among others, in Moshe Idel's *Alte Welten Neue Bilder: Jüdische Mystik und die Gedankenwelt des 20. Jahrhunderts* (Frankfurt am Main: Jüdischer Verlag im Suhrkamp Verla, 2012), p. 373.

29 Scholem, "*Es gibt ein Geheimnis in der Welt*," p. 12.

30 Ibid., p. 12.

31 Ibid., p. 14f.

32 Ibid., p. 84.

33 Ibid., p. 29.

34 Erich Neumann, "Man and Meaning, " in *The Place of Creation: The Essays of Erich Neumann*, vol. 3 (Princeton, NJ: Princeton University Press, 1989), p. 207f.; originally published as "Mensch und Sinn," in *Der schöpferische Mensch* (Zurich: Rascher Verlag, 1959).

35 The term is from Eric Santner's cultural theory, cited here from Dominik Finkelde's *Politische Eschatologie nach Paulus* (Vienna: Turia & Kant, 2007), p. 109.

36 Ibid.

37 The letter continues as follows: "I take the view, however, that I may collect materials for my living psychological work, even as a layman, as far as they are accessible to me and useful. This incursion into theological, religious, and historical areas is of course dillettantist in a certain sense. But the urgency of these problems for the Jewish situation seems so huge to me that even the inevitable arbitrariness of such an attempt is permitted, as long as it is conscious of its preliminariness and relativity" (JNC, p. 142).

38 This idea and account differ at best in their understated tone from a passage in Ernst Bloch's *Spirit of Utopia* (1918): "If air and soil are taken away from us, the sun turns black as sackcloth of hair, and the moon becomes as red as blood; if for us who are incomplete and unsheltered from the world's time, the world's entire countenance thus dies out in the raging thunderstorms, led by the devil himself, of the world's midnight

hour, in the immeasurable collapse of every foundation and every firmament; then we stand naked before the end, half, tepid, unclear and yet 'consummated,' consummated as by a tragic situation"; see Ernst Bloch, *The Spirit of Utopia*, trans. Anthony A. Nassar (Stanford: Stanford University Press, 2000), p. 272.

39 Rudolf Otto, cited in Gerd Mattenklott, "Mythologie, Messianismus, Macht," p. 182.

40 Ibid, p. 183.

41 Erich Neumann, "Man and Meaning," in *The Place of Creation: The Essays of Erich Neumann*, vol. 3, pp. 237–238.

42 On the themes of Jewish thought in modern philosophy, see Joachim Valentin and Saskia Wendel (eds.), *Jüdische Traditionen in der Philosophie des 20. Jahrhunderts*, p. 4: (1) Prohibition of images, prohibition of naming God, the impossibility of "saying the unsayable." (2) The meaning of God's name as a "nameless name" and the mystical-kabbalistic concept of the symbol. (3) God as a hidden God, who nevertheless proves to be a living God, i.e. "I am there for you." (4) The historicity of the experience of God (e.g. the experience of Exodus) and the associated messianic hope for liberation, reconciliation, redemption and the prophetic traditions of protest and promise; the resulting understanding of faith, which implies historical remembrance, a willingness to listen, receive and understand (the name of God, the gift of the covenant and the land, the law, the Scriptures) and upright action in response to God's claim and call. (5) Exile, the threat to identity and homelessness as a historically overwhelming imprinting of Jewish culture. (6) Rabbinic hermeneutics.

43 See Moshe Idel and Bernhard McGinn (eds.), *Mystical Union in Judaism, Christianity and Islam: An Ecumenical Dialogue* (1996). Referring to Neumann's "Mystical Man," Idel, who teaches the Kabbalah at the University of Jerusalem, attests Neumann's "congeniality of description to Jewish mysticism," in connection with the typically Hasidic approach to mystic experience.

44 Dvora Kutzinski, "Neumann as my Supervisor," *Harvest* 52, no. 2 (2006).

45 Giorgio Agamben, *The Time That Remains: A Commentary on the Letter to the Romans*, trans. Patricia Dailey (Stanford: Stanford University Press, 2005), p. 1.

46 Ibid., p. 18.

47 Ibid., p. 68; original emphasis.

48 Ibid., p. 69.

49 *The Trial of Adolf Eichmann, Record of Proceedings in the District Court of Jerusalem*, vol. 5 (Jerusalem, 1994), p. 2146; cited in Dori Laub, "Kann die Psychoanalyse dazu beitragen, den Völkermord historisch besser zu verstehen?" *Psyche, Sonderheft, Vergangenheit in der Gegenwart 6, Zeit, Narration, Geschichte*, 57 (September/October 2003).

50 Paul Celan, "Büchner-Preisrede," in *Büchner-Preis-Reden 1951–1971* (Stuttgart: Reclam, 1972), p. 96f. See also "Paul Celans Psalm, Eine Offenbarung des Nichts," in Moshe Idel, *Alte Welten, neue Bilder, Jüdische Mystik und die Gedankenwelt des 20. Jahrhunderts*, pp. 308–317; cited here from the English edition: "The Meridian," in *Paul Celan: Collected Prose*. Translated by Rosemary Waldrop (New York: Routledge, 2006), pp. 47–48.

"... on the side of the inner voice and against the conscience of his time"

Depth Psychology and a New Ethic in the context of the Jewish reception of Nietzsche

"During the Second World War and under its direct impact:" This is how Neumann describes the conditions under which he wrote *Depth Psychology and a New Ethic*.[1] The preface, dated "Tel Aviv May 1948," expresses his apocalyptic concern of living in "an age dominated by a dance of death, to which National Socialism in Germany was little more than a prelude" (DPNE, p. 19). "What is the point, in a world situation such as this," Neumann asks in the same passage, "of the ridiculous 'ethical' question and still more ridiculous answer, 'It all depends on the individual'?"

Neumann's attempt to devise an ethics is suspended within a specific paradox: namely, of rescuing the individual in the face of the world's total eclipse. However, he approaches this challenge from a dynamic principle inherent in human history[2]—and this is most certainly not the principle of reason—according to which the world is embroiled in a "collective disintegration of standards" (DPNE, p. 30). At the heart of ethics stands the phenomenon of evil, whose "collective outbreak ... brands our epoch" (ibid., p. 25). Thus, Neumann is highly critical of contemporary society and its moral crisis, which Nietzsche had "anticipated" 50 years earlier (ibid., p. 30).

The moral crisis of the 20th century, so Neumann, is the product of the "old ethic," by which he means Western ethics in its Judeo-Christian form (DPNE, p. 33f). This is characterised chiefly by the "denial of the negative" while rendering absolute the good (ibid.). The splitting of good and evil into two hostile principles has rendered ineffectual the old ethic, whose consequence and expression is the present catastrophe (ibid.).[3] The old ethic "has proved itself incapable of mastering the destructive forces in man" (ibid., p. 26). Or, in even starker terms, "wars are the correlative of the old ethic" (ibid., p. 45).

For Neumann, the precarious ethical state of Western humanity had escalated during the previous 150 years, that is, during the "bourgeois epoch." This or its dark side represents a deterrent conglomerate of hubris, delusion and cruelty:

> Western man's illusory self-identification with positive values, which conceals the real state of affairs, has never been more widespread than in the bourgeois epoch which is now coming to an end.
>
> (DPNE, p. 41)

He sees executions, prisons, welfare institutions, but also schools and families, as representative institutional forms in which the dark side of the ethical collective finds powerful expression (DPNE, p. 57). This finding is overshadowed even further by the " *'recollectivisation' process* of modern times" (ibid., p. 70; original emphasis).

Thus, where might newness spring from? Based on his idea of a dialectics of forces that has been triggered by a series of ruptures (see Chapter 11), Neumann believes that the "basic elements of a new ethic" (DPNE, p. 29) emerge from the depths of the unconscious. In this respect, he assumes that the individual is always far ahead of the collective, "that external collective developments are decades behind the development of the individual" (ibid.). His reflections on a new ethic turn entirely on the individual, whose "fate is the prototype for the collective." The individual, moreover, is the "retort in which the poisons and antidotes of the collective are distilled" (ibid., p. 30).

If we search for the intellectual signature of Neumann's radical reckoning with Western cruelty and his turn towards the individual, in which newness announces itself, thus leaving behind old values that have grown futile, we come across the work of Friedrich Nietzsche. It is no coincidence that Nietzsche's name appears at the very beginning of Neumann's *Depth Psychology and a New Ethic*, where he characterises those individuals who serve as "forerunners": They are the "sensitive, psychically disturbed and creative people," whose "enhanced permeability by the contents of the collective unconscious, the deep layer which determines the history of happenings in the group" predestines them for "emerging new contents of which the collective is not yet aware" (DPNE, p. 30). Their most striking features are their "lack of contemporaneity, remoteness and eccentric isolation—but also their prophetic role as forerunners" (pp. 30–31).

Here, Neumann's methods for transposing the basic contents of his *Roots of Jewish Consciousness* (originally conceived of as "The Psychology of the Jewish Person") become evident: He regards the prophet, first and foremost the figure of Moses, as the prototype and ethical precursor of the permeable individual, who is capable of initiating new historical orientations. Thus, Neumann draws a line from Moses to Nietzsche as it were.

His personal equation, to a certain extent his life's mission, became to eradicate the alienation of the modern human being. This, he felt, linked his own work to Jung's view of the individuation process. On 2 May 1934, Jung began delivering his *Zarathustra Lectures* at the Psychological Club in Zurich, a marathon undertaking that lasted until 1939. Although Neumann was listed among the seminar participants,[4] he left Zurich for Palestine in May 1934, and we may surmise that his luggage also included a copy of Nietzsche's works. Commenting briefly on Jung's *Zarathustra Lectures*, Steven Aschheim observes: "Jung simultaneously fashions Nietzsche into a prescient forerunner of the notion of the collective unconscious as well as living example of its inner workings, a confirmation of Jung's own system of analysis."[5]

In Neumann's work, particularly his early writings, which emerged amid great spiritual isolation in Palestine, and which were accompanied by his correspondence with Jung, two directions of thought intersect in an unconventional fashion: Jung's and (the previously ignored) *Jewish Nietzscheanism*. Coined by Achad Ha'am,[6] this term intends to capture the intellectual proximity of Judaism to Nietzsche's intellectual world on the one hand, and the rebellion against conventional Judaism on the other. For decades, Nietzsche's work exerted a powerful and significant influence on Jews, whether traditionalist, secular, Eastern or Western European, nationalist or assimilated, although in very different ways.[7]

Nietzsche enabled late-19th and early-20th century Jewish intellectuals to discover a new, liveable form of Jewish self-determination. He proclaimed the "revaluation of all values," which subsequently gave rise to Jewish Nietzscheanism. "The moral and cultural-critical, militant, prophetic, apocalyptic Nietzsche" knew how to kindle new thoughts.[8] Amid great tension and conflict, Nietzsche encouraged others to abandon the old and to strike out in search of new shores. The intellectual elite of this generation questioned the tradition of rationalist Enlightenment and its values. The anti-bourgeois, neo-romantic mood of those years, not least through highlighting the creative role of myth, combined reformist Zionist aspirations with the need for personal and collective renewal in terms of a nation of free and creative individuals who have been awakened to new life.[9] Nietzschean thinking asserted itself in this "Renaissance of Judaism," which had been largely initiated by Martin Buber. Essentially, Nietzsche was assimilated to German Zionism through Buber,[10] whose reading of *Zarathustra* had "acted like a revelation."[11] Nietzsche assumed the prophet's persuasive guise in *Zarathustra* and proclaimed: "You solitaries of today, you who have seceded from society … you shall one day be a people: from you, who have chosen out yourselves, shall a chosen people spring—and from this chosen people, the Superman" (Z, p. 103).

And, even more so, the Jews as a people, which had always demonstrated the greatest possible capacity in history for revaluing values, would be able, according to Nietzsche, to become the moral "legislator." Zarathustra's summons—"O my brothers, shatter, shatter the old law-tables" (Z, p. 219)—became the slogan of Jewish Nietzscheans.[12] Thus, Neumann's contrast "Old Ethic versus New Ethic" probably emerged in analogy to Nietzsche's famous chapter "The Old and New Law-Tablets" in Part Three of *Zarathustra*.

Neumann's *Depth Psychology and a New Ethic* follows Nietzsche's call to break the old tablets in a literal sense, for instance, when he mentions the "disintegration of the old values" (DPNE, p. 59). Or, for instance, when he mentions Abraham, "who broke his father's idols into pieces" (p. 39). Citing Nietzsche, Neumann refers to the former's play on words: *Brecher* (tablet-breaker) versus *Verbrecher* (law-breaker, "criminal") (ibid.).[13] *Depth Psychology and a New Ethic* became Neumann's most controversial book. It caused a storm of indignation, most of all in Zurich, and almost led to a break with the Jungians there. Its publication was also accompanied by a dramatic exchange of letters between Neumann and Jung. I will return to this point after discussing the Jewish-Nietzschean traces in Neumann's ethics.

Both Neumann's title and chapter headings indicate that *Depth Psychology and a New Ethic* is about overcoming the old and creating the new.[14] The catastrophes of the early and mid-20th century had disavowed the old ethic, and a nihilistic mentality emerged from the prevailing values. This old ethic, so Neumann, was accountable for those disasters. He substantiates this idea by referring to the adaptation strategies demanded by that ethic, and which had imposed themselves upon the individual with a view to fulfilling collective norms. The outcomes, so Neumann, were heteronomy and alienation. Characteristic of a personality thus shaped is an "'as if' attitude to sanctimonious hypocrisy and downright lying" (DPNE, p. 41). This is "symptomatic, in every case, of a split in the structure of the collective psyche" (ibid., p. 52).

In terms of depth psychology, this amounts to a "split between the world of ethical values in the conscious mind and a value-negating, anti-ethical world in the unconscious." This "generates guilt feelings in the human psyche and accumulations of blocked energies in the unconscious" (DPNE, p. 58). But can this split be prevented and, if so, how? Neumann detects an emerging reorientation. This is induced by "psychic crises," that is, the nihilistic positioning of modern humanity, by individuals who, provided they possess a deep psychological orientation, experience a specific disillusionment, namely, as "evil and sick in mind, antisocial and a prey to neurotic suffering, ugly and narrow-minded—an analytical technique which punctures the inflation of the ego" (ibid., p. 79).

Assimilating "the primitive side of our nature" is indispensable to making a fundamental ethical correction, for only this is capable of creating a "stable feeling of human solidarity and co-responsibility with the collective" (DPNE, p. 97). Building on these ideas, Neumann distinguishes different levels of moral development. In higher personality structures, he speaks of the authority of the "voice," which eliminates the collective law of conscience (see Chapter 11). He views conscience, a representative of the collective super-ego, as a heteronomous external influence. Its antagonist is the "voice," as an expression of an inner revelation of the new and the evolving, "of that which is to come, in fact" (DPNE, p. 122).[15] This radically individualised form of the new ethic "cannot be codified and made the basis of a general law" (ibid., p. 112). It lies beyond the scope of this chapter to discuss the aporias arising from Neumann's approach.

This brings us to Nietzsche's reception, the same Nietzsche who had proclaimed the "revaluation of all values," and whose intellectual radiance brought forth Jewish Nietzscheanism. Daniel Krochmalnik has highlighted the phenomenon of "counter-history" as "the preferred form of expression of Jewish Nietzscheanism."[16] This, he argues, needs to be understood in structural terms as a forum for accusation: "History is subjected to judgment from the standpoint of a counter-history," in order to break its spell. Counter-history thus functions as emancipatory rebellion. History and its course are perceived from the perspective of the excluded, not least from the perspective of the Bible. This opens up not only a new perspective but also a new concept of history.[17] But the criterion of "counter-history," which serves the project of describing history, amounts to the "revaluation of all values."[18]

Let us first consider the principle of "counter-history" from the perspective of the Bible. As mentioned, the Jewish Nietzscheans regarded themselves as the "breakers of the old tablets," as the founders of the new tablets or as the discoverers of ancient "hidden tablets."[19] The latter gave rise to a strong commitment to the "rebirth of the Jewish myth."[20] Many intellectual Jews of the generation born around 1900 consciously chose the "religion of myth based on Judaic sources" as an anti-liberal programme. Thus, the Pentateuch (for Oskar Goldberg), the Bible and the Hasidic tales (for Buber), the legends of the Midrash and Aggada (for Micha Josef Berdyczewski), and the Kabbalah (for Gershom Scholem) represented suppressed sources of Jewish mythology. At the same time, these endeavours can be seen as "reactive remythisation thrusts in response to rabbinical rationalism."[21]

In *The Roots of Jewish Consciousness*, Neumann expressed his belief in a revival of Judaism through a specific reading of the Bible, whose proximity to Nietzsche's stance towards the Old Testament (*Antichrist*, chapters 25–26) is plainly evident:[22]

> It has always been the incomparable charm and awe-inspiring greatness of the Bible—disregarding its determinative religious content for a moment— that it is governed by a powerful closeness to the earth, an undistorted view of good and evil, which no other people or time in the world knows. This ultimately quite untheological stance has always aroused the resentment of Christian and Jewish moralizers. Entangled with the here and now, this unconcern and piety are great enough to permit the tribal father, who wrestles with and defeats the angel, nevertheless to skillfully increase his property, just as they allow the law-giver of Sinai to be a manslaughterer and at the same time a timid person.

This long passage continues as follows:

> It is a powerful vitality that lets the God-filled Samson, a Nazarite, be killed by a foreign prostitute, while still holding him to be filled with God, and that almost grants permission to King David, the people's and God's favorite, to commit adultery, to murder, and to be a coward. If one compares this with the heroic endeavors of other peoples, for instance, the Neo-Germanics, one understands a point that is striking but otherwise not immediately obvious: namely, how passionately a mistaken theology bestowed its poison upon the Jewish people of the Old Testament, whose lack of feigning evoked its disapproval and misjudgment. Here, too, Nietzsche saw both sides correctly: the greatness and autochthony of the Old Testament on the one hand, and the clericalizing of its critics on the other.
>
> (Roots I, p. 36; see also DPNE, p. 129f.)

Nietzsche's view not only accompanied Neumann's outline of a depth psychology of the Jewish person, but it also appears in his ethical reflections. In this vein, *Depth Psychology and a New Ethic* represents a transposition of his reading of Nietzsche, particularly of *Zarathustra*, into a depth-psychological and philosophical score. Its thematic backdrop—along with the traumatisation inflicted by the Holocaust—involves engaging with the family constellation specific to Neumann and many Zionists. That constellation includes its indissoluble nature and the resulting unbearable feelings of guilt. The generational conflicts in early 20th century Jewish homes—and Neumann's was prototypical in this respect—often assumed highly complex forms:

> If the fathers remained orthodox, they had to reckon with their sons' rebellion. Whereas if they assimilated, they were discredited by anti-Semitism, and their sons returned to Judaism. Under no circumstances could they turn their backs on Judaism. ... anti-Semitism would not allow that to happen.[23]

Nietzsche's thinking promised a way out of these indissoluble tensions: His *Zarathustra* was viewed as a prophet whose second coming marked a fundamental ethical correction:

> Nietzsche's Zarathustra represents an individual who, at his own peril, formed concepts of good and evil, which subsequently evolved into ever more general concepts. Thus, he was the one who would cancel out those terms of reference. Having been a teacher for thousands of years, he would create a new future.[24]

With the return of *Zarathustra* as the transformer, as the destroyer of obsolete, unusable and now rigid ethical principles, Nietzsche devised a time frame within which he could think in terms of millennia and settle accounts with their ethical principles, particularly those of Western-Christian morality, the "old ethic." Thus, Nietzsche develops a brilliantly provocative critique of this morality that radically questions traditions while delineating the contours of a new morality. Similarly, Neumann's writing, whose decisive coordinates form the conceptual pair of good and evil, is pervaded by a general accusation against Western-Christian morality.

Let me turn to three pairs of contrasting concepts central to Neumann's ethics, whose structure is largely indebted to the Jewish-Nietzschean principle of "counter-history" outlined earlier.

Conscience versus voice

The figure of *Zarathustra* as a powerful destroyer of old values and prophet of new life enabled Neumann and other Zionists, whose lives were marked by truncations, upheavals and new beginnings, to feel entitled to entertain a central idea: namely, interrupting one's directly experienced tradition in order to revive it elsewhere—inspired, as mentioned, by a re-reading of the Bible.

The wisdom proclaimed as revelation, as well as those revolutionary, subversive features of *Zarathustra*,[25] made it possible for the Jewish Nietzscheans to return to the transformative forces of the prophetic word. In Neumann's work, the prophet—analogously to Zarathustra, the outcast—is the prototypical "Great

Individual"; his voice, which reveals the word of God, is paradigmatic of the original potential lying dormant in the individual. A prescient understanding, indeed anticipating the deepest contents as the rule of the creative unconscious, is one of the central thoughts on which Neumann's ethics hinges and which he calls the "Voice." This idea culminates in the antithesis between the voice and a critique of conscience, which is collectively oriented, bound by tradition and heteronomous. In contrast, the "voice" at work in the individual is forward-looking, creative, individual and self-responsible.

Essentially, Neumann's *Roots of Jewish Consciousness* amounts to a phenomenology of prophethood and the prophetic word:

> Behind the prophet's state of possession, as behind anything possessed by the spirit, stands that which wants to become loud, which wants to express itself, which is destined to intervene in life as word or saying.[26]

(Roots I, p. 38)

Neumann's rejection of conscience and its power as the central authority of the "old ethic" draws on Nietzsche's summary (in *Ecce Homo*) of the second part of his *Genealogy of Morality*. As Nietzsche writes:

> The second essay contains the psychology of conscience: this is not, as you may believe, "the voice of God in man"; it is the instinct of cruelty, which turns inwards once it is unable to discharge itself outwardly. Cruelty is here exposed, for the first time, as one of the oldest and most indispensable elements in the foundation of culture … But above all, until the time of *Zarathustra* there was no such thing as a counter-ideal.[27]

According to Neumann, the very cruelty that expresses itself in Nietzsche's formula of conscience qua resentment represents the "old ethic": "Puritanism and the Inquisition, the legalistic Judaism of the Pharisees and the parade-ground discipline of the Prussian mentality are all subject to the same psychological law" (DPNE, p. 56). This cruelty must be overcome, in what constitutes a revolutionary act, whose sole basis is "the original revelation to the Great Individual" (ibid., p. 63). Moreover: "The revolutionary (whatever his type) always takes his stand on the side of the inner voice and against the conscience of his time, which is always an expression of the old dominant values" (ibid., p. 39). The "criminals" (*Verbrecher*) of the inner voice are the "forerunners of a new ethic" (ibid.), since ethical values have always emerged "as a result of a revelation by the 'Voice' to the Founder Individual" (ibid., p. 62).

Father versus son

The contrast between conscience and voice is analogous to a new accentuation of the generational conflict in terms of the following model: The old stands opposed to the new, the past to the future and intuiting, the sclerotic and traditional to the creative and living, the conventional to the individual. Neumann sees the rigidifying into conventional traditionalism as a consequence of "absolute obligation," whose unattainability is reflected in the curse of "original sin" (DPNE, p. 116). This, he asserts, inevitably leads to a rejection of "'life in this world,'" to the "rejection of earth and the earthly, and, not least, the rejection of man himself" (ibid.).

These oppositions are typical of Neumann's generation and, as he knew from his own, assimilated home, of a specific problem of early 20th century Jewish families: loyalty to the German emperor. Here, Nietzsche's *Zarathustra* acted as a "destroyer of the morals of pious hillbillies," since he dared to denounce the commandments of the Decalogue as being hostile to life.

The chapter titled "Of Old and New Tables" in Part Three of *Zarathustra* begins: "Here I sit and wait, old shattered law-tables around me and also new, half-written law-tables" (Z, p. 214). These new, half-written tables no longer mention the importance of honouring father and mother. They instead emphasise the need to "make amends to your children for being the children of your fathers: thus you shall redeem all that is past! This new law-table do I put over to you!" (ibid, p. 221).

Neumann's "new table" reads: "Always and inevitably, the Voice possesses the character of a 'son' vis-à-vis the 'father' character of the law" (DPNE, p. 122). This new tablet can be read as a deliberate counterbalancing of Freud's "old tablet," particularly with regard to "the drama of parricide, as depicted by Freud in *Totem and Tabu*" (ibid., p. 120). This, in turn, needs to be seen as the "origin of the super-ego" (ibid.). As such, it falls under Nietzsche's previously cited "cruel verdict" against the old morality, which must be overcome (ibid.).

The original, or what in Jungian language are "archetypal tablets," now need to be contrasted with the legal formalism of the ethical principles formulated in the Decalogue. If the present and future belong to the child archetype, that is, the son in Neumann's language, overcoming the old is always contained in the archetypal image of patricide. Neumann does not believe that this image should be confused with the relationship to the personal father, because

> from the point of view of historical development, the supra-personal collective contents appear both phylogenetically and ontogenetically before the formation of the personal contents relating to the ego … The myth precedes the family romance.
>
> (DPNE, p. 121)

In this sense, "the murder of the father by the son will always remain an eternal primordial image of the inner history of mankind and individual man" (DPNE, p. 122). Neumann mentions the following examples of this archetypal and revolutionary event:

> This relationship is by no means peculiar to the son-religion of Christianity and the father-religion of Judaism. The same archetype governs the murder

of the Pope-Father (this, of course, is what the Pope really is) by Luther the heretic and, in Judaism (looking at it from the opposite point of view), the son-revolution of Hasidism against the typical paternal position of rabbinism.

(DPNE, p. 122)

"The ugliest man"

The usurpatory intention of the "criminal" son is now directed against the Western, Judeo-Christian ethic (DPNE, pp. 26ff.). Its essential thrust, so Neumann, is the "denial of the negative," while it also insists on the "absolute character" of the good (ibid., p. 34). Neumann's idea of revolution first refutes negativity, which he characterises as the "breakthrough of the dark side into Western consciousness" (ibid., p. 82). This dark side is represented by Jung's concept of the shadow (ibid., p. 78). The shadow is the outcast *par excellence*: "anti-social and greedy, cruel and malicious, poor and miserable … a beggar, a negro or a wild beast" (ibid., p. 95), a "hunchback" (ibid., p. 81). "The shadow … is the outcast of life" (ibid., p. 95f.).

In socio-political and cultural terms, however, this outcast attracts attention; he exercises a "deep, uncanny and perilous fascination" (DPNE, p. 84). Moreover: "The sick, the psychopath and the psychotic, the degenerate and the cripple, those in need of care and attention, the abnormal and the criminal arouse the interest and sympathy of contemporary man as never before" (ibid., p. 83).

Consequently, "ugliness, dissonance and evil are forcing their way into art." Examples include "atonality in music" and "Dostoievsky, in whose work man— sick, evil and abandoned—stands naked at the very heart of despair" (DPNE, p. 83). Now, however, this outcast can also be experienced by the individual as "the dark brother" residing in his own soul:

> The encounter with the "other side," the negative component, is marked by an abundance of dreams in which this "other" confronts the ego in such guises as the beggar or cripple, the outcast or bad man, the fool or ne'er-do-well, the despised or the insulted, the robber, the sick man."
>
> (DPNE, p. 79)

Moreover, "the personality experiences its relationship with the enemy of mankind, the drive to aggression and destruction, in the structure of its own being" (DPNE, p. 80). It is here, in this momentous clash with the unconscious, in which the "inflationary exaltation of the ego has to be sacrificed" (ibid.), that Neumann identifies an opportunity for "reconciliation with the dark brother of the whole human race" (ibid., p. 95).[28]

At key junctures in Neumann's reflections on the "dark brother," Nietzsche appears as an intellectual mentor, in the company of other "destroyers of old values":

> Darwin's "proof" of man's kinship with the apes, Biblical criticism and the thesis which interprets spirit as an epiphenomenon of the economic process,

Nietzsche's Beyond Good and Evil, and Freud's Future of an Illusion—all these have contributed to the destruction of the old values.[29]

(DPNE, p. 83)

Neumann explicitly refers to Nietzsche's "ugliest man," who appears in the fourth part of *Zarathustra*.[30] In his correspondence with Jung, Neumann makes a crucial point about the "discovery of the 'ugliest man,'"[31] who "occupies a far larger part of … the cultural life of our time than we normally realise" (DPNE, p. 82).[32] In his letter of 25 May 1957, Neumann alludes to the conditions under which he wrote his *New Ethic*. He first refers to Jung's "fine text *Present and Future*," before adding:

For me personally it was a pleasure, besides, that your text extends hand to my *New Ethic*, which fared so badly, even if in secret, of course. For if a reader of your work now asks himself, so what can actually be done, then he comes up against the problems that compelled me to this work back then in the second world war, with Rommel at the door. But, in fact, this genesis is not quite correct, for the deeper causes were [inner] images where it was all about evil and the "ape man" as destroyers, internally and externally.[33]

(JNC, pp. 324–325; translation modified)

Three weeks later (on 14 June 1957), Neumann was meant to provide more detailed information about these "inner images" in response to Jung's enquiry, which deeply "moved" Neumann:

The New Ethic was the attempt to process a series of phantasies that roughly corresponded timewise with the exterminations of the Jews, and in which the problem of evil and justice was being tossed around in me. I am still gnawing away at these images at the end of which, in brief, stands the following. I seemed to be commissioned to kill the ape man in the profound primal hole. As I approached him, he was hanging, by night, sleeping on the cross above the abyss, but his—crooked—single eye was staring into the depths of this abyss. While it at first seemed that I was supposed to blind him, I all of sudden grasped his "innocence," his dependence on the single eye of the Godhead, which was experiencing the depths through him, which was a human eye. Then, very abridged, I sank down opposite this single eye, jumped into the abyss, but was caught by the Godhead, which carried me on the "wings of his heart." After that, this single eye opposite the ape man closed and it opened on my forehead. (Bit difficult to write this, but what should one do.) Working outward from the attempt to process this happening, I arrived at *The New Ethic*. For me, since then, the world looks different.[34]

(JNC, p. 331)

Based on the experience that he had gained through his imagination, Neumann develops two further thoughts that can be traced back to Nietzsche: The first refers to what the experience of the primitive re-established in the individual: the connection with "nature and earth." Neumann describes this as a "basic shift ... in a downward direction, towards the earth, on such a scale as has never previously been experienced by the Christian world of the West" (DPNE, p. 82). A few pages later, he adds a second thought:

> When the ego realises its solidarity with the evil "ugliest man," the predatory man and the ape man in terror in the jungle, its stature is increased by the accession of a most vital factor, the lack of which has precipitated modern man into his present disastrous state of splitness and ego-isolation—and that is, a living relationship with nature and the earth.
>
> (DPNE, p. 96f.)

Only the "secular concentration on this earth characteristic of modern man" (DPNE, p. 134) makes it possible to envision a "stable feeling of human solidarity and co-responsibility with the collective" (ibid., p. 97).

In his Prologue, in a passage also considering evolution, from worm to monkey, from man to Superman, Zarathustra ponders the "meaning of the earth":

> I entreat you, my brothers, *remain true to the earth*, and do not believe those who speak to you of superterrestrial hopes! They are poisoners, whether they know it or not.[35]
>
> (Z., p. 42; original emphasis)

In its reference to body, earth and nature, which for Neumann represent the healing aspects of psychic depth, the "ground of one's own being" (DPNE, p. 96), life inevitably involves the question of evil, a subject that he addresses at the beginning of the *New Ethic*. The experience of the dark brother within oneself or the encounter with the ugliest man makes individuals work on and accept their "own evil." Crucially, "the individual is brought face to face with the necessity for 'accepting' his own evil" (ibid., p. 80). In the same section, he observes:

> The differentiation of "my" evil from the general evil is an essential item of self-knowledge from which no-one who undertakes the journey of individuation is allowed to escape. But as the process of individuation unfolds, the ego's former drive towards perfection simultaneously disintegrates.
>
> (DPNE, p. 80)

Thus, the new ethic extends "the responsibility of the personality ... to include the unconscious or at any rate the personal component of the unconscious, that part of it which contains the figure of the shadow" (DPNE, p. 93). This involves a "hard task" for the individual. To return to Nietzsche one last time: The concept of one's own evil can be placed in the context of the chapters "Self-Overcoming" and "Of

Old and New Law-Tables," in which Nietzsche demands the individualisation of values.[36]

Pervading Neumann's new ethic is Nietzsche's "pathos of distance,"[37] which, as Volker Gerhardt has noted, he "elevates to the maxim of every extraordinary life."[38] This pathos, so Nietzsche, is "the basic ethical rule" for the "sovereign person."[39] Thus, he demands the philosopher to possess this quality.[40] Neumann's tone, which resonates with his contempt of tradition,[41] irritated the Jungians in Zurich. Among others, he was accused of adhering to an "old testament perspective" (JNC, p. 249). Neumann was utterly astonished by the outrage at the newly founded Jung Institute in Zurich. He characterised its adversariness as "intellectual disingenuousness" and, as his letter to Jung reveals, was in a belligerent mood:

> I am willing to defend *The New Ethic*—which apparently no longer has any friends in Switzerland—in open battle against the whole institute. Protestants, Catholics, baptized Jews, unbaptized Jews, and even Jungian analysts if any show up.
>
> (JNC, p. 248f.)

When he first read *Depth Psychology and a New Ethic*, Jung agreed that "its effect will be like that of a bomb" (JNC, p. 236). He felt "a secret pleasure" and saw his role in the anticipated discussion as that of a "commandant of the fire brigade" (ibid., p. 237). Yet Neumann's reply (1 January 1949) asks Jung "not to extinguish too enthusiastically," since a cleansing fire might "eradicate some filth" (ibid., p. 239). His main accusation was directed against what he considered the misunderstood function of the unconscious:

> They smiled in a rather superior way about my provincial attitude, which was thought not quite up to it simply because I made a value judgment about where one ought to allow the wisdom of the unconscious to prevail, beyond good and evil. But they seemed to me all too often to mistake the unconsciousness of the ego for the wisdom of the unconscious.
>
> (JNC, p. 239)

Further:

> Some of the reservations against your teaching are based on the unrevolutionary and all too bourgeois stance of your students who always wish to anticipate the wisdom of the "third half of life" before they have the struggles of the first behind them. ... I do not wish to conceal from you that it sometimes seems to me that you are yourself rather complicit in this.
>
> (JNC, p. 239)

And then, towards the end of this lengthy letter, he adds the following assurance:

At the same time, though, I would like to assure you that my fervent efforts will continue to prove myself worthy of the "hate of the pussyfooters".

(JNC, p. 241)

Since the material concerned has only recently been published, neither this fierce controversy at the time, nor Jung's and Neumann's debate on the concepts of morality and ethics, has yet been discussed.[42] Roman Lesmeister's discussion of Jung's views on morality and ethics[43] suggest just how strongly Jung himself was moved by the idea of a "radical individualisation of ethics," an "ethics *beyond good and evil* in the conventional sense of these terms," an "ethics of the radical self-empowerment of the subject," from which "some of Nietzsche's spirit wafts over."[44]

The previous observations suggest what remains to be done to fathom the highly complex facts, in terms of their reception history, in both Jung's and Neumann's works.

Notes

1 Erich Neumann, *Depth Psychology and a New Ethic* (Boston: Shambala, 1990), p. 39; hereafter cited as DPNE.
2 See Walter Schulz, *Philosophie in der veränderten Welt* (Pfullingen: Neske Verlag), 1972, p. 691f.
3 Neumann also mentions the "basic Iranian concept of the battle between light and darkness," and thus refers directly to Zarathustra: "Mankind is confronted with the strange and, for the old ethic, paradoxical problem that the world, nature and the human soul are the scene of a perpetual and inexhaustible rebirth of evil" (DPNE, p. 46).
4 Jung's *Seminar on Nietzsches Zarathustra*, edited and abridged by J.L. Jarrett, Bollingen Series XCIX (Princeton, NJ: Princeton University Press 1998), p. XXV.
5 Steven Aschheim, *The Nietzsche Legacy in Germany, 1890–1990* (Berkeley: University of California Press, 1992), p. 9.
6 Friedrich Niewöhner, "Jüdischer Nietzschanismus seit 1888: Ursprünge und Begriff," in Werner Stegmaier and Daniel Krochmalnik (eds.), *Jüdischer Nietzscheanismus* (Berlin, New York: De Gruyter, 1997), p. 22.
7 Ibid., p. XX.
8 Ibid., p. XVII.
9 Aschheim, *The Nietzsche Legacy*, p. 105; see also his *Brothers and Strangers: The East European Jew in German and German Jewish Consciousness, 1800–1923* (Madison: University of Wisconsin Press, 1982), esp. chapters 4 and 5.
10 Nietzsche made a lasting impact on Buber's work; see, among others, Paul Mendes-Flohr, *Von der Mystik zum Dialog: Martin Bubers geistige Entwicklung bis hin zu 'Ich und Du'* (Königstein/Taunus: Jüdischer Verlag, 1978). The subjects and language of Buber's early works exhibit many similarities with Nietzsche's writings; see also Aschheim, *Brothers and Strangers*, p. 107. One notable instance is Buber's "Ein Wort über Nietzsche und die Lebenswerte," in *Die Kunst im Leben* (Berlin, December 1900).
11 Stegmaier and Krochmalnik, *Jüdischer Nietzscheanismus*, p. XXIX.
12 For a discussion, see Daniel Krochmalnik, "Neue Tafeln: Nietzsche und die Jüdische Counter History," in Stegmaier and Krochmalnik, *Jüdischer Nietzscheanismus*, p. 56f.

13 The passage in Nietzsche reads: "They hate the *creator* most: him who breaks the law-tables and the old values, the breaker—they call him the law-breaker" (Z, p. 229).

14 Neumann's *Depth Psychology and a New Ethic* is divided into four chapters: "The Old Ethic," "Stages of Ethical Development," "The New Ethic" and "The Aims and Values of the New Ethic."

15 See also the following passage: "In earlier times, this phenomenon only occurred or was observable in ethical geniuses; today, however, it is already affecting far wider circles in the individualised population of the West" (DPNE, p. 112).

16 Krochmalnik, "Neue Tafeln," p. 59. David Biale coined this term in his biography of Gershom Scholem: *Gershom Scholem: Kabbalah and Counter-History* (Cambridge, MA: Harvard University Press, 1979).

17 Krochmalnik, "Neue Tafeln," p. 81.

18 Ibid., p. 74.

19 Ibid., pp. 74ff.; see also section 26 of *The Antichrist*, where Nietzsche addresses a Jewish priest: "Out of the powerful and *wholly free* heroes of Israel's history they fashioned, according to their changing needs, either wretched bigots and hypocrites or men entirely 'godless.' They reduced every great event to the idiotic formula: 'obedient *or* disobedient to God.'"

20 Krochmalnik, "Neue Tafeln," p. 70f.

21 Ibid., p. 71.

22 In *Beyond Good and Evil,* Nietzsche states: "In the Jewish 'Old Testament,' the book of divine justice, there are men, things, and sayings on such an immense scale, that Greek and Indian literature has nothing to compare with it. One stands with fear and reverence before those stupendous remains of what man was formerly, and one has sad thoughts about old Asia and its little out-pushed peninsula Europe, which would like, by all means, to figure before Asia as the 'Progress of Mankind' ... the taste for the Old Testament is a touchstone with respect to 'great' and 'small'" (chapter 3, section 52).

23 Krochmalnik, "Neue Tafeln," p. 76f.

24 Werner Stegmaier, *Hauptwerke der Philosophie: Von Kant bis Nietzsche* (Stuttgart: Reclam, 2005), p. 409.

25 In *Ecce Homo*, Nietzsche observed that Zarathustra came over him like a "revelation" (in the section "Why I Write Such Excellent Books").

26 See also the following passage: "For the Jew, attached to the earth and to the here and now, a steadying counterweight is formed by the prophets, who, in their primordial experience of YHWH as the irruptive God, are seized by the numinous supremacy of his ambivalent spirit-nature" (Roots I, p. 37). Connecting the Bible, primeval religious experience and C.G. Jung, Neumann observes: "However, as Jung has again recently pointed out [A.L.], this side of the divinity, as *deus absconditus*, is an inescapably real experience for the religious person, who does not have idyllic religious experiences, but has been beheld and called from the abyss within ... All prophetic experience is based on this primary experience of the numinous" (Roots I, p. 38).

27 See *Ecce Homo*, "The Genealogy of Morals: A Polemic." See also this passage in the *Genealogy of Morals*: "This *instinct of freedom* forced into being latent—it is already clear—this instinct of freedom forced back, trodden back, imprisoned within itself, and finally only able to find vent and relief in itself; this, only this, is the beginning of the 'bad conscience'" (Second Essay, "Guilt," "Bad Conscience," and the Like, section 17).

28 See also: "To be obliged to admit that one is infantile and maladjusted, miserable and ugly, a human animal related to the monkeys, a sexual beast and a creature of the herd is in itself a shattering experience for the ego" (DPNE, p. 80).

29 A few pages later, Neumann refers to the "ideal of the blond beast" (DPNE, p. 85).

30 In *Zarathustra*, Part Four, Chapter 7, "The Ugliest Man," Zarathustra comes to a valley where he encounters a hideous creature. Deeply ashamed, Zarathustra averts his gaze. The being, the ugliest man, is God's murderer: "He had killed God because his compassion for his ugliness and shame had been shameless: even in the last corners of his misery this God had looked and recognized him in everything. The ugliest man could not bear such a witness to his tormented existence. He thanks and praises Zarathustra for his contempt of compassion"; see Barbara Himmelmann, "Zarathustras Weg," in Volker Gerhardt (ed.), *Friedrich Nietzsche: Also sprach Zarathustra* (Berlin: De Gruyter, 2000), p. 42—Trans.

31 See Jung's lecture of 24 June 1936 in his *Seminar on Nietzsche's Zarathustra*, in which he refers to questions raised by Neumann, who evidently participated in the seminar by letter. One question explicitly refers to "the rejection of the inferior function or *the ugliest man*"; see *Jung's Seminar on Nietzsche's Zarathustra*, abridged edition, ed. by James L. Jarrett, Bollingen Series XCIX (Princeton, NJ: Princeton University Press, 1988), p. 247ff.

32 In connection with Nietzsche's "ugliest man," Neumann considers the term "earth" and the theme of evil, which also occur in *Zarathustra*.

33 Jung replied almost immediately, on 3 June 1957, which suggests his keen interest in the topic; see JNC, pp. 327–330.

34 It is no coincidence that Neumann here recalls aphorism 146 from Nietzsche's *Beyond Good and Evil*: " He who fights with monsters should be careful lest he thereby become a monster. And if thou gaze long into an abyss, the abyss will also gaze into thee." Neumann's vision might also be seen as an analogy to Zarathustra's "most oppressive dream." The passage in context is: "Truly, you have dreamed *your enemies themselves*: that was your most oppressive dream!" (Z, p. 158; original emphasis). It also echoes Zarathustra's prologue: in his attempt to teach the Superman to the people, Zarathustra takes up the theory of evolution: "You have made your way from worm to man, and much in you is still worm. Once were you apes, and even now man is more of an ape than any ape" (Z, p. 42). See Stegmaier, *Interpretationen Hauptwerke der Philosophie*, p. 425f.

35 The passage continues: "To blaspheme the earth is now the most dreadful offence, and to esteem the bowels of the Inscrutable more highly than the meaning of the earth. Once the soul looked contemptuously upon the body … So the soul thought to escape from the body and from the earth" (Z, p. 42). Fettered to his body, his nature and the earth in rejection of supernatural salvation leads Zarathustra to express his idea of "eternal recurrence" (Z, p. 237). I am unable to pursue this idea in more detail here. But let me nevertheless mention that in the end *the ugliest man*, almost devoured by his self-loathing, surprisingly speaks of his love of life: He wants to live it again in the same way. As Zarathustra's dark brother, the ugliest man takes up Zarathustra's struggle for the idea of *eternal recurrence*. This is the struggle to free oneself from weariness after realising that all things return forever: the hopeful and forward-looking but also the ugly, the small, the mediocre, the inferior, the evil.

36 See the end of the section titled "Of Self-Overcoming: "Truly, I say to you: Unchanging good and evil does not exist! From out of themselves they must overcome themselves again and again! And he who has to be creator in good and evil, truly, has first to be a destroyer and break values. Thus the greatest evil belongs with the greatest good: this, however, is the creative good" (Z, p. 139).

37 See *Genealogy of Morals*, First Essay, "Good and Evil," "Good and Bad," (section 2).

38 Volker Gerhardt, *Pathos der Distanz* (Stuttgart: Reclam, 1988), p. 6.

39 Ibid.

40 Referring to Nietzsche's posthumous fragments, Stegmaier and Krochmalnik note: "According to Nietzsche, it was again the Jews who, since ancient times, understood

'the pathos of distance': the permanent 'foreign rule' to which they opposed the arrogance of a spiritual aristocracy had educated them this way" (p. XV)—Trans.

41 The majestic plural (*we*) underscores this gesture: "This type of holiness has become loathsome in our eyes," *Depth Psychology and a New Ethic*, p. 115.

42 The response to Neumann's treatise was also marginal beyond psychoanalytic circles. One exception is Walter Schulz's brief contribution to *Philosophie in der veränderten Welt* (Pfullingen: Klett-Cotta, 1972). More recently, Neumann's ethics has attracted criticism from Jungians; see, for instance, Roman Lesmeister, "Grundlagen von Moral und Ethik in der Analytischen Psychologie," *Analytische Psychologie* 39 (2008), pp. 52–69. See also the contributions by Anita von Raffay and Gerhard Burda to *Zur Utopie einer neuen Ethik: 100 Jahre Erich Neumann, 130 Jahre C.G. Jung: Kongressband zur Dreiländertagung der deutschsprachigen Gesellschaften für Analytische Psychologie* (Vienna: Österreichische Gesellschaft für Analytische Psychologie, 2005).

43 Lesmeister, "Grundlagen von Moral und Ethik in der analytischen Psychologie."

44 Ibid., pp. 62–63.

Chapter 13

"... all of a sudden I grasped his innocence"[1]

A vision

Neumann's letter to Jung of 25 May 1957 is highly interesting since it articulates his "deeper reasons" for writing his controversial *Depth Psychology and a New Ethic*. He describes the book as

> the attempt to process a series of phantasies that roughly corresponded time-wise with the exterminations of the Jews, and in which the problem of evil and justice was being tossed around in me.
>
> (JNC, p. 329)

The thinking of French philosopher Emmanuel Lévinas provides a helpful context for gauging Neumann's underlying motivations. Here, in 1957, he alludes to the conditions under which he wrote his *New Ethic*. He first refers to Jung's "fine text *Present and Future*":[2]

> For me personally it was a pleasure, besides, that your text extends hand to my *New Ethic*, which fared so badly, even if in secret, of course. For if a reader of your work now asks himself, so what can actually be done, then he comes up against the problems that compelled me to this work back then in the second world war, with Rommel at the door. But, in fact, this genesis is not quite correct, for the deeper causes were [inner] images where it was all about evil and the "ape man" as destroyers, internally and externally.
>
> (JNC, pp. 324–325)

As observed in the previous chapter, Neumann sent Jung more detailed information about these "inner images," in response to Jung's reply, which had deeply "moved" him. His letter continues as follows:

> I am still gnawing away at these images at the end of which, in brief, stands the following. I seemed to be commissioned to kill the ape man in the profound primal hole. As I approached him, he was hanging, by night, sleeping on the cross above the abyss, but his—crooked—single eye was staring into the depths of this abyss. While it at first seemed that I was supposed to blind him, I all of sudden grasped his "innocence," his dependence on the single

eye of the Godhead, which was experiencing the depths through him, which was a human eye. Then, very abridged, I sank down opposite this single eye, jumped into the abyss, but was caught by the Godhead, which carried me on the "wings of his heart." After that, this single eye opposite the ape-man closed and it opened on my forehead. (Bit difficult to write this, but what should one do.) Working outward from the attempt to process this happening, I arrived at *The New Ethic*. For me, since then, the world looks different.[3]

(JNC, p. 331)

Today's reader might feel alienated, or perhaps even dismayed, by Neumann's pathos and his pictorial motif of the imagination. Just as we might find the notion of the "ape man" embarrassing. The term recalls the zoomorphisms of anti-Semitic political propaganda, in which the "dehumanisation" of the Jews found its outrageous expression.[4] Anti-Semitic agitation and dehumanisation doubtless climaxed in *Der Stürmer*, the anti-Semitic weekly founded by Julius Streicher on 20 April 1923.[5]

Does Neumann's vision constitute more than a legitimate attempt to escape from hate-filled images and slogans? What does his reference to his monstrous, yet innocent counterpart suggest? Does it contain more than the cheap "exculpation" of a barbarian opposite, combined with impending self-pathologisation, that is, another variation on so-called Jewish self-hatred, a concept en vogue ever since Theodor Lessing? "We must change," Arnold Zweig had declared as early as 1913. Numerous literary sources point to the defensive strategies that were deployed by Jewish people to maintain an identity now acutely threatened with extinction. One of these strategies was to appropriate the gaze of others.[6]

We might easily settle for this line of interpretation. And yet, does Neumann's text not perhaps extend even further? His *New Ethic* offers various clues to interpreting encounters with the monstrous, including the "predatory man" and the "ape man," two metaphors of the "'ugliest man'" (DPNE, p. 96). As I mentioned in the previous chapter, Neumann took the figure of the "ugliest man" from Nietzsche's *Zarathustra*. This figure exists beyond the pressure of anti-Semitic stereotypes, since his monstrosity is not politically contextualised. This, among others, indicates the difficulty of distinguishing various semantic levels without neutralising them.

Neumann's vision points to an asymmetrical encounter: an evidently superior figure—the "I" in the vision—approaches a sleeping, one-eyed ape man with the intention of killing him. This juxtaposition—cultural supremacy versus primitivism—already surfaced in one of Jung's well-known papers ("The Role of the Unconscious," published in 1918), which is controversial from a modern perspective. Reflecting on World War I, Jung discusses the distinction between the "Jewish" and the "Germanic" peoples:

> Christianity split the Germanic barbarian into an upper and a lower half, and enabled him, by repressing the dark side, to domesticate the brighter half and

fit it for civilization. But the lower, darker half still awaits redemption and a second spell of domestication. Until then, it will remain associated with the vestiges of the prehistoric age, with the collective unconscious, which is subject to a peculiar and ever-increasing activation. As the Christian view of the world loses its authority, the more menacingly will the "blond beast" be heard prowling about in its underground prison, ready at any moment to burst out with devastating consequences. When this happens in the individual it brings about a psychological revolution, but it can also take a social form.

(CW 10, §17)

He adds:

In my opinion this problem does not exist for the Jews. The Jew already had the culture of the ancient world and on top of that has taken over the culture of the nations amongst whom he dwells. He has two cultures, paradoxical as that may sound. He is domesticated to a higher degree than we are, but he is badly at a loss for that quality in man which roots him to the earth and draws new strength from below. This chthonic quality is found in dangerous concentration in the Germanic peoples. Naturally the Aryan European has not noticed any signs of this for a very long time, but perhaps he is beginning to notice it in the present war; and again, perhaps not. The Jew has too little of this quality—where has he his own earth underfoot? The mystery of earth is no joke and no paradox.

(CW 10, §18)

Neumann quotes this passage in June 1933, in his dispute with James Kirsch. Their exchange was published in the *Jüdische Rundschau*, the journal of the German Zionist Association. Neumann placed himself protectively in front of Jung by presenting him as a spiritual precursor of Zionism.[7] The antagonism evident in Jung's assertions upends the anti-Semitic stereotype: not the Jews, but the Germanic peoples are the primitives, the barbarians. The Jew, on the other hand, is "domesticated to a higher degree," by ancient culture and by the culture of the "host people."

Jung's claims suggest that the monstrous counterpart of the imagination is a screen figure of the barbaric Teuton, whose single eye recalls Polyphemus. His intention to kill—secretly, as his counterpart is asleep—casts Neumann in the role of Odysseus, through whom this cultural antagonism has come down to us. This wise and agile figure knows how to keep himself and his companions safe whatever the threat. He eventually (and very cunningly!) frees himself and his companions from the power of Polyphemus, the uncouth monster. Odysseus also appears in Adorno's and Horkheimer's *Dialectic of Enlightenment*, where Homer's *Odyssey* exemplifies the "raveled skein of prehistory, barbarism, and culture,"[8] from which the dialectic of the Enlightenment takes its momentous course. Adorno and Horkheimer regard Ulysses, one of the fathers of Western culture, as one of the first executors of the power relations perpetuated to the present day—on account of his intellectual superiority, which nurtured his self-confidence.[9]

Considering this dialectical, yet asymmetrical relation between superiority and violence makes those contemplating Neumann's vision aware of what might transcend the entanglement of barbarism and culture, since something new and unexpected happens. The killing fails to take place and is replaced by an experience that is shifted into the superior protagonist. For Neumann, the "face to face" (Lévinas) initiates an experience that is perceived as diametrically opposed to the original instinct of killing one's adversary. This experience prevents the impulse to kill. In the protagonist's encounter with the ape man, the other's monstrosity—which is exaggerated by his one-eyedness—shifts into a human dimension. The other person's eye becomes a human eye. After the gaze sinks into the other's single eye, an exchange occurs: The single eye now opens on Neumann's forehead while it closes on his counterpart's. This eye constellates a new semantics. It becomes a metaphor of seeing things as the other does, of seeing more or even differently than previously, which Neumann captures in three verbs: "grasping, sinking, opening." The process of understanding and perception through encountering the other initiates ethical change. In Homer's *Odyssey*, the sleeping Polyphemus is blinded, loses his power of vision, enabling Odysseus and his companions to escape from captivity. Neumann's version of this encounter stands in the strongest possible contrast with the Homeric original.

Let me briefly digress to the work of the French philosopher Emmanuel Lévinas, whose phenomenological exploration of the other, whom he calls "fellow man," offers an alternative approach to Neumann's account of his vision. Lévinas's thinking turns on the constitution of the ethical subject and on the question of intersubjectivity. This question has equated his work, since its reception in Germany in the 1970s, with a hitherto unsurpassed exploration of justice, and with coming to terms with guilt and responsibility.

Lévinas was born in 1906.[10] His parents, brothers and other members of his family were murdered by the Nazis. Exploring the horror of extermination is one of the central aspects of his philosophy. He argues that understanding, indeed the capacity to understand in the first place, occurs through interpersonal relations. For Lévinas, these assume a particular shape, since they extend beyond conceptual or philosophical interpretation from the outset:

> The other. Our relation with him certainly consists in wanting to understand him, but this relation exceeds the confines of understanding. Not only because, besides curiosity, knowledge of the other also demands sympathy or love, ways of being that are different from impassive contemplation, but also because, in our relation to the other, the latter does not affect us by means of a concept. The other is a being and counts as such.[11]

Lévinas's key metaphor of our fellow human being is the face: "The Face of the Other is perhaps the very beginning of philosophy."[12] This philosophy, at whose beginning stands the experience of the other, is intimately related to ethics. Lévinas grounds this new philosophical perspective in the fundamental human experience of proximity, in which the distinction between what lies within and beyond our skin becomes questionable:

> An awakening to the other man, which is not knowledge. Precisely the approach to the other man—the first one to come along in his proximity as fellowman—irreducible to knowledge ... Thought that is not an adequation to the other, for whom I can no longer be the measure, and who precisely in his uniqueness is refractory to every measure, but nonetheless a non-indifference to the other.[13]

The experience of the other, as Lévinas puts it, is associated with direct encounter. Thus, the other is the stranger who suddenly appears before us and disturbs our peace (of mind). The other in Lévinas's sense is anything but the person we choose or prefer to associate with. This "awakening" wrenches us out of our sleep and out of predictability. It interrupts the "familiar" and the "ordinary." By approaching the "first one to come along," we have entered an asymmetrical relation. For us, the "first one to come along" represents a "face" without "a plastic form like a portrait."[14] Thus, we neither know or recognise that person. Our "relationship with the other is not symmetrical, it is not at all as in Martin Buber."[15]

Lévinas also describes this awakening, which we might best understand as a shock, as the "epiphany of the face." Here, proximity and separation, encounter and defencelessness, clash:

> This otherness and this absolute separation manifest themselves in the epiphany of the face, in the face to face. Being a grouping quite different from the synthesis, it initiates a proximity different from the one that presides over the synthesis of data, uniting them into a "world" of parts within a whole. The "thought" awakened in the face or by the face is commanded by an irreducible difference: thought which is not a thought of, but, from the very beginning, a thought *for* ... a non-in-difference for the other breaking the equilibrium of the equal and impassive soul of knowledge.[16]

Lévinas speaks of encounters and discrepancies that "decentre the subject," that undermine feelings of security and eventually make the self become unsure of itself. The inner movement appearing in "the thought for" delineates the balancing act of a shaken self whose convulsion triggers an ethical impulse. Yet that is not all. Lévinas seeks to heighten this idea into a radical-ethical conflict, one caused by the other's "exposure." On an archaic level, this nakedness activates an impulse to kill:

> The relation to the Face is both the relation to the absolutely weak—to what is absolutely exposed, what is bare and destitute, the relation with bareness

and consequently with what is alone and can undergo the supreme isolation we call death—and there is, consequently, in the Face of the Other always the death of the Other and thus, in some way, an incitement to murder, the temptation to go to the extreme, to completely neglect the other—and at the same time (and this is the paradoxical thing) the Face is also the "Thou Shalt not Kill."[17]

This "incitement to murder," the attempt to exterminate the other—which both Lévinas and Neumann consider the primordial ethical scene, in which the human makes its first appearance—is a scene of temptation, to be imagined quite biblically, and its inhibition. The temptation lies in the desire to triumph, which leads to annihilating the other. Contemplation involves intuiting difference as a basic relationship. This, however, can never become relational:

> The temptation of total negation, which spans the infinity of that attempt and its impossibility—is the presence of the face. To be in relation with the other face to face—is to be unable to kill. This is also the situation of discourse.[18]

For, as Lévinas adds: "At the very moment when my power to kill is realized, the other has escaped ... The immediate is not an object of understanding."[19]

Thus, what is the most radical form of nakedness? For Lévinas, it is that moment when we are caught in the other's gaze. When that gaze falls upon me, I experience affirmation. The gaze of the other, with whom I come face to face, constitutes within me the prohibition to kill, beyond friendship or enmity:

> The face that looks at me affirms me ... it is only the noumenal glory of the other that makes the face to face situation possible. The face to face situation is thus an impossibility of denying, a negation of negation ... the "thou shalt not murder" is inscribed on the face and constitutes its very otherness ... Neither hostile nor friendly, all hostility, all affection would already change the pure vis-à-vis of the interlocutor.[20]

Recognition, which is constituted through us looking at each other, is based on experiencing ourselves as existing in and through the gaze. Another's gaze enables me to experience myself as someone who exists. And yet, Lévinas's reflections extend even further, beyond the present encounter, by placing the gaze within a concept of time in which time "opens up." In the gaze, as we have seen, the principle of "thinking for" another, which forms the basis of responsibility, opens up:[21]

> In my responsibility for the other, the past of the other, which has never been my present, "concerns me": it is not re-presentation for me. The past of the other and, in a sense, the history of humanity in which I have never participated, in which I have never been present, is my past.[22]

Lévinas speaks of "my *nonintentional* participation in the history of humanity, in the past of the others, who 'regard/look at me,'" and through which the "sovereign *I* is put into question."[23] The radical alienness of the other, implicit in his gaze, which—paradoxically—recognises me, and vice versa, has to do with his story, which is foreign to me. The gaze establishes a closeness with an alien narrative, with which I am related, both unintentionally and involuntarily.

Let us return to Neumann's vision. We can now associate his encounter with the "ape man" with Lévinas's phenomenological "textual threads": We can understand the ape man in the context of experiencing "the first one who comes along," as a "face ... with no plastic form," as a metaphor of a radical "nakedness," which inhibits the impulse to kill.

Complete asymmetry becomes evident: On the one hand, the protagonist, superior in every respect, who is preparing to become a murderer; on the other, albeit with open eyes, the sleeping ape man, who is at the mercy of the other. This rapprochement occurs under the sign of power and violence. The moment in which the situation keels over is fragile; it occurs when the protagonist is seized by the unknown, which Neumann calls "innocence," so as to express the immediacy of the situation.

How might we understand the other's "innocence"? Let us recall what constituted ethics first and foremost for Lévinas:

> In my responsibility for the other, the past of the other, which has never been my present, "concerns me": it is not re-presentation for me. The past of the other and, in a sense, the history of humanity in which I have never participated, in which I have never been present, is my past.[24]

Unquestionably, the mysterious centre of Neumann's text is the cyclopic, dormant and yet alert gaze. The other's strange, rigid gaze opens up a window of time in which his past, and moreover human history, is contained. Looking into this window of time, or rather through it, interrupts the impulse to kill, as Neumann remarked in his letter to Jung of 14 June 1957: "I all of sudden grasped his 'innocence,' his dependence on the single eye of the Godhead, which was experiencing the depths through him, which was a human eye" (JNC, p. 331).

Now, exchange takes place: The figure imagining this sinks into the other's single eye, whereupon the eye closes and opens on the other's forehead. To speak of an "epiphany of the face" seems warranted here, given this sudden opening in the protagonist, which occurs through his encounter with his counterpart's nakedness, his radical otherness.

Responsibility replaces violence in the above sense: as the "nonintentional participation in the history of humanity, in the past of other, in relation to a past that is not a personal past."[25] And yet, this is no ordinary experience. According to Lévinas, it "does not come from the world," but instead marks "a breach made by humanness in the barbarism of being."[26]

This epiphany is the nucleus of philosophising, also for Neumann. It is pre-ceded—prior to any thinking—by a profound experience of the unconscious—"the encounter with the 'other side,'" as Neumann explains in *Depth Psychology and a New Ethic* (p. 79), in which the "inflationary exaltation of the ego has to be sacrificed" (p. 80). He describes this encounter as follows:

> The encounter with the "other side," the negative component, is marked by an abundance of dreams in which this "other" confronts the ego in such guises as the beggar or cripple, the outcast or bad man, the fool or ne'er-do-well, the despised or the insulted, the robber, the sick man, etc. etc.
>
> (DPNE, p. 79)

At that point "where the personality experiences its relationship with the enemy of mankind, the drive to aggression and destruction, in the structure of its own being" (DPNE, p. 80), Neumann recognises a bridge to achieve "reconciliation with the dark brother of the whole human race" (ibid., p. 86).[27] Or as Lévinas says: "*Thou shalt not murder* is inscribed on the face."

Like Lévinas, Neumann's authority in this respect is Dostoievsky, "in whose work man—sick, evil and abandoned—stands naked at the very heart of despair" (DPNE, p. 83). What Lévinas describes (in various places) and interprets as the "epiphany of the face," in Neumann's depth-psychological terminology becomes the experience of the unconscious and the encounter with the shadow. This expe-rience determines responsibility, both for Lévinas and for Neumann.[28]

Neumann describes being taken possession of by the other as the appearance of the latter's eye on "my forehead," as an "encounter with the dark brother inside me." This seizure inverts the original power relations because it bears the traits of stigmatisation: Not I do something onto the other, but something is done onto me. What is gained thereby? The philosopher and psychoanalyst Rudolf Bernet raises this question in his essay "Das traumatisierte Subjekt" ("The traumatised subject"). Taking Lévinas as his starting point,[29] Bernet observes that

> any attempt to summarise the psychoanalytic view of psychological trauma is reminiscent of the language of Lévinas. In fact, trauma, in psychoanalytic terms, denotes the subject's encounter with something completely foreign, which affects it, inevitably and most intimately.[30]

In *Otherwise than Being or Beyond Essence* (1981), Lévinas describes the human subject as "traumatically commanded."[31] The neighbour summons and "assigns me before I designate him."[32] This appropriation of the subject means that it is "set up as it were in the accusative form," without, however, "being able to slip away."[33] Thus, for Lévinas, the subject is taken hostage by the other.[34] His claim that the other comes from an "immemorial past," which is never present,[35] recalls Freud's claim about posteriority: We can neither remember nor forget trauma.[36]

We need to understand Lévinas's and Neumann's thinking against the back-ground of a massive historical break: the Holocaust. They both consider how the traumatised subject responds to its traumatisation. This, in turn, raises another fundamental question: What constitutes subjectivity?

Bernet suggests that we ought to speak of the "traumatisable" rather than of the "traumatised" subject. The transition from the traumatised to the traumatisable ego involves thinking of the subject not as what pre-exists trauma, that is, on what underlies it, but as what constantly reconstitutes itself through "being called" and "answering." For Lévinas, the subject, as an I, is unjustifiably subject to another's "call," to which I submit. Further, the I that "answers" this call is no longer what it was before. It transforms into "being-for-the-other." In this thinking, the subject is constituted in terms of an asymmetrical dialogue, and as such in terms of "calling and answering."

With regard to this asymmetrical dialogue, Neumann's approach to human experience and thought is structurally related to Lévinas's. Both refer to the human being's constitutive vulnerability, which makes us a "traumatisable subject." They also regard this as a condition of and as an empowerment to being and to becoming human. We need to understand this vulnerability as an opening that is constitutive of the subject. There must, according to Bernet, "already exist a fissure in the I that allows the voice of the other to echo in me without losing its otherness and its power to bring about change."[37] The asymmetry presents itself as follows: "The subject who responds to the trauma does not respond on its own; its response comes from the trauma and therefore remains dependent on it."[38]

Or, as Lévinas puts it, the one who responds to the trauma is a "subject against his will."[39] This anticipates a certain difference between Lévinas and Neumann. Lévinas is aware of the "appropriation" by the other as an "affront," even if this involves change, that is, the basic impulse of ethical action *par excellence*. Being a "subject against one's will" indicates the boundary at which the subject is painfully constituted. Neumann, on the other hand, lends his experience a programmatic dimension. His heroic, captivating language, very much true to the vitalist spirit of Jewish-Nietzschean thought, which sees itself as laying the ethical foundations of the future, drowns out the quiet truth of "being a subject against one's will."

To return to Neumann's vision one last time: After sinking into the other's single eye, "he jumped into the abyss, was caught by the deity who … [carried him] on the wings of the heart." What Neumann describes here eludes final understanding. A secret remains, namely, how the "perished" subject—reappearing from the abyss—reassembles itself and finds a language in which its vulnerability can find expression.

Notes

1 Neumann to Jung, 25 May 1957; see *Analytical Psychology in Exile: The Correspondence of C. G. Jung and Erich Neumann.* Edited by Martin Liebscher. Translated by Heather McCartney (Princeton, NJ: Princeton University Press, 2015), p. 331.
2 See C.G. Jung (1957), "The Undiscovered Self (Present and Future)," CW 10.
3 As mentioned in Chapter 12, it is no coincidence that Neumann's vision recalls aphorism 146 in Nietzsche's *Beyond Good and Evil*: "He who fights with monsters should

be careful lest he thereby become a monster. And if thou gaze long into an abyss, the abyss will also gaze into thee."

4   Alongside the figure of the devil, these zoomorphisms included various animals traditionally assigned negative traits. The pig is of particular importance, as it is considered impure in Jewish religious law and is therefore well suited to defamation. The widespread motif of the *Judensau* ("Jewish pig") has been part of the "classical" repertoire of anti-Semitic stereotypes since the Middle Ages. Others, for instance, ugly, purportedly treacherous, unpredictable or monstrous animals, also appear preferentially in the arsenal of anti-Semitic representations. They include spiders, snakes, giant octopuses, vampires, monkeys and ravens.

5   The articles published in *Der Stürmer* were accompanied by large-format headlines and anti-Semitic cartoons by Philip Rupprecht (pseudonym: Fips) or by photographs visually reproducing the established anti-Semitic stereotypes.

6   Nicolas Berg, *Luftmenschen, Zur Geschichte einer Metapher* (Göttingen: Vandenhoeck und Ruprecht, 2008), p. 115ff.

7   Neumann, *Jüdische Rundschau* (1934), p. 5; see also Chapter 4.

8   Max Horkheimer and Theodor W. Adorno, *Dialectic of Enlightenment*, trans. Edmund Jephcott (Stanford: Stanford University Press, 2002), p. 62.

9   Ibid., pp. 35ff. Like Neumann's ethics, the *Dialectic of Enlightenment* was also written in the early 1940s. The foreword was written in 1944 and the volume was published in Amsterdam in 1947. Neumann wrote his preface to *Depth Psychology and a New Ethic* in 1948.

10   According to the Julian Calendar, Lévinas was born on 30 December 1905 in Kaunas in Lithuania (i.e. 12 January 1906 in the Gregorian Calendar); see Salomon Malka, *Emmanuel Lévinas: Eine Biographie* (Munich: Beck, 2003).

11   Emmanuel Lévinas, "Is Ontology Fundamental," in *Entre Nous: On Thinking-of-the-Other*, translated by Michael B. Smith and Barbara Harshav (New York: Columbia University Press, 1998), p. 5.

12   Ibid., "Philosophy, Justice, and Love," p. 103.

13   Ibid., "Diachrony and Representation," p. 168.

14   Ibid., "Philosophy, Justice, and Love," p. 104.

15   Ibid., p. 105.

16   Ibid., "The Philosophical Determination of the Idea of Culture," p. 185f.; my emphasis.

17   Ibid., "Philosophy, Justice, and Love," p. 104.

18   Ibid., "Is Ontology Fundamental," p. 10.

19   Ibid., p. 10f.

20   Ibid, "The I and the Totality," *Entre Nous*, pp. 34–35.

21   Ibid., "Philosophy, Justice, and Love," *Entre Nous*, p. 115.

22   Ibid., p. 115.

23   Ibid., "Diachrony and Representation," p. 171; original emphasis. See also the following passage: "A significance in ethics of a pure past irreducible to my present, and thus, of an originating past. An originating significance of an immemorial past, in terms of responsibility for the other man. My unintentional participation in the history of humanity, in the past of others which has something to do with me" ("From the One to the Other," *Entre Nous*, p. 150).

24   Ibid., "Philosophy, Justice, and Love," p. 115.

25   Ibid, "From the One to the Other," p. 150.

26   Ibid., "The Philosophical Determination of the Idea of Culture," p. 187.

27   See also: "To be obliged to admit that one is infantile and maladjusted, miserable and ugly, a human animal related to the monkeys, a sexual beast and a creature of the herd is in itself a shattering experience for any ego (DPNE, p. 79f.).

28 Neumann asserts that the new ethic extends the "responsibility of the personality ... so as to include the unconscious or at any rate the personal component of the unconscious, that part of it which contains the figure of the shadow" (DPNE, p. 93).

29 Rudolf Bernet, "Das traumatisierte Subjekt," in Matthias Fischer, Hans-Dieter Gondek and Burkhard Liebsch (eds.), *Vernunft im Zeichen des Fremden, Zur Philosophie von Bernhard Waldenfels* (Frankfurt am Main: Suhrkamp, 2001), pp. 225ff.

30 Ibid., p. 227.

31 Emmanuel Lévinas, *Otherwise than Being, or Beyond Essence*, trans. Alphonso Lingis (The Hague: Martinus Nijhoff, 1981), p. 87.

32 Ibid., p. 86.

33 Ibid., p. 85.

34 See Bernet, "Das traumatisierte Subjekt," pp. 225ff.

35 Lévinas, *Otherwise than Being*, p. 89.

36 Bernet, "Das traumatisierte Subjekt," p. 235.

37 Lévinas, *Otherwise than Being*, p. 240.

38 Ibid., p. 246.

39 Ibid., p. 246.

Chapter 14

"Oedipus the vanquished, not the victor"[1]

The Origins and History of Human Consciousness and Neumann's critique of Freud

In his letter of 4 June 1946, Neumann told Jung that he had sent him the first part of a manuscript titled "Über die archetypischen Stadien der Bewusstseinsentwicklung" ("The Archetypal Stages of Conscious Development"): "As you can imagine, this work is very important to me and I would like to publish this work this time. I think it is now ready to come out" (JNC, p. 166). Neumann is referring to *The Origins and History of Human Consciousness*. Published by Rascher in 1949, this became one of his most important works. The following dream played a crucial role in its emergence:

> I once dreamed, almost three years ago, that you said to me: "I would like to eat some more fruit with you." This sentence got into me in its own or in my own way, and independently of the complexity of its meaning, it has been a strong incentive for me. For, as paradoxical as it may be, it was a challenge to me, and for me, the book is a fruit, which I am sending you herewith "to eat." Should you have a taste for it, it would be a great pleasure for me. And if "eating together" could find expression in an introduction from you, my egotistic interpretation of the dream would come fully true.
>
> (JNC, p. 168)

For Neumann, Jung's failure to respond to the manuscript was "a little bitter." He vented this feeling by lamenting the difficult conditions under which he was having to conduct his research:

> The isolation of my existence in Palestine is probably greater than you imagine, and I fear a part of the deficiencies of which I was fully conscious on sending the manuscript to you has to do with this basic fact of my life. I have virtually no opportunity of discussing any scientific matters with peers, and this may be evident.
>
> (JNC, p. 166)

This isolation also left Neumann feeling uncertain about his "self-evaluation," which he describes as "quite shaky" (JNC, p. 166). Sometimes he finds his work important, "at other times everything becomes doubtful once again" (ibid.). Jung did not reply until 5 August 1946: Neumann's complaint about his intellectual isolation resounds in Jung's own lamentation:

> I have also been giving some thought to how we can get you back to Europe again. But for the time being I can't see any way this can be done. The situation is extremely difficult and everything is uncertain. While we are still living on our cultural island as before, everything around us is nothing but destruction, physically as well as morally. To do something reasonable oneself, you have to close your eyes. Germany is indescribably rotten.
>
> (JNC, p. 171)

Jung responds neither to Neumann's implicit request to intervene with potential publishers on his behalf, nor to his explicit request that he (Jung) should write an introduction to *Origins and History*. Instead, he praises Neumann's manuscript after a first reading: "I am especially impressed by the clarity and precision of your formulations" (JNC, p. 171).

Less than a year later—having meanwhile studied the first part of Neumann's manuscript in detail and still full of admiration—Jung wrote to Neumann on 1 July 1947, saying that he had spoken to Rascher, who were prepared to publish the book. Apologising for the delay in communication, which was due to his ill health, Jung added: "So you see, since I have been better, I have been engaged with your affairs and am doing my best to facilitate publication" (JNC, p. 196).

Neumann responded very promptly, on 8 July 1947, and expressed his delight at this positive development:

> You can imagine how pleased I was about your letter letting me know that Rascher has accepted my book. What is more, I am really touched by the active engagement you are showing toward me and my productions.
>
> (JNC, p. 197)

As Neumann later told Jung, he urged Rascher to make haste with printing his *Origins* and *New Ethic* because he feared that postal services between Palestine and Europe would soon be interrupted (see his letter of 3 April 1948; JNC, p. 219). The fact that a dark shadow clouded the publication of these works in 1949 had to do with the founding of the C.G. Jung Institute in 1948. This event appeared to restrict Jung's freedom of opinion and action: He changed his previous, enthusiastic foreword to *Origins and History* into a significantly more reserved version, very much to Neumann's disappointment (see Chapters 8, 9 and 12).

In his letter of June 1946, Neumann had mentioned three works that had exerted a particular influence on his work: Jung's "Transformations" and "Book on Alchemy," as well as Thomas Mann's novel *Joseph and his Brothers*.[2] The first part of Jung's "Transformations" had appeared in 1911, in the *Jahrbuch für psychoanalytische und psychopathologische Forschungen* (Yearbook for psychoanalytical and psychopathological research) published by Eugen Bleuler and Freud.[3] Shortly afterwards, its publication soon put the seal on Jung's break with Freud. The work was titled *Wandlungen und Symbole der Libido. Beiträge zur Entwicklungsgeschichte des Denkens* ("Transformations and Symbols of Libido. Contributions to the History of the Development of Thought"). In his preface to the fourth edition, published in 1950, Jung observed:

> The whole thing came upon me like a landslide that cannot be stopped. The urgency that lay behind it became clear to me only later: it was the explosion of all those psychic contents which could find no room, no breathing-space, in the constricting atmosphere of Freudian psychology and its narrow outlook. I have no wish to denigrate Freud, or to detract from the extraordinary merits of his investigation of the individual psyche. But the conceptual framework into which he fitted the psychic phenomenon seemed to me unendurably narrow. I am not thinking here of his theory of neurosis, which can be as narrow … One of my principal aims was to free medical psychology from the subjective and personalistic bias that characterized its outlook at that time, and to make it possible to understand the unconscious as an objective and collective psyche … Thus this book became a landmark, set up on the spot where two ways divided. Because of its imperfections and its incompleteness it laid down the programme to be followed for the next few decades of my life.
>
> (CW 5)

In *Origins and History*, whose mythological material was indebted to important works in the fields of religious philosophy, anthropology, ethnology and archaeology, Neumann consciously addressed Jung's work and thus also his criticism of Freud's psychoanalytical approach.[4] According to Neumann, Freud's thinking contains a "concretistic and narrowly personalistic theory of libido" (OHC, p. xviii). Analogously to the subtitle chosen by Jung at the time, *Beiträge zur Entwicklungsgeschichte des Denkens* ("Contributions to the History of the Development of Thought"), Neumann chose the concept of *consciousness*, probably also to distinguish his work from Karl Abraham's *Versuch einer Entwicklungsgeschichte der Libido* ("A Short Study of the Development of Libido"), in which human "symbolic products are misunderstood and depreciated" (OHC, p. 32, n. 48).[5]

In Neumann's theory of conscious development, the "ego complex," the "central complex of the psyche," forms the "theater for the events," insofar as this is supported by an incessant emancipatory-creative dynamics (OHC, p. 262). In his introduction to *Origins*, he observes:

> The evolution of consciousness as a form of creative evolution is the peculiar achievement of Western man. Creative evolution of ego consciousness means that, through a continuous process stretching over thousands of years, the conscious system has absorbed more and more unconscious contents.
>
> (OHC, p. xviii)

In the Western cultural canon, the "creativity of consciousness" (OHC, p. xix) is central to individual development. In *Origins*, Neumann sets out to systematically demonstrate to what extent "a priori transpersonal dominants—archetypes—which, being essential components and organs of the psyche from the beginning, mold the course of human history" (ibid., p. xxi). They are "constituents of psychic development" in the consecutive stages of child development (ibid., p. 264).

Jung's preface expressed his appreciation of Neumann's work:

> He has woven his facts into a pattern and created a unified whole, which no pioneer could have done nor could ever attempted to do. As though in confirmation of this, the present work opens at the very place where I unwittingly made landfall on the new continent long ago, namely the realm of *matriarchal symbolism* ... Upon this foundation he has succeeded in constructing a unique history of the evolution of consciousness, and at the same time in representing the body of myths as the phenomenology of this same evolution.
>
> (OHC, pp. xiii–xiv; original emphasis)

Neumann, in contrast to Freud, opposes the "personalistic" reduction of the castration threat and patricide. Further, the "early history of humanity" should not be understood "in the likeness of a patriarchal bourgeois family of the nineteenth-century" (OHC, p. xxi–xxii). Instead, he embeds these terms in a transpersonal framework, in which their destructive–regressive or emancipatory–progressive character becomes evident in the dialectical interplay with the individual psyche's conscious realisation.

Neumann's theoretical conception is based on the dominance of the transpersonal, from which the personal and the individual have developed only slowly in the history of humanity and whose stages—by analogy—need to be passed through again in the ontogenetic development of the individual (OHC, p. xvi).[6] Using a wealth of material and considerable interpretative acumen, Neumann maps out a large-scale panorama of archetypal stages through which he describes the development of consciousness. My brief overview attempts to illuminate Neumann's criticism of Freud, in particular of the Oedipus complex, and to indicate how Neumann's thinking is related to Jung's work.

The drama in which the ego complex is involved bears witness to both entanglement and emancipation. If the ego, in its mythical place of origin, is at first wholly contained in the unconscious, it soon strikes out—as verifiable mythological evidence attests—on its path as a hero who must battle unconscious forces. Emancipation from this envelopment only marks one stage in the hero's path. The heroic canon of culture is transformed at a well-defined point through its own activity, which considerably expands the hero's horizon of experience: "Consciousness = deliverance: that is the watchword inscribed above all man's efforts to deliver himself from the embrace of the primordial uroboric dragon" (OHC, p. 105).

Nevertheless, containment in the uroboros, which represents the bisexual World Parents, meant a deep connection with nature and with the unconscious.

It meant existing in *participation mystique* as a unified being. Neumann finds dramatic words for the bursting open of the "fluid continuum," the unity in which early humans were enclosed:

> Differentiation of the ego, separation of the World Parents, and dismember-ment of the primordial dragon set man free as a son and expose him to the light, and only then is he born as a personality with a stable ego.
>
> (OHC, p. 106)

Only the "separation of the World Parents" made the world "dual, as is said in the Jewish midrash" (OHC, p. 116). The human being "objectifies" the world, confronts it and is confronted by it. The "son," who is placed centre stage, now stands between the opposites: between the World Parents and between the bright heaven (above) and the dark earth (below). In this way, he simultane-ously experiences powerlessness, fear, loss, the threat of death and, in the final instance, guilt. Neumann also describes this primordial loss as "primary castra-tion" (ibid., p. 118) and points to the "theologisation" of this essential stage of conscious development:

> Interpreted as sin, apostasy, rebellion, disobedience, this emancipation is in reality the fundamental liberating act of man which releases him from the yoke of the unconscious and establishes him as an ego, a conscious individual.
>
> (OHC, p. 120)

In this self-imposed loss, the ego appropriates the instruments of negativity, which springs from its ability to say no. These instruments include "to discriminate, to distinguish, to mark off, to isolate oneself from the surrounding context … for the motto of all consciousness is *determinatio est negatio*" (OHC, p. 121).

This distinction also includes the masculine and the feminine principles. The unconscious is experienced as feminine in the course of the separation of the World Parents, in that it is birth-giving and generative, yet also absorbing and devouring. This conception of the feminine needs to be understood archetypally: The spiritual constellations, which are governed by the unconscious, are under the dominance of the Great Mother. According to the mythological canon, the counterpart is consciousness, which is experienced as archetypal and masculine. These archetypal dominants are experienced and worked through differently in the developing female psyche than in the male psyche. Neumann articulates this difference as follows:

> Man experiences the "masculine" structure of his conscious as pecu-liarly his own, and the "feminine" unconscious as something alien to him, whereas woman feels at home in her unconscious and out of her element in consciousness.
>
> (OHC, p. 125, n. 13)

The archetypal images of mother and father also rest on this original matrix of opposites (male versus female):

> In relation to the ego, the mother image has both a productive and a destructive aspect, but over and above that, it preserves a certain immutability and eternality. Although it is two-faced and can assume many shapes, for the ego and consciousness it always remains the world of the origin, the world of the unconscious ... Whereas man's ego and his consciousness have changed to an extraordinary degree during the last six thousand years, the unconscious, the Mother, is a psychic structure that would seem to be fixed eternally and almost unalterably.
>
> (OHC, p. 171)

After the "separation" of the World Parents, the second, mythologically well-documented stage, now involves the confrontation with these opposites, the dragon fight. In this struggle, patricide and matricide (that is, both types of murder) occupy a "sacred place" (OHC, p. 172). If, however, we are to better understand and classify the "sanctity" of these murders, we need to take account the "dual structure" of heroism (ibid, p. 136f.). To begin with, the problem of dual parentage is important for the hero's path. Having two fathers or two mothers is "a central feature in the canon of the hero myth":

> Besides his personal father there is a "higher," that is to say an archetypal father figure, and similarly an archetypal mother figure appears beside the personal mother. This double descent, with its contrasted personal and suprapersonal parental figures, constellates the drama of the hero's life.
>
> (OHC, p. 132)

In addition to his dual parentage, another essential attribute of the hero is his "double nature":

> He is a human being like the others, mortal and collective like them, yet at the same time he feels himself a stranger to the community. He discovers within himself something which, although it "belongs" to him and is as it were part of him, he can only describe as strange, unusual, god-like. In the process of being exalted above the common level, in his heroic capacity as doer, seer, and creator, he feels himself like one "inspired," altogether extraordinary and the son of a god.
>
> (OHC, p. 136)

The third doubling of the hero archetype is that he is "twice-born." Only the twice-born, the born-again, can be described as a hero (OHC, p. 148). This explicit reference to the hero's dual structure (or double nature) enables the distinction between the transpersonal and the personal. It also opens up a symbolic understanding of the focal points of murder, incest and castration, which become important in the "dragon fight."

Neumann first put this dual structure to the test with totemism. While he criticises Freud's interpretation, he admits that Freud "made a vital discovery" before adding that he had, however, also "distorted and misunderstood something even more vital" (ibid., p. 144). In male societies, which once played a secondary role in matriarchy, a developmental step takes place through initiation rites gravitating round "higher masculinity." These rites have no "phallic-chthonic" emphasis, but instead occupy a spiritual position, one associated symbolically with light and the sun, the head and the eye. The men are now connected via their fathers to a world structure that appears as "heaven" in contrast to the feminine earth. This heaven is not yet the seat of a deity, but needs to be understood as "air – spirit – pneuma – principle," which will eventually lead to patriarchy and the enthronement of patriarchal deities in the following cultural stage. In the initiation rites of male societies, young men are devoured by a spirit associated with the masculine world. When they are reborn, they are no longer born by the mother, but by the spirit; they are no longer sons of the earth, but sons of heaven. To this day, initiation rites for young men have the character of initiations into the world of the male spirit and intellect. The male world represents the ancestral tradition, the law and the world of the gods (ibid., p. 143). Moreover:

> It is no accident that all human culture, and not Western civilization alone, is masculine in character, from Greece and the Judaeo-Christian sphere of culture to Islam and India. Although woman's share in this culture is invisible and largely unconscious … The masculine trend, however, is towards greater co-ordination of spirit, ego, consciousness, and will.
>
> (OHC, p. 143)

For Neumann, male societies are the birthplace of consciousness, "higher masculinity" and finally also of individuality. Decreasing unconsciousness makes the totem a content that can be experienced as a projection and is represented by an animal, a plant or a "thing." As an "indefinable quantity," the totem represents wholeness as a tangible group; it represents the ancestral as an experienceable inter-generational relationship. Neumann describes the totem as a "transpersonal, spiritual being" (OHC, p. 145). Moreover: "This totemic being forms the basis of a whole, a totem community which is not so much a natural biological unit as a spiritual or psychic structure" (ibid.).

This transpersonal or spiritual interpretation of the totem leads Neumann to criticise Freud. The totem "never has a personal character, let alone that of the personal father" (OHC, p. 144):

> On the contrary, the whole point of the ritual is that the procreative spirit should be experienced as something remote and different … The initiations

of puberty, like all initiations, aim at producing something suprapersonal, namely that part of the individual which is transpersonal and collective. Hence the production of this part is a second birth.

(OHC, p. 144)

Neumann rejects Freud's interpretation of totemism, which is associated with the latter's theory of patricide. This, in turn, is also a key element of the Oedipus complex, since Freud misunderstands the hero motif as wishful thinking rather than as an archetype of masculine, patriarchal consciousness. Even anthropologically, Freud succumbs to a personalistic misinterpretation with his "hypothesis of a gorilla father." Freud argued that overcoming the apelike patriarch, who is slain by the brotherly band, is the origin of totemism, from which in turn the main features of religion and culture can be derived (OHC, p. 153).

The fight with the dragon is thus the fight with the First Parents, a fight in which the murders of both father and mother, but not of one alone, have their ritually prescribed place. The dragon fight forms a central chapter in the evolution of mankind as of the individual.

(OHC, p. 153)

In contrast, Neumann finds Jung's interpretation, substantiated in the *Psychology of the Unconscious*, convincing:

He shows, first, that the hero's fight is the fight with a mother who cannot be regarded as a personal figure in the family romance. Behind the personal figure of the mother there stands ... what Jung was later to call the mother archetype.

(OHC, p. 154)

The bisexual structure of the uroboric dragon means that the Great Mother possesses not only feminine but also masculine features (OHC, p. 155). These, however, should not be misinterpreted as paternal ones. Thus, the fear of the dragon "does not correspond to the fear of the father, but to something far more elemental, namely the male's fear of the female in general" (ibid). Against this background of fear, the hero's incest is "regenerative" (ibid., p. 154), and thus constitutes a form of rebirth. It is not—as Freud claimed—the young boy's fantasy, which only his fear of the castrating father is able to temper. Thus, incest needs to be seen as a stage in vanquishing the mother. It involves "actual entry into her" and thus brings about rebirth (ibid.).

Two qualities distinguish the hero: first, active incest, that is, his conscious exposure to the "dangerous influence of the female," as represented by the "womb, the pit, and hell"; second, his overcoming the fear of the feminine (OHC, p. 158): "The incest produces a transformation of personality which alone makes the hero a hero, that is, a higher and ideal representative of mankind" (ibid., p. 154).

Here, Neumann offers a fundamental critique of Freud's theory of the Oedipus complex, which he contrasts with his own interpretation. This rests on his insistence that the hero's drama unfolds in mythologically distinct stages of development. Neumann interprets the Oedipus myth in terms of its outcome, from the perspective of failure, that is, in terms of Oedipus's lack of consciousness. This deficiency marks a certain stage within the development of consciousness. For Neumann, Oedipus is "only half a hero" (OHC, p. 164), whose progression stalled, who thus regressed to being a son and who eventually suffered the fate of the son-lover. In context, this line of interpretation reads as follows:

> Though Oedipus conquers the Sphinx, he commits incest with his mother, and murders his father, unconsciously. He has no knowledge of what he has done, and when he finds out, he is unable to look his own deed, the deed of the hero, in the face. Consequently he is overtaken by the fate that overtakes all those for whom the Eternal Feminine reverts to the Great Mother: he regresses to the stage of the son, and suffers the fate of the son-lover. He performs the act of self-castration by putting out his own eyes … It signifies the destruction of the higher masculinity, of the very thing that characterizes the hero; and this form of spiritual castration cancels out all that was gained by his victory over the Sphinx. The masculine progression of the hero is thrown back by the old shock, the fear of the Great Mother which seizes him after the deed. He becomes the victim of the Sphinx he had conquered.
>
> (OHC, p. 163)

Thus, Oedipus failed to commit active, conscious matricide, that is, to slay the motherly aspect that is projected onto the father. He also failed to perform incest as a ritual of rebirth, since he did not identify with the "father-god." Only by belonging to "heaven," and by his "sonship with God," does the hero, the intruder into dark Earth Mother, once again "hack his way out of the darkness" (OHC, p. 165). According to Neumann, Oedipus lacks all the features typical of the hero's birth, and which would have established his connection with the divine. Thus Sophocles's tragedy is also a "myth of early times." Situated between "the epoch of the Great Mother and the intermediate stage of the dragon fight" (ibid., p. 168), it does not represent a real heroic tragedy, "but the glorification of a fate beyond the control of man" (ibid., p. 164). Moreover, the "drama contains the traces of the early matriarchal epoch," in which appears the "dominance of the Great Mother, with a philosophical coloring, as total dependence upon fate" (ibid.).

In contrast, the *Oresteia* marks a new developmental stage in the heroic canon. In Sophocles, the son kills his mother, avenges his father and thus completes his identification with him. Aided by the "paternal-solar principle," Orestes ushered in a new era of the "patriarchate," which Neumann defines in Bachofen's sense, as "the predominantly masculine world of spirit, sun, consciousness, and ego" (OHC, p. 168). This culture has a strong masculine emphasis, whereas "in the matriarchate, the unconscious reigns supreme, and the predominant feature here is a preconscious, prelogical, and preindividual way of thinking and feeling" (ibid.).

This raises a crucial question: In which sense can we speak of "patricide" if Oedipus did not murder his father, but his mother, although in a fragmented and ultimately unsuccessful way— that is, the bisexual uroboric dragon at the level of the matriarchal stage of culture? Neumann asserts that answering this question requires a fundamental inquiry into the father principle. Like the mother principle, its personal and transpersonal structure is positive and negative, that is to say, ambiguous. Mythological evidence exists both for the murderous, destructive father and for the generative-protective father. Nevertheless, the ego's relation to the father and the father image calls for a different psychological interpretation than its relation to the mother and the mother image. The latter's relation to the ego can be defined in terms of "its productive and destructive aspect." This image can assume many shapes, "but over and above that, it preserves a certain immutability and eternality." It always remains "the creative background" (OHC, p. 171).

This timeless character of the mother principle means that the personal mother is far less significant than the mother archetype than it is with the father. In addition to the archetypal father image, the personal father image is quite significant, according to Neumann—not as an individual person, yet as "the character of the culture and the changing cultural values which he presents" (OHC, p. 172). This different structural emphasis on the mother and father image is part of Neumann's own theoretical approach, which reaffirms, "in a most surprising way one of Jung's central discoveries: the anima psychology of man and the animus psychology of woman" (ibid.).

As I have mentioned, the cultural canon of the patriarchate is represented by male societies. These are the origin of all taboos, legislations and institutions, through which the dominance of the Great Mother begins to dissolve (OHC, pp. 146 and 173). Thus, the father world is

> the world of collective values; it is historical and related to the fluctuating level of conscious and cultural development within the group. ... [The fathers] preside over the upbringing of each individual and certify his coming of age. Always the fathers see to it that the current values are impressed upon the young people ... The advocacy of the canon of values inherited from the fathers and enforced by education manifests itself in the psychic structure of the individual as "conscience".
>
> (OHC, p. 173)

That is to say, the father world needs to be defined in terms of the transfer of cultural values. The hero as son, who challenges and overcomes this paternal world, breaks down the old laws and opposes the fathers "and their spokesman, the personal father" (OHC, p. 174). Neumann agrees with Otto Rank's description of patricide in the hero myth, even though he rejects its narrow, personalistic interpretation.[7] In this context, the threat emanates from the old paternal system, which strives for the son's death and ruin. Symbolically, it concerns the struggle between an old and a new system of rule. This power struggle is evident both in the history of Moses and in the myth of Heracles (ibid.).

The "creative" hero's refusal to adjust to the cultural canon transmitted by the fathers reflects an element of discontinuity. The hero points towards the future and gives "the world a new and better face" (OHC, p. 174). Understanding this heroic deed presupposes a transpersonal father. As the "'inner voice'" or "command" within the son, this figure wants the world to change, yet clashes with the personal father, who represents the old law (ibid.). This interpretation of the father–son conflict, so Neumann, refutes Freud's view:

> It is no uxorious gorilla father who, as paterfamilias, drives out his son ... no wicked king packs off his son to slay the monster, which is himself, as the nonsensical psychoanalytical interpretation would have us believe.
>
> (OHC, p. 176)

Eventually, Oedipus succumbed to the mother world of early times. In the patriar-chate, the fatal attraction to the Great Mother corresponds to what Neumann calls "patriarchal castration." Now held captive,

> the ego remains totally dependent upon the father as the representative of the collective norm—that is, it identifies with the lower father and thus loses its connection with the creative powers ... it remains bound by traditional morality and conscience, and, as though castrated by convention, loses the higher half of its dual nature.
>
> (OHC, p. 187)

These fathers' sons are the "parallels of the mothers' sons" (OHC, p. 189). They suffer from what Neumann calls the "'Isaac complex'" (ibid.): While they corre-spond to the father, and worship the patriarchal canon of values, they do not gain independence. Nor do they possess the "inner voice," that is, the authority "that announces the new manifestation of the Divine" (ibid.).

The concept of castration becomes the subject of an extensive debate in Neumann's correspondence with Jung, which includes the latter's sole objection to Neumann's *Origins and History of Consciousness*. In his letter of 1 July 1947 (see earlier), Jung writes:

> Having read your first volume, the only troubling terminology to strike me was that of the "castration complex." I consider the use of this term to be not only an aesthetic error, but also an erroneous overvaluation of the sexual symbolism. This complex is a matter of the archetype of sacrifice, a term that is much more comprehensive, and that takes into account the fact that, for the primitive, sex does not have, by far, the same significance as it does for the modern individual ... The expression "castration complex" is, to my

taste, much too concretistic and therefore one-sided, even though it definitely proves to be applicable in a whole series of phenomena ... We must place the existence of the psyche as a sui generis phenomenon in the first place and understand the instincts as being in a specific relationship to this.

(JNC, p. 195f.)

A week later, Neumann's reply rejected the accusation of "concretism." He disagreed with Jung's suggestion to speak of an "archetype of sacrifice" instead. As far as the concretistic is concerned, Neumann argues that no "'genital' misunderstanding of castration" could occur, "especially as the symbolic meaning of the sexual is explored at length" (JNC, p. 199f.). Further, he considers it "absolutely necessary to retain the sexual symbols that are interpreted in a personal way by psychoanalysis" (ibid.). He adds that this also explains his decision to preserve the term "incest." "Castration," so Neumann, is what threatens masculinity in various ways; "sacrifice," on the other hand, is merely a "subsuming concept," yet not a symbol:

In castration, there is the threat to the ego and consciousness by the terrible mother of the unconscious. The ego is supposed to be sacrificed, against which it defends itself. This dramatization of the situation, as an expression of the conflict of the psyche is not in any way denoted by the concept of sacrifice, but it is very much so by the castration symbol. Not until the hero stage does the archetype of sacrifice become relevant, it seems to me, as a fulfilled act assumed by the ego ... The concept of sacrifice belongs, just like the taboos etc. to the "offering" in the sense of a positive relationship of the ego to the Self and thus belongs on the side of consciousness—strengthening—expansion, etc. The castration symbol stands in the first part where it is a question of a disempowerment of the ego-consciousness and of a danger of violation by the unconscious.

(JNC, p. 200)

Neumann hopes to have persuaded Jung and invites suggestions if he has failed in his attempt. Jung replied 11 days later. Expressing his understanding of Neumann's request, he uses their discussion to expand and clarify his own terminology and to introduce a possible correction:

I cannot repudiate the justification of "castration complex" terminology and even less its symbolism, but I must take issue with "sacrifice" not being a symbol. In the Christian sense it is even one of the most significant symbols ... With incest it is the same thing, which is why I had to use the additional term *hierosgamos*. Just as only the twin concepts "Incest-Hierosgamos" describe the whole situation, so also "castration-sacrifice." Could one say *castration symbol* instead of castration complex, to be on the safe side? Or castration *motif* (like incest motif)?

(JNC, p. 202; original emphases)

Neumann took up Jung's suggestion, in particular his caveat about unnecessary misunderstandings. In a footnote in *Origins and History*, he explains that "whenever in our discussion we speak of castration we mean a symbolic castration, and never a personalistic castration acquired in childhood and having concretistic reference to the male genitalia" (OHC, p. 53, n. 16).

The brief summary of this discussion reveals two points: On the one hand, Neumann was his teacher's equal—even if living and working in Palestine denied him opportunities for sustained professional exchange. On the other, their debate reflects a productive turn of events: While Jung expanded his conceptual repertoire, Neumann took Jung's fear of being misunderstood seriously.

Let us return to Neumann's critique of Freud's interpretation of the Oedipus complex and totemism.[8] Neumann's deliberations are exceptional in psychoanalytic literature: They are the only sustained cultural-historical examination of the underlying mythological matrix, and hence the only qualified assessment of Freud's interpretation. Unquestionably, Neumann's cultural-historical approach is captivatingly clear. Nevertheless, it still raises the question whether it is not precisely Oedipus's "succumbing"—when placed within the mythological context specified by Neumann—that provides a highly suitable backdrop against which average human entanglement in compulsive repetition is experienced as fate. Its recognition does not rule out the possibility of considering further mythological models of heroic struggle as a basis for personal development. However, this idea eludes Neumann for two reasons: On the one hand, because he seeks to distinguish Freud's basic "personalistic" assumptions from the "family romance"; and on the other, and this reason is more far-reaching, because he refused to consider individual therapy as an option in light of the devastation wreaked by the Third Reich and the Holocaust.

Neumann's attitude towards psychoanalysis can also be interpreted in generational terms. The generation born around 1900 in Germany spent its youth and its formative years in the shadow of two world wars, that is, amid the horror of an unbridled collective catastrophe. No intellectual penetration of that reality could ignore the need to assess this problem. Thus, Neumann devotes four chapters of *Origins and History* to diagnosing his times. Their most prevalent phenomena, as he emphasises, are the "aggregation of the masses, the decay of the old canon, the schism between conscious and unconscious, and the divorce between individual and collective" (OHC, p. 383). More specifically: "Psychologically a primitive collective situation predominates, and in this new collective the old laws of *participation mystique* are more prevalent than at any time during the last few centuries of Western development" (ibid).

Neumann further elucidates this diagnosis by referring to the Wotan phenomenon (CW 10). While Jung described this as a symbolic manifestation, Neumann defined it as castration by the Great Mother. The coalescing, regressive identification with the Great Mother, which precipitates the ego's demise, is as destructive in evolutionary history as its complimentary problem, namely, the desire for the unconscious to be split off from the ego. Neumann describes this as a sclerosis of consciousness, where the ego identifies with consciousness as a form of spirit. In most cases this means identifying spirit with intellect, and consciousness with thinking. Such a limitation is utterly unjustified, but the patriarchal trend of development "away from the unconscious" and towards consciousness and thinking makes the identification understandable.

(OHC, p. 386)

The separation of the individual from the collective eventually makes itself felt as "isolation," as "individualism," as a life characterised by "restlessness, discontents, excesses, formlessness and meaninglessness" (OHC, p. 391). This entails the "activation of the deeper-lying layers which, now grown destructive, devastate the autocratic world of the ego with transpersonal invasions, collective epidemics, and mass psychoses" (ibid., p. 388).

Neumann's cultural diagnosis, of a deeply regressive society dominated by mass phenomena, and in which the individualistic overemphasis on the self spells simultaneous self-alienation, is far from untypical of the 1940s. Though diametrically opposed to Neumann's thinking and language, yet belonging to the same generation (born around 1900), Theodor Adorno reached structurally similar conclusions in his *Minima Moralia* (written between 1942 and 1949). For instance: Adorno's diagnosis of the "bourgeois subject" resembles Neumann's man of the crowd, whom he pits as a distorted image of supposed individuality against Freud and psychoanalysis. Adorno's critique distrusts any individual-therapeutic viewpoint, and even seeks to expose it as mendacious and as an adjustment required by mainstream society:

> A connection is commonly drawn between the development of psychology and the rise of the bourgeois individual, both in Antiquity and since the Renaissance. This ought not to obscure the contrary tendency also common to psychology and the bourgeois class, and which today has developed to the point of excluding all others: the suppression and dissolution of the very individual in whose service knowledge was related back to its subject ... This is flagrantly apparent in psycho-analysis. It incorporates personality as a lie needed for living, as the supreme rationalization holding together the innumerable rationalizations by which the individual achieves his instinctual renunciation, and accommodates himself to the reality principle. But precisely in demonstrating this, it confirms man's non-being.[9]

In contrast to Adorno, who lost faith in humanity after Auschwitz, Neumann sought to develop "a collective and cultural therapy adequate to cope with the mass phenomena that are now devastating mankind." This therapy, he explained, "has to correct and prevent the dislocation of collective life, of the group, by applying its specific points of view" (OHC, p. xxiv).

Essential to this cultural therapy is the need to recall Western cultural achievements, in particular after the horrific rupture in civilisation. This explains

Neumann's outright refusal of half-hearted heroic endeavours—the two world wars had, after all, provided more than sufficient evidence of a misunderstood, failed heroism. The correction of which Neumann speaks leads to consciously remembering those mythological moments in the canon of heroes that reveal the capacity to establish relations, that is, to integrate "the Other," in particular the feminine, and to relativise the ego in the context of experiencing the self.

Neumann's correction refers to these two elements in the canon of heroes because they counterbalance his cultural diagnosis of the present. Thus, they bear the potential of cultural emancipation. Neumann considers the "sanctity of the individual soul" (OHC, p. 382) within the Western cultural canon as relevant to cultural therapy, and thus as worth reactivating. With regard to the cultural canon, he refers to the following stages of mythological development (as mentioned earlier).

First, "overcoming" mother and father, as a symbolic event, is prerequisite for developing the personality. The symbolism of attaining a treasure, an elusive precious object, which the Western cultural canon often represents as the liberation of a captured virgin, heralds the "discovery of a psychic world":

> It is a tremendous step forward when a feminine, "sisterly" element—intangible but very real—can be added to the masculine ego consciousness as "my beloved" or "my soul." The word "my" separates off from the anonymous, hostile territory of the unconscious a region which is felt to be peculiarly "my" own, belonging to "my" peculiar personality.
>
> (OHC, p. 204)

Opening a sphere within oneself, in order to experience the Other, may also be described as the "discovery of the reality of the psyche" (OHC, p. 210). Psychic creativity, previously projected into cosmic space as creation myths, can only be "experienced as part of man's personality, as his soul" (ibid.). This female Other refers to Jung's discovery of the anima as the spiritual counterpart of the male psyche. Neumann expresses particular interest in people capable of maintaining access to this "primary reality of the soul," the creative unconscious, at the height of the current development of consciousness. The creative individual is the "bringer of culture": "Every culture-hero has achieved a synthesis between consciousness and the creative unconscious" (ibid., p. 212).

For Neumann, the myth of Perseus represents a corresponding ancient model of this stage of development:

> His father a god and his mother the bride of a god, a personal father who hates him, then the killing of the transpersonal First Parents, and finally the liberation of the captive—these are the stages that mark the progress of the hero.
>
> (OHC, p. 216)

Perseus kills the Gorgon, whose head springs from Pegasus, the winged horse. Neumann interprets Pegasus's ascent as "the freeing of libido from the Great Mother and its soaring flight" (OHC, p. 218). He continues:

Pegasus is the libido which, as winged spiritual energy, carries the hero Bellerophon ... to victory, but he is also inward-flowing libido that wells forth as creative art. In neither case is the release of libido undirected; it rises up in the direction of spirit ... Pegasus is therefore a spiritual and transcendent symbol in one.

(OHC, p. 219)

The characteristic "directedness" of everything psychic, which Jung contrasts with a "reductive causalism" in his preface to the fourth edition of *Transformations and Symbols of the Libido*, is also centrally important to Neumann (OHC, p. 12). Thus, in developmental terms, he describes the path of the libido as a path of transformation:

The path of evolution, leading mankind from unconsciousness to consciousness, is the path traced by the transformations and ascent of the libido. On either side there stand the great images, the archetypes and their symbols. As man progresses along this path, ever greater units of libido are supplied to his ego consciousness.

(OHC, p. 342)

As I have mentioned, the image of Pegasus rising from the head of the Gorgon symbolises the libido that is set free by the Great Mother. Its counterpart, for Neumann, is the myth of Osiris, which he considers to be the last stage in the hero's canon of transformation and which exerted "prodigious influence" on the ancient mysteries, Gnosis, Christianity, alchemy and mysticism (OHC, p. 253).[10] If the heroic deeds involved in overcoming the Great Mother are associated with attaining a positive-nurturing, creative-generative, protective stage in the natural cycle, the events surrounding Osiris can be understood as an *opus contra naturam*. The decisive aspect of the transformation and rebirth mystery of Osiris is the liberation from nature symbolism, which can be only attained through recourse to paradoxical symbols: "The dead person is alive, the one without a phallus begets, the buried rises to heaven, transience becomes eternal, man becomes God, God and man are one."[11]

The patriarchal king, the son of Horus, no longer marks the new year, and thus is not assigned the role of temporary impregnator, which would confirm his affiliation with the matriarchate. Rather, he has freed himself from the cycle and rhythm of the course of nature. This is only possible with the help of an authority that asserts its independence from the periodic process of nature. This stability exists in the spiritual principles of duration, timelessness and eternity, as represented by Osiris. Under the sign of Osiris, resurrection no longer occurs on the matriarchal, earthly plane; instead, it now means "his eternal and lasting essence, becoming a perfected soul, escaping from the flux of natural occurrence." He is "conjoined to the father, the everlasting and unchanging father who rules over the spirits" (OHC, p. 249).

We can place the myth of Osiris in the context of a patriarchal father–son relationship, which replaced Isis, the ruling mother figure. Horus, Osiris's son, enters into a mythologically complex relationship with his father, at whose centre stands the ritual identification with the dead (OHC, p. 252). Osiris, now dead, has become mummified: "The dead man who begets is a spirit ancestor. He is spermatic spirit, blowing where he listeth, invisible as the wind spirit" (ibid., p. 249).

In this myth, the roles of father and son are interdependent: Horus, the son, struggles against Seth for recognition as a son; as the "higher man," he is Osiris, symbolised by *djed*, the phallus transformed into the spirit. At the same time, he is also Horus, as symbolised in the Eye of Horus. Finally, Horus is also the father of Osiris, whom he brings to life through the Eye of Horus while being reborn through his ritual identification with the dead Osiris.

To Osiris, the father, who is endowed with a spirit phallus has "his counterpart in the chthonic-phallic son" (OHC, p. 250). Both refer to one another and together form a mutually penetrating and transforming unity in a ritual process of transformation. Neumann here cites a formula familiar from the New Testament: "I and the father are one" (ibid., p. 250).

In this creative act, both sides refer to each other—the worldly Horus as the master of the earthly and Osiris as the representative of eternity. Here, in this creative act of identification, Neumann, mythologically speaking, identifies the relationship between self and ego. First described by Jung, it was subsequently adopted and systematically expanded by Neumann (OHC, p. 250). He then returns once again to the human being's dual structure in order to establish a framework for the essential interdependence of Horus and Osiris: "Only in this paradoxical situation, when the personality experiences dying as a simultaneous act of self-reproduction, will the twofold man be reborn as the total man" (ibid., p. 255).

Philosophically speaking, Neumann here attempts to describe the significance of this paradoxical connection between self and ego for psychic development:

> As though a Copernican revolution had taken place within the psyche, consciousness faces inward and becomes aware of the self, about which the ego revolves in a perpetual paradox of identity and nonidentity. The psychological process of assimilating the unconscious into our present-day consciousness begins at this point, and the consequent shifting of the center of gravity from the ego to the self signalizes the latest stage in the evolution of human consciousness.
>
> (OHC, p. 256)

Jung described the possibility of conscious development, for which Osiris serves as a mythological model, as a process of individuation (OHC, p. 255). In the archetypal stages of the hero's path, Neumann observes a tendency towards stabilising consciousness. This, in turn, strengthens the ego in its struggle with the world and the unconscious and thus prevents its disintegration. He calls this tendency "centroversion" (ibid., p. 286f.). In the first half of life (Neumann follows Jung's division into several stages), conscious development proceeds archetypally, that is, collectively, as an ontogenetic process; the individual's possibilities of assimilation and working through become evident only in the second half of life. Neumann, however, advances a highly ambitious definition of the concept of individuality: as the highest good, the treasure to be attained after a protracted, arduous struggle with the world and the inner forces. It is not given. Contemplating it is worthwhile, since it constitutes a radical rejection of the deceptive splendour in which the 19th-century bourgeois subject once shone. In terms of his cultural criticism, Neumann seeks to stand the concept of the individual on its head: Being an individual is a postulate of development, that is, a project or a possibility created within the human soul. By no means does it pre-exist.

The path of individuation is the path of the individual. It is burdensome, and ultimately incomparable with the path of others. Moreover, it is associated with the capacity for self-reflection and with a way of knowing that is capable of grasping the numinous. Neumann's description of centroversion, as "the innate tendency of a whole to create unity with its parts" (OHC, p. 286), reflects how he formulates the connection between ego and self in terms of the Osiris cult and its symbolism:

> After passing through all the phases of world-experience and self-experience, the individual reaches consciousness of his true meaning. He knows himself the beginning, the middle, and end of the self-development of the psyche, which manifests itself first as the ego and is then experienced by this ego as the self.
>
> (OHC, p. 416)

And yet, this consciousness can be attained only with the help of the images of the soul. They are the "creative centre." These psychic images form the actual reality of every culture, whose task is to help this psychic reality to achieve "realisation." Art, religion, science: Everything draws on these images. As Neumann concludes:

> The self-generating power of the soul is man's true and final secret, by virtue of which he is made in the likeness of God the creator and distinguished from all other living things.
>
> (OHC, p. 211)

Notes

1 Erich Neumann, *The Origins and History of Consciousness* (New York: Pantheon Books, 1954), p. 168; cited hereafter as OHC.
2 C.G. Jung, *Symbole der Wandlung* (1911), published in English as *Psychology of the Unconscious: A Study of the Transformations and Symbolisms of the Libido* (New York: Moffat Yard, 1916; and London: Kegan Paul, 1917); see also CW 5; C.G. Jung, *Psychologie und Alchemie* (1944); see CW 12. See Neumann's letter of 3 April 1948: "As the third in the league I love, by the way, Mann's *Joseph* novel. I express a quiet wish that I would love to read something from you about it. Jung-Kerenyi, Mann-Kerenyi, but why not Jung-Mann? To my mind, Mann has been confusing Freud with

you for a long time, but, anyway, the history of ideas will not be disturbed by that" (JNC, p. 167f.).

3 *Jahrbuch für psychoanalytische und psychopathologische Forschungen III*. The second part followed in 1912 in *Jahrbuch IV* (Leipzig and Vienna: Deuticke Verlag).

4 Among others, these were Jung-Kerényi's *Einführung in das Wesen der Mythologie*, Briffaut's *The Mothers*, Bachofen's *Mutterrecht und Urreligion* and *Urreligion und antike Symbole*, Adolf Erman's *Die Religion der Ägypter* and James Frazer's *The Golden Bough*.

5 Karl Abraham, *Versuch einer Entwicklungsgeschichte der Libido auf Grund der Psychoanalyse seelischer Störungen* (Leipzig, Vienna, Zurich: Internationaler Psychoanalytischer Verlag, 1924).

6 See Wolfgang Giegerich, "Ontogeny = Phylogeny? A Fundamental Critique of Erich Neumann's Analytical Psychology," *Spring, an Annual of Archetypal Psychology and Jungian Thought* (New York: Spring Publications, 1975).

7 Otto Rank, *Mythos von der Geburt des Helden* (Vienna: Turia und Kant, 1922); published in English as *The Myth of the Birth of the Hero: A Psychological Exploration of Myth*, trans. Gregory C. Richter and E. James Lieberman (Baltimore: Johns Hopkins University Press, 2004).

8 In describing uroboric incest, which, as a longing for death, is a symbolic expression of the tendency of the ego and consciousness towards dissolution, Neumann expresses further criticism of Freud. The uroboros represents "the world of origination and regeneration, from which life and the ego are eternally reborn." Thus, "many creation myths have as their emblem the uroboros: for while uroboric incest is the symbol of death, the maternal uroboros is the symbol of rebirth, of the nativity of the ego, and of the dawn of consciousness, the coming of light" (OHC, p. 278). Neumann considers the assumption of a death instinct mistaken. The fact that the ego experiences this uroboric-incestuous state symbolically as death is rooted in this archetypal phase of conscious development. Neumann expands this idea in a footnote that further criticises Freud's interpretation in *Civilization and its Discontents*: "Uroboric incest is the sole psychological ground we have for postulating a 'death instinct,' and it is wrong to mix it up with aggressive and destructive tendencies. A deeper understanding of uroboric incest, which is by no means only a pathological phenomenon, would prevent us from confusing it with a psychically nonexistent instinct … The 'death instinct' of uroboric incest is not the 'adversary of instinct,' but one of its primordial forms" (OHC, p. 280, n. 20). Finally, Neumann's essay "Leonardo da Vinci and the Mother Archetype," published in *Art and the Creative Unconscious: Four Essays*, Bollingen Series LXI (Princeton, NJ: Princeton University Press, 1959), also critiques Freud's interpretation of Leonardo.

9 Theodor W. Adorno, *Minima Moralia: Reflections on a Damaged Life*, trans. E.P.N. Jephcott (London: Verso, 2005), pp. 63–64.

10 See Richard Reitzenstein, *Die hellenistischen Mysterienreligionen: Ihre Grundgedanken und Wirkungen*, (Leipzig and Berlin: Teubner, 1920).

11 Translator's note: This passage in Neumann's *Ursprungsgeschichte des Bewusstseins* (p. 272) is missing from the English translation.

"... a new principle of love"

Neumann's *Amor and Psyche*

In 1956, on the centenary of Freud's birth, Neumann paid tribute to his work, in particular Freud's heroic struggle to free humanity "from the oppression of the old father figure."[1] He adds, slightly more critically, that Freud had remained "deeply fixated" to this figure, whose shackles he had so momentously shaken (FFI, p. 245). Yet Neumann also acknowledges that "Western culture (religion, society, and morals) is mainly formed by this father image and the psychic structure of the individual is partly damaged by it" (ibid., p. 244).

Neumann's approach, in contrast, is grounded in a layer that forms the "sediment" of the manifest father problem, and thus precedes it. He first considers the following symbolic conflict: "Today, as always, the battle of Western consciousness is fought in the spirit of the Old Testament war against the Mother-Goddess" (FFI, p. 244). For Neumann, Freud made highly important theoretical contributions to understanding the struggle with the father. While the "Jewish taboo of the Mother-Goddess, that is, of the unconscious, prevailed with [Freud] to the end" (ibid.), he always lent it overwhelmingly negative connotations. Neumann continues:

> His psychology of the feminine is therefore a patriarchal misconception and his lack of understanding of the nature of religion and of artistic creation comes from the same unawareness of the creative psyche which, mythologically, is connected with the Mother-Goddess and the prepatriarchal level of the unconscious.
>
> (FFI, p. 245)

Neumann posits that the paternal and maternal principles are polar aspects of the divine, and that each fulfils a different psychic function.[2] This enables him to establish an argumentative framework in which to consider Jung's theorising.

In a letter to Jung dated 5 December 1951, Neumann mentions his book about Apuleius's tale of *Amor and Psyche*, which was published the following year by Rascher in Zurich. The letter is highly interesting because, in addition to referring to his own work, Neumann expresses his appreciation of Jung's recently published *Answer to Job*. He implicitly treats the two works as counterparts. In terms of substance, the drama of the opposing male and female principles unfolds in the space between God (the Father) and a woman (Psyche), who brings redemption. Neumann comments on Jung's *Answer to Job* as follows:

> Firstly it is a book that grips me deeply … It is—for me personally—especially also an argument against God who allowed 6 million of "His" people to be killed, for Job is precisely also Israel … I know we are the paradigm for the whole of humanity in whose name you are speaking, protesting, and consoling. And exactly the conscious one-sidedness, yes, often the inaccuracy of what you are saying is, to me, an inner proof of the necessity and justice of your attack —which is, of course, not one, as I well know.
>
> (JNC, p. 271)

After Jung's lack of empathy, which he bemoaned on several occasions, in particular during the November pogroms of 1938 (see Chapter 7), Neumann is grateful that Jung confronts that God whose chains Freud had already shaken. But his recognition is intended for Sophia, who plays an important role in Jung's work. In *Answer to Job*, Jung dedicates a whole chapter to Sophia, whom he regards as the authority that ultimately enables YHWH's self-reflection. Jung describes Sophia's workings (and effect) as follows:

> God was now known, and this knowledge went on working not only in Yahweh but in man too. Thus it was the men of the last few centuries before Christ who, at the gentle touch of the pre-existent Sophia, compensate Yahweh and his attitude, and at the same time complete the anamnesis of Wisdom. Taking a highly personified form that is clear proof of her autonomy, Wisdom reveals herself to men as a friendly helper and advocate against Yahweh, and shows them the bright side, the kind, just, and amiable aspect of their God.
>
> (CW 11, §623)

The preeminent importance of Sophia in Jung's thinking leads Neumann, in his letter of 5 December 1951, to the following assessment:

> In reality, you believe in the feminine Sophia as the highest authority without admitting it. Perhaps it only seems to me to be so because this is how it is for me personally. Only the matriarchal psychology of the psyche and the Holy Ghost is comprehensible.
>
> (JNC, p. 272)

For Neumann, whose correspondence with Jung, in particular from the mid-1940s, focused increasingly on discussing each other's works, Jung's account of YHWH's conscious realisation through the mediation of Sophia bears a structural relationship to the myth of Eros and Psyche, which Apuleius masterfully recounts in the form of a fairy tale in his novel *The Golden Ass*:

> In the *Psyche*, which Rascher will send you as soon as it comes out (which should happen any day), a similar process of an archetypal nature seems to me to exist. But taking place in the feminine and at the edge of antiquity. But I have only been able to hint at it and for sure it is a problem of apparently smaller numinosity. But who knows, even the divine daughter is not without deep significance. The rebirth of Sophia in ecstasy is still quite puzzling to me, but there is something about it.
>
> (JNC, pp. 275–276)

Neumann dedicated the last chapter of *The Great Mother: An Analysis of the Archetype* (1956) to Sophia. He describes this figure as follows:

> in the generating and nourishing, protective and transformative, feminine power of the unconscious, a wisdom at work that is infinitely superior to the wisdom of man's waking consciousness, and that, as source of vision and symbol, of ritual and law, poetry and vision, intervenes, summoned or unsummoned, to save man and give direction to his life.

He adds:

> This feminine-maternal wisdom is no abstract, disinterested knowledge, but a wisdom of loving participation ... Sophia is living and present and near, a godhead that can always be summoned and is always ready to intervene ... Thus the spiritual power of Sophia is living and saving; her overflowing heart is wisdom and food at once. The nourishing life that she communicates is a life of the spirit and of transformation, not one of earthbound materiality.
>
> (GM, pp. 330–331)

Through his studies on prehistoric matriarchal culture,[3] Neumann developed an understanding of the feminine as the actual agency of psychic mutability. Thus, in his foreword to Neumann's *Origins and History of Consciousness*, Jung had already noted that "the present work opens at the very place where I unwittingly made landfall on the new continent long ago, namely the realm of *matriarchal symbolism*" (OHC, p. xiii; Jung's emphasis).

Towards the end of the 1940s, Neumann began devoting himself increasingly to this particular symbolism. From 1950, he systematically published texts on the psychology of the feminine. These publications peaked in his comprehensive *The Great Mother* (1956). For Neumann, the female psyche and human creative powers are intimately related. Hence, he does not see his reflections being limited to individual psychological practice, but rather as central to a cultural psychology, since "the peril of present-day mankind springs in large part from the one-sidedly patriarchal development of the male intellectual consciousness, which is no longer kept in balance by the matriarchal world of the psyche" (GM, p. xlviii).

Only exploring the archaic world of archetypes makes it possible to grasp the expressions of the matriarchal world of the psyche, which have drifted into the unconscious. Neumann emphasises that rather than this being an abstruse preoccupation, it involves opening a worldview that enables a "new approach to life." Moreover, the integration of the archetypal into the inner world is an "inner form of humanization" that might prove "more reliable" than an intellectually acquired humanism (GM, p. xlix).

Neumann introduces the nature of the archetype as follows: Structurally, it presents itself as a structure of psychodynamics, symbolism and meaning—the archetype itself remains essentially inconceivable. Its constellation in humankind expresses itself as a state of emotional possession—on the affective and the emotional level (GM, p. xlix). The archetype becomes visible on the "image plane" (pictorial level) as a symbol, as which unconscious activity, as far as it is capable of consciousness, manifests itself. The symbols take hold of the whole human personality, while consciousness tries to interpret them. However, the effect of the symbol is not at all soothing. Rather, it "disturbs" consciousness. In this way, it builds up consciousness and transforms energy, and thus urges the psyche to work on the unconscious contents contained in the symbol (ibid., p. 27f.). Their superordinate character makes symbols difficult to assimilate. Certain pictorial elements can only be grasped in the course of a longer development, that is, some elements continue to transcend consciousness and are numinous.

The symbol is not only the origin of consciousness, but also of religion, ritual, cult and art. Language is first of all also symbolic language (GM, p. 17). For Neumann, the transformation associated with the power of the symbol is bound to the productive, synthesising power of the *transcendent function* (MEA, p. 223). This mediates between "bright" consciousness and the unconscious hidden in mystery and "darkness." As he suggested in *Krise und Erneuerung* ("Crisis and Renewal"), the emerging symbol refers pictorially to the absence of the collective, which can lead to the correction or also to the upheaval of a previous cultural canon (KUE, p. 75f.).

We need to see Neumann's "collective and cultural therapy" (OHC, p. xxiv) against the background of a problem that he struggled with for many years. It provides an answer to a conflict that long seemed insoluble to him, and into which his devotion to what became his two-volume *The Roots of Jewish Consciousness* had plunged him.

In the dialectics between the development of male or patriarchal consciousness and its counterpart, the female path of development, which proves accessible through the matriarchal matrix, Neumann identifies the possibility of developing a more comprehensive view of the cultural constitution of the West, which he considers responsible for the dominance of solar, patriarchal consciousness and the suppression of female wisdom. According to Neumann, this repression sheds light in particular on the relationship with the unconscious: He regards woman as the "earthly-human vehicle of this numinous principle" (GM, p. 287). Thus,

> for while the specific achievement of the male world lies in the development of masculine consciousness and the rational mind, the female psyche is in far greater degree dependent on the productivity of the unconscious, which is closely bound up with what we accordingly designate as the matriarchal consciousness.
>
> (GM, pp. 292–293)

This "matriarchal consciousness," Neumann adds, "with its great receptivity toward the powers of the unconscious, is stronger than woman and less overlaid by the abstracting form of the patriarchal consciousness" (GM, p. 293). On a large historical scale, Neumann regards the repression of this female quality as disastrous:

> In the patriarchal development of the Judeo-Christian West, with its masculine, monotheistic trend toward abstraction, the goddess, as a feminine figure of wisdom, was disenthroned and repressed. She survived only secretly, for the most part on heretical and revolutionary bypaths.
>
> (GM, p. 331)

He maintains that women are able to access this specifically female matrix more directly than men. And yet, this must be rediscovered and reopened through depth-psychological work, since this approach is fundamentally responsible for individuation, insofar as it represents a creative process. Based on his interpretation of Apuleius's tale, Neumann calls this femininity—which simultaneously represents the self and wholeness—*Psyche*. Ego consciousness, on the other hand, is "the masculine":

> In all these processes where "Psyche leads" and the masculine follows here, the ego relinquishes its leading role and is guided by the totality. In psychic developments which prove to be centered around the nonego, the self, we have creative processes.
>
> (AP, p. 151)

His discovery, that the deep layer of *Eros and Psyche*[4] is (emphatically) "pagan," seems to have relieved Neumann of a double burden he had been shouldering for years, one that resembled an inner mission: On the one hand, to provide evidence of a positive-feminine principle that was equal to the male principle in Western tradition; on the other, to furnish proof of a principle of love and encounter that unfolds and is realised in secular space.

This burden first appeared in *The Roots of Jewish Consciousness*, where the following opposition serves as the starting point for his further conclusions:

The fundamental contrast between YHWH and the principle of the Earth Mother becomes obvious once again. This contrast alone explains why the Hebrews, surrounded by mother-cults, remained the only tribe, among the Semitic tribes, that possessed no female deity.

(Roots I, p. 62)

This deficiency—Neumann maintains—explains the dominant negative mother archetype eventually adopted by Christianity in the Jewish tradition:

For Jews, Christians and Gnostics, the archetype of the negative Mother and the anima, representing the natural and earthly aspect of the unconscious, became the basis for a negative image of woman … The left side of the Kabbalistic tree is feminine. Detached from the positive, masculine side, it is the origin of the "other side," meaning evil. Here, too, the masculine conception of the story of creation remains in effect, according to which the female is secondary, originating from the side of the male, Adam.

(Roots II, p. 96f.)

Yet Neumann's assessment proved to be mistaken. Research findings on the Hebrew mother goddess, first published in 1967 by Raphael Patai,[5] refuted Neumann's claim that the Hebrews had no female deity or were permeated by the negative mother archetype on account of their religion.[6] Patai, a Jew born in Budapest in 1910, emigrated to Palestine in 1933, where he taught as an ethnologist. He emigrated to the USA in 1947. As a professor of anthropology, he wrote numerous books on Jewish and Arab history and culture, Eastern mythology, and anthropology, including biblical studies. However, his seminal work, *The Hebrew Goddess*, failed to establish further research interest in the subject. In a sense, his work represents a pioneering achievement, comparable to Neumann's *The Great Mother*, to which Patai refers in various passages (Patai and Neumann never met).

Patai demonstrated that for many centuries after the revelation on Sinai religious currents were alive in which the worship of goddesses played an important role.[7] He established the importance of Ashera, Astarte, Anat and Shekhinah-Matronit, who, in this historical sequence, occupied a place equal to YHWH as goddesses of the biblical, Hellenistic, Talmudic and eventually the Kabbalistic periods.[8] Nevertheless, he acknowledged that in the post-Talmudic period in particular the female element of the deity moved into the background, only to be completely eliminated in the recent past by the concept of God prevailing among Reform Jews, conservative or non-Hasidic Orthodox Jews.[9]

Patai's historical findings refute Neumann's overriding claim, yet not his assessment, of the marginal role occupied by the feminine in the Judaism of his time. Let us return to Neumann, who was aware of the positive achievements of the patriarchal heritage—that is, stabilising the ego and safeguarding the light of consciousness against the devouring uroboric-archetypal forces as a male heroic deed. Yet he sought to place the complementary power of the feminine on a par with this "solar achievement." From the forward-looking, consciousness- and morality-expanding experience with YHWH, Neumann thus looked back at the "fate" that nature, the earth and, along with them, the feminine had suffered as a result of their repression:

> Of particular importance … is the loss of the feminine side of consciousness in favor of radical masculinization, an extreme emphasis on active and rational components. This is particularly evident with regard to introversion. Originally, Judaism had consciously emphasized an inner, feminine stance toward the irradiating impulse and the word of God. This stance had been symbolized most strongly in the image of the people as the bride of God. This attitude of stillness, maintaining silence and preparing oneself for inner experience, poses no contradiction to the active assimilation and realization that are then demanded, but this attitude now began to disappear. Even introversion became active, speculative, and rational, geared toward working through what was found, rather than being expanded by a new thing breaking in.
>
> (Roots I, p. 129)

Thus, Neumann deplores the rigidity of solar consciousness towards new things, the disappearance of the assimilating forces towards unforeseeable and ineffable experiences, and the disappearance of emotional openness. He links this to the historical and social findings concerning the marginal status of the fundamental qualities of the feminine. Hence, Neumann's interpretation of Apuleius's tale is an attempt to depict an alternative discourse of the feminine that can be found in mythology, namely, a "heroic struggle of the feminine" (AP, p. 93), which stands in complementary opposition to that of the solar hero. His postscript notes that he is drawing on the research findings of his time, in particular the works of Bachofen, Reitzenstein and Kerenyi.[10]

Let me first briefly summarise the tale: Psyche, a king's daughter, is worshipped like a goddess. While this provokes the wrath of the goddess Aphrodite, it does not make her more desired by men. She remains lonely and unloved, and begins to hate herself for her beauty. Her parents consult Apollo's oracle to appoint a husband. The oracle commands Psyche to lead a marriage of death with a monstrous bridegroom. Zephyr kidnaps Psyche, who miraculously experiences an intoxicating erotic life with her invisible husband, the alleged fiend. In truth, it is Eros who has chosen Psyche as his wife. The envious sisters advise Psyche to kill the "monster." At night, Psyche wounds Eros in an attempt to murder him with a burning drop of oil. She loses him, yet burns with love for him when she sees him. Eros escapes. Next follow Psyche's search for her beloved, her despair at Aphrodite's continuing anger and at the tasks imposed upon her. Although she succeeds at first, Psyche eventually fails in her final task, as she opens Persephone's box in Hades without permission, which brings a deathlike sleep upon her. Eros redeems Psyche and takes her to Mount Olympus as his immortal wife (AP, pp. 57–58).

Neumann's interpretation highlights three typical aspects of the myth: Psyche's "humanity"; a transitional situation, which we may describe in historical terms as a precarious starting point; and, finally, losing the beloved and the love resulting from this loss, which Neumann describes as the "archetype of relatedness" (AP, p. 109).

Psyche is worshipped as another goddess, as another "Aphrodite": She is no longer divine, "born from the spray of the foaming waves," but mortal, "born of the earth" (ibid., pp. 58f.). Characteristically, humanity, in this case the feminine, must travel the path of individuation. Neumann describes Psyche's path as a pro-totypical model of female individuation: He considers Psyche's sojourn in the "dark Paradise of Eros" to be a variation on the hero's devouring by the whale–dragon–monster (AP, p. 74, n. 7).

Psyche does not heed Eros's advice to sever ties with the sisters as little as the prohibition to keep receiving him only in complete darkness. The conflict height-ens Psyche's ambivalence—"she hates the beast and loves her husband"—and "leads to the deed," through which she loses her beloved. Neumann locates this event in the transition from matriarchy to patriarchy: Psyche is "no longer the languorously ensnared being"; rather, she "assumes the cruel militancy of the matriarchate as she approaches the bed to kill the monster, the male beast who has torn her from the upper world in a marriage of death and carried her off into darkness" (ibid., p. 78).

This expansion of consciousness leads Psyche to realise that the polarisation between beast and husband is untrue. It arouses her curiosity and she injures her-self more unintentionally than intentionally with God's arrow: Or, as the original says, "So all unwitting, yet of her own doing, Psyche fell in love with Love" (AP, p. 26).

Thus, a decisive caesura has occurred: Psyche is no longer a victim, nor the object of a foreign will, but from now on an active lover. Her love, which erupts when she sees "Eros," is an Eros that she has created within herself. This figure is no longer identical with the sleeping, outer Eros. "This inner Eros … is the adult Eros which pertains to the conscious, adult psyche" (AP, p. 80). As such, however, she loses Eros: "The loss of her lover in this moment is among the deep-est truths of this myth; this is the tragic moment in which every feminine psyche enters upon its own destiny" (ibid., p. 81).

I will return to Neumann's central claim later. He interprets Psyche's (outer) loss while preserving her (inner) love as that which places her on an equal foot-ing with her absconded husband. Eros has lost his divine supremacy. Love, then, has become a human affair and must as such be fought for, painfully endured and suffered.

> With Psyche's heroic act suffering, guilt, and loneliness have come into the world. For Psyche's act is analogous to the deed of the hero who separated the original parents in order to produce the light of consciousness.
>
> (AP, p. 82)

In recounting the story of Psyche as a secular myth, Neumann contrasts it with the biblical story of creation, whose "masculine conception of the story of creation remains in effect, according to which the female is secondary, originating from the side of the male, Adam" (Roots II, p. 96f.). Further, he contrasts the dialectic of Enlightenment, which had deployed the solar hero, who knew the craft of killing, with the lunar-feminine principle, whose blind murderous impulse is interrupted by insight and knowledge, prior to being rejected, and whose capacity for love develops amid separation and loneliness:

> And whereas the masculine goes on from this act of heroic slaying to conquer the world, whereas his *hieros gamos* with the anima figure he has won constitutes only a part of his victory, Psyche's subsequent development is nothing other than an attempt to transcend, through suffering and struggle, the separation accomplished by her act.
>
> (AP, p. 83; original emphasis)

Thus, Neumann distinguishes the masculine–solar principle, which strives to conquer and to assert itself, in what constitutes the heroic struggle of the masculine, from the original experience of the feminine, insofar as this, in confronting the other, corrects its actions from a primary reference to otherness and assumes responsibility for the relationship to the other in the name of a shared vulnerability, which comes to replace the principle of anonymous lust. For Neumann, this "heroic struggle of the feminine ... ushers in a new human era" (AP, p. 93). This creates the paradoxical experience that loneliness is one of the conditions of both love and individuation: "With Psyche, then, there appears a new principle of love, in which the encounter between feminine and masculine is revealed as the basis of individuation" (ibid., p. 90)

This new principle of love follows a "psychology of encounter" whose characteristics include uniqueness and individuality. The myth describes the recognition of the other—"Psyche's act"—as the act of "making visible": "But the coming of light makes Eros 'visible,' it manifests the phenomenon of psychic love, hence of all human love, as the human and higher form of the archetype of relatedness" (AP, p. 109).

Psyche's path of individuation, which leads her into loneliness, is depicted in the myth as the flight of the lover, as his loss. Overcoming separation thus becomes Psyche's overriding goal. The seemingly unsolvable tasks imposed upon Psyche by her adversary, Aphrodite, represent the steps towards the overcoming of separation. For Neumann, the tasks on Psyche's path constitute "the formation of hitherto unformed uroboric powers" (AP, p. 108). Yet the "solution" to these problems "consists not in struggle but in the creation of a fruitful contact between feminine and masculine" (ibid., p. 102).

Nevertheless, Psyche seems to—or in fact does—fail when confronted with her final task: She is supposed to steal Persephone's beauty ointment. But she opens the box without permission, anoints herself with "divine beauty" (AP, p. 122) and falls into a deathlike sleep. The ointment represents "Persephone's eternal youth of death," "the beauty of Kore." Yet Psyche is now doubly endangered: She risks regressing to "natural maidenly perfection," that is, becoming a "barren frigid beauty ... without love for a man, as exacted by the matriarchate." And she faces the risk of becoming "inhuman," of living in "divine perfection" (ibid., p. 118). Here, Neumann speaks of being entrapped, in narcissistic love, as if in "a glass coffin," a term that recalls the fate of Sleeping Beauty (ibid.). Psyche fails (Neumann highlights the verb) and is "overpowered by the death aspect of Aphrodite ... the victorious Great Mother" (ibid., p. 119).

But why does Psyche fail at this particular time, of all times? "Because," as Neumann replies, "she is a feminine psyche." He adds: "The story began with the motif of beauty, which now reappears on a new plane" (AP, p. 121). In the beginning, Psyche had grown lonely and estranged from the world because of her beauty. She had only experienced jealousy or admiration. Now, however, in a reversal of circumstances (*peripeteia*), the desire for beauty combined with love represents a new stage of development. Neumann associates the theme of beauty with bodily experience on the one hand and with an amorous relationship on the other.

According to Neumann, we ought to understand Psyche's paradoxical behaviour as her attempt to renew "her bond with her feminine center, her self" (AP, p. 123). Yet her real task is to transcend her entrapment in the "negative unity of Aphrodite-Persephone" (ibid., p. 128). This she needs to accomplish without, however, placing herself above nature, that is, above her own body through ascetic abstinence. As Neumann adds, the "superior though still nameless unity of a Great Goddess as guiding Sophia-Self" also has a hand in the solution (ibid.). Thus, Neumann interprets Psyche's failure not as a "regressive, passive sinking," but rather as a "dialectical reversal of her extreme activity into devotion." He concludes that "abandoning herself out of love, she unwittingly achieves redemption through love" (ibid., p. 125f.).

Psyche's "paradoxically feminine failure" compels Eros to intervene himself. This turns "the boy into a man, and transforms the burned fugitive into a savior" (AP, p. 124). "The supreme masculine authority," Neumann asserts, "bows to the human and feminine, which by its superiority in love has proved itself equal to the divine" (ibid., p. 125). He concludes his observations on Psyche's path of individuation as follows:

> The human has conquered its place on Olympus [*Himmel*, "heaven," in the German—Trans.], but this has been done not by a masculine deified hero, but by a loving soul. Human womanhood as an individual has mounted to Olympus ... And paradoxically enough, she has gained this divine place precisely by her mortality.
>
> (AP, p. 137)

In *Amor and Psyche*, Neumann moves beyond Jung's concept of animus and anima (AP, p. 142), among others, by presenting Psyche's path of individuation as the highest level of spiritual development. It is precisely from this path that the "creative person"—the prototype of the receptive person, whose creativity is able to express unconscious contents—draws his or her actual strength and essential impetus:

> It is no accident that we speak of the "soul" of man as well as woman … This psyche as the whole of the personality must be characterized in man as well as in woman as feminine, because it experiences that which transcends the psychic as numinous, as "outside" and "totally different" … Where this psyche undergoes experience, the symbolically masculine structure of the ego and of consciousness seems, both in man and woman, to be so relativized and reduced that the feminine character of psychic is predominant. Thus the mystical birth of the godhead in the man does not take place as birth of the anima, i.e., of a partial structure of psychic life, but as the birth of totality, i.e., of the psyche.
>
> (AP, pp. 141–142)

Neumann's interpretation of Apuleius's tale points to the "Great Individual," who occupies the key role of cultural transformer in *Depth Psychology and a New Ethic* and in *The Origins and History of Consciousness*. His typical—sudden, surprising—manifestation is related to experiences of the numinous. For Neumann, both domains have the same origin:

> Such developments, in which "the spontaneity of the psyche" and its living guidance are the crucial determinants in the life of the masculine, are known to us from the psychology of the creative process and of individuation. In all these processes where "Psyche leads" and the masculine follows her, the ego relinquishes its leading role and is guided by the totality. In psychic developments which prove to be centered round the nonego, the self, we have creative processes and processes of initiation in one.
>
> (AP, p. 151)

Neumann substantiates his perspective and interpretation by referring to the impressive religious and cultural development of the West. He sees human-feminine "primordial receptivity" as one of the highest assets of Western cultural development, whose "ensoulment" and "spirituality" is indebted to that disposition:

> The triumph of Psyche's love and her ascension to Olympus were an event that has profoundly affected Western mankind for two thousand years. For two millenniums the mystery phenomenon of love has occupied the center of psychic development and of culture, art, and religion.
>
> (AP, p. 139)

This, moreover, "has brought both good and evil, but in any event it has been an essential ferment of the psychic and spiritual life of the West down to the present day" (AP, p. 139f.). In conclusion, he writes:

> This love of Psyche for her divine lover is a central motif in the love mysticism of all times, and Psyche's failure, her final self-abandonment, and the god who approaches as a savior at this very moment correspond exactly to the highest phase of mystical ecstasy, in which the soul commends itself to the godhead.
>
> (AP, p. 140)

Let me offer some critical remarks on the tale, or rather refer to other interpretations: Neumann's claim about woman's redemptive role, his most revolutionary and at the same time most far-reaching thesis, seems to have gone largely unnoticed in theory for the following reason: The masculine–feminine polarity, which he consistently posited, leads into a theoretical impasse, since Neumann's interpretation links biological gender, social gender or gender construction and the associated gender role, thus creating a somewhat simplistic complementary system that lacks sufficient scope. In spite of the important role that Neumann assigns to the feminine, that is, "woman" in the process of cultural development, it once again finds itself "measured," that is, assigned a place alongside the masculine aspect. Its heroic-emancipatory potential is not evident to begin with, and thus it is no accident that Neumann's account has attracted feminist criticism.[11] Subsequent Jungian interpretations have interpreted Psyche as the man's anima.[12]

James Hillman, whose extensive study of Apuleius's tale relies on classical sources (1972), contributed to reviving the ancient myth.[13] Like other critics, Hillman also mentions the theme of female inferiority in Greek, Jewish and Christian contexts. The tale, as he puts it, resonates with the "desperate compulsive for *psychic relatedness* and erotic identity."[14] Nevertheless, he rejects Neumann's interpretation of the tale as the feminine path to heroism and individuation. Hillman's straightforward assertion, that the heroic age of psychology is a thing of the past, also passes judgment on Neumann's interpretive approach.[15] For Hillman, the tale of Eros und Psyche represents a "new myth," which makes it possible "to meet the new problems in the analysis of today."[16] It is a paradigm for a "creative psychology" of the present.

In *The Inner World of Trauma* (1996), Jungian analyst Donald Kalsched offers an extensive interpretation of the tale that contrasts with Neumann's reading and those mentioned earlier.[17] Kalsched sees Psyche as a traumatised, innocent ego and Eros as the demonic lover endowed with salvific and diabolical traits. Psyche, as a trauma victim, could only save her innocence and vitality through a dissociative system, which Kalsched calls the *self-care system* of the soul. This system protectively splits off the wounded part, yet at great expense. Kalsched regards the soul's self-care system as a core complex, into which the "dissociating psyche falls if it falls prey to a complex." This system—a universal complex similar to

Freud's Oedipus complex—constitutes "the archetypal and mythical background for the more prosaic and familiar complexes into which the dissociating psyche fragments."[18] In view of these clinical findings, Kalsched, unlike the other critics mentioned here, detects the dark side of Apuleius's tale, which manifests itself in particular in Aphrodite's raging fury and Psyche's helplessness and ongoing suicidality.

Drawing on one of the central ideas of the French philosopher Emanuel Lévinas, I wish to outline another possible interpretation of the myth, one actually intuited by Neumann (see also Chapter 13). Neumann's juxtaposition of masculine and feminine principles clearly favours the latter:

> And whereas the masculine goes on from this act of heroic slaying to conquer the world, whereas his *hieros gamos* with the anima figure has won constitutes only a part of his victory, Psyche's subsequent development is nothing other than an attempt to transcend, through suffering and struggle, the separation accomplished by her act.
>
> (AP, p. 83)

One cannot help thinking that Neumann is to some extent suspicious of the archetype of the victorious hero to whom he dedicated one of his most brilliant works, *The Origins and History of Consciousness*. And yet, the figure of the hero is indispensable to Neumann's thinking. It seems that the counter-project of the feminine heroine, who bears all those attributes that are essential to the solar hero, ultimately satisfies him. Let us consider this subtle, yet audible criticism of the solar hero, once again by referring to the work of Lévinas.

In *Totality and Infinity* (first published in French in 1961), Lévinas juxtaposes the two principles announced in his title.[19] The killing hero in myth-interpreting archetypal psychology, who hastens from conquest to conquest, subjugating object after object to his will in his relentless struggle for freedom, eventually also makes the highest good, the virgin qua anima, his own. In Lévinas's philosophical language, this means: Affected just as deeply by the trauma of two world wars as Neumann, Lévinas regards what philosophers call "being" as war. This, he argues, is forever possible and more likely to occur than peace. It overrides morality and ultimately mocks it. Lévinas regards this relentless belligerence as the matrix of the essential concepts of Western thought; it becomes concrete in the concept of totality, which dominates philosophy and its history.[20] Lévinas speaks of the ego as an active force, one that is accustomed to taking, taking hold of, understanding and making the world its own.[21] The ego's implicit claim to control returns in philosophical systematics as a unifying principle, which ultimately obliterates the individual through a tendency towards generalisation. The power of the ego, its embodying gesture, as the cause of identity thinking, assimilates everything foreign. The stranger no longer remains foreign. On the contrary, singular existence becomes part of the system. Intellectual totality, a claim familiar to the West, can now be interpreted as an attitude that subjugates and objectifies others.

According to Lévinas, Socrates taught this appropriating principle as the "primacy of the same." This means "to receive nothing of the Other but what is in me, as though from all eternity I was in possession of what comes to me from the outside!" From this follows Lévinas's explanation of reason:

> That reason in the last analysis would be the manifestation of a freedom, neutralizing the other and encompassing him, can come as no surprise once it was laid down that sovereign reason knows only itself, that nothing other limits it.[22]

Consequently, to know, to "illuminate is to remove from being its resistance ... its alterity."[23] In a further step, Lévinas opposes another principle to this totalising, subordinating and classificatory principle: *infinity*, that is, transcendence.

This requires a brief explanation: infinity breaches totality.[24] Hence, "what remains ever exterior to thought is thought in the idea of infinity." This, Lévinas explains, is "the mind before it lends itself to the distinction between what it discovers by itself and what it receives from opinion."[25] Or, more concisely, the idea of infinity reveals that the ego "nonetheless contains in itself what it can neither contain nor receive solely virtue of its own identity."[26] Human subjectivity, however, is capable of leapfrogging the "barriers of immanence."[27]

This capacity expresses itself as desire and "is produced as Desire."[28] Desire strives for the totally other.[29] The desired is invisible and inexpressible as an idea.[30] Hence, there is no knowledge of the other. The desired is far removed, since desire lacks the capacity to anticipate the desirable.[31] Desire seeks neither satisfaction nor fulfilment. Nor does it demand nourishment. All these qualities distinguish it radically from need. Moreover, only desire understood thus provides a starting point for friendship and love. In this respect, Lévinas speaks of the mythical parents of the god Eros—Penia (poverty) and Poros (abundance)—who appear in Plato's *The Banquet*: "Might the Platonic myth of love as offspring of abundance and poverty be interpreted as the indigence of wealth itself, as the desire not what one has lost, but absolute Desire?"[32]

The horizon of infinity, which opens in the ego's desire for the elusive, which at the same time represents abundance, although this is not the answer to any concrete deficiency, inevitably places the ego in a welcoming, receiving position. Infinity is what the ego consumes itself for, allows itself to be challenged by and is unable to apprehend. In this desire, according to Lévinas, the Other constellates itself as one whose relation to the ego is the "curvature of the intersubjective space."[33] Only here can encounter take place beyond power and claim. The space thereby opened is completely different from that of the appropriating subject, whose mythological counterpart is the solar hero.

The tale of Eros and Psyche, or at least so it seems to me, could be situated within this infinity: The connection of Eros and Psyche can be understood as the emergence of human desire in the sense outlined earlier. The asymmetry between Psyche and Eros is fundamental and marks the transcendent space that opens. This perspective suggests that not the active Psyche, who contemplates murder, is a heroine, but rather that Psyche who is willing to submit to a process of dissolution, *solutio*, and eventually *mortificatio* (whereas the solar hero seems to be entrapped in the incessant process of separation).

Reading the tale reminds us of the overriding importance of the death metaphor: a marriage with death, Psyche's constant thoughts of suicide, and in the end the entrance to Hades. Death, for Psyche, is ever present. Her existence is determined by pain, loneliness and despair. She might be said to represent the human capacity for self-transformation, through deprivation, misfortune and sorrow, in the psychic realm. Metaphysically or theologically, this capacity is directed towards the hereafter, whose constitution is indeterminable, however. Yet this longing is caused by none other than Eros. Hence, he might be seen as that divine-demonic principle that implants itself as desire in the human soul. In this way, a desire for what cannot be desired as material possession may emerge and take effect. If, like Neumann, we read the tale as the developmental history of the female soul, we remain on the personal level. The relationship between Eros and the Psyche, conceived of as a love story, seems to represent an allegorical connection, one arising from the power of beauty and situated between human finiteness and divine infinity in the psychic realm: Beauty pervades the tale as its central theme.

The meaning of beauty for human desire is the theme of Plato's *Phaedrus*.[34] There, beauty is what reminds the soul of the archetype of beauty that it once beheld. This memory makes the soul erotically desirous. Yet the desired also lies far removed, at an infinite distance; it is divine beauty, the idea of beauty, in a transcendent realm impenetrable to the human eye. Thus, the tale could be read as a transformation of erotic desire into a desire utterly detached from anything earthly, in an interpretation that does justice to the Platonic background of poetry. Hades as a place of death finally proves to be a place of transformation: Persephone's ointment represents a beauty that no longer belongs to the earthly sensual realm. Sleep, into which Psyche falls after applying the ointment, marks a state of renewed letting go. Further psychoanalytical theories could investigate how the life and death instinct interlock and which role the latter plays in the process of sublimation from erotic desire to other objectives.[35] Unusually enough, Eros and Psyche are reunited in Hades. One relevant question in this respect is how much Eros as *daimon* projects into the sphere of death. Psyche does not return to lead a fulfilled life at her husband's side, as is usually expected in fairy tales with a happy ending. There is no return to earth from the realm of death, but instead apotheosis: Psyche is accepted into the pantheon, which in antiquity was reserved for important figures after death.[36] In other words, Psyche's death in the tale becomes the prerequisite for her eternal life with Eros and their daughter Voluptas in the pantheon.

What remains as an earthly legacy is the capacity to transform desire, symbolised in Psyche's persistent quest, for which the object of desire is only symbolised in a sphere beyond the visible and formative. This is symbolised in Eros-cum-Thanatos, who emerges at the very moment when the possessive part of desire has lapsed. This interpretation brings us full circle to Neumann. He concludes his commentary on the tale of *Amor and Psyche* by observing that "the mystery phenomenon of love has occupied the center of psychic development" and of the "psychic and spiritual life of the West." Psyche's love, so Neumann, is a "central motif in the love mysticism of all times" (AP, p. 140).

This, I suggest, reveals a problem in Neumann's interpretation, which seeks to depict Psyche as the strong, unyielding lover whose desire to be united with her lover is ultimately fulfilled and who is rewarded for her steadfastness and independence when she ascends Mount Olympus. But how does this vital, self-confident image of the heroine go together with the union in Hades, which Neumann interprets as an image of mystical union? This transformation process remains intangible in Neumann's interpretation, since he ignores the stages of the metaphor of death as an expression of Psyche's inner dissolution.

Let us take one final look at the theme of the hero in Neumann's writings. First, he confines himself to that hero who is capable of giving "the world a new and better face" (OHC, p. 174; see also Chapter 14). Only one heroic action qualifies as heroic, namely, that which establishes a "connection with the creative powers" (GM, p. 187). This type of hero already exists and is waiting to be called upon by culture.

Neumann's canon of heroes in *The Origins and History of Consciousness*, which Wolfgang Giegerich has characterised as an "archetypal fantasy,"[37] is hence oriented exclusively towards that hero who promises liberation, redemption and ultimately transformation; or, in archetypal terms, who helps overcome the Great Mother.[38] The theme of transformation is most impressive in the image of Pegasus rising from the severed head of the Gorgon.

On the other hand, Neumann rejects Oedipus, whose existence is marred by failure. He sees Oedipus, whose tragedy still moves us today, as a hero who failed because of his great mother complex. Consequently, he does not point to the future. As Donald Kalsched suggests, Psyche may also be seen to fail, whereas Neumann regards her as a "conqueror" of poverty and loneliness, and thus as epitomising "a new principle of love."

One cannot help but perceive Neumann's mythological scheme as a realm purged of human suffering and misery, or as one not significantly affected by these forces and in which only heroic action and achievement matter. We can read these secular images of redemption, affixed to the archetypal sky, as counter-images to real historical destruction and annihilation; they are the content of an ideological construct in the guise of a mythopoetic work. These images counter the "cultural break," the "schizophrenic episode" of the Germans, to whom Neumann at the same time nevertheless feels "a debt of gratitude" (as he told Jung in his letter of 5 December 1938; JNC, p. 140). The word "counter-image," in Jungian terms, resonates with the compensatory function of the unconscious. This alone, Neumann is convinced, could counter the "modern decay of values," and the subsequent regression of the cultural canon, as he observed in *Origins and History* (OHC, p. 390).

Neumann, who was deeply convinced that the transpersonal ultimately precedes the individual's development and determines his or her existence, saw his work as re-establishing a connection with a constructive, creative archetypal canon that comes before the break in civilisation and exerts a positive cultural influence on the history of the Western world (see Chapter 14).[39]

We can understand this perspective as Neumann's attempt to link his work to the educational ideal internalised already in the 19th century by German-Jewish culture. Central to that ideal was systematic progress. Neumann therefore implicitly presupposes a principle of development that is characterised by continual progress. This enables him to uphold the utopian idea that what inheres in the archetypal circle of creative forms contains the seed of a new beginning and of cultural progress. Ideas, myths and the works of great masters all bear the archetypal potential of entering human history in the future. Dedicated to creativity, Neumann's world of heroes is immersed in the bright light of hope. This originates in a way of thinking that considers the redemption of the world to be an inalienable fact.[40]

Let us recall a letter that Neumann wrote to Jung in 1959, one year before Neumann's death (Chapter 11):

> For me in any case, it is a fact that the Jewish historical "development" in this mortal world is becoming ever more problematic for me, the "actualization of messianism" in individuation is becoming ever more crucial … What is relevant are the stages of development of consciousness in the development of the individual, otherwise everything "historical" belongs to the constellation of the ego as time, like family and constitution. The realization of the ego-Self unity is vertical.
>
> (JNC, p. 345)

The less Neumann, a Jewish émigré to Palestine, could identify with actual historical conditions—in spite of his sense of belonging—the more he concentrated on the "vertical ego-Self axis."[41] On the one hand, as an analyst and writer living an "insular" life in Tel Aviv, he lamented "the isolation of my existence in Palestine" (JNC, p. 166). On the other, distancing himself from "horizontal" everyday and contemporary events seemed to provide him with a protective retreat and at the same time with a mystical source of inspiration and life.

In fact, Neumann's heroes seem enraptured, as if they have been liberated from the earthly slag. In this respect, I am reminded of Walter Benjamin's remarks on Robert Walser's characters: They have "already gone mad" and are "all healed." As for Neumann's heroic figures (and to modify Benjamin's words), "they have already suffered and are redeemed."[42]

This book intends to contribute to understanding Neumann's theorising in the context of its genesis. Works in cultural theory written during the period of cultural disruption always ought to be read as an answer to this rupture. They do not escape the dialectic that unfolds within historical facticity.

It was only at the Eranos round table, through dialogue with others, that Neumann was able to reconcile his life, thought and vision—at least briefly. This is the same round table at which we are still able to engage in dialogue with Neumann and his work.

Notes

1 "Freud and the Father Image," *Creative Man: Five Essays*, trans. Eugene Rolfe, Bollingen Series LXI:2 (Princeton, NJ: Princeton University Press, 1979), pp. 232–255; originally published in German as "Freud und das Vaterbild, *MERKUR, Deutsche Zeitschrift für europäisches Denken*, 10, no. 8 (August 1956); cited hereafter as FFI.

2 Neumann raises this issue for the first time in his correspondence with Jung; see his letter of 1 January 1949 (see JNC, pp. 238–42). In October 1950, Neumann taught a course on Apuleius's *Amor and Psyche* at the Küsnacht Institute; see JNC, p. 241, n. 457.

3 Today's scientific community rejects the hypotheses of the classic works on matriarchy, in particular any speculations that seem to be based on mythology. See, for instance, Margaret Ehrenberg, *Women in Prehistory* (London: British Museum Publications, 1989).

4 In his "Editorial Note," Neumann mentions that Apuleius mixes Roman and Greek elements, as reflected by the name "Eros," whom Apuleius calls Amor or Cupid, whereas he (Neumann) consciously speaks of Eros; see AP, pp. 56 and 155, n. 9.

5 Raphael Patai, *The Hebrew Goddess*, 3rd enlarged ed. (Detroit, MI: Wayne State University Press, 1990; first published 1967).

6 Another, more recent standard work is William G. Dever's *Did God Have a Wife? Archeology and Folk Religion in Ancient Israel* (Grand Rapids, MI: Eerdmans, 2008). Gerda Weiler's *Das Matriarchat im alten Israel* (Stuttgart, Berlin, Cologne: Kohlhammer, 1989) does not refer to Patai's seminal research and therefore did not build on the state of research at the time.

7 Patai, p. 25f.

8 Ibid., p. 278f.

9 Ibid., p. 279.

10 Johann Jakob Bachofen, *Das Mutterrecht* (Stuttgart: Verlag von Krais und Hoffman, 1861) and *Versuch über die Gräbersymbolik der Alten* (Basel, 1859; reprinted Munich: Beck, 1923); Richard Reitzenstein, *Das Märchen von Amor und Psyche bei Apuleius* (Berlin & Leipzig: Teubner, 1912); Karl Kerenyi, *Der große Daimon des Symposion* (Amsterdam, Leipzig: Pantheon, Albae Vigiliae XIII, 1942).

11 Heide Göttner-Abendroth, *Die Göttin und ihr Heros: Die matriarchalen Religionen in Mythen, Märchen, Dichtung* (Munich: Frauenoffensive, 1980; expanded and updated edition, Stuttgart: Kohlhammer, 2011); see also Gerda Weiler, *Der enteignete Mythos: Eine feministische Revision der Archetypenlehre C.G. Jungs und Erich Neumanns* (Frankfurt/Main, New York: Campus, 1991).

12 Marie-Luise von Franz, *A Psychological Interpretation of the Golden Ass of Apuleius* (Zurich: Spring Publications, 1970); see also Ann Ulanov, *The Feminine in Jungian Psychology and in Christian Theology* (Evanston, IL: Northwestern University Press, 1971).

13 James Hillman, *The Myth of Analysis: Three Essays in Archetypal Psychology* (New York: Harper & Row, 1972), pp. 74–107. This volume is based on three Eranos lectures delivered in the years 1966, 1968 and 1969.

14 Ibid., p. 59.

15 Ibid.

16 Ibid.
17 Donald Kalsched, *The Inner World of Trauma, Archetypal Defenses of the Personal Spirit* (London and New York; Routledge 1996), pp. 166–184.
18 Donald Kalsched, "Trauma, Unschuld und der Kernkomplex der Dissoziation," *Analytische Psychologie,* 47, No. 188, 2/2017.
19 Emmanuel Lévinas, *Totality and Infinity: An Essay on Exteriority*, trans. Alphonso Lingis (Pittsburgh, PA: University of Pittsburgh Press, 2011).
20 Ibid., p. 22.
21 Ibid., p. 35.
22 Ibid., p. 43f.
23 Ibid., p. 43f.
24 Ibid., p. 35.
25 Ibid., p. 31f.
26 Ibid., p. 27.
27 Ibid., p. 27.
28 Ibid., p. 50.
29 Ibid., p. 33.
30 Ibid., p. 29f.
31 Ibid., p. 40.
32 Ibid., p. 63.
33 Ibid., p. 291.
34 Apuleius referred to himself as a "Platonic philosopher."
35 See Roman Lesmeister, "Jenseits des Gesetzes: Sublimierung, Todestrieb und Exzess," in Angelica Löwe, Roman Lesmeister and Daniel Krochmalnik (eds.), *Gewalt, Sublimierung, Glaube* (Freiburg: Alber, 2017).
36 On the concept and function of apotheosis, see David Engels, "Entrückung, Epiphanie und Consecration," in Dominik Gross and Jasmin Grande (eds.), *Objekt Leiche* (Frankfurt a.M., New York: Campus Verlag, 2010).
37 Wolfgang Giegerich, *Ontogeny=Phylogeny? A Fundamental Critique of Erich Neumann's Analytical Psychology* (Dallas, TX: Spring Publications, 1975), pp. 110–129.
38 Neumann's most pronounced discussion of this liberation can be found in his Eranos lecture "The Meaning of the Earth Archetype for Modern Times" (orig. *Die Bedeutung des Erdarchetyps für die Neuzeit*; see Chapter 10).
39 Wolfgang Giegerich has criticised this historical enslavement of the archetypal by arguing that this is an inadmissible amalgamation of the imaginary with the empirical world. The gods are essentially timeless. In his opinion, in archetypal psychology there is no principle of development, no regular sequence of archetypes nor archetypal phases. Further, the implantation of the idea of development in archetypal space is reductive; see his essay "Ontogeny=Phylogeny?" (1975). Now it might be objected that Jung paved the way for this trend, among others, with his Wotan essay. Nor did he voice any criticism along these lines in his preface to Neumann's *Origins and History*. Therefore, the discussion on the "historicisation" of the archetype would need to be conducted on a broader level.
40 Seemingly unaware of this background, Giegerich speaks of a "'fixed order'" in Neumann, which "finally helps sustain a fundamental ideological optimism, by making light of all the trials of history, of all suffering and imperfection"; see Giegerich, "Ontogeny=Phylogeny? A Fundamental Critique of Erich Neumann's Analytical Psychology," *Spring* (1975), pp. 110–129; cited here from http://web.utanet.at/salzjung/ontogeny.htm.
41 Giegerich also cites this passage. As he was only familiar with excerpts of Neumann's correspondence with Jung when writing his essay, and unaware of Neumann's

unedited manuscripts, Giegerich believes that Neumann's account is a late idea. In fact, it is a very early idea, which Neumann expanded on in his Hasidism manuscript, now published as *The Roots of Jewish Consciousness* (2019); see Giegerich, "Ontogeny=Phylogeny?".

42 Walter Benjamin, "Robert Walser" (1929), in *Gesammelte Schriften* Vol. I/II (Frankfurt am Main: Suhrkamp, 1980), pp. 324–328—Trans.

Appendix I

The Life of Erich Neumann

23 January 1905: Erich Neumann is born as the third child of Eduard Neumann and Selma Neumann, née Brodnitz, in Berlin-Charlottenburg, Joachimsthaler Strasse 30.

Siblings: Lotte, born 1 August 1897 and Franz, born 3 March 1899 (both later became physicians).

Mother: Selma Neumann, née Brodnitz, born 21 May 1872 in Poznan.

Father: Eduard Neumann, born 29 March 1866 in Schlochau/Poznan; a wealthy grain merchant and assimilated Jew.

Erich attended the humanistic Mommsen-Gymnasium (liberal arts grammar school) on Wormserstrasse 11 in Berlin-Charlottenburg; many Jewish classmates; average school reports; his favourite subject is German, but his reports in mathematics are poor; he frequently plays "truant" to participate in group debates on Jewish topics.

He undertakes his first writing experiments in year 12, producing prose and above all poems; at the age of 16, he meets Erwin Loewenson, 17 years his senior, who becomes his philosophical-Zionist mentor and friend.

1920: Erich meets Julie Blumenfeld at a local dance school. They begin dating but split up after six months. On 28 April 1921, Erich presents Julie with a book by Martin Buber as a farewell gift and birthday present with the dedication: "Our ways will cross again! Your Erich."

1923: Erich is awarded his school-leaving certificate, qualifying for entrance into university.

1921–1929: Erich writes poetry (their Expressionist style echoes Erwin Loewenson's literary activities).

2 March 1924: Erich joins the Berlin Zionist Association.

1923: Erich enrols at Erlangen University where he spends six semesters studying philosophy, psychology, education studies, history of literature and art, Semitic studies under professors Hensel, Leser and Hell.

He develops an interest in Freud's psychoanalysis and Jung's theory of the collective unconscious.

1925: After four years of separation, Erich meets Julie again.

1926: Erich meets Hannah Arendt in Heidelberg.

2 March 1927: Erich submits his dissertation at the Faculty of Philosophy in Erlangen: "Johann Arnold Kanne. A forgotten romantic. A contribution to the history of mystical philosophy of language." He majors in philosophy, with pedagogy and Arabic as his minors.

September 1928: Erich and Julie are married.

1928: Erich enters medical school in Berlin with the intention of becoming a psychoanalyst. He sits his finals on 24 April 1933, without obtaining his doctorate in medicine, as Jews were no longer allowed to do the necessary internships.

17 June 1932: Julie gives birth to Micha, their first child.

1932: Erich completes his (unpublished) commentary on Franz Kafka's stories and novels, applying a Kabbalistic approach to interpretation. A reply from Martin Buber dated 1935 indicates that Erich had sent him his Kafka manuscript for review.

1932: Two chapters of Erich's novel *Der Anfang* (The Beginning) are published in a anthology of young Jewish authors (*Zwischen den Zelten*).

October 1933: Erich meets C.G. Jung and spends eight months stay in Zurich for training analysis. Julie leaves Switzerland with Micha in February 1934. Jung encourages Erich Neumann to settle in Palestine in order to lead a life in his "own country."

May 1934: Erich leaves Zurich to travel to Palestine; his life in Tel Aviv begins.

Between 1934 and 1940: Erich works on his unpublished "Jewish" manuscript. Originally planned as a three-volume work, it comprises two volumes:
I. "Contributions to the Depth Psychology of the Jewish Person and the Problem of Revelation"
II. "Hasidism and its Psychological Significance for Judaism."

Erich runs a joint private psychotherapy practice with Julie, who is also a well-known chirologist in Israel.

He holds seminars in Tel Aviv and Jerusalem on various topics such as the collective unconscious, Kabbalah, Hasidism.

1934–1959: Correspondence with C.G. Jung.

1936: Erich and Julie visit C.G. Jung during a two-month stay in Switzerland. They do not return to Europe again until the summer of 1947.

1936: The Neumann's move to Gordonstrasse 1 in Tel Aviv, into a four-room apartment where the family lives until Julie's death in 1985. The apartment soon became an "institution," initially among German émigrés; the circle later expanded. During the Second World War, the apartment became a small-scale "cultural centre," where Erich held seminars and classical music could be heard.

1936: Erich's parents visit Tel Aviv and try to take their grandson Micha back to Germany, "where he belongs."

25 March 1937: Erich's father Eduard Neumann dies as a result of a Gestapo interrogation.

8 May 1938: Julie gives birth to their daughter Rali.

1939: Publication of *Tiefenpsychologie und Neue Ethik* (published in English as *Depth Psychology and a New Ethic*). The book sparks outrage at the Jung Institute in Zurich.

1945–1948: Neumann writes *Ursprungsgeschichte des Bewusstseins*; published in 1949 with a favourable preface by Jung, who tones down its message, however, due to tensions at the Jung Institute; published in English as *The History and Origins of Consciousness.*

1947: Erich's mother moves from London (where she had lived with Franz, Erich's brother, after leaving Germany) to Tel Aviv. She lived with Erich and his family until her death in 1955.

1947: Erich and Julie travel to Switzerland to "work" with Jung. They meet Olga Fröbe-Kapteyn, the organiser of the Eranos conferences in Ticino. Fröbe-Kapteyn shows Erich her large archive of images dealing with the "Great Mother."

1948: Erich travels alone to Switzerland because of the war in Israel. He gives his first lecture ("Mystical Man") at the Eranos conference in Ascona at the invitation of Fröbe-Kapteyn and Jung. He is invited to write a foreword to a project titled *The Great Mother*, from which one of his most important works was to emerge.

Annual participation in the Eranos conferences from 1948.
A scholarship from the Bollingen Foundation enables Erich to work on *The Great Mother* and to travel to Switzerland.

1949: The outcry against Erich had meanwhile subsided.
He is invited to hold seminars and lectures at the C.G. Jung Institute.
He rejects the position of institute director.

From 1949: Erich lectures in Zurich and Basel, later also in Holland. Julie and Erich spend about two months every summer travelling in Europe, staying with friends and family members.

1952: Publication of *Amor und Psyche* (published in English as *Amor und Psyche*).

1953–1954: Publication of *Umkreisung der Mitte: Aufsätze zur Tiefenpsychologie der Kultur*, three volumes.

8 December 1955: Erich's mother Selma dies in Tel Aviv.

1955: Founding of the International Association for Analytical Psychology (IAAP). Erich becomes a member.

1956: Publication of *Die Grosse Mutter* (published in English as *The Great Mother*).

1958: The first IAAP Congress at which Erich gives a lecture.

18 November 1958: Erich receives official recognition for his doctorate from Hamburg Faculty of Medicine. *The Origins and History of Consciousness* is approved as a doctoral thesis; the oral examination was waived. He describes this as "an act of cultural restitution."

1959: Publication of *Der Schöpferische Mensch* (published in English as *Creative Man: Five Essays*).

Erich spends the last years of his life writing, doing therapeutic work and training therapists, especially child therapists.

1959: Foundation of the Israeli Association of Analytical Therapists, of which Erich becomes president.

1959: Erich rejects the offer to found the Psychological Institute at Tel Aviv University and become its director.

1960: Travels to Germany and gives various lectures.

5 November 1960: Erich Neumann dies of cancer.

1961: Publication of *Krise und Erneuerung.*

1961: Publication of *Die archetypische Welt Henry Moores.*

1963: Publication of *Das Kind* (published posthumously, edited by Julie Neumann).

The Life of Julie Neumann, née Blumenfeld

28 April 1905: Julie Blumenfeld is born as the fourth child of the merchant Julius Blumenfeld (born 21 June 1863) and his wife Ida, née Silbermann (born 14 June 1863), at Pariserstrasse 4, Berlin-Wilmersdorf.

Julie's siblings: Martin, Lotte, Paul and Ruth.

She attends Hohenzollern Lyceum until Year 1; joins the Zionist Youth Federation "Blue-White."

1920: Julie meets Erich Neumann, who is the same age, at dance school. They separate after half a year.

October 1921–Easter 1922: Julie works as a volunteer in a home for East Jewish refugees in Berlin, Augustastrasse 14/15.

Easter to October 1922: Julie works as a maid in Lübeck.

Six-month apprenticeship at the *Mütter-und Säuglingsheim Berlin*, Brunnenstrasse 41; passes her finals.

Easter 1923–1924: Works for one and a half years as an assistant nurse at Friedrich-Luisen hospice in Bad Dürrheim.

1924: Meets Erich Neumann again.

1925: Ward nurse at the *Mütter- und Säuglingsheim* in Berlin, Brunnenstrasse 41.

Julie runs a day nursery in Berlin before moving to Berlin Polyclinic on Augustastrasse 17. She expresses her desire to earn A-levels to be able to work as a psychologist and special needs teacher.

Easter 1926: Works as a children's nurse at Mannheim General Hospital.

1926: Passes her state examination in child and infant care.

1927: Runs a day nursery in Berlin until her marriage to Erich Neumann.

September 1928: Marries Erich Neumann.

The couple first lives at Hindenburgerstrasse 86 (now Volkspark 73); later Weimarische Strasse 26.

Undergoes training in chirology with Julius Spier, a student of C.G. Jung.

Easter 1929: Enters the Pädagogium Thie, Berlin.

1932: Graduates from Pädagogium Thie.

17 June 1932: Julie gives birth to Micha.

October 1933: Emigration to Switzerland; training analysis with Emma Jung and Toni Wolff.

February 1934: Emigration to Palestine; life in Tel Aviv.

Establishes a joint psychoanalytical practice with Erich. Becomes a very successful and highly recognised chirologist.

Julie's youngest sister, Ruth, marries an Englishman in the early 1930s and moves to London.

1936: Julie and Erich move to Gordonstrasse 1 in Tel Aviv, which serves as an apartment and practice.

1936: The couple visits C.G. Jung during a two-month stay in Switzerland.

1938: Martin, Julie's eldest brother, emigrates to Australia; two other siblings (Lotte and Paul) emigrate to England before the outbreak of war.

Julie's parents emigrate to England shortly before the outbreak of war assisted by their English son-in-law.

8 May 1938: Julie gives birth to Rali.

1947: Erich Neumann's mother emigrates to Israel. She lived with Erich and Julie until her death in 1955.

Summer 1947: The Neumann's meet Olga Fröbe-Kapteyn, the organiser of the Eranos conferences, in Moscia–Ascona.

28 April 1949: Julie's father dies.

1949: Julie accompanies Erich from now on every year to Switzerland and takes part in the Eranos conferences.

From 1949: Long stays (August to October) with Erich in Switzerland, trips to Austria, France and England, Holland, Spain and Italy.

July 1955: IAAP membership.

1959: Member of the Israel Association of Analytical Psychology.

5 November 1960: Erich dies of cancer in Tel Aviv.

1960: Erich's mother dies a few days later.

1960: After Erich's death, Julie served as chair of the Israel Association of Analytical Therapists for several years.

1985: Julie Neumann dies in Tel Aviv.

Appendix 2: German-Jewish dialogue: Neumann, Jung and the Jungians

An Address delivered on the Occasion of the Inauguration of the Commemorative Plaque for Erich and Julie Neumann in Berlin on 6 May 2007.

We have gathered today for what is undoubtedly a very pleasant and festive occasion. This occasion provides us with an opportunity to contribute to an area of life that likes to adorn itself with names such as "culture of remembrance" or "German-Jewish dialogue." We should, however, take joy, which ought not come up short, in today's occasion, behind whose radiant façade a polyphony of voices can be heard, quietly, perhaps barely audible, and which is slightly drowned out by overly objective or even by overly affected speech, a "hollow space" of language.[1] These quiet tones can, however, shift our contemporary recollection and thinking towards a point that has become anaesthetised: the point of mutual immeasurable loss.

In gathering here today, to remember Erich Neumann and Julie Blumenfeld, who emigrated from this city in 1933, first to Zurich, then to Tel Aviv, we are inevitably reminded of the destruction and extermination that began in 1933. That year marked the beginning of the exodus of the spirit, when the Weimar Republic gave way to a dawning inferno of persecution, expulsion, oppression and the systematic murder of millions of Jews.

The house whose yard we are standing in belonged to Julie Blumenfeld's parents. Pleasingly, it is still standing—whereas the house in which Erich Neumann was born is now a bombed-out, gaping construction site. And yet, this house also tells the story of emigration, flight, expulsion and expropriation.

Mr Krochmalnik, our host and the house's present owner, attaches great importance to documenting its history. Before so-called "Aryanisation," the former owners, the Tennenbaums, sold the house to Allianz, a major German insurance company, and emigrated to South America. As is well known, such emergency sales fetched no more than rock-bottom prices. The caretakers and their children moved to the stately fourth floor, where all the furniture had been left behind. Allianz owned the house on Pariser Strasse 4 until 1996, when it was sold to its present owners, the Krochmalniks and Salzers. The building formerly housed a private school for Jewish and Christian children, which had been founded in 1918 by Mrs Anne Peletson, a Jewish woman who had converted to Protestantism. Mrs Peletson was murdered in Theresienstadt.

In 1936, approval was granted to establish a Jewish house of prayer in Pariser Strasse 4. When Mr Krochmalnik took over the house, the wall paintings of the former synagogue had been painted over—and all the Jewish traces obliterated. Now these paintings have been uncovered and restored.

Ruth Goldstone, Julie Neumann's youngest sister—whose advanced age and poor health unfortunately prevent her from celebrating with us today—visited Berlin when the house was still owned by Allianz. When she wanted to visit her parents' house, she was denied admission. When she next returned to Berlin, in 2001, the new owner, Mr Krochmalnik, opened its doors to her. He also organised a visit to the school that Ruth and her sister Julie had visited, and invited a teacher and her students for a return visit to Pariser Strasse 4.

Julie and Erich Neumann, who were both born in 1905, belonged to a generation whose youth and early adult life were overshadowed by unprecedented social and political upheavals. Both came from assimilated homes and already turned to Zionism at a young age. Basically, they owe it to this fact that they got to know each other. Julie was only permitted to remain an active member of the Zionist *Wanderbund Blau-Weiss* if she cultivated ladylike elegance, among other things, by taking dance lessons. So she attended the dance school located here in this house. And got to know Erich Neumann. Both were 15 years old at the time. Their budding relationship lasted six months. Then, for four years, they had no contact. During this time, Julie lived and worked in various cities across Germany and earned a diploma as a paediatric nurse. Her commitment to East Jewish refugees is worth mentioning in this context. For example, she worked in the Eastern Jewish children's home on Auguststrasse in Berlin.

One day Erich called Julie. Both were now 20 years old.

Erich became the most important person in Julie's life, and vice versa: his companion, the mother of their two children, a professional colleague and the woman who remained at his side until his early death and who survived him by 25 years.

Many young people who joined Zionism were interested primarily in searching for their Jewish identity. The movement's purely political or international law aspect often mattered less to them. Rather, Zionism became a catalyst for personal development, especially for young Jews rebelling against their bourgeois parents. The desire to realise the potential slumbering in Judaism seemed attainable only because "the Jew would encounter himself, his people, and his roots."[2] Kurt Blumenfeld, a "Zionist by Goethe's Grace," as he called himself, and the intellectual leader of German Zionists, warned his followers against false religiosity and recommended reading Fichte, Nietzsche and Hölderlin.[3]

Erich and Julie were also moved by this endeavour to "liberate the individual personality" (see the Blumenfeld Resolution of 1912, presented at the Delegates Conference of the Zionist Federation of Germany that year). They were, however, also concerned about their future—unfortunately, their fears were justified.[4] The anti-Semitic agitation that reached extreme proportions after the First World War spread insecurity, helplessness and insult, which no appeasement could disguise.

Julie later spoke of her "unrequited love for Germany." And yet, emigrating to Eretz Israel (Palestine) was far from easy. The political situation there was difficult, the standard of living extremely modest, the future uncertain. Erich received information from the Zionist Federation that therapists would probably not be needed in Palestine, so to be on the safe side he gained training in manual nerve massage.

He had obtained a doctorate in philosophy in Erlangen, before studying medicine in Berlin with a view to becoming a psychoanalyst. His doctorate was not recognised because—as a Jew—he was no longer permitted to do a clinical internship. Nor were any university degrees earned by Jews in the Weimar Republic recognised in the Third Reich. Shortly before his death, Neumann managed to regain his doctorate with *The Origins and History of Consciousness*. The fact that he had to pursue this goal himself ought to give us even more pause for thought.

In 1933, the couple first travelled to Zurich for psychoanalytical training, which Erich completed with C.G. Jung and Julie with Toni Wolff. In February 1934, Julie embarked for Israel with their little son, who had been born in Berlin. Erich followed three months later.

While working with C.G. Jung, Neumann set out to "demonstrate the collective predeterminedness of a part of the problem of the modern Jew" (JNC, p. 140–141).

Neumann's work with Jung was not without friction, as the latter had published an article titled "Zur gegenwärtigen Lage in der Psychotherapie" ("The State of Psychotherapy Today") in March 1934. From a Jewish perspective in particular, its contents moved Jung into the Nazi-friendly, anti-Semitic camp.

In response, Neumann wrote a letter to Jung that left nothing to be desired in terms of clarity. He reminds Jung of his humanistic background, their common bourgeois education and the "Goethean gaze," which actually ought to be capable of diagnosing the "dirt, blood and filth" in the "Germanic soul," which had calamitously fallen prey to National Socialism. Furthermore, he accuses Jung's lacking knowledge "of Jewish things, and of harbouring a secret and medieval disgust for them, which leads to knowing everything about India and nothing about Hasidism."[5]

In June of the same year—Neumann had meanwhile arrived in Tel Aviv—he defended Jung in the *Jüdische Rundschau*, the newspaper of the German Zionist Association, against the allegations made by James Kirsch by turning Jung into a spiritual precursor of Zionism. I quote:

> All of us belong to the phenotype of the Jew living in the banishment of the Shekhinah. Jung's work with Jewish people has made him see this fateful tendency. … Jungian psychology will be decisive in the effort of the Jews to reach their foundations. The "Zionist" character of his findings, which, like Zionism, include the irrational of the primordial creative ground, will prove groundbreaking in this respect.[6]

The theme of the soil or the earth is pivotal in this regard. Jung calls it "something in man that touches the earth, that receives new power from below. The mystery of the earth is neither a joke nor a paradox."[7]

The Neumanns were among the nearly 2,000 German Jews who had emigrated by 1933—at the time, only a tiny percentage of Zionists seriously considered moving to Palestine as part of their life plan (see Blumenfeld Resolution of 1912).[8]

The Zionists merely held a minority position among the plethora of German-Jewish views on several vital issues: coexistence, assimilation, symbiosis or separation. The Zionist Federation of Germany, which had been headed by Kurt Blumenfeld since 1924, was relatively small. In 1930, it had about 20,000 members, that is, 3.5 per cent of German Jews.[9] Nevertheless, we should not underestimate the Zionist influence on the debates over the position of Jews within the field of culture, since many of their followers were intellectuals.

The Neumanns founded a psychoanalytical practice in Tel Aviv. This became their main source of income. Moreover, Julie was a widely recognised chirologist in Israel. In addition to his courses and lectures, Erich began producing that body of work whose conceptual and linguistic distinctiveness we know and appreciate today as Jungians, and which is also known far beyond Jungian circles.

We know him as the author of *Depth Psychology and a New Ethic*, which he "conceived during the Second World War and under its direct impact," as Neumann observed in his preface. This book, which gravitates around the Holocaust, caused a storm of indignation, especially in Zurich.

Neumann had met Jung at a time when his life was undergoing complete transformation on the outside, which also questioned his inner being—his existence as a galut Jew, a Jew living in exile—which seemed deeply alien to him, and which he was keen to leave behind. Eliminating this alienation became his personal equation, his mission in life as it were. One of his main concerns was to redefine Jewish identity. He grappled with anti-Jewish stereotypes to the point of seemingly and painfully exaggerated self-criticism. The anti-Semitic stereotypes had changed decisively in the first decades of the 20th century.[10] Jews now represented the antithesis to the dominant neo-romantic ideal of the time: They were mostly urbanised, not bound to *terra firma*, homeless and had no living folk traditions. Judaism, once reviled and attacked for its superstition, was now criticised for being a religion of reason. This illustrates how much the perception and evaluation of Judaism were determined by a dual schematism, with Judaism figuring as a counter-image or antithesis to its own ideal and self-understanding while always forming the negative pole regardless of content.[11]

Thus, for example, the "restless age" and the "restless Jew," two key notions of the cultural pessimism *en vogue* at the time, blended into the signature of a disastrous epoch. The gentrified Jews in the large cities had become the "distorted image of modernity," especially for these neoconservative ideologues. Nor did this distortion stop at those whose image was distorted. We may also attribute Jung to this position. Unfortunately, his psychological view on this subject was a poor imitation of the prevailing, that is, anti-Semitic stereotypes.

It seemed reasonable to Neumann that the other side, the once so cultivated Western world, especially the "Germanic soul," needed to engage with its "shadow problem." From this point of view, the *New Ethic* can be seen as a Jewish Jungian offering German and Swiss Jungians an opportunity for dialogue. He was therefore completely astounded by the outrage at the newly founded Swiss Jungian Institute. He was accused of having an "old testament perspective."

Neumann characterised the uproar in Zurich as "intellectual disingenuousness" and was combative:

> I am willing to defend The New Ethic—which apparently no longer has any friends in Switzerland—in open battle against the whole institute. Protestants, Catholics, baptized Jews, unbaptized Jews, and even Jungian analysts if any show up.
>
> (JNC, p. 248f.)

His main accusation was directed at the function of the unconscious, which in his opinion was misunderstood:

> They smiled in a rather superior way about my provincial attitude, which was thought not quite up to it simply because I made a value judgment about where one ought to allow the wisdom of the unconscious to prevail, beyond good and evil. But they seemed to me all too often to mistake the unconsciousness of the ego for the wisdom of the unconscious ... Some of the reservations against your teaching are based on the unrevolutionary and all too bourgeois stance of your students who always wish to anticipate the wisdom of the "third half of life" before they have the struggles of the first behind them ... I do not wish to conceal from you that it sometimes seems to me that you are yourself rather complicit in this ... At the same time, though, I would like to assure you that my fervent efforts will continue to prove myself worthy of "the hate of the pussyfooters".
>
> (JNC, p. 239ff.)

When Jung first read the *New Ethic*, he sensed that "its effect will be like that of a bomb." He felt "a secret pleasure" and saw his role in the anticipated discussion as that of a "commandant of the fire brigade" (JNC, pp. 236–237). Neumann, however, asks Jung not to limit himself to putting out the fire, as a cleansing blaze could "eradicate some filth" (ibid., p. 139). So this is what the Jewish-German dialogue, or rather the Jewish-Swiss dialogue, looked like a few years after the end of the Second World War. It took the form of fierce controversy.

On the subject of dialogue, let me refer you to a passage in a letter by Gershom Scholem, another Zionist from Berlin. Like Neumann, Scholem had also emigrated to Israel. Scholem had been asked to collaborate on a commemorative publication which, as the invitation stated, was meant to be "a document of a German-Jewish dialogue that was essentially indestructible."

Scholem describes this formula in his letter as blasphemous. He insists that "the entire eerie German-Jewish dialogue is taking place in an empty, fictitious space." He closes his letter as follows:

> The allegedly indestructible spiritual commonality of the German essence with the Jewish one has, as long as these two sages have lived together in reality, always only consisted of a chorus of Jewish voices and was, on the level of historical reality, never anything but a fiction, one about which I will be granted the view that its price has been too high.[12]

Neumann's astonishment at the reaction of the Swiss Institute suggests that his offer for discussion was based on a fiction, the fiction of a willingness to engage with one's counterpart on equal terms.

His second work, *The Origins and History of Consciousness*, also published in 1949, earned Neumann widespread recognition. In his preface, Jung praised the "conclusions and insights" of this work as "among the most important ever to be reached in this field." Neumann's third major work was *The Great Mother: An Analysis of the Archetype*, published in 1956.

Since 1947, Neumann had participated in the Eranos conferences in Ascona, where he gave his first lecture in 1948. From 1953 until his death, he was the opening speaker. The line running through Neumann's work is that of a Humboldtian humanistic educational canon. The belongings that the emigrants had shipped to Palestine included not only furniture but also well-stocked personal libraries. The silent presence of books and the sounds of classical music connected Neumann with his origins. Some of his lectures, in which he interprets poetry by Goethe, Rilke and Trakl, among other important authors, and which tangibly illustrate his own hypotheses, reveal the tradition in which he stood. Is not this, too, a sign of the Jewish-German dialogue, the outer side of the inner one, that took place in Neumann himself?

In 1951, he wrote to Olga Fröbe-Kapteyn, the founder of the Eranos conferences:

> You know that I am not in Israel by chance, and a sizeable part of me comes from the ancestors and proceeds, via the children, into the future. But another, more unconditional or otherwise conditioned part, which seemed basically homeless and for which not Israel, nor Europe and certainly not America could be home, found, surprised and delighted, a piece of soil on the reality of the occidental spirit is alive, as Eranos in your heart, as a large roundtable inviting discussion … and as a constant endeavour of many speakers and conferences.[13]

The roundtable discussion, as a symbol of home, which the homeless, uprooted person can only find in the spiritual realm, and who felt he did not belong in Germany because his identity formation—this complex mediation process between being-at-home, familiarity, as well as wanting and being able to differentiate and to be different—was overlaid, damaged and ultimately rendered impossible by the historical situation.

The roundtable was a symbol of conversation, of dialogue.

In speaking of a Jewish-German, German-Jewish dialogue today, we can mean nothing that is certain or unequivocal. Rather, we are moving on unsecured terrain, close to the abyss of a possible "counter-fiction"—to modify Scholem's terminology.

This dialogue—as seen from today's cultural-historical perspective—lay at the heart of the European intellectual tradition. It decisively determined the culture of the Weimar Republic and thus the reciprocal, cross-fertilising influence of Jews and Germans on the level of art, literature and philosophy.[14]

How much and in what way Neumann's work stands in the German tradition of thought has not yet been investigated and would make a worthwhile scientific undertaking. Even less attention, however, has been given to Neumann's intense preoccupation with his Jewish roots. This endeavour was first reflected in his unpublished *Kafka Commentaries* from the early 1930s, in which he seeks to decipher Kafka's work with the help of Kabbalistic figures of thought. This approach to interpretation arises from the fact that Kafka, himself desperately searching for (his) Jewish identity, immersed himself in the world of mysticism conveyed by Eastern Judaism. It is perhaps worth mentioning that Kafka moved to Berlin for a short time to learn Hebrew; Berlin had become the centre of the modern Hebrew Renaissance during the Weimar Republic.

Neumann had already taken private Hebrew lessons at grammar school. In Israel, he wrote two large manuscripts, both dedicated to a "depth psychology of the Jewish person," in which Hasidic mysticism plays an essential role.

Thus, once again: Jewish-German dialogue, at first by letter, and now offered by Neumann to Jung, his first and most important addressee, with whom he corresponded for many years.

Neumann wrote his decisive letter about his "Jewish" manuscripts on 5 December 1938, shortly after the *Reichspogromnacht.* It makes shocking reading. He asks Jung to represent a "piece of Europe" for him in the face of the "terrible torture" depicted in the reports that were pouring in "on a daily or hourly basis." Neumann is reluctant to "simply pass a judgment" on the "German event" because he owes "a great debt of gratitude" to the German people. He places his hopes in "the inner source energies of Judaism"—without knowing whether he will survive the upheaval (JNC, p. 140). To combat this agony, to oppose it somewhat, he discusses the work mentioned earlier in further detail.

Jung replied two weeks later, on 19 December 1938. In view of the terrible political situation, he writes that everyone is "shocked to their core as it were by what is happening in Germany" and adds that he has a lot to do with Jewish refugees (JNC, p. 145). Regarding the manuscripts, he advises Neumann to move away from a specifically Jewish accentuation of his experiences. And now follow momentous words:

It is a question of a general and identical revolutions of minds … The whole problem is itself of paramount importance for humanity that is why individual and racial difference only play a small part.

(JNC, p. 145)

It is perhaps worth recalling that four years earlier Jung, in his aforementioned article "Zur gegenwärtigen Lage der Psychotherapie" ("The State of Psychotherapy Today"), had said that the "'Aryan' unconscious has a higher potential than the Jewish" (CW 10, §354).

Now, after the catastrophe, after the historical events had borne out Neumann's diagnosis in the saddest possible way, can the "identical revolution of minds" suddenly proclaimed by Jung be understood differently than as reality being disguised in the form of a spiritually and historically exaggerated defence against guilt as far as the perpetrators and the victims are concerned?

A year of silence ensued.

Neumann wrote again to Jung in November 1939. He highlights rootlessness as a central Jewish problem. His letter seems as if Neumann had lost his footing. While he had engaged with Jung under the premise of working on his personal and at the same time collective problem, he now stands, in view of the complete relativisation of Jung's own therapeutic approach, "without preconceptions before something that is incomprehensible to me" (JNC, p. 149).

Deep down, the rootlessness about which Neumann speaks seems to point not only to the impossibility of grasping the unleashed violence in Germany, but also to Jung's lack of ideological differentiation and support in the face of that violence.

The experience of being thrown back upon himself, existentially, and the effect of Jung's words make Neumann doubt whether continuing to attach importance to considering the history of Judaism makes sense.

Jung could not respond to Neumann's offer of dialogue. Neumann discontinued the project he had been pursuing since arriving in Israel.

His offer, however, remains valid: The manuscripts are still unpublished, and a worthwhile step would be to create a broad basis of interest for their publication.[15]

A culture of remembrance only makes sense if it is alive and lived. Aside from some works still awaiting publication, this would mean setting Erich Neumann's work in relation to his biographical fault lines. It also means beginning to understand how Neumann's theories emerged and evolved in light of a severed, interrupted and hopefully non-futile German-Jewish dialogue, which we are still obliged to engage in.

Notes

1 Theodor W. Adorno, "Was bedeutet Aufarbeitung der Vergangenheit?" In *Eingriffe, Neun kritische Modelle* (Frankfurt/Main, 1963), p. 126.
2 Gershom Scholem, *From Berlin to Jerusalem* (Philadelphia, PA: Paul Dry Books, 2012), p. 54.

3 Amos Elon, *Zu einer anderen Zeit* (Munich, 2005), p. 284.

4 Ibid., p. 285.

5 Erich Neumann, in Micha Neumann, "Die Beziehung zwischen C.G. Jung und Erich Neumann auf Grund ihrer Korrespondenz," in *Zur Utopie einer neuen Ethik* (Kongressband ÖGAP Vienna: Mandelbaum Verlag, 2005).

6 Erich Neumann, Leserbrief *Jüdische Rundschau*, 1934, p. 5

7 Ibid.

8 Amos Elon, *Zu einer anderen Zeit*, p. 285.

9 Jost Hermand, *Judentum und deutsche Kultur, Beispiele einer schmerzhaften Symbiose* (Cologne, Weimar, Vienna: Böhlau, 1996), p. 147.

10 Michael Brenner, *The Renaissance of Jewish Culture in Weimar Germany* (New Haven and London: Yale University Press, 1996).

11 Christhard Hoffmann, "Das Judentum als Antithese: Zur Tradition eines kulturellen Wertungsmusters," in Wolfgang Benz (ed.), *Antisemitismus in Deutschland* (Munich, 1995), pp. 25ff.

12 Gershom Scholem, "Wider den Mythos vom deutsch-jüdischen Gespräch," in *Bulletin des Leo Baeck Instituts 27*, 1964 (originally a letter written by Scholem dated 18 December 1962), p. 278f.

13 H. Dieckmann, C.A. Maier and H.J. Wilke (eds.), *Kreativität des Unbewussten. Zum 75. Geburtstag von Erich Neumann* (Basel, 1980), p. 187.

14 George L. Mosse, *Jüdische Intellektuelle in Deutschland, Zwischen Religion und Nationalismus* (Frankfurt/Main, 1992), p. 19.

15 Translator's note: As mentioned elsewhere in this volume, the manuscripts referred to here were published in 2019 as *The Roots of Jewish Consciousness*, edited by Ann Lammers and translated by Mark Kyburz and Ann Lammers.

Appendix 3: Documents

Document 1
Birth certificate

Document 2
Certificate of entrance into the Zionist Association

Berliner Zionistische Vereinigung

Fernsprecher: Zentrum 3614—3615

Postscheck-Konto: Berlin Nr. 12006
Kassenverwaltung der B. Z. V.

Bank-Konto:
Direktion der Disconto-Gesellschaft
Dep.-Kasse Leipziger Strasse Nr. 66

Betrifft:
(In der Antwort anzugeben)

BERLIN C.19, den   2. März 1924.
Seydelstrasse 3 III.

Herrn

E r i c h   N e u m a n n

B e r l i n

Lietzenburgerstr.

Wir freuen uns, dass Sie   durch Herrn Loewensohn
Ihren Beitritt zu der "Berliner Zionistischen Vereinigung" erklärt haben und überreichen Ihnen in der Anlage eine Beitrittserklärungskarte
mit der Bitte, uns dieselbe ausgefüllt bald zurücksenden zu wollen.

Es wird Ihnen klar sein, dass mit einer rein organisatorischen An
gliederung weder Ihnen noch der Sache hinreichend gedient ist. Sie wer
den sicher den Wunsch haben, in enge persönliche Fühlung mit Ihren Par
teigenossen zu treten und Gelegenheit zur Arbeit zu finden. Sollten Si
irgend welche Auskunft zu erhalten wünschen, so steht Ihnen der Unter-
zeichnete in unserem Büro täglich von 10-5 Uhr zur persönlichen Rück-
sprache zur Verfügung.
Besonders möchten wir Sie schon heute auf die Wichtigkeit der Mit
arbeit in den Bezirksgruppen aufmerksam machen, die den wirklichen Mit
telpunkt des zionistischen Lebens und der Arbeit bilden müssen und die
diesen Zweck andererseits nur dann erfüllen können, wenn immer neue vo
frischer Begeisterung getragene Kräfte ihnen zuströmen. Sie gehören de
Gruppe   West.   an, deren Vorsitzende

Herr   Dr.-Alfred Apfel, Friedrichstr. 59/60.   is

Die Veranstaltungen der Gruppe werden durch unser Ihnen 14 tägig koste
los zugehendes Nachrichtenblatt "Die B.Z.V.", den Versammlungskalender
der "Jüdischen Rundschau" oder durch persönliche Einladungen bekannt g
macht.
Die "Jüdische Rundschau" unser zweimal wöchentlich erscheinendes
Parteiorgan, ermöglicht Ihnen eine rasche und genaue Orientierung in a
len Fragen des jüdischen Lebens. Zwecks Zustellung derselben wollen Si
sich direkt an den Verlag der Jüdischen Rundschau, W.15, Sächsischestr
wenden.
Den Beitrag für das 1 Quartal wollen Sie uns frdl. unter Benutzu
beiliegender Zahlkarte einsenden.
Wir würden uns freuen, Sie recht oft bei den Versammlungen Ihrer
Gruppe begrüssen zu können und verbleiben

mit Zionsgruss

Jede Adressenveränderung bitten
wir schnellstens aufzugeben.

hochachtungsvoll

Lichtenstein

1 Beitrittskarte
1 Zahlkarte   Wir bitten Sie, beiliegenden Fragebogen
                ausgefüllt zurückzusenden.

Document 3
Curriculum vitae (included in doctoral dissertation)

Lebenslauf!

Am 25. Januar 1905 wurde ich als Sohn des Kaufmanns Eduard Neumann und seiner Ehefrau Selma geb. Brodnitz in Berlin-Charlottenburg geboren. Ich bin Jude und habe die preußische Staatsangehörigkeit. Von der untersten Klasse an besuchte ich das humanistische Mommsen-Gymnasium in Charlottenburg, das ich Ostern 1923 mit dem Zeugnis der Reife verließ. Meine ersten 6 Semester studierte ich in Berlin und zwar Philosophie, Psychologie, Pädagogik, Literatur- und Kunstgeschichte sowie Semitistik. Im Jahre 1926 ging ich an die Universität Erlangen, wo ich im Sommersemester 1926 und im Wintersemester 1926/27 die Vorlesungen und Seminare von Herrn Geheimrat Professor Hensel, Professor Leser und Professor Hell besuchte, bei denen ich auch am 2. März 1927 in Philosophie als Hauptfach, Pädagogik und Arabisch als Nebenfach, die mündliche Doktorprüfung ablegte.

Es sei mir gestattet, an dieser Stelle Herrn Geheimrat Professor Dr. Hensel für die vielfachen Anregungen zu danken, die ich durch seine Vorlesungen und Seminare, sowie durch seinen persönlichen Verkehr empfangen durfte.

Referent: Geheimrat Prof. Dr. Hensel.

Dekan: Prof. Dr. v. Negelein.

485613

1929: Gvd.

Document 4
Letter: Martin Buber to Erich Neumann, 13 November 1935

Heppenheim a.d.B., 13. Novb. 1935

Herrn

Dr. E. Neumann

Tel Aviv

Sehr geehrter Herr Doktor!

Dass ich Ihnen bisher nicht geschrieben habe, liegt daran,
dass ich durch Arbeiten und Reisen übermässig beansprucht war.
Ihr Manuskript habe ich seinerzeit erhalten, konnte es aber, da es
einer flüchtigen Lektüre widerstrebt, erst jetzt lesen.

Ihre Art, Kafka zu behandeln, hat mich sehr interessiert. Sie
werden mit Ihrer klaren und exakten Methodik manchen Bezügen und
Zusammenhängen in einer bemerkenswerten Weise gerecht. Am glück-
lichsten erscheint mir die Kommentierung solcher Stücke, die wie
etwa "Die Brücke" einen eindeutig symbolischen Charakter haben.

Nicht ebenso uneingeschränkt kann ich Ihnen überall da
zustimmen, wo – wie sehr häufig bei Kafka – die Dichtungen durch
ihren Stil die geradlinige Deutung ablehnen und eine mehr fliessen-
de, mehr musikalische fordern. Auch scheint es mir, dass mitunter
ein theologischer Begriff, den Sie aus einer mir wohl verständlichen
Scheu meiden, das Gemeinte, so weit es überhaupt begrifflich zu
erreichen ist, eher treffen würde als der von Ihnen verwendete
metaphysische. So müsste z.B. meines Erachtens bei der Kommentierung von "Das Ehepaar" angedeutet werden, dass die Gestalt des
kranken Sohnes von einer christologischen Atmosphäre umspielt ist.
Es liegt hier freilich eine besonders schwierige Aufgabe vor, da

– 2 –

sich in diesen Punkten am eindringlichsten zeigt, wie Kafka als
ein bewusster oder unbewusster Gegner seines Kommentators arbeitet
und ihm alle möglichen Schwierigkeiten bereitet, – worin sich aber
eben nicht Willkür, sondern Grundwesen äussert.

Vorerst nur dies. Ich bin aber gerne bereit, mich mit
Ihnen weiter über Ihre wertvolle Arbeit zu unterhalten.

In vorzüglicher Hochachtung

Buber

Document 5
Letter: Thomas Mann to Erich Neumann, 31 May 1952

Document 6
Letter: Henry Moore to Erich Neumann, 22 December 1954

2nd December, 1954.

Dear Dr. Neumann,

I was very pleased to get your letter which reached me the other day.

Mr. Gregory told me that he had seen you when you were in England and I am very glad that he is planning for an extra publication of your essay on me. He tells me that when he receives from you the list of the necessary pictures for the publication he will pass the list on to me and I will then-send you the pictures.

I am looking forward to reading your essay when it has been translated and I shall also look forward very much to our meeting, whenever that is.

Very sincerely yours,

with best wishes

Henry Moore

Document 7
Letter: Henry Moore to Erich Neumann, 2 June 1959

HOGLANDS,
PERRY GREEN,
MUCH HADHAM,
HERTS.

2nd June 1959.

Dear Mr. McGuire,

I expect it was through you that
I received a complimentary copy of
THE ARCHETYPAL WORLD OF HENRY MOORE,
Bollingen Series LXV3, by Eric Neumann.

I am very happy indeed with the
book and would like to order four extra
copies to distribute to my friends.

Could you please send them by
air-mail, as i would like to receive
them as soon as possible.

Also, could you please send the
bill, including the air-mail postage
charge, to my dealers, M.Knoedler & Co.
Inc., 14 East 57th Street, New York 22,
New York.

With many thanks.

Yours sincerely,

Henry Moore

P.S.

If there is any occasion for you
to be in touch with Mr.Neumann, will
you please tell him how delighted I am
with his book.

References

Works about Erich Neumann

Abramovitch, Henry. "Erich Neumann, Theorist and Analyst: A Brief Introduction." *Harvest* 52(2), 2006, pp. 19–25.

Abramovitch, Henry. "Erich Neumann and the Search for a New Ethic." *Harvest* 52(2), 2006, pp. 130–147.

Abramovitch, Henry and Marian Badrian. "Neve Ze'elim. Children's Home: A Unique Long-term Treatment Centre Inspired by the Teachings of Erich Neumann." *Harvest* 52(2), 2006, pp. 182–199.

Adler, Gerhard. "Erich Neumann: 1905–1960." *Anal. Psychol.* 11(3), 1980, pp. 181–186; reprinted in: H. Dieckmann, C. A. Meier and H. J. Wilke (eds.). *Kreativität des Unbewussten. Zum 75. Geburtstag von Erich Neumann (1905–1960).* Basel: S. Karger Verlag, 1980.

Arendt, Hannah. *Denktagebuch.1950–1973.* Vol. 1. Munich: Piper, 2002.

Bar Kochba (Verein jüdischer Hochschüler, Prague). *Vom Judentum. Ein Sammelbuch.* Leipzig: Kurt Wolff Verlag, 1913.

Baumann, Avi. "Erde, Mystik, Friede von Erich Neumann." In: Margarethe von Maldegern (ed.). *Zur Utopie einer neuen Ethik. Kongressband zur Drei-Länder-Tagung der deutschsprachigen Gesellschaften für Analytischen Psychologie zum Thema 100 Jahre Erich Neumann, 130 Jahre C.G. Jung.* Vienna: Mandelbaum Verlag, 2005. English version: "Erich Neumann on Freud, Earth, Mysticism and Peace." Harvest 52(2), 2006.

Burda, Gerhard. "Ethik im Schatten des Vaters." In: Margarethe von Maldegern (ed.). *Zur Utopie einer neuen Ethik. Kongressband zur Drei-Länder-Tagung der deutschsprachigen Gesellschaften für Analytischen Psychologie zum Thema 100 Jahre Erich Neumann, 130 Jahre C.G. Jung.* Vienna: Mandelbaum Verlag, 2005.

Dieckmann, Hannes. "Zu Erich Neumanns Arbeit über 'Das Gericht' von Franz Kafka." *Anal. Psychol.* 7(4), 1974, pp. 249–251.

Dreifuss, Gustav. "Erich Neumanns jüdisches Bewusstsein." *Anal. Psychol.* 11(3), 1980, pp. 239–247; reprinted in: H. Dieckmann, C. A. Meier and H. J. Wilke (eds.). *Kreativität des Unbewussten. Zum 75. Geburtstag von Erich Neumann (1905–1960).* Basel: S. Karger Verlag, 1980.

Frankenstein, Carl. "Echtheit und Falschheit." *Anal. Psychol.* 11(3), 1980, pp. 297–311; reprinted in: H. Dieckmann, C. A. Meier and H. J. Wilke (eds.). *Kreativität des Unbewussten. Zum 75. Geburtstag von Erich Neumann (1905–1960).* Basel: S. Karger Verlag, 1980.

Frankenstein, Carl. "Gedenkrede nach dem Tode Erich Neumanns 1960." *Anal. Psychol.* 11(3), 1980, pp. 297–311; reprinted in: H. Dieckmann, C. A. Meier and H. J. Wilke (eds.). *Kreativität des Unbewussten. Zum 75. Geburtstag von Erich Neumann (1905–1960).* Basel: S. Karger Verlag, 1980.

Giegerich, Wolfgang. "Ontogeny=Phylogeny? A Fundamental Critique of Erich Neumann's Analytical Psychology." In: *Spring, An Annual of Archetypal Psychology and Jungian Thought.* New York: Spring Publications, 1975.

Jacoby, Mario. "Urbeziehung und Kulturkanon." *Anal. Psychol.* 11(3), 1980, pp. 282–296; reprinted in: H. Dieckmann, C. A. Meier and H. J. Wilke (eds.). *Kreativität des Unbewussten. Zum 75. Geburtstag von Erich Neumann (1905–1960).* Basel: S. Karger Verlag, 1980.

Jacoby, Mario. "Erich Neumanns Konzept der Urbeziehung im Lichte der neueren Kleinkindforschung." In: *Zur Utopie einer neuen Ethik. Kongressband zur Drei-Länder-Tagung der* deutschsprachigen Gesellschaften für Analytischen Psychologie *zum Thema 100 Jahre Erich Neumann, 130 Jahre C.G. Jung.* Vienna: Mandelbaum Verlag, 2005. English version: "Neumann's Concept of the Primary Relationship in the Light of Contemporary Infant Research." Harvest 52(2), 2006.

Jaffé, Aniela. "Die Einheitswirklichkeit und das Schöpferische." *Anal. Psychol.* 11(3), 1980, pp. 312–320; reprinted in: H. Dieckmann, C. A. Meier and H. J. Wilke (eds.). *Kreativität des Unbewussten. Zum 75. Geburtstag von Erich Neumann (1905–1960).* Basel: S. Karger Verlag, 1980.

Kalsched, Donald. *The Inner World of Trauma. Archtypal Defenses of the Personal Spirit.* London und New York: Routledge, 1996.

Kalsched, Donald. "Trauma, Unschuld und der Kernkomplex der Dissoziation." *Analytische Psychologie,* (47)188, 2/2017, pp. 226–272.

Kerenyi, Karl. *Der große Daimon des Symposion.* Amsterdam, Leipzig: Pantheon, Albae Vigiliae Heft XIII, 1942.

Kutzinski, Dvora "Neumann As My Supervisor: An Interview with Dvora Kutzinski (Henry Abramovitch)." *Harvest* 52(2), 2006, pp. 162–181.

Lesmeister, Roman. "Über-Ich, Stimme des Selbst und depressive Position." *Anal. Psychol.* 26, 1995, pp. 1–18.

Lesmeister, Roman. "Grundlagen von Moral und Ethik in der Analytischen Psychologie." *Anal. Psychol.* 39(1), 2008, pp. 52–69.

Lesmeister, Roman. "Jenseits des Gesetzes: Sublimierung, Todestrieb und Exzess." In: Angelica Löwe, Roman Lesmeister and Daniel Krochmalnik (eds.). *Gewalt, Sublimierung, Glaube.* Freiburg: Alber, 2017.

Liebscher, Martin (ed.). *C.G. Jung und Erich Neumann: Die Briefe 1933–1959. Analytische Psychologie im Exil.* Ostfildern: Patmos, 2015.

Liebscher, Martin (ed.). *Analytical Psychology in Exile: The Correspondence of C. G. Jung and Erich Neumann.* Edited by Martin Liebscher. Translated by Heather McCartney. Princeton, NJ: Princeton University Press, 2015.

Löwe, Angelica. "Deutsch-jüdischer Dialog: Neumann, Jung und die Jungianer." *Anal. Psychol.* 39(1), 2008, pp. 17–27.

Löwe, Angelica. "Wir waren ein zufriedene und glückliche Familie. Interview mit Ruth Goldstone. *Anal. Psychol.* 39(1), 2008.

Löwe, Angelica. "Aktualisierter Messianismus: Zur theologischen Konzeptualisierung von Krisenerfahrung, Identität und Wandlung bei Erich Neumann." *Anal. Psychol.* 40(2), 2009, pp. 178–202.

Löwe, Angelica. "Erich Neumanns *Tiefenpsychologie und Neue Ethik* im Kontext jüdischer Nietzscherezeption." In: Roman Lesmeister and Elke Metzner (eds.). *Nietzsche und die Tiefenpsychologie*. Freiburg/Munich: Karl Alber Verlag, 2010.

Löwe, Angelica. "'… erfasste mich mit einmal seine Unschuld …' Annäherungen an eine Imagination Erich Neumanns." *Anal. Psychol.* 42(1), 2011, pp. 59–72.

Löwe, Angelica. "' … eine allgemeine und identische Revolution der Geister … Der Briefwechsel zwischen Erich Neumann und C. G. Jung anlässlich der Novemberpogrome 1938." *Psycho-logik 7, Erinnern und Vergessen*, Jahrbuch für Psychotherapie, Philosophie und Kultur. Freiburg/Munich: Karl Alber Verlag, 2012.

Meier-Seethaler, C. "Das Kind. Erich Neumanns Beitrag zur Psychopathologie der Entwicklung." *Anal. Psychol.* 11(3), 1980, pp. 250–273; reprinted in: H. Dieckmann, C. A. Meier and H. J. Wilke (eds.). *Kreativität des Unbewussten. Zum 75. Geburtstag von Erich Neumann (1905–1960)*. Basel: S. Karger Verlag, 1980.

Mendelsohn, J. "Das Phänomen der Stimme im Werk Erich Neumanns und in jüdische Legende und Mystik." *Anal. Psychol.* 11(3), 1980, pp. 199–221; reprinted in: H. Dieckmann, C. A. Meier and H. J. Wilke (eds.). *Kreativität des Unbewussten. Zum 75. Geburtstag von Erich Neumann (1905–1960)*. Basel: S. Karger Verlag, 1980.

Neumann, Micha. "Die Beziehung zwischen Erich Neumann und C.G. Jung und die Frage des Antisemitismus." *Anal. Psychol.* 23(1), 1992, pp. 3–23.

Neumann, Micha. "On the Relationship between Erich Neumann and C.G. Jung." In: Aryeh Maidenbaum (eds.). *Jung and the Shadow of Anti-Semitism*. Berwick: Nicolas Hays, Inc., 2002.

Neumann, Micha. "Die Beziehung zwischen C.G. Jung und Erich Neumann auf Grund ihrer Korrespondenz." In: Margarete von Maldegern (ed.). *Zur Utopie einer neuen Ethik*. Kongressband ÖGAP Vienna: Mandelbaum Verlag, 2005. English Version: "The Relationship Between C.G. Jung and Erich Neumann According to Their Correspondence." Harvest 52(2), 2006.

Neumann, Micha. "Erinnerung an Erich und Julie Neumann." *Anal. Psychol.* 39(1), 2008, pp. 35–39.

Neumann-Loewenthal, Rachel. "My Father, Dr. Erich Neumann." *Harvest* 52(2), 2006.

Patai, Raphael. *The Hebrew Goddess*, 3rd enlarged edition. Detroit, MI: Wayne State University Press, 1990 (first published 1968).

Reitzenstein, Richard. *Das Märchen von Amor und Psyche bei Apuleius*. Leipzig: Teubner, 1912.

Riedel, Ingrid. "Geschwistersymbolik und Geschwisterinzest. Erich Neumanns Trakl-Interpretation." In: Margarete von Maldegern (ed.). *Zur Utopie einer neuen Ethik. Kongressband zur Drei-Länder-Tagung der deutschsprachigen Gesellschaften für Analytischen Psychologie zum Thema 100 Jahre Erich Neumann, 130 Jahre C.G. Jung*. Vienna: Mandelbaum Verlag, 2005.

Scholem, Gershom. "Erich Neumann, Nachruf November 1960." In: *Mitteilungsblatt. Wochenzeitung des Irgun Olej Merkas Europa* 28, 47 (18 November 1960), p. 4; also published in: Das neue Israel 13 (1960/1), p. 313.

Shalit, Erel and Murray Stein (eds.). *Turbulent Times, Creative Minds: Erich Neumann and C.G. Jung in Relationship (1933–1960)*. Asheville: Chiron, 2016.

Shalit, Erel (ed.). *Jacob and Esau: On the Collective Symbolism of the Brother Motif*. Translated by Mark Kyburz. Asheville: Chiron, 2016.

Vitolo, Antonio. *Un esilio impossibile. Neumann tra Freud e Jung*. Rome: Edizioni Borla, 1990.

Von Raffay, Anita. "Gedanken zum Gewissenskonzept bei C.G. Jung und Erich Neumann." In: Margarete von Maldegern (ed.). *Zur Utopie einer neuen Ethik. Kongressband zur Drei-Länder-Tagung der deutschsprachigen Gesellschaften für Analytischen Psychologie zum Thema 100 Jahre Erich Neumann, 130 Jahre C.G. Jung.* Vienna: Mandelbaum Verlag, 2005.

Walch, Gerhard M. *Wandlungen des Bewusstseins: Erich Neumanns Tiefenpsychologie der Kultur.* Stuttgart: Opus Magnum Verlag, 2010.

Weiler, Gerda. *Der enteignete Mythos. Eine feministische Revision der Archetypenlehre C. G. Jungs und Erich Neumanns.* Frankfurt/Main, New York: Campus Verlag, 1991.

Zielen, Viktor. "Gedanken zur Ich-Psychologie von Erich Neumann." *Anal. Psychol.* 11(3), 1980, pp. 274–281; reprinted in: H. Dieckmann, C. A. Meier and H. J. Wilke (eds.). *Kreativität des Unbewussten. Zum 75. Geburtstag von Erich Neumann (1905–1960).* Basel: S. Karger Verlag, 1980.

Other references

Abraham, Karl. *Versuch einer Entwicklungsgeschichte der Libido auf Grund der Psychoanalyse seelischer Störungen.* Leipzig, Vienna, Zürich: Internationaler Psychoanalytischer Verlag, 1924.

Adler, Gerhard. "Junge Generation über sich selbst." In: *Die Literarische Welt, Unabhängiges Organ für Deutsches Schrifttum*, 19 February 1932.

Adler-Rudel, Salomon. *Ostjuden in Deutschland.* Tübingen: Mohr-Verlag, 1959.

Adorno, Theodor W. *Minima Moralia.* Frankfurt/Main: Suhrkamp Verlag, 1951. English edition: *Minima Moralia: Reflections from Damaged Life.* London/New York: Verso, 1974.

Adorno, Theodor W. "Was bedeutet Aufarbeitung der Vergangenheit?" In: *Eingriffe, Neun kritische Modelle.* Frankfurt/Main: Suhrkamp Verlag, 1963.

Agamben, Giorgio. *The Time That Remains: A Commentary on the Letter to the Romans.* Translated by Patricia Dailey. Stanford: Stanford University Press, 2005.

Albertz, Anuschka. *Exemplarisches Heldentum. Die Rezeptionsgeschichte der Schlacht an den Thermopylen von der Antike bis zur Gegenwart.* Munich: Oldenbourg Verlag, 2006.

Arendt, Hannah. *Die verborgene Tradition. Acht Essays (1932–1948).* Frankfurt/Main: Suhrkamp Verlag, 1976.

Arendt, Hannah. *Thinking without a Banister: Essays in Understanding 1953–1975*, ed. Jerome Kohn. New York: Schocken Books, 2018.

Aschheim, Steven, *Brothers and Strangers, The East European Jew in German and German Jewish Consciousness, 1800–1923.* Madison, WI: The University of Wisconsin Press, 1982.

Aschheim, Steven. *The Nietzsche Legacy in Germany, 1890–1990.* Berkeley, CA: University of California Press, 1992.

Aschheim, Steven. "German Jews beyond Bildung and Liberalism: The Radical Jewish Revival in the Weimar Republic." In: K.L. Berghahn (ed.). *The German-Jewish Dialogue Reconsidered, A Symposium In Honor Of George L. Mosse*, N.Y., Washington, D.C./ Baltimore, Bern, Frankfurt am Main, Berlin, Vienna, Paris: Peter Lang Verlag, 1996.

Aschheim, Steven. *Nietzsche und die Deutschen, Karriere eines Kults.* Stuttgart, Weimar: Verlag Metzler, 2000.

Bachofen, Johann Jakob. *Das Mutterrecht: eine Untersuchung über die Gynaikokratie der alten Welt nach ihrer religiösen und rechtlichen Natur.* Stuttgart: Verlag von Krais und Hoffmann, 1861.

Bachofen, Johann, Jakob. *Versuch über die Gräbersymbolik der Alten.* Basel 1859. Reprinted: Munich: Beck, 1923.

Badiou, Alain. *Paulus: Die Begründung des Universalismus.* Zürich: Diaphanes 2009.

Baioni, Giuliano. *Kafka, Literatur und Judentum.* Stuttgart-Weimar: Metzler Verlag, 1994.

Bair, Deirdre. *Jung: A Biography.* New York: Back Bay Books, 2004.

Balke, Ralf. *Tel Aviv, das Open Air Museum des Bauhauses.* Website der Deutsch-Israelischen Gesellschaft E.V., 2003.

Bargur, Ayelet. *Ahawah heißt Liebe. Die Geschichte des jüdischen Kinderheims in der Berliner Auguststrasse.* Munich: dtv, 2004.

Barone, Elisabetta (ed.). *Pioniere, Poeten, Professoren: Eranos und Monte Verità in der Zivilisationsgeschichte des 20. Jahrhunderts.* Würzburg: Königshausen und Neumann, 2004.

Baynes, Helton Godwin. *Mythology of the Soul, Mythology of the Soul; a research into the unconscious from schizophrenic dreams and drawings,* London: Baillière, Tindall and Cox, 1940.

Beck-Gernsheim, Elisabeth. *Juden, Deutsche und andere Erinnerungslandschaften,* Frankfurt/Main: Suhrkamp Verlag, 1999.

Benjamin, Walter. "Robert Walser" (1929). In: Rolf Tiedemann and Hermann Schweppenhäuser (eds.). *Gesammelte Schriften I/II,* Frankfurt am Main: Suhrkamp, 1980.

Benjamin, Walter. *The Correspondence of Walter Benjamin and Gershom Scholem.* Edited by Gershom Scholem. Translated by Gary Smith and Andre Lefevere. Cambridge, MA: Harvard University Press, 1992.

Berdyczewski, Micha Josef. *Die Sagen der Juden.* Gesammelt und bearbeitet von Micha Josef Bion Gorion, 5 vols. Frankfurt/Main, Rütten & Loening, 1913–1927.

Berg, Nicolas. *Luftmenschen, Zur Geschichte einer Metapher.* Göttingen: Vandenhoeck und Ruprecht, 2008.

Berghahn, Klaus L. (ed.). *The German-Jewish Dialogue reconsidered: A Symposium in Honor of George L. Mosse.* New York, Vienna: Peter Lang Verlag, 1996.

Bernet, Rudolf. "Das traumatisierte Subjekt." In: M. Fischer, H.-D. Gondek and B. Liebsch (eds.). *Vernunft im Zeichen des Fremden: Zur Philosophie von Bernhard Waldenfels.* Frankfurt/Main: Suhrkamp Taschenbuch Verlag, 2001.

Bernstein, Richard J. *Freud und das Vermächtnis des Moses.* Berlin/Vienna: Philo Verlagsgesellschaft, 2003.

Betten, Anne and Miryam Du nour. *Wir sind die Letzten. Fragt uns aus. Gespräche mit den emigranten der dreißiger Jahre in Israel.* Gießen: Haland und Wirth im Psychosozial Verlag, 2004.

Biale, David. *Gershom Scholem, Kabbalah and Counter-History.* Cambridge, MA: Harvard University Press, 1979.

Biale, David (ed.). *Cultures of the Jews: a New History.* New York: Schocken, 2002.

Bohnet, H. and K. Stadler. *Hannah Arendt, Denken ohne Geländer, Texte und Briefe.* Munich: Piper Verlag, 2010.

Bloch, Ernst. *Durch die Wüste: frühe kritische Aufsätze.* Frankfurt/ Main: Suhrkamp Verlag, 1964.

Bloch, Ernst. *The Spirit of Utopia*. Translated by Anthony A. Nassar. Stanford: Stanford University Press, 2000.

Blumenfeld, Kurt. *Erlebte Judenfrage- ein Vierteljahrhundert deutscher Zionismus*. Stuttgart: Deutsche Verlagsanstalt, 1962.

Bracher, Karl Dietrich. *Zeit der Ideologien: eine Geschichte politischen Denkens im 20. Jahrhundert*. Stuttgart: Deutsche Verlagsanstalt, 1982.

Brenner, Michael. *Nach dem Holocaust: Juden in Deutschland 1945–1950*. Munich: Beck'sche Reihe, 1995.

Brenner, Michael. *The Renaissance of Jewish Culture in Weimar Germany*. New Haven, CT and London: Yale University Press, 1996.

Brenner, Michael. *Geschichte des Zionismus*, Munich: H.C. Beck Verlag, 2005.

Brenner, Michael and Yfaat Weis (eds.). *Zionistische Utopie-israelische Realität. Religion und Nation in Israel*. Munich: Beck'sche Reihe, 1999.

Brody, Daniel. "Das Eranos-Jahrbuch." In: Walter Curti (ed.). *Du, Schweizerische Monatszeitschrift*, Zürich, April 1955, 15. Jahrgang.

Brokoff, Jürgen. *Die Apokalypse in der Weimarer Republik*. Munich: Fink, 2001.

Brumlik, Micha. *Kritik des Zionismus*. Hamburg: europäische Verlagsanstalt, 2007.

Buber, Martin. "Ein Wort über Nietzsche und die Lebenswerte." In: *Die Kunst im Leben* I,2, Berlin: Schenk, Dezember 1900.

Buber, Martin. *Dissertation über den Begriff der Individuation bei N. Cusanus und Jakob Böhme*. Vienna: Unpublished PhD diss., University of Vienna, 1904.

Buber, Martin. *Die Geschichten des Rabbi Nachman / ihm nacherzählt von Martin Buber*. Frankfurt/Main: Rütte und Loening, 1906.

Buber, Martin. *Die Legende des Baal-Schem*. Frankfurt /Main: Rütte und Loening, 1908.

Buber, Martin. "Das Land der Juden" (1910). In: *Die jüdische Bewegung*, Vol. I., Gesammelte Aufsätze und Ansprachen 1900–1915. Berlin: Jüdischer Verlag, 1916.

Buber, Martin. *Vom Geist des Judentums*. Leipzig: Wolff Verlag, 1916.

Buber, Martin. *Die jüdische Bewegung. Gesammelte Aufsätze und Ansprachen (1900–1914) Erste Folge*. Berlin: Jüdischer Verlag, 1920.

Buber, Martin. "Jüdische Renaissance" (first published in Ost-West), reprinted in Buber: *Die jüdische Bewegung. Gesammelte Aufsätze und Ansprachen (1900 – 1914) Erste Folge*. Berlin: Jüdischer Verlag, 1920.

Buber, Martin. *Tales of the Hasidim*. Foreword by Chaim Potok. Translated by Olga Marx. New York: Schocken Books, 1947/1991.

Buber, Martin. *Der Jude und sein Judentum; gesammelte Aufsätze und Reden*. Cologne: Melzer, 1963.

Buber, Martin. *On Judaism*, Edited by Nahum N. Glatzer. Translated by Eva Jospe. New York: Schocken Books, 1967/1995.

Burckhardt, Jacob. *Die Kultur der Renaissance in Italien*. Frankfurt/Main: Fischer Taschenbuch Verlag, 2009.

Butler, Judith. *Kritik der ethischen Gewalt, Adorno –Vorlesungen 2002*. Frankfurt/Main: Suhrkamp Taschenbuch Wissenschaft, 2003.

Campbell, Joseph. *The Hero with a Thousand Faces*. Bollingen Foundation. New York: Pantheon Books, 1949.

Campell, Joseph (ed.). *Spiritual Disciplines, Papers from the Eranos Yearbooks*. Bollingen Series XXX, Volume 4. Princeton, NJ: Princeton University Press, 1960.

Cassirer, Ernst. *Philosophie der symbolischen Formen*, 3 Vols. Hamburg: Meiner Verlag, 2010 (originally published 1923–29).

Celan, Paul. "Büchner-Preisrede." In: Ernst Johann (ed.). *Büchner-Preis-Reden 1951–1971*. Stuttgart: Reclam, 1972.

Celan, Paul *Collected Prose*. Translated by Rosemary Waldrop. New York: Routledge, 2006.

Cowan, Lyn (ed.). *Barcelona 04, Edges of Experience: Memory and Emergence, Proceedings of the Sixteenth International Congress for Analytical Psychology*. Einsiedeln: Daimon Verlag, 2006.

Dachs, Gisela (ed.). *Die Jeckes*. Frankfurt/Main: Jüdischer Verlag im Suhrkamp Verlag, 2005.

Davidowicz, Klaus Samuel. *Gershom Scholem und Martin Buber. Die Geschichte eines Mißverständnisses*. Neukirchen-Vluyn: Neukirchener Theologie, 1995.

Dever, Wiliam G. *Did God Have a Wife? Archaeology and Folk Religion in Ancient Israel*, Grand Rapids, MI: Eerdmans, 2005.

Diner, Dan and Dirk Blasius (ed.). *Zerbrochene Geschichte. Leben und Selbstverständnis der Juden in Deutschland*. Frankfurt/Main: Fischer Taschenbuch Verlag, 1991.

Ehmann, Annegret. *Juden in Berlin 1671–1945. Ein Lesebuch*. Berlin: Nicolaische Verlagsbuchhandlung, 1988.

Ehrenberg, Margaret. *Women in Prehistory*. London: British Museum Publications, 1989.

Elberfelder Bibel. Witten: SCM R. Brockhaus, 1985.

Elder, G.R. *The Body: An Encyclopedia of Archetypal Symbolism*. Boston, MA: Shambala, 1996.

Elon, Amos. *Zu einer anderen Zeit, Porträt der jüdisch-deutschen Epoche 1743–1933*. Munich: dtv, 2002.

Eloni, Yehuda. *Zionismus in Deutschland: von den Anfängen bis 1914*. Gerlingen: Bleicher, 1987.

Engels, David. "Entrückung, Epiphanie und Consecration." In: Dominik Gross and Jasmin Grande (eds.). *Objekt Leiche*. Frankfurt a.M., New York: Campus Verlag, 2010.

Erman, Adolf. *Die ägyptische Religion*. Berlin: Reimer Verlag, 1905.

Evers, Timann. *Mythos und Emanzipation. C.G. Jung: eine kritische Annäherung*. Hamburg: Junius Verlag, 1998.

Finkelde, Dominik. *Politische Eschatologie nach Paulus*. Vienna: Turia, 2007.

Fordham, Michael (ed.). *Contact with Jung: Essays on the Influence of his Work and Personality*. London: Tavistock Publications, 1963.

Franz, Marie-Luise von. *The Psychological Interpretation of the Golden Ass of Apuleius*, Zürich: Spring Publications, 1970; Aktualisierte deutsche Neuauflage unter dem Titel: *Die Erlösung des Weiblichen im Manne*. Der goldene Esel von Apuleius in tiefenpsychologischer Sicht, Frankfurt am Main: Insel 1980.

Franz, Marie-Luise von. *A Psychological Interpretation of the Golden Ass of Apuleius*. Zurich: Spring Publications, 1970.

Frazer, James George. *Der goldene Zweig. Das Geheimnis von Glauben und Sitten der Völker*. Leipzig: Hirschfeld Verlag, 1928.

Freud, Sigmund. *Eine Kindheitserinnerung des Leonardo da Vinci*, GW VIII, Frankfurt/Main: Fischer Verlag, 1945.

Freud, Sigmund. *Der Moses des Michelangelo*, GW X, Frankfurt/Main: Fischer Verlag, 1946.

Freud, Sigmund. *Der Mann Moses und die monotheistische Religion*, GW XVI, Frankfurt/Main: Fischer Verlag, 1950.

Freud, Sigmund. *Totem und Tabu*, GW IX. Frankfurt/Main: Fischer Verlag, 1954.

Freud, Sigmund. *Freud/Jung Letters*. Edited by William McGuire. Translated by Ralph Manheim and R.F.C. Hull. Bollingen Series XCIV. Princeton, NJ: Princeton University Press, 1974.

Friedländer, Saul. *Das Dritte Reich und die Juden*. Munich: dtv, 2006.

Friedländer, Saul and Orna Kenan. *Das Dritte Reich und die Juden 1933–1945 (abbreviated version)*. Munich: Verlag C.H. Beck, 2010.

Fröbe-Kapteyn, Olga. "Brief an Walter Robert Corti." In: Walter Curti (ed.). *Du, Schweizerische Monatsschrift*, Zürich, April 1955, 15. Jahrgang.

Frobenius, Leo. *Das Zeitalter des Sonnengottes*. Berlin: G. Reimer Verlag, 1904.

Gay, Peter. *Die Republik der Außenseiter: Geist und Kultur in der Weimarer Republik 1918–1933*. Frankfurt/Main: Fischer Verlag, 1970.

Gay, Peter. *Freud, Juden und andere Deutsche. Herren und Opfer in der modernen Kultur*. Munich: dtv, 1989.

Gelber, Mark H. *Melancholy Pride: Nation, Race and Gender in the German Literature of Cultural Zionism*. Tübingen: Niemeyer (Conditio Judaica), 2000.

Gerber, U. and R. Hoberg (ed.). *Sprache und Religion*. Darmstadt: Wissenschaftliche Buchgesellschaft, 2009.

Gerhardt, Volker. *Pathos und Distanz, Studien zur Philosophie Friedrich Nietzsches*. Stuttgart: Reclam Verlag, 1988.

Gerhardt, Volker (ed.). *F. Nietzsche, Also sprach Zarathustra*. Berlin: Akademie-Verlag, 2000.

Goldberg, Oskar. *Die Wirklichkeit der Hebräer*. Edited by Manfred Voigts. Wiesbaden: Harrasowitz, 2005.

Göttner-Abendroth, Heide. *Die Göttin und ihr Heros. Die matriarchalen Religionen in Mythen, Märchen, Dichtung*. Munich: Kohlhammer, 2011.

Grab, Walter and Julius H. Schoeps (eds.). *Juden in der Weimarer Republik*. Tel Aviv: Univ. Jahrbuch des Instituts für Deutsche Geschichte, 1986.

Greif, Gideon, McPherson, Colin and Laurence Weinbaum (eds.). *Die Jeckes. Deutsche Juden aus Israel erzählen*. Cologne, Weimar, Vienna: Böhlau, 2000.

Grözinger, Karl Erich. *Kafka und die Kabbala. Das Jüdische im Werk und Denken von Franz Kafka*. Frankfurt/Main, Eichborn Verlag, 1992.

Grubitz, Christoph. "Erwin Loewenson (Golo Gangi)." In: Andreas Kilcher (ed.). *Metzler-Lexikon der deutsch-jüdischen Literaturgeschichte. Jüdische Autorinnen und Autoren deutscher Sprache von der Aufklärung bis zur Gegenwart*. Stuttgart: Metzler, 2000.

Hackeschmidt, Jörg. *Von Kurt Blumenfeld zu Norbert Elias. Die Erfindung einer jüdischen Nation*. Hamburg: Europäische Verlagsanstalt, 1997.

Hakl, Hans Thomas. *Der verborgene Geist von Eranos, eine alternative Geistesgeschichte des 20. Jahrhunderts*. Bretten: Scientia Nova, Verlag Neue Wissenschaft, 2001.

Hermand, Jost. *Judentum und deutsche Kultur. Beispiele einer schmerzhaften Symbiose*. Cologne, Weimar, Vienna: Böhlau, 1996.

Hermand, Jost and Frank Trommler. *Die Kultur der Weimarer Republik*. Munich: Nymphenburger Verlagshandlung, 1978.

Herzig, Arno. *Jüdische Geschichte in Deutschland. Von den Anfängen bis zur Gegenwart*. Munich: Beck'sche Reihe, 2002.

Hetkamp, Jutta. *Die jüdische Jugendbewegung in Deutschland zwischen 1913–1933*. Münster: Lit., 1994.

Heuer, Renate (ed.). *Lexikon deutsch-jüdischer Autoren*. Munich: Walter de Gruyter, 1992–2012.

Heuer, W., B. Heiter and S. Rosenmüller (eds.). *Arendt Handbuch. Leben-Werk-Wirkung.* Stuttgart: Metzler Verlag, 2011.

Hillman, James. *The Myth of Analysis: Three Essays in Archetypal Psychology.* New York: Harper & Row, 1972.

Himmelmann, Barbara. "Zarathustras Weg." In: Volker Gerhardt (ed.). *Friedrich Nietzsche, Also sprach Zarathustra.* Berlin: Akademie-Verlag, 2000.

Hinshaw, R., P. Kugler, H. Kawai, D. Miller and G. Quispel. "Walking in the Footsteps of Eranos." In: Lyn Cowan (ed.). *Barcelona 04, Edges of Experience: Memory and Emergence, Proceedings of the Sixteenth International Congress for Analytical Psychology.* Einsiedeln: Daimon Verlag, 2006.

Hobsbawm, Eric. "Inventing Traditions." In: Eric Hobsbawm and Terence Ranger (ed.). *The Invention of Tradition.* Cambridge: Cambridge University Press, 1984.

Hoeller, Stephan A. *The Gnostic Jung and the Seven Sermons to the Dead.* Wheaton, IL: Quest Books, 1982.

Hoffmann, Christhard. "Das Judentum als Antithese. Zur Tradition eines kulturellen Wertungsmusters." In: Wolfgang Benz (ed.). *Antisemitismus in Deutschland.* Munich: dtv, 1995.

Hoffmann, Daniel (ed.). *Handbuch zur deutsch-jüdischen Literatur des 20. Jahrhunderts.* Paderborn, Munich, Vienna, Zurich: Schöningh, 2002.

Hofmannsthal Hugo von. "Das Schrifttum als geistiger Raum der Nation." In: Fritz K. Ringer (ed.). *Die Gelehrten. Der Niedergang der deutschen Mandarine 1890 –1933.* Stuttgart: Klett Cotta, 1983.

Horch, Otto (ed.). *Antisemitismus und europäische Kultur.* Tübingen: Francke, 1988.

Horkheimer, Max and Theodor W. Adorno. *Dialectic of Enlightenment.* Translated by Edmund Jephcott. Stanford: Stanford University Press, 2002.

Huizinga, Johan (1924). *Herbst des Mittelalters.* Stuttgart: Kröner, 2006 (12th ed.).

Idel, Moshe. *Alte Welten – Neue Bilder, Jüdische Mystik und die Gedankenwelt des 20. Jahrhunderts.* Frankfurt/Main: Jüdischer Verlag im Suhrkamp Verlag, 2012.

Idel, Moshe (ed.). *Mystical Union in Judaism, Christianity and Islam. An Ecumenical Dialogue.* New York: Continuum Publishers, 1996.

Jacobi, Jolande. "Eranos – vom Zuhörer aus gesehen." In: Walter Curti (ed.). *Du Schweizerische Monatszeitschrift,* Zürich, April 1955, 15. Jahrgang.

Jaffé, Aniela. *Jung and Eranos.* Zürich: Spring Publications, 1977.

Jaffé, Aniela. *Parapsychologie, Individuation, Nationalsozialismus. Themen bei C.G. Jung.* Zürich: Daimon, 1985.

Jung, C. G. *Memories, Dreams, Reflections.* Recorded and edited by Anielà Jaffé. Translated by Richard and Clara Winston. New York: Pantheon Books, 1962.

Jung, C. G.. *Letters.* 2 Vols. Edited by Gerhard Adler and Aniela Jaffé. Translated by R.F.C. Hull. Bollingen Series XCV. Princeton, NJ: Princeton University Press, 1973.

Jung, C. G. und Adolf Weizsäcker. "Zwiegespräch." In: Tilmann Evers (ed.). *Mythos und Emanzipation: Eine kritische Annäherung an C. G. Jung.* Hamburg: Junius, 1987.

Jung, C. G. *The Red Book: Liber Novus.* Edited by Sonu Shamdasani. Translated by Mark Kyburz, John Peck and Sonu Shamdasani. New York: W.W. Norton, 2009.

Jung, C. G. *Collected Works: Complete Digital Edition.* Edited by Gerhard Adler, Michael Fordham and Herbert Read. Translated by R.F.C. Hull. Princeton, NJ: Princeton University Press, 2014.

Jung's Seminar on Nietzsches Zarathustra. Edited and abridged by James L. Jarrett. Bollingen Series XCIX. Princeton, NJ: Princeton University Press, 1998.

Kafka, Franz. *Brief an den Vater (1919)*. Frankfurt/Main: Fischer Verlag, 1999.

Kalsched, Donald. *The Inner World of Trauma: Archetypal Defenses of the Personal Spirit*. London & New York: Routledge, 1996.

Kalsched, Donald. "Trauma, Unschuld und der Kernkomplex der Dissoziation." *Analytische Psychologie*, 47(188), 2/2017, pp. 226–272.

Kamber, Peter. *Geschichte zweier Leben: Wladimir Rosenbaum und Aline Valangin*. Zürich: Limmat Verlag, 1990.

Kampmann, Wanda. *Deutsche und Juden*. Frankfurt/Main: Fischer, 1979.

Karady, Victor. *Gewalterfahrung und Utopie, Juden in der europäischen Moderne*. Frankfurt/Main: Fischer Taschenbuch Verlag, 1999.

Katz, Jacob. *Zwischen Messianismus und Zionismus: zur jüdischen Sozialgeschichte*. Frankfurt/Main: Suhrkamp Verlag, 1993.

Kessler, Harry Graf. *Walther Rathenau, Sein Leben und sein Werk*. Frankfurt: Fischer, 1988.

Kirsch, Thomas B. *C.G. Jung und seine Nachfolger*. Giessen: Psychosozial Verlag, 2000.

Kirsch, T. and G. Hogenson (eds.). *The Red Book. Reflections on C.G. Jung's Liber Novus*. London & New York: Routledge, 2014.

Knopp, Guido and Ralf Piechowiak (eds.). *Heimkehr in die Fremde. Die Gründung des Staates Israel*. Recklinghausen: Bitter, 1992.

Koch, Hans-Gerd. *Kafka in Berlin*. Berlin: Wagenbach, 2008.

Koebner, Thomas, R.P. Janz and F. Trommler (eds.). *Mit uns zieht die neue Zeit. Der Mythos Jugend*. Frankfurt/Main: Suhrkamp Verlag, 1985.

Koestler, Arthur. *Promise and Fulfilment: Palestine 1917–1949*. London: Macmillan, 1949.

Krochmalnik, Daniel. "Neue Tafeln, Nietzsche und die jüdische Counter-History." In: Stegmeier, Werner and Daniel Krochmalnik (eds.). *Jüdischer Nietzscheanismus*. Berlin & New York: Walter de Gruyter Verlag, 1997.

Krochmalnik, Daniel. "Vierfacher Schriftsinn in Judentum und Christentum." In: U. Gerber and R. Hoberg (ed.). *Sprache und Religion*. Darmstadt: Wissenschaftliche Buchgesellschaft, 2009.

Langbehn, Julius. *Rembrandt als Erzieher*. Weimar: Duncker, 1928.

Laqueur, Walter. *Linksintellektuelle zwischen den beiden Weltkriegen*. Munich: Nymphenburger Verlagshandlung, 1969.

Laqueur, Walter. *Der Weg zum Staat Israel: Geschichte des Zionismus*. Vienna: Europa-Verlag, 1975.

Laqueur, Walter. *Die Kultur der Weimarer Republik*. Frankfurt/Main: Ullstein, 1976.

Laqueur, Walter. *Die deutsche Jugendbewegung: eine historische Studie*. Cologne: Verlag Wissenschaft und Politik, 1978.

Laub, Dori. "Kann die Psychoanalyse dazu beitragen, den Völkermord historisch besser zu verstehen?" *Psyche*, Sonderheft, Vergangenheit in der Gegenwart 6, Zeit, Narration, Geschichte, 57. Jahrgang, September/ Oktober 2003, pp. 938–959 (The Trial of Adolf Eichmann, Record of Proceedings in the District Court of Jerusalem, Vol. 5, 1994, Jerusalem, p. 2146.).

Lévinas, Emmanuel. *Otherwise than Being, or Beyond Essence*. Translated by Alphonso Lingis. The Hague: Martinus Nijhoff, 1981.

Lévinas, Emmanuel. "Diachrony and Representation." In *Entre Nous: On Thinking-of-the-Other*. Translated by Michael B. Smith and Barbara Harshav. New York: Columbia University Press, 1998.

Lévinas, Emmanuel. "From the One to the Other." In *Entre Nous: On Thinking-of-the-Other*. Translated by Michael B. Smith and Barbara Harshav. New York: Columbia University Press, 1998.

Lévinas, Emmanuel. "Is Ontology Fundamental." In *Entre Nous: On Thinking-of-the-Other*. Translated by Michael B. Smith and Barbara Harshav. New York: Columbia University Press, 1998.

Lévinas, Emmanuel. "Philosophy, Justice, and Love." In *Entre Nous: On Thinking-of-the-Other*. Translated by Michael B. Smith and Barbara Harshav. New York: Columbia University Press, 1998.

Lévinas, Emmanuel. "The I and the Totality." In *Entre Nous: On Thinking-of-the-Other*. Translated by Michael B. Smith and Barbara Harshav. New York: Columbia University Press, 1998.

Lévinas, Emmanuel. "The Philosophical Determination of the Idea of Culture." In *Entre Nous: On Thinking-of-the-Other*. Translated by Michael B. Smith and Barbara Harshav. New York: Columbia University Press, 1998.

Lévinas, Emmanuel. *Die Spur des Anderen: Untersuchungen zur Phänomenologie und Sozialphilosophie*. Freiburg: Karl Alber Verlag, 2007.

Lévinas, Emmanuel. *Totality and Infinity: An Essay on Exteriority*. Translated by Alphonso Lingis. Pittsburgh, PA: University of Pittsburgh Press, 2011.

Lichtheim, Richard. *Rückkehr. Lebenserinnerungen aus der Frühzeit des deutschen Zionismus*. Stuttgart: Deutsche Verlags-Anstalt, 1970.

Livné-Freudenthal, Rachel, Monika Richarz, Julius H. Schoeps, Raymond Wolff and Annegret Ehmann. *Juden in Berlin 1671–1945. Ein Lesebuch*. Berlin: Nicolai, 1988.

Lockot, Regine. *Erinnern und Durcharbeiten. Zur Geschichte der Psychoanalyse und Psychotherapie im Nationalsozialismus*. Frankfurt/Main: Fischer Taschenbuch, 1985.

Lockot, Regine. *Die Reinigung der Psychoanalyse*. Tübingen: Ed. Diskord, 1994.

Loewenson, Erwin. *Der Weg zum Menschen, Philosophische Fragmente*. Herausgegeben von Carl Frankenstein. Hildesheim: A. Lax Verlag, 1970.

Löwith, Karl. *Weltgeschichte und Heilsgeschehen: die theologischen Voraussetzungen der Geschichtsphilosophie*. Stuttgart: Metzler, 2004.

MacGuire, William. *Bollingen. An Adventure in Collecting the Past*. Bollingen Series. Princeton, NJ: Princeton University Press, 1982.

Maidenbaum, Aryeh (ed.). *Jung and the Shadow of Anti-Semitism*. Berwick: Nicolas-Hays, 2002.

Malka, Salomon. *Emmanuel Lévinas. Eine Biographie*. Munich: C.H. Beck Verlag, 2003.

Mannheim, Karl. *Das Problem der Generationen in Wissenssoziologie. Auswahl aus dem Werk*. Berlin: Herausgegeben von K.H. Wolff, 1964.

Mattenklott, Gert. "Nicht durch Kampfesmacht und nicht durch Körperkraft. Alternativen jüdischer Jugendbewegung in Deutschland vom Anfang bis 1933." In: Koebner, Janz, Trommler (eds.). *Mit uns zieht die neue Zeit*. Frankfurt/Main: Der Mythos Jugend, 1985.

Mattenklott, Gert. "Mythologie, Messianismus, Macht." In: E. Goodman-Thau and W. Schmied-Kowarzik (eds.). *Messianismus zwischen Mythos und Macht. Jüdisches Denken in der europäischen Geistesgeschichte*. Berlin: Akademie Verlag, 1994.

Maurer, Trude. *Ostjuden in Deutschland 1918–1933*. Hamburg: Hans Christians Verlag, 1986.

Maurer, Trude. "Die Juden in der Weimarer Republik." In: Dirk Blasius and Dan Diner (eds.). *Zerbrochene Geschichte Leben und Selbstverständnis der Juden in Deutschland.* Frankfurt/Main: Fischer, 1991.

Maurer, Trude. *Die Entwicklung der jüdischen Minderheit in Deutschland (1780–1933); neuere Forschung und offene Fragen.* Tübingen: Niemeyer, 1992.

McLynn, Frank. *Carl Gustav Jung.* New York: St. Martin's Griffin, 1996.

Mendes-Flohr, Paul. *Von der Mystik zum Dialog, Martin Bubers geistige Entwicklung bis hin zu Ich und Du. Königstein/Taunus:* Jüdischer Verlag, 1978.

Meyer, Michael A. *Jüdische Identität in der Moderne.* Frankfurt/Main: Jüdischer Verlag, 1992.

Mommsen, Hans. "Generationskonflikt und Jugendrevolte in der Weimarer Republik." In: Koebner, Janz, Trommler (eds.). *Mit uns zieht die neue Zeit.* Frankfurt/ Main: Der Mythos Jugend, 1985.

Moon, Beverly (ed.). *Encyclopedia of Archetypal Symbolism.* Boston, MA: Shambala, 1991

Mosse George, L. *Jüdische Intellektuelle in Deutschland, Zwischen Religion und Nationalismus.* Frankfurt/Main: Campus Verlag, 1992.

Nietzsche, Friedrich. *Sämtliche Werke. Kritische Studienausgabe in 15 Bänden.* Edited by Giorgio Colli and Mazzino Montinari. Munich: DTV; Berlin and New York: de Gruyter, 1980.

Niewöhner, Friedrich. "Jüdischer Nietzschanismus seit 1888: Ursprünge und Begriff." In: Stegmeier, Werner and Daniel Krochmalnik (eds.). *Jüdischer Nietzscheanismus.* Berlin, New York: Walter de Gruyter Verlag, 1997.

Otto, Rudolf (1917). *Das Heilige. Über das Irrationale in der Idee des Göttlichen und sein Verhältnis zum Rationalen.* Munich: C.H. Beck, 2004.

Patai, Raphael. *The Hebrew Goddess,* 3rd enlarged ed. Detroit: Wayne State University Press, 1990; first published 1967.

Peukert, Detlev J.K. *Die Weimarer Republik. Krisenjahre der Klassischen Moderne.* Frankfurt /Main: Suhrkamp, 1987.

Portmann, Adolf. "Eranos." In: Walter Curti (ed.). *Du, Schweizerische Monatsschrift,* Zürich, April 1955, 15. Jahrgang.

Rebiger,Bill. *Das jüdische Berlin, Kultur, Religion und Alltag gestern und heute.* Berlin: Jaron Verlag, 2002.

Rabinbach, Anson. *In the Shadow of Catastrophe. German Intellectuals between Apocalypse and Enlightenment.* Berkeley, CA: University of California Press, 1997.

Rank, Otto (1922). *Mythos von der Geburt des Helden.* Vienna: Turia und Kant, 2000. English edition: *The Myth of the Birth of the Hero: A Psychological Exploration of Myth.* Translated by Gregory C. Richter and E. James Lieberman. Baltimore, MD: Johns Hopkins University Press, 2004.

Reitzenstein, Richard (1910). *Die hellenistischen Mysterienreligionen: Ihre Grundgedanken und Wirkungen.* Zweite Auflage. Leipzig/Berlin: Teubner, 1920.

Rilke, Rainer Maria. *Briefe aus Muzot 1921–1926.* Herausgegeben von Ruth Sieber-Rilke und Carl Sieber. Leipzig: Insel Verlag, 1935.

Ringer, Fritz K. *Die Gelehrten. Der Niedergang der deutschen Mandarine 1890–1933.* Stuttgart: Klett-Cotta, 1983.

Ritter, Henning. "Von Berlin-Lichterfelde nach New York." In: *Frankfurter Allgemeine Zeitung.* 28 November 2007.

Rosenbaum-Kroeber, Sybille. "Was ist Eranos und wer war Olga Fröbe-Kapteyn?" In: Harald Szeemann (ed.). *Monte Verità. Der Berg der Wahrheit*. Milan. Locarno: Dadò; Milano: Electa, 1978.

Rosenzweig, Edith (in assocation with Ernst Simon, ed.). *Franz Rosenzweig, Briefe*. Berlin: Schocken, 1935.

Samuels, Andrew. *Jung und seine Nachfolger. Neuere Entwicklungen der Analytischen Psychologie*. Stuttgart: Ernst Klett Verlag, 1989.

Santner, Eric. *The Psychotheology of Everyday Life, Reflections on Freud and Rosenzweig*. Chicago, IL & London: University of Chicago Press, 2001.

Scherpe, K. R. "Dramatisierung und Entdramatisierung des Untergangs – zum ästhetischen Bewußtsein von Moderne und Postmoderne." In: A. Huyssen and K.L. Scherpe (eds.). *Postmoderne, Zeichen eines kulturellen Wandels*. Reinbek bei Hamburg: Rowohlt, 1986.

Schlör, Joachim. *Tel Aviv. Vom Traum zur Stadt*. Frankfurt/Main: Insel Verlag, 1999.

Schluchter, Wolfgang (ed.). *Max Webers Studie zum antiken Judentum: Interpretation und Kritik*. Frankfurt/Main: Suhrkamp Verlag, 1981.

Schmied-Kowarzik, W. "Franz Rosenzweig: Der Stern der Erlösung." In: J. Valentin and S. Wendel (eds.). *Jüdische Traditionen in der Philosophie des 20. Jahrhunderts*. Darmstadt: Wissenschaftliche Buchgesellschaft, 2000.

Schoeps, Julius H. *Zionismus: Texte zu seiner Entwicklung*. Wiesbaden: Fourier, 1983.

Scholem, Gershom. "Zur Neuauflage des Stern der Erlösung." In: *Frankfurter Israelitisches Gemeindeblatt*, September 1931.

Scholem, Gershom. *Major Trends in Jewish Mysticism*. New York: Schocken Verlag, 1946.

Scholem, Gershom. "Wider den Mythos vom deutsch-jüdischen Gespräch. In: *Bulletin des Leo Baeck Instituts* 27, 1964 (originally a letter dated 18 December 1962).

Scholem, Gershom. *Die jüdische Mystik*. Frankfurt/Main: Suhrkamp Verlag, 1967.

Scholem, Gershom. *On Kabbalah and its Symbolism*. Translated by Ralph Manheim. New York: Schocken Books, 1969.

Scholem, Gershom. "Identifizierung und Distanz, ein Rückblick." In: A. Portmann and R. Ritsema (eds.). *Eranos 1979*. Frankfurt/ Main: Insel Verlag, 1981.

Scholem, Gershom. *Zwischen den Disziplinen*. Frankfurt/Main: Suhrkamp Verlag, 1989.

Scholem, Gershom. *Briefe*. Vol. III, Munich: Beck Verlag, 1999.

Scholem, Gershom. *"Es gibt ein Geheimnis in der Welt": Tradition und Säkularisation*. Edited by Itta Shedletzky. Frankfurt/Main: Jüdischer Verlag im Suhrkamp Verlag, 2002.

Scholem, Gershom. *From Berlin to Jerusalem*. Philadelphia, PA: Paul Dry Books, 2012.

Schürr, F. (1942). "Sprachwissenschaft und Zeitgeist: eine sprachphilosophische Studie." In: Fritz K. Ringer (ed.). *Die Gelehrten. Der Niedergang der deutschen Mandarine 1890–1933*. Stuttgart: Klett-Cotta, 1983.

Schulte, Christoph. *Die jüdische Aufklärung*. Munich: C.H. Beck Verlag, 2002.

Schulz, Walter. *Philosophie in der veränderten Welt*. Pfullingen: Neske Verlag, 1972.

Sheppard, Richard. *Die Schriften des Neuen Klubs 1908–1914*. Hildesheim: Gerstenberg, 1980.

Simon, Ernst. "Martin Buber und das deutsche Judentum." In: Deutsches Judentum. Aufstieg und Krise (ed.). *Gestalten, Ideen, Werke*. Stuttgart: Herausgegeben von Robert Weltsch, 1963.

Slezkine, Yuri. *Das jüdische Jahrhundert*. Göttingen: Vandenhoeck &Ruprecht, 2006.

Sorge, Giovanni. "Lettere Ernst Bernhard – Carl Gustav Jung 1934–1959." Vivarium, Roma 2001, Beiheft zur Rivista di Psicologia analitica (32) 64/2001 – Nuova serie N. 12.

Spier, Julius (1944). *The Hands of Children: An Introduction to Psycho-Chirology.* Abingdon, Oxon: Routledge, 1999.

Stegmaier, Werner. *Hauptwerke der Philosophie, Von Kant bis Nietzsche.* Stuttgart: Reclam Verlag, 2005.

Stegmeier, Werner and Daniel Krochmalnik (eds.). *Jüdischer Nietzscheanismus.* Berlin & New York: Walter de Gruyter Verlag, 1997.

Taguieff, Pierre André. "Die Metamorphose des Rassismus und die Krise des Antirassismus, 1991." In: Ullrich Bielefeld (ed.). *Das Eigene und das Fremde – neuer Rassismus in der Alten Welt?* Hamburg: Hamburger Edition, 1998.

Theison, Philipp. *Die Urbarkeit der Zeichen: Zionismus und Literatur – eine andere Poetik der Moderne.* Stuttgart: Metzler, 2005.

Tramer, Hans. "Berliner Frühexpressionisten. Leben und Schaffen von Erwin Loewenson." In: *Bulletin des Leo Baeck Instituts* 6, 1963.

Ulanov, Ann. *The Feminine in Jungian Psychology and in Christian Theology.* Evanston, IL: Northwestern University Press, 1971.

Valentin, J and S. Wendel (eds.). *Jüdische Traditionen in der Philosophie des 20. Jahrhunderts.* Darmstadt: Wissenschaftliche Buchgesellschaft, 2000.

Voigts, Manfred. *Oskar Goldberg: Der mythische Experimentalwissenschaftler. Ein verdrängtes Kapitel jüdischer Geschichte.* Berlin: Agora,1992.

Voigts, Manfred. *Die deutsch-jüdische Symbiose: zwischen deutschem Sonderweg und Idee Europa.* Tübingen: Niemeyer, 2006.

Volkov, Sulamith. *Antisemitismus als kultureller Code.* Munich: Beck'sche Reihe, 1990.

Volkov, Shulamit. "Jüdisches Leben und Antisemitismus in Deutschland im 19. und 20. Jahrhundert." In Ibid. *Antisemitismus als kultureller Code.* Munich: Beck'sche Reihe, 1990.

Volkov, Shulamit. "Die Dynamik der Dissimilation. Deutsche Juden und osteuropäische Einwanderer." In: Dan Diner and Dirk Blasius (eds.). *Zerbrochene Geschichte. Leben und Selbstverständnis der Juden in Deutschland*, Frankfurt/Main: Fischer, 1991.

Volkov, Shulamit. *Die Juden in Deutschland 1780–1918*, Enzyklopädie deutscher Geschichte. Edited by L. Gall. Munich: R.Oldenbourg Verlag, 1994.

Volkov, Shulamit. *Das jüdische Projekt der Moderne.* Munich: Beck'sche Reihe, 2001.

Volkov, Shulamit. "Die Erfindung einer Tradition: zur Entstehung des modernen Judentums in Deutschland." In: Ibid. *Das jüdische Projekt der Moderne.* Munich: Beck'sche Reihe, 2001.

Vosswinckel, Ulrike. *Freie Liebe und Anarchie. Schwabing – Monte Verità. Entwürfe gegen das etablierte Leben.* Munich: Allitera Verlag, 2009.

Warhaftig, Myra. *Sie legten den Grundstein. Leben und Wirken deutschsprachiger jüdischer Architekten in Palästina 1918–1948.* Tübingen: Wasmuth, 1996.

Wassermann, Jakob (1923). *Mein Weg als Deutscher und Jude.* Munich: dtv, 2005.

Weber, Max (1919). *Politik als Beruf.* Stuttgart: Reclam Verlag, 1995.

Weiler, Gerda. *Das Matriarchat im alten Israel.* Stuttgart, Berlin, Cologne: Kohlhammer, 2006.

Weltsch, Robert. *Deutsches Judentum. Aufstieg und Krise. Gestalten, Ideen, Werke.* Stuttgart: Deutsche Verlagsanstalt, 1963.

Wilhelm, Richard. *Das Geheimnis der Goldenen Blüte.* Olten: Walter Verlag, 1971.

Wilhelm, Richard. *I Ging, Das Buch der Wandlungen*. Cologne: Eugen Diederichs Verlag, 1973.

Witte, Bernd. *Jüdische Tradition und literarische Moderne: Heine Buber, Kafka, Benjamin*. Munich: Hanser, 2007.

Wolff, Raymond. "Zwischen formaler Gleichberechtigung, Zionismus und Antisemitismus." In: Rachel Livné-Freudenthal, Monika Richarz, Julius H. Schoeps, Raymond Wolff, Annegret (AutorInnen) Ehmann von Nicolai (eds.). *Juden in Berlin 1671–1945. Ein Lesebuch*. Berlin: Nicolaische Verlagsanstalt, 1988.

Wurmser, Léon. *Ideen- und Wertewelt des Judentums. Eine psychoanalytische Sicht*. Göttingen: Vandenhoeck und Ruprecht, 2001.

Yerushalmi, Hayim Yosef. *Freuds Moses, Endliches und unendliches Judentum*. Frankfurt/Main: Fischer Taschenbuch Verlag, 1999.

Young-Bruehl, Elisabeth. *Hannah Arendt. Leben Werk und Zeit*. Frankfurt/Main: Fischer Verlag, 2004.

Zimmermann, Moshe. *Die Deutschen Juden 1914–1945*. Munich: Oldenbourg Verlag, 1997.

Zizek, Slavoj. *Die Puppe und der Zwerg: Das Christentum zwischen Perversion und Subversion*. Frankfurt/Main: Suhrkamp Verlag, 2003.

Zweig Arnold (1919). *Das ostjüdische Antlitz*. Zu zweiundfünfzig Zeichnungen von H. Struck. Wiesbaden: Fourier Verlag, 1992.

Index

Page numbers in *italics* indicate figures.

Printed in Great Britain
by Amazon

80747679R00188